MEDIA BACKENDS
Digital Infrastructures and Sociotechnical Relations

Edited by
**LISA PARKS,
JULIA VELKOVA, AND
SANDER DE RIDDER**

© 2023 by the Board of Trustees
of the University of Illinois
All rights reserved
Manufactured in the United States of America
1 2 3 4 5 C P 5 4 3 2 1
♾ This book is printed on acid-free paper.

Library of Congress Cataloging-in-Publication Data
Names: Parks, Lisa, editor. | Velkova, Julia, editor. | De Ridder, Sander, editor.
Title: Media backends : digital infrastructures and sociotechnical relations / edited by Lisa Parks, Julia Velkova, and Sander De Ridder.
Description: Urbana : University of Illinois Press, [2023] | Series: The geopolitics of information | Includes bibliographical references and index.
Identifiers: LCCN 2023007532 (print) | LCCN 2023007533 (ebook) | ISBN 9780252045349 (cloth) | ISBN 9780252087462 (paperback) | ISBN 9780252054877 (ebook)
Subjects: LCSH: Information society. | Information technology—Social aspects. | Digital media—Social aspects. | Mass media—Technological innovations.
Classification: LCC HM851 .M4239 2023 (print) | LCC HM851 (ebook) | DDC 303.48/33—dc23/eng/20230628
LC record available at https://lccn.loc.gov/2023007532
LC ebook record available at https://lccn.loc.gov/2023007533

MEDIA BACKENDS

THE GEOPOLITICS OF INFORMATION

Edited by Dan Schiller, Amanda Ciafone, and Yuezhi Zhao

A list of books in the series appears at the end of this book.

CONTENTS

Acknowledgments   vii

Introduction   1
   Lisa Parks, Julia Velkova, and Sander De Ridder

PART I: SENSING, AUTOMATING, MEDIATING

1. Atmospheric Mediation: From Smart Dust to Customizable Governance   25
   Mark Andrejevic and Zala Volcic

2. The Other Side of the Smart Phone: MEMS Sensors and the Tiny Matters of Mediation   42
   Lisa Parks

3. EugenicTech: Three Perspectives on the (B)anality of AI   62
   Jonathan Cohn

4. Coding and Encoding Streamed Media: The Cultural Infrastructure of the Netflix Recommender System   80
   Fatima Gaw

5. Engaging Opacity: Spotify and the Poiesis of Algorithmic Backends   95
   Tim Markham

PART II: DATAFYING, SERVING, DISTRIBUTING

6. The Social Mapping of Hyperscale Data Center Regions: Placemaking, Infrastructuring, Curating   113
   Vicki Mayer and Julia Velkova

7 Cross-sectoral Relations in VoD Markets:
   Frontend, Backend, and Deepend in India   129
   Vibodh Parthasarathi, Philippe Bouquillion, and Christine Ithurbide

8 Serving Machines and Heterotopias: Data Entry Work
   in Prisons and Refugee Camps in the US and Uganda   144
   Anne Kaun, Alexis Logsdon, Philipp Seuferling, and Fredrik Stiernstedt

9 Mythical Media Backends: Human-Machine
   Communication's Cruel Promises   162
   Sander De Ridder

10 Black Living Data Booklet   177
    Faithe J. Day

PART III: SUBJECTING, HUMANIZING, REPAIRING

11 Sonorous Surfaces, Biased Backends:
    The Gendered Voices of AI Assistants as Existential Media   193
    Amanda Lagerkvist, Jacek Smolicki, and Matilda Tudor

12 On Meaning and Exploitation:
    Everyday AI and Productivity Tracking in Denmark   214
    Stine Lomborg

13 The Backend Work of Data Subjects:
    Ordinary Challenges of Living with Data in India and the US   229
    Ranjit Singh

14 Repairing Algorithms, Rebuilding Data Paths:
    Digital Infrastructures, Public Service Media,
    and Material Solidarity in Europe   245
    Kaarina Nikunen

Afterword: Theorizing across and between Media Backends   263
Rahul Mukherjee

Contributors   271

Index   275

ACKNOWLEDGMENTS

This book emerged from a conference called "Infrastructures and Inequalities: Media Industries, Digital Cultures, and Politics" held at the University of Helsinki in October 2019, convened by the Media Industries and Cultural Production thematic section of the European Communication Research and Education Association (ECREA). The event gathered more than one hundred participants from fifteen countries and three continents, launching discussions about the diversity of media studies perspectives as our field contends with emergent objects such as clouds, platforms, algorithms, artificial intelligence, virtual assistants, and more. The conference also addressed the various kinds of inequalities that have been reinforced and created by ongoing processes of digitalization. In the months after the conference, the world became a much different place; as we scattered to our home countries a global pandemic took shape. Despite the grave challenges it posed, we sought to keep the conference's intellectual threads and arguments alive to share them with others in media studies and beyond. We worked on this book across three countries and time zones amid the contingencies and individual pressures we each faced during the pandemic, and tried our best to make the book evocative, multidisciplinary, and inclusive. We thank all participants of the conference as well as the institutions that supported it, including the Center for Consumer Society Research at the University of Helsinki; the Finnish Learning Society; and the co-organizing thematic sections of ECREA: Digital Culture and Communication and Communication and Democracy. Special thanks to Minna Ruckenstein and Kaarina Nikunen for being excellent hosts in Helsinki and for making the conference a memorable experience.

We also deeply thank all of our wonderful contributors who have been a pleasure to work with as we developed this book. In addition, we thank Daniel

Nasset, editor-in-chief at University of Illinois Press, associate editor, Megan Donnan, and editors of the Geopolitics of Information series for their support of this work. We also are grateful to anonymous readers who reviewed the proposal and manuscript and offered helpful feedback. Rahul Mukherjee generously wrote the book's afterword, and we thank him for his powerful critical insights. Thanks also to Shaoni Chattopadhyay White and Marilyn Campbell for their helpful feedback and attentive copyediting.

Before we share our individual acknowledgments, we would like to publicly thank one another for an enriching editorial collaboration. We found it intellectually stimulating to edit this book together and are deeply grateful for the camaraderie we formed and all we learned from one another. It was a privilege to work together, and we felt fortunate to build a caring, creative, and supportive partnership.

Lisa Parks thanks the Comparative Media Studies/Writing department at MIT, where her work on this project began, and the Film and Media Studies Department at UC Santa Barbara, where it was completed. She is deeply grateful to her colleagues and graduate students in both departments and to the following scholars for their inspiring tech-related research: Darin Barney, Simone Browne, Jenna Burrell, Alenda Chang, Wendy Chun, Nick Couldry, Tarleton Gillespie, Orit Halpern, David Hesmondhaulgh, Jennifer Holt, Carlos Jimenez, Caren Kaplan, Kara Keeling, Vicki Mayer, Patrick McCray, Lisa Nakamura, Safiya Noble, Rita Raley, Sarah Roberts, Laila Shereene Sakr, Jim Schwoch, Jeff Sconce, Lynn Spigel, Nicole Starosielski, Jonathan Sterne, TL Taylor, Fred Turner, Cristina Venegas, and France Winddance Twine. Parks also thanks Kim Yasuda for inviting her to the Underworlding residency at the Montalvo Arts Center in Saratoga, California, in June 2022, which provided a quiet place to work during this project's final phases. Parks is grateful to the MacArthur Foundation for a fellowship that supports her Global Media Technologies and Cultures Lab and ongoing research on media infrastructures and backends. Finally, she thanks Constance Penley, Bhaskar Sarkar, and Janet Walker for their friendship and support over the years, and John, Luna, Jenna, Cristy for their love and solidarity. Parks dedicates her portion of this book to two beloved friends and tech experts who left our planet too soon: Myron Dewey and Jing Wang.

Julia Velkova thanks the Center for Consumer Society Research at the University of Helsinki in Finland for providing a welcoming and vibrant environment where the seeds of this work were planted, and her current department—TEMA-T at Linköping University in Sweden—for welcoming her during the pandemic to an academic home built around an ethics of care and solidarity. Both departments and all colleagues there offered generous support, the privilege of enjoying intellectual freedom, and inspiration. Velkova is particularly grateful to Cathy Johnson and Maria Michalis for excellent teamwork, program coordination, and engagement with the conference in Helsinki and for great time together co-chairing the Media Industries and Cultural Production section of ECREA; to the STRIPE seminar group at Tema-T for discussions; and to the Technologies in Practice group at the IT University in Copenhagen for hosting her in June 2022 at the final stages of this book project. Thanks to Minna Ruckenstein, Anne Kaun, Nanna Bonde Thylstrup, Thomas Keating, and Ekaterina Tarasova for friendship and good talks; Harald Rohracher, Anna Storm, Ericka Johnson, Lars Lundgren, Stine Lomborg, and Patrik Åker for their generosity and good advice; to Jonas, Adrian, and Vera for much needed distractions and love; and to the following scholars for their inspiring work: A.R.E. Taylor, Pat Brodie, Mél Hogan, Marisa Cohn, Jean-Christophe Plantin, Maria Bakardjieva, Göran Bolin, Alex Johnson, Vicki Mayer, Fernanda Rosa, Nicole Starosielski, Rahul Mukherjee, Sarah Pink, Laura Watts, Kat Jungnickel, as well as all colleagues in the "Reimagine ADM," and "Earth Stations to Data Centers" projects. Julia dedicates her part of the book to the Ukrainian victims of the Russian war in Ukraine that broke out as this manuscript was being finished.

Sander De Ridder is grateful for the time he spent at the Centre for Cinema and Media Studies at Ghent University where he was working when this project started. During this project he made the switch to the University of Antwerp, finding a new home at the Antwerp Media in Society Centre—thanks for the very warm welcome. Special thanks to the Research Foundation Flanders for supporting six years of postdoctoral research and providing the opportunity to do research. He would also like to thank the many people that stimulated him over the past years. Thanks to Sofie Van Bauwel, Frederik Dhaenens, Stijn Joye, Tonny Krijnen, Sofia P. Caldeira, Ana Jorge, Daniel Bilteresyt, Ranjana Das, Kevin Smets, Joke Hermes, Marco Scarcelli, Tereza Pavlíčková, Jonathan Corpus Ong, Pieter Verdegem, Sonia Livingstone, Peter Lunt, Susanna Paasonen, Jaap Kooijman, Thomas Poell, Mark Deuze, Alexander Dhoest, Steve Paulussen, and Pieter Maeseele. He also wants to thank his partner, Thomas Jans, for everything.

INTRODUCTION

LISA PARKS,
JULIA VELKOVA, AND
SANDER DE RIDDER

Screens and interfaces have long been the focus of media studies researchers. For some there has been a parallel curiosity about the electronic gadgetry, labor, and operations behind the screen—a domain we conceptualize in this book as "media backends." This other side of media is key to understanding the sociotechnical relations, economies, and operations of media, yet is often relegated to spheres of electrical engineering, software development, telecom operation, or electronics manufacturing. Most digital media use today takes place through a mobile phone, a "smart" device, or an app. These devices serve as the main interfaces through which many consumers interact with everyday services, whether music listening, ride sharing, or home heating. What consumers do not perceive, however, is the complex "stack" of software, hardware, and network systems distinct from, if related to, the interface or screen.[1] This multilayered domain of digital infrastructures and sociotechnical relations has augured a media environment defined by a proliferating array of automated extractions and transactions.

Once organized around technologized spectacles and rituals of mass consumption, media industries have shifted dramatically over the past twenty years. National telecommunication and broadcast providers have been subsumed into the global internet. Network standards have been switched over from analog to digital. Content distribution now occurs as "streaming" across multiple competing platforms. And mobile internet has become the primary media gateway for many citizen-consumers. In some countries, privatized social media platforms such as WhatsApp and Facebook have all but replaced national telecom operators. Most media scholars and publics are familiar with these transformations through the brand names and services of Big Tech companies, whether Amazon, Netflix, or Tik Tok. And they are familiar with streaming, social media, and app interfaces. They are less familiar, however, with what we call the "backends" of media—the parts of media systems that are not accessible to most users. Media backends include electronic components in devices, network equipment and linkages, data centers and storage facilities, and algorithmic processes and software, as well as the ways these components and processes are designed, imagined, and communicated about, and the hierarchies of power/knowledge that they enact. While the frontends of media—the screens, monitors, and interfaces—have remained relatively constant in their enframed shape and form, the backends have undergone major transformations during the past two decades in the context of digitalization.

Media scholars have referred to these macrolevel transformations as processes of "convergence," "distribution revolution," "streaming," "ensensing," "platformization," "appification," and media automation.[2] A range of scholarly works have conceptualized the various dimensions and politics of these transformations. Within the field of platform studies, for instance, scholars have engaged with the interrelations between computer hardware and software, and the media content produced therein;[3] the orientation of the web to a logic of programmability;[4] and the articulation of this logic to an array of sectors that become interlinked with data markets and platforms.[5] Scholars of critical data studies and algorithmic cultures have explored how relations of power and knowledge between citizens and states are shifting through processes of datafication and algorithm-driven decision making.[6] They have also examined the forms of resistance that these relations generate[7] and the role that human labor plays in automated, predictive systems, which increasingly organize human and more-than-human life.[8]

Within the field of media infrastructure studies, scholars have studied large sociotechnical systems that unevenly organize the global distribution of content across time/space. They have considered how power dynamics of the state, settler-colonialism, capitalism, and militarism materialize in, around, and through objects such as satellites, fiber optic cables, data centers, or internet exchange points.[9] In parallel, media industry studies scholars have analyzed transformations in ownership structures and content distribution evoked by the entry of new actors such as content delivery networks (CDNs) and streaming platforms.[10] Addressing issues ranging from labor to regulation to digital rights, these analyses offer crucial context for understanding industrial and technological shifts in the media sector.

Our attempt to grapple with these infrastructural and industrial issues is informed at a deep level by feminist, queer, and intersectional criticism. Scholarship on digital technologies and design bias has revealed what is at stake in who designs the backend, what decisions are made in that process, and who is allowed to know about them.[11] We are concerned about systemic inequalities that emerge when tech company owners and tech designers persistently fail to address workplace discrimination and algorithmic violence and exclusions. In media studies, it is vital that we ask, following the work of scholars such as Anne Balsamo, Safiya Noble, Ruha Benjamin, and Sasha Costanza-Chock:[12] Who is designing media systems? What experience and knowledge do designers have of social differences and power structures? To what ends and for whom are these systems being designed? While media and communication scholars have begun to investigate these issues across a proliferation of subfields in our discipline, more work needs to be done on infrastructures and struggles for equality and justice.

Beyond the politics of design, processes of conglomeration and digitalization are continuing to change the backends of media systems in ways that reinforce inequalities. Big Tech corporations have come to exert significant dominance over the infrastructural layer of much media production and distribution. Amazon, for instance, owns both Amazon Web Services (AWS), data centers, wind power plants, and content delivery networks in various parts of the world, and Amazon Prime, which produces original audiovisual content.[13] The political economy of "cloud" infrastructure ownership activates social struggles around internet access, energy distribution and digital service provision, the sourcing of local versus global labor, and the new cultural and class identities of small towns converted by Big Tech into nodal points in their global data infrastructure networks, as Vicki Mayer and Julia Velkova discuss in chapter 6. These authors emphasize the need to engage closely with people who have rarely, if ever, been consulted about the substantial changes brought by Big Tech to their towns and livelihoods. Corporate efforts to control the collection and storage of data, as well as the histories of systemic racism, prompted Faithe Day's manifesto in chapter 10, which calls on Black communities and others to adopt heightened awareness and hands-on practices relative to the production and use of data.[14] Thinking about what is behind the interface may expose the dynamic and differential impacts of media conglomeration, and digitalization, and support further investigations of what Wendy Chun calls "discriminating data."[15]

As we grapple with ongoing global crises such as systemic racism, climate disruption, and pandemics, we need critical models for studying how media industries affect and are affected by such conditions. Often media and information technologies are positioned as idealized solutions to complex problems. Yet such techno-solutionism, as Sander De Ridder argues in chapter 9 of this book, must be critically questioned. In moments of crisis or uncertainty, controversial technologies may slip into public acceptance, legacy media may be revived, or genuinely new media uses may emerge. The point is that a medley of conditions has challenged existing industrial models and produced the need for greater public knowledge and control of media backends, as Kaarina Nikunen argues in chapter 14 of this book.

While there is often a celebration of greater "flexibility," "choice," "convenience," and "engagement" for media consumers in the digital era, there is a parallel move toward regimented platformization, formatting, templating, and automation of media experiences.[16] Today, media content is produced for distribution to "niched" viewers/users/demographics whose tastes and preferences are already "known." Consumption of one media product automatically "pushes" or triggers the distribution of another. And media content is stored in and streamed from geographically dispersed data centers that rely on cloud administration services and content delivery networks.[17] All along the media supply chain, metadata is generated, collected, and used to train algorithms. Those algorithms suggest media content to users and signal which parts of the global media economy are lucrative and which are not. Backend processes are reshaping and being reshaped by the political economic and infrastructural contours of media globalization.

Computing equipment and software are increasingly organized in the form of digital services called "the cloud," whose ownership and maintenance are dominated by a handful of global corporations.[18] These companies structure access to computation resources in a way similar to that of traditional public utilities such as electrical and water service providers. Yet because they are privatized and operate regionally according to the logics of digital capitalism, they often accrue enormous value and end up superseding state-owned or public sector services. In South Asian countries like India, this mode of organizing cloud access has broadened the possibilities for smaller media companies to reduce their infrastructural ownership costs and build new digital services, while bringing local and national content into new international, online media markets, as Vibodh Parthasarathi, Philippe Bouquillion, and Christine Ithurbide demonstrate in their analysis of Indian video-on-demand services in chapter 7.[19]

In the context of these transformations, deregulation and conglomeration in the media and high-tech sectors have enabled new cross-sector collaborations, infrastructure bundling, and system interoperabilities, making it increasingly challenging to differentiate the "media industries" from other sectors, whether energy, data management, transportation, agriculture, military, or surveillance. Industrial developments in sensing technologies, computational media, data storage, and software are not only affecting the content and form of mediated communication but also redrawing relations across various sectors of the economy. As authors explore in this book, cross-sector relations—such as those between the prison, refugee camp, and software industry, as discussed by Anne Kaun and her colleagues in chapter 8—often manifest and materially come together on the backends of media. Such cross-sectional relations have long existed, but have arguably intensified and shifted in the contexts of neoliberalism, globalization, and digitization.

Conceptualizing Media Backends

We develop the term "media backends" to emphasize the need for further thinking and critical inquiry regarding the sociotechnical relations that enable mediation.[20] We find the term "backend" an evocative metaphor for multiple reasons. The word's etymology points to its functions as both a noun and verb with spatial and temporal connotations. According to the *Oxford English Dictionary*, the term emerged in the 1600s to describe the rear part of a "lord's coach" or horse carriage; by the 1800s backend also meant the latter part of a season or year. Over time, the noun "backend" has come to refer generically to technical parts or processes that are inaccessible, imperceptible, or irrelevant to most users yet are integral to a technology's or system's operation. Colloquial meanings of the term include another form of income or "side hustle," and, of course, the gluteus maximus. In the field of computing, the backend refers to the support components of an information system, specifically to the database management system (DBMS) or the storehouse of data residing in a server.[21] Though less common, backend is also a verb: to backend is to hide something in space or delay in time. Suffice it to say, given its use as noun and verb, its spatial and temporal connotations, and its articulation with technical matters, we adopt the term "backend" to describe and analyze contemporary industrial and technological conditions on the other side of the screen.

We also believe there are productive conceptual affinities between the terms "backend" and "infrastructure," which has been described as the uninteresting, boring, invisible, or concealed parts of media operations.[22] The term "backend," we contend, not only encompasses the materialities (including labor and energy) of "the stack" of systems and sociotechnical relations on the other side of interfaces, but also includes strategic efforts by corporations to privatize, conceal, suppress, or regulate access to information about them. In this sense, media backends are sites where the politics of technology and knowledge can be interrogated, and where public interests in transparency, opacity, equality, and justice may emerge. As Erving Goffman argues, a "back region" or "backstage" is a place "where the suppressed facts make an appearance."[23] Susan Leigh Star and Martha Lampland have described practices of quantification and classification as "boring backstage elements" yet emphasize the importance of the stories we tell about them.[24] Even if the backstage (or backend) is imagined as a site of suppression or boredom, it is still worthy of critical attention. In the current conjuncture, the terms "backstage" or "backend" are closely related to what Frank Pasquale calls "black-boxing"—containing or sequestering information about how a sociotechnical system works as well as making intellectual property claims to that information.[25] The backend is not just a set of technical objects that we need to "see" or "make visible" in order to grapple with—it is the place where the sociotechnical politics of opacity and transparency, knowing and nonknowing emerge and converge. As Tim Markham suggests in chapter 5 with a focus on Spotify music listening, the goal is not to do away with opacity since it can be a precondition of investigating these relations.[26]

Put another way, to direct attention to the backends is to suggest a different orientation toward the study of media and mediation. As Sara Ahmed reminds us in her writing about queer phenomenology, in everyday acts of perception we "bracket" certain objects and relegate them to a "background," but this does not mean that these objects do not exist or matter. As Ahmed writes, "some things are relegated to the background in order *to sustain* a certain direction; in other words, in order to keep attention on what is faced [emphasis in original]."[27] By focusing on the backends, our book suggests that what media and communication studies—as a field or discipline—faces or does not face is important to think about. Moreover, Ahmed argues that a particular orientation toward an object depends on work to sustain it.[28] We might consider all the work that is done—whether by designers, advertisers, or scholars—to keep media backends out of sight, mind, or interest. Endowing virtual assistants with anthropomorphized personalities and voices, for instance, becomes a way of effacing their machinic properties.[29] Simone Natale refers, in this context, to the "banal deception" of "everyday situations in which technologies and devices mobilize specific elements of the user's perception and psychology" in ways that impact the technologies' uses and appropriations.[30] Relatedly, in chapter 11 of this book, Amanda Lagerkvist, Jacek Smolicki, and Matilda Tudor demonstrate, in their study of femininized voices in personal devices, that by changing our orientation toward the media object it becomes possible to confront the gendered ideologies, ethics, and values encoded into the backends of consumer devices such as AI assistants.

The conceptualization of media backends involves a critical focus on sites, objects, practices, and relations that have been ignored or occluded for various reasons as well as a recognition of the importance of dynamisms within and across disciplines. As Ahmed reminds us, "Disciplines . . . have a specific 'take' on the world, a way of ordering time and space through the very decisions about what counts within the discipline."[31] Thus media backends can become a site for thinking through what directions the discipline has and has not taken; by bringing what is backstage to the front we can reorient, diffract, and think about media and mediation from different angles. In pursuit of this approach, authors in this book experiment with various critical practices and methods—ranging from phenomenology to drawing, from storifying to manifesto-writing, from speculating to queering—to investigate a realm many of us have been socialized to turn away from. The question of which methods are most appropriate for researching media backends is an open one and we encourage further thinking and experimentation in this regard.

The Politics of Technological Knowing and Nonknowing

When thinking about media backends, it is important to link the question of technology to power and knowledge. Power is constituted through legitimated forms of knowledge, scientific understanding, and "truth," which can function as sources of social discipline, control, and normalization.[32] As feminist science and technology studies (STS) scholars have argued, it is crucial that social differences be considered in relation to questions of power/knowledge and technology: the sites, bodies, practices, and objects used to investigate and "know" technology certainly matter.[33] In the context of this book, we are interested in the ways that power is mobilized to hierarchize and sanction particular ways of knowing technological systems and phenomena, while devaluing, ignoring, or dismissing others. For instance, technology designers or engineers typically possess the most formalized and legitimated understandings of a given technology and the actions it has been delegated to perform. Once a technology circulates within a marketplace and user economy, however, the knowledges and practices surrounding it can proliferate and shift.[34] In contexts of everyday life, technologies are shaped by a broad spectrum of user dispositions and material conditions.

While some users may operate a technology without ever asking a single question about its design, materiality, or function, others may be much more inquisitive. They may disassemble it to improve the design, augment it with other materials, or rebuild it to serve other purposes. Or users may undertake their own "teardowns" or repairs as interventions into technological power/knowledge.[35] As Lisa Parks demonstrates in chapter 2 in an analysis of tiny MEMS sensors, there are multiple ways of investigating a smart phone, ranging from drawing its interior parts to studying the ways it collects data. Embodied experimentation, Parks argues, can help to generate diverse kinds of technological power/knowledge, including drawing, inferring, and speculating. User orientations toward technology vary greatly across local and regional contexts and are often correlated with socioeconomic hierarchies and gender, racial, class, and bodily differences.[36] Some people are socialized into the world with technological access, curiosity, and skill, and others learn to inhabit positions of nonknowing or uninterest. There is more to learn about the power/knowledges and sociotechnical relations of diverse users and non-users.

Although humans are socialized into thinking that we live in a "knowledge society," many of the spheres of our mediated lives are in fact conditioned by nonknowing. Renata Salecl, who approaches ignorance as a complex phenomenon, reminds us that it is not possible nor even desirable to know everything about a given topic or domain.[37] Nonknowing is not merely a temporary condition that anticipates that something will become known over time. It involves the power to recognize the uncertainties that prompt and shape contemporary life, as well as science and technology.[38] In an era in which "smart machines" and predictive analytics are mobilized to determine the past, present, and future, positions of uncertainty and nonknowing can activate important political potentials aligned with acts of skepticism, inquiry, and opting out.

Increasingly, uncertainty is managed by computational processes operating on the backends of screens and interfaces. These processes are designed to approximate and produce "certainties" about issues ranging from user preferences to climate change, from criminal recidivism to election returns.[39] The production of such "certainties" is a mediated process that is materialized across data sets and centers, algorithms, and machine learning systems. This process has the potential to reshape hierarchies of power/knowledge, social norms, subjectivities, and actions. To trace these conditions and their politics we need methods that foreground how modes of uncertainty, such as doubt, skepticism, and hesitation, are effaced or suppressed by automated systems that output decisions about individuals and collectives as "truths."

Computerized forms of "objective knowledge" have become a dominant mode of governing "nonknowing." In data-governed societies, the politics of knowing and nonknowing shape the very production of governable subjects, collective identities, and politics of nationhood, belonging, and exclusion. Such structures might seem today algorithmically overdetermined, but they are still unfolding and thus open to change and intervention. Stine Lomborg demonstrates in chapter 12 how uncertainty and error are negotiated every day by white-collar workers whose actions are monitored by AI systems that track their workplace productivity. Glitches and errors in such environments can compel workers to interrogate media backends and learn about their own positionality within sociotechnical systems.[40] To think in relation to media backends, then, is to account for a dynamic and shifting politics around technological knowing and nonknowing. It is to analytically "decode" the phenomenological, ethico-political, and material ramifications of an infrastructurally reconfigured/ing media landscape.

When considering issues of technological knowledge/power we see productive openings offered by media scholars who have theorized, historicized, and empirically studied the material and discursive conditions of various "networks" of communication, focusing on transmitters, fiber optic cables, satellites, and data centers.[41] Scholars such as Dan Schiller, José van Dijck, Tarleton Gillespie, and Jennifer Holt have brought refined understandings of terms such as public utilities, platforms, and pipelines.[42] We build on this work to consider how emergent relations of power/knowledge are generated through distributed microsensors, chips and other digital devices, consumer platforms for streaming content, community apps, algorithms and AI systems, national databases, artworks, virtual assistants and social robots. Media backends evoke a consideration of technology and power/knowledge at multiple scales, from the small scale of microscopic sensors and individuals' unique encounters with media technologies to the meso and macro scales of data-driven platforms and infrastructures. An underlying goal here is to bring research on media industries more fully into dialogue with research on sociotechnical systems.

Media Industries and Infrastructures: Toward the Study of Productive Relations across Sites

We are deeply interested in the ways media technologies dynamically interface with multiple fields and matters. We understand the backend as a site for bridging various media subfields and concerns often lumped together under the common umbrella of "digital media studies." In bringing together subfields such as media industries and media infrastructure studies and drawing on insights from fields such as STS, critical data studies, software studies, etc., we explore how multifaceted and complex the digital infrastructures and sociotechnical relations of media have become. Practices and tools that bring digital media into being are distributed across sites and involve various kinds of actors, resonating with what Jane Bennett calls "vibrant matter."[43] Ironically, some of the most vibrant matter of media may exist behind the screen. It includes algorithms, code and AI, content delivery networks, interconnection protocols and infrastructure workers, prisoners, scholars and artists, research labs and exhibition galleries. It involves policy and legislation, electricity grids, cables, antennas, rare earth minerals, and feminized voices of AI assistants. The ways in which these "multiples" intra-act give vitality and power to media, which affects everyone but not equally and not always knowingly.

Researchers in subfields of media industries and media infrastructure studies have already begun to address issues concerning the ways digital media are materialized, such as through cross-sector relations, technopolitics, and supply chains, as well as through the organizing logics, institutions, economies, and policies that come together on the backends of media. As Charles Acland has acknowledged, studying media production not only involves media commodities, but also entails probing "the dirt and depth of economic systems."[44] That is, it involves recognizing media industries' reliance on and relation to other economic sectors, from real estate to e-waste disposal, from food to transportation, from advertising to electricity. Other scholars of media industries who focus on technopolitics show that there is much to be gained by asking questions about industrial and institutional logics, policies, labor politics, distribution practices, and interconnections on the backend.[45] Scholarly work on logistics and supply chains has in turn demonstrated the value in examining the multiple sites and cross-sector relations that shape and inform sociotechnical relations of media. Crucially, the latter work also situates media industries and infrastructures in relation to broader histories of global, racial, and digital capitalism.[46] It critically interrogates "how contemporary mediation is haunted by its logistical substructures, from the slave ship to the supply chain" and tracks how "systems of coordination modulate flows across infrastructure, reinforce the dominance of some companies, and connect media production to a multitude of other forms of commodity production."[47] These perspectives shed light on the ways in which such systems reproduce and reinforce historical and contemporary forms of power, inequality, and injustice.

We find this work inspirational for research on media backends. At the same time, we notice a sedimented industrial approach to media production that tends to dominate scholarly understandings of media technologies and cultural forms (radio, film, television, or music) and foci of our field, despite the fact that there are many sites and modes of "media production." Moreover, there is a tendency to privilege the study of media capitals in industry research, which excludes much of the mediated world. What if we build from models in media industry and infrastructure studies to unbracket other sectors and sociotechnical relations of "media production"? This could involve exploring how sectors of cloud computing, electronics manufacturing, or system dismantling help to support or materialize certain processes of mediation. Or it could prompt investigations of media production in different kinds of institutions, whether the hospital, the science lab, the military unit, or the prison.[48] The "media productivities" generated on the backends of media systems—such as massive datasets, acts of encoding, server activities, repair labor, or sensor operations—are not only part of media industries and infrastructures; they often take shape or occur unevenly across various milieus. Focusing on the differential materialities of backend processes can help to build on and extend media research.

Toward that end, we suggest shifting perspective beyond singular or fixed industrial "sites of media production/consumption/exhibition" to a model that attends to the productive relations across the multiple sites along the supply chain in which media are made, enacted, stored, streamed, and even dismantled and discarded.[49] Our analytic attention is focused, then, on the sociotechnical systems of media—the systems that support and organize processes of mediation. We are setting out to problematize discrete categories of "production," "consumption," and "exhibition," as they have become increasingly integrated, multivalent, extensive, and difficult to pin down. Put simply, we suggest a relational approach to backend objects and processes, acknowledging the scattered materials, practices, and time/spaces through which media "become media," and attend to the ways power/knowledge differentials shape sociotechnical relations on the other side of the screen. With this approach we hope to open space for pluriversal understandings of media, breaching some of the silos that have formed within media research.[50]

Approaching media in this way, of course, also prompts continuous reengagement with core concerns of critical media studies—including questions of ownership, power, meaning, representation, audiences, and value. Sociotechnical transformations put pressure on diverse strands of media research and theorizing, confronting scholars with the dilemma of what to face and what to bracket. For instance, backend transformations have brought about new issues for media scholars engaged in aesthetic and representational analysis. Digital content is now presented to consumers on streaming platforms in flexible modes and formats that change dynamically depending on who is consuming and for what purpose. To put it another way, a video shown on a streaming platform may appear as a form of "television," but it is also an assemblage of algorithms, brands, code, policy, as well as a product of the synchronous operation of multiple computational and materializing processes. How do media scholars study aesthetics and representation in this sociotechnical context? Jonathan Cohn addresses some of these questions in his analysis of AI-generated art and media in chapter 3, emphasizing the need to recognize the "individuality, personality, and specificity of each AI" in studies of digital aesthetics and representation.

Critical approaches are also challenged by sociotechnical relations on the consumer side, as digital assistants, cookies, sensors, recommender systems, or other things not traditionally categorized as "media" become part of everyday life. Indeed, a focus on the backends brings a variety of emergent processes and eclectic objects within the purview of media studies—from the voices of virtual assistants to the network infrastructures that stream media; from gadgets that promise to make the home "smarter" to satellite constellations that bring high-speed internet connectivity. A focus on media backends brings forward the objects and sociotechnical relations that enable various kinds of mediation. This focus can also direct attention to new administrative, cultural, and economic realities brought about by data collection, machine learning, and automated decision-making. Understanding media in this way situates the study of media content and audiences in relation to emergent sociotechnical processes and explores their power dynamics and mutual co-shaping.

The Objects, Concepts, and Publics of Media Studies

In the current era, it is increasingly challenging to identify objects/people/relations that exist beyond media.[51] Having said this, we want to resist totalizing claims about media and mediation, and instead recognize and inflect difference within these concepts and practices. By difference we are referring not only to entangled social/national/bodily singularities but to disciplinary ones as well. We posit the backend as a space for reflecting upon, critiquing, and expanding disciplinary approaches. At the same time, we want to recognize how important past scholarship and thinking have been in building and defining the field of media studies.

In an era in which "everything is mediated" what constitutes a media object? What makes something legible as an object of media studies? To make something legible is to make it recognizable, readable or interpretable, discernible. Legibility involves identifying and bringing forth an object and making the case for its relevance, significance, and salience within a given field. Given the poststructuralist foundations of humanities-based media studies and its expanded foci over the past twenty years—from digital platforms to media infrastructures to elemental media—media researchers are constantly challenged to establish the legibility of their objects of study rather than presume their relevance or take them for granted. The field of media studies is no longer limited to screens and speakers, studios and theaters, content and viewing or listening; rather, as Mark Andrejevic and Zala Volcic suggest in chapter 1, "media" now include "smart dust" electronics and industrial fantasies of automatically collecting, analyzing, and governing "everything." Indeed, media have been conceptualized as oceans and forests, platforms and posts, ice and clouds. Rather than patrol the ontological boundaries of what media and mediation are and can be, it is important that researchers across disciplines and subfields undertake and support creative acts of conceptualization and articulation, since a multitude of media objects, practices, and sites matter in media studies.

In relation to recent media scholarship on algorithms, for instance, we might ask: How, why, and when did the algorithm become legible as an object of media studies? There is a technological, industrial, and intellectual history here and the algorithm's status as an object of media studies should itself be subject to scrutiny and reflection.[52] In making the algorithm legible, media scholarship has also made broader points about the shifting materialities of media systems, patterning, sorting, and ordering, and their relations to the evolving cultural, financial, and computation-intense industries.[53] As Fatima Gaw explores in chapter 4, the Netflix recommender system is setting the possibilities and boundaries of users' cultural experiences. And, again, in his study of Spotify streaming environments, Tim Markham enacts digital agility and curiosity "by acting with and among" algorithms in an effort to carve out new paths of relating to and living with them.

Another way of approaching the changing objects of media studies might be to consider scholarship focused on elemental and nonrepresentational media where oceans, air, fire, ice, and geological formations are studied as the matter of mediation.[54] This research has opened up frontiers of media theorizing, and, in the process, has made the case that various elements and relations mediate life on earth. Scholars who work in the areas of new materialisms, media phenomenology, and environmental media too have expanded the ways objects and technologies are imagined and approached within media studies.[55] This work has brought forth new thinking around the deep time of media/mediation and planetary sensorium. It has challenged scholars to rethink the properties and sites of media and mediation across territorial and aquatic contexts, underground and into the air and orbit, resonating with what Andrejevic and Volcic call in chapter 1 "atmospheric mediation." At the same time, however, elemental media scholarship tends to sidestep media industry research even as it implicitly recognizes the extractive and transformative forces of global capitalism. The backend may be an evocative site for thinking through questions of matter, media, and legibility as it is a domain where different and often ignored objects, labor, and practices emerge and intersect. We are interested in the question of how media scholars select and define objects, sites, or practices as relevant or in the purview of media studies, as well as the consequences of relegating some of these beyond this purview.

Relatedly, a focus on media backends suggests the need to broaden the conceptual vocabulary of media studies and find terms that specify the materialities and complexities of media systems.[56] Too often media backends are imagined as seamlessly operating and sustaining themselves when, in fact, they are reliant on meticulous organizations of labor, energy, time/space, and materials. Metaphors in media studies, such as "flow," help perpetuate such understandings. New industry jargon and catchwords, such as "streaming," "cloud," or "platform," if used without critical reflection, can further naturalize and obscure power relations and ongoing material reconfigurations of media, suppressing their contingency, fragility, and reversibility.[57] A focus on backends could encourage media scholars to create and build new metaphors and concepts, as well as tell different kinds of stories about media technologies, industries, cultures, and actors. Relatedly, there is a need for more empirical research on the ways intersectional differences are both woven into and ignored in understandings of media backends.

The introduction of new language intervenes in the politics of knowing and nonknowing by taking up active space in it.[58] For example, it makes a difference when processes of automation are uncritically ascribed intelligence when mediated through "AI." It matters if scholars criticize the deceptive flatness of the term "platform," but keep reinvoking it as an explanatory or rhetorical device in their writings. It also matters if media scholars refer to "the cloud" yet do not have a concrete sense of where or what it is. Even the term "infrastructure" runs the risk of becoming diffuse if it is used as too much of a catchall.[59] Using new metaphors—or even referring to media through their materialities (metal cabinets, aluminum screens, electronic bits, circuit charts and diagrams, low-voltage electronics, etc.)—can help generate responses and response-abilities to media objects whose futures and role in society often appear overdetermined.[60] Concepts can also be used to trouble, expand, or unlearn particular modes of thought. What if we think about artificial intelligence not as the brains of a system but as its guts and groins, as evocatively suggested by Cohn in chapter 3 of this book?[61] What if we approach platforms as trees and trace the political-economic and social relations at their deeply material, dirty roots?[62]

New metaphors and concepts can help to make objects legible in media studies, motivate new empirical research, and challenge sedimented assumptions. They can intensify the sense of possibilities contained in an empiric situation, make that situation exist in other ways, and dwell within immanent becomings.[63] It is our hope that the concept of media backends can be an expansive term associated with a shift in focus to devices and operations of media that are often imperceptible or unknown to most people. Critical inquiry into the fluctuating and differential conditions of technological knowing/unknowing are integral to the conceptualization of media backends. We also hope this call for attention to the other side of the screen will encourage thinking between and across various subfields of media studies, such as media industry, infrastructure, and environmental media studies, as well as further engagement with science and technology studies and design studies.

In addition to prompting a reconsideration of the objects of media studies, backend operations are reconfiguring the meanings and functions of media publics. We use the term "publics" to signal the expansive realm of entities—human, nonhuman, and more-than-human—positioned wittingly or unwittingly on the "receiving" side of media. These include people who consume media but also algorithms and devices that are programmed to operate on people's behalf. While middle class human consumers watch a movie, listen to music, or eat a meal in the private space of their home, voice speakers and sensors placed in their surroundings listen to sounds too, register and interpret human movements, temperatures, and ambience. In this context, the private space of the home becomes simultaneously more "smart," public, and privatized. Backend processes turn the home into a frontline for the extractive logics of digital capitalism.[64]

Media publics are no longer defined only as people who consume or create media content. This term also includes nonhuman data, algorithms, sensors, and bots that play a role in shaping media publics. The agencies of media publics are shifting as well; "audiences" are also "users" whose lives are appropriated, structured, and administered by backend processes. This transformation requires a shift away from thinking with concepts such as "mediated public spheres" or "nationwide audiences" toward a recognition of the ways that publics are produced, used, and reorganized by sociotechnical relations on the backends of media.⁶⁵ Contemporary media infrastructures define, assemble, and "reutilize publics as part of the base of their operations." Media publics are being replaced by "utility publics"—publics that are fragmented and instrumentalized to perform specific roles and tasks for commercial providers, whether to provide personal data, give attention, or create content.⁶⁶ Increasingly, "utility publics" erode shared and collective media experiences and support the attention economy rather than democratic participation and the common good.

Various countries are using tracking devices and social credit systems to control media publics, using backend data to determine who is a "responsible citizen" and who is not. Social credit algorithms process various kinds of data, including whether the person actively uses technology, upgrades software, generates content, acts as an influencer, "hosts communities," and more. Socially responsible "publics" are produced, sorted, and recombined by backend processes to support various industries, including energy, pharmaceuticals, transport, food, and agriculture as much as media conglomerates. In this context, it is urgent to consider what inequalities and forms of discrimination arise, what "acts of citizenship"⁶⁷ are possible, and how publics can struggle over their subjectivities and agencies, which are being defined more and more by transactional data. As Ranjit Singh suggests in chapter 13 in the context of the Aadhaar biometric system in India and credit scoring in the United States, ordinary citizens have to continuously trick and find workarounds in order to secure representation and enact their civic rights in datafied bureaucracies.

To investigate acts of citizenship in relation to media backends is to attend to the situations when individual or collective deeds can transform the ethico-political conditions of possibility in relation to digital machines. Such situations can, for instance, include making a public service algorithm, or building infrastructures of solidarity to resist hate, racism, homophobia, and polarization in media culture, as Nikunen discusses in chapter 14 of this book. Acts of responsibility, she argues, necessarily require "courage, bravery, indignation, or righteousness to break" with the habitus of a person or the inertia of governance. How do publics become aware of, comply with, resist, or redefine their changing sociotechnical roles? A foundation for this work can be located in past debates over what audiences, consumers, and publics do with media⁶⁸ as well as how they are "worked upon" by giving up their "free labor" to support and sustain television programs and network cultures.⁶⁹ While these debates have been extended by research on "platform" labor and gig-economy work, we find this work helpful in thinking about the ways in which new publics are constructed on the backends. Media publics are no longer produced by virtue of their shared consumption of screened content; backend operations now create new relations between content producers and audiences, and reorganize time and attention in ways that serve digital capitalism first and foremost.⁷⁰ For instance, backend operations determine who is similar to whom,[71] what kind of transaction is likely to lead to another,[72] and how to categorize and order data to generate the most profit.[73] By discussing the backend, then, this book points to the reorganization of media publics into utility publics, the growing potential for media industries to participate in cross-sector economies, and the proliferation of social constellations made up of different kinds of actors.

To underscore the importance of media concepts, the book is organized into three sections that foreground particular backend operations. These sections are: I. "Sensing, Automating, Mediating"; II. "Datafying, Serving, Distributing"; and III. "Subjecting, Humanizing, Repairing." These action-oriented terms specify and make legible distinct processes that materialize on the backends of media. This list of processes is by no means exhaustive; rather, it intends to build momentum and provide inspiration for further investigations of the digital infrastructures and sociotechnical relations on the other side of the screen.

Notes

1. Benjamin Bratton, *The Stack: On Software and Sovereignty* (Cambridge, MA: MIT Press, 2015).

2. Mark Andrejevic, *Automated Media* (London: Routledge, 2020); Michael Curtin, Jennifer Holt, and Kevin Sanson, eds., *Distribution Revolution: Conversations about the Digital Future of Film and Television* (Oakland: University of California Press, 2014); Henry Jenkins, *Convergence Culture: Where Old and New Media Collide* (New York: New York University Press, 2006); Lynn Spigel and Jan Olsson, eds., *Television after TV: Essays on a Medium in Transition* (Durham, NC: Duke University Press, 2004); José van Dijck, Thomas Poell, and Martijn de Waal, *The Platform Society: Public Values in a Connective World* (Oxford: Oxford University Press, 2018); Jeremy Wade Morris and Sarah Murray, eds., *Appified: Culture in the Age of Apps* (Ann Arbor: University of Michigan Press, 2018).

3. Ian Bogost and Nick Montfort, "Platform Studies: Frequently Questioned Answers," *Digital Arts and Culture* (2009); Thomas Poell, David B. Nieborg, and Brook Erin Duffy, *Platforms and Cultural Production* (Malden, MA: Polity, 2021).

4. Anne Helmond, "The Platformization of the Web: Making Web Data Platform Ready," *Social Media + Society* (2015).

5. Jean-Christophe Plantin and Aswin Punathambekar, "Digital Media Infrastructures: Pipes, Platforms, and Politics," *Media, Culture & Society* 41, no. 2 (2019): 163–74.

6. Arne Hintz, Lina Dencik, and Karin Wahl-Jorgensen, *Digital Citizenship in a Datafied Society* (Malden, MA: Polity 2018). Evelyn Ruppert and Stephan Scheel, eds., *Data Practices: Making Up a European People* (London: Goldsmiths Press/MIT Press, 2021); Nick Couldry and Ulises Ali Mejias, *The Costs of Connection: How Data Is Colonizing Human Life and Appropriating It for Capitalism* (Stanford, CA: Stanford University Press, 2019).

7. Aymar Jean Christian, Faithe Day, Mark Díaz, and Chelsea Peterson-Salahuddin, "Platforming Intersectionality: Networked Solidarity and the Limits of Corporate Social Media," *Social Media + Society* 6, no. 3 (July 2020); Stefania Milan and Emiliano Treré,

"Big Data from the South(s): Beyond Data Universalism," *Television & New Media* 20, no. 4 (2019): 319–35; Julia Velkova and Anne Kaun, "Algorithmic Resistance: Media Practices and the Politics of Repair," *Information, Communication & Society* 24, no. 4 (2021): 523–40.

8. Kylie Jarrett, *Digital Labor* (Medford, MA: Polity Press, 2022); Sarah Pink, Martin Berg, Deborah Lupton, and Minna Ruckenstein, eds., *Everyday Automation: Experiencing and Anticipating Emerging Technologies* (London: Routledge, 2022).

9. Miriyam Aouragh and Paula Chakravartty, "Infrastructures of Empire: Towards a Critical Geopolitics of Media and Information Studies," *Media, Culture & Society* 38, no. 4 (2016); Cristina Venegas, *Digital Dilemmas: The State, the Individual, and Digital Media in Cuba* (New Brunswick, NJ: Rutgers University Press, 2010); Rahul Mukherjee, *Radiant Infrastructure: Media, Environment, and Cultures of Uncertainty* (Durham, NC: Duke University Press, 2020); Nicole Starosielski, *The Undersea Network: Sign, Storage, Transmission* (Durham, NC: Duke University Press); Fernanda R. Rosa, "Internet Interconnection Infrastructure: Lessons from the Global South," *Internet Policy Review* 10, no. 4 (2021); Mél Hogan, "Big Data Ecologies," *Ephemera* 18, no. 3 (2018): 631–57; James Schwoch, *Wired into Nature: The Telegraph and the North American Frontier* (Urbana: University of Illinois Press, 2018).

10. Fernanda R. Rosa and Janice A. Hauge, "GAFA's Information Infrastructure Distribution: Interconnection Dynamics in the Global North versus Global South," *Policy & Internet* 14, no. 2 (2021); Ramon Lobato, *Netflix Nations: The Geography of Digital Distribution* (New York: New York University Press, 2019).

11. Safiya Umoja Noble, *Algorithms of Oppression: How Search Engines Reinforce Racism* (New York: New York University Press, 2018); Sasha Costanza-Chock, *Design Justice: Community-Led Practices to Build the Worlds We Need* (Cambridge, MA: MIT Press, 2020); Virginia Eubanks, *Automating Inequality: How High-Tech Tools Profile, Police, and Punish the Poor* (New York: St. Martin's Press, 2017); Cathy O'Neil, *Weapons of Math Destruction: How Big Data Increases Inequality and Threatens Democracy* (New York: Crown, 2016); Ruha Benjamin, *Race after Technology: Abolitionist Tools for the New Jim Code* (Medford, MA: Polity, 2019); Joy Buolamwini and T. Gebru, "Gender Shades: Intersectional Accuracy Disparities in Commercial Gender Classification," *Proceedings of Machine Learning Research* 81 (2018): 77–91.

12. Anne Marie Balsamo, *Designing Culture: The Technological Imagination at Work* (Durham, NC: Duke University Press, 2011); Noble, *Algorithms of Oppression*; Benjamin, *Race after Technology*; Costanza-Chock, *Design Justice*. Also see Jonathan Cohn, *The Burden of Choice: Recommendations, Subversion, and Algorithmic Culture* (New Brunswick, NJ: Rutgers University Press, 2019); and France Winddance Twine, *Geek Girls: Inequality and Opportunity in Silicon Valley* (New York: New York University Press, 2022).

13. Nathan Ensmenger, "The Cloud Is a Factory," in *Your Computer Is on Fire*, ed. Thomas S. Mullaney, Benjamin Peters, Mar Hicks, and Kavita Philip (Cambridge, MA: MIT Press, 2021), 29–50.

14. Also see Shaka McGlotten, "Black Data," *S&F Online*, no. 13.3–14.1 (2016), https://sfonline.barnard.edu/traversing-technologies/shaka-mcglotten-black-data/.

15. Wendy Hui Kyong Chun, *Discriminating Data: Correlation, Neighborhoods, and the New Politics of Recognition* (Cambridge, MA: MIT Press, 2021).

16. Amanda Lotz, *Portals: A Treatise on Internet-Distributed Television* (Ann Arbor: Michigan Publishing, University of Michigan Library, 2017); Andrejevic, *Automated Media*.

17. Jennifer Holt and Patrick Vonderau, "'Where the Internet Lives': Data Centers as Cloud Infrastructure," in *Signal Traffic: Critical Studies of Media Infrastructures*, ed. Lisa Parks and Nicole Starosielski (Urbana: University of Illinois Press, 2015), 71–93; Mél Hogan, "Facebook Data Storage Centers as the Archive's Underbelly," *Television & New Media* 16, no. 1 (2015): 3–18; Vicki Mayer, "From Peat to Google Power: Communications Infrastructures and Structures of Feeling in Groningen," *European Journal of Cultural Studies* 24, no. 4 (2020): 901–15; Sebastián Lehuedé, "Territories of Data: Ontological Divergences in the Growth of Data Infrastructure," *Tapuya: Latin American Science, Technology, and Society* (2022); Alix Johnson, "Data Centers as Infrastructural In-Betweens: Expanding Connections and Enduring Marginalities in Iceland," *American Ethnologist* 46, no. 1 (2019): 75–88.

18. In the spring of 2022, Amazon, Google, and Microsoft owned 65 percent of the global cloud infrastructure services market and more than 50 percent of the large-scale data centers around the world. See "Huge Cloud Market Still Growing at 34% Per Year; Amazon, Microsoft & Google Now Account for 65% of the Total," *Synergy Research Group*, April 28, 2022, https://www.srgresearch.com/articles/huge-cloud-market-is-still-growing-at-34-per-year-amazon-microsoft-and-google-now-account-for-65-of-all-cloud-revenues.

19. Also see Devika Narayan, "Platform Capitalism and Cloud Infrastructure: Theorizing a Hyper-Scale Computing Regime," *Environment and Planning A: Economy and Space* 54, no. 5 (2022), https://doi.org/10.1177/0308518X221094028.

20. By "mediation" we refer to the dynamic processes and unique temporalities of "media," including the multiple ways "media" can come into being, effect power relations, affect subjects, and/or alter material conditions. See Jesús Martín-Barbero, *Communication, Culture, and Hegemony: From the Media to Mediations* (London: Sage Publications, 1993); Sarah Kember and Joanna Zylinska, *Life after New Media: Mediation as a Vital Process* (Cambridge, MA: MIT Press, 2012).

21. Bernhard Rieder, *Engines of Order: A Mechanology of Algorithmic Techniques* (Amsterdam: Amsterdam University Press, 2020).

22. Susan Leigh Star, "The Ethnography of Infrastructure," *American Behavioural Scientist* 43, no. 3 (1999): 377–91.

23. Erving Goffman, *The Presentation of Self in Everyday Life* (London: Penguin Books, 1990), 112.

24. Susan Leigh Star and Martha Lampland, eds., *Standards and Their Stories: How Quantifying, Classifying, and Formalizing Practices Shape Everyday Life* (Ithaca, NY: Cornell University Press, 2009), 21.

25. Frank Pasquale, *The Black Box Society: The Secret Algorithms That Control Money and Information* (Cambridge, MA: Harvard University Press, 2015).

26. On this point, also see Louise Amoore, *Cloud Ethics: Algorithms and the Attributes of Ourselves and Others* (Durham, NC: Duke University Press, 2020).

27. Sara Ahmed, *Queer Phenomenology: Orientations, Objects, Others* (Durham, NC: Duke University Press, 2006), 31.

28. Ibid., 30.

29. Kelly Wagman and Lisa Parks, "Beyond the Command: Feminist STS Research and Critical Issues for the Design of Social Machines," *Proceedings of the ACM on Human Computer Interaction* 5, no. CSCW1 (2021): article no. 101, 1–20.

30. Simone Natale, *Deceitful Media: Artificial Intelligence and Social Life after the Turing Test* (New York: Oxford University Press, 2021), 7.

31. Ahmed, *Queer Phenomenology*, 22.

32. Michel Foucault, *The Foucault Reader: An Introduction to Foucault's Thought*, ed. Paul Rabinow (London: Penguin Books, 1991).

33. Donna Haraway, "Situated Knowledges: The Science Question in Feminism and the Privilege of Partial Perspective," *Feminist Studies* 14, no. 3 (1988): 575; Judy Wajcman, *TechnoFeminism* (Cambridge: Polity, 2004); Lisa Nakamura, *Digitizing Race: Visual Cultures of the Internet* (Minneapolis: University of Minnesota Press, 2008).

34. Roger Silverstone and Eric Hirsch, eds., *Consuming Technologies: Media and Information in Domestic Spaces* (London: Routledge, 1992); Nelly Oudshoorn and Trevor Pinch, eds., *How Users Matter: The Co-construction of Users and Technologies* (Cambridge, MA: MIT Press, 2003); Jenna Burrell, *Invisible Users* (Cambridge, MA: MIT Press, 2012).

35. Steven J. Jackson, "Rethinking Repair," in *Media Technologies: Essays on Communication, Materiality, and Society*, ed. Tarleton Gillespie, Pablo Boczkowski, and Kirsten Foot (Cambridge, MA: MIT Press, 2014), 221–40; Daniela Rosner, *Critical Fabulations: Reworking the Methods and Margins of Design* (Cambridge, MA: MIT Press, 2018).

36. See, for instance, Kishonna L. Gray, *Intersectional Tech: Black Users in Digital Gaming* (Baton Rouge: Louisiana State University Press, 2020); Christine Hine, "Strategies for Reflexive Ethnography in the Smart Home: Autoethnography of Silence and Emotion," *Sociology* 54, no. 1 (2020): 22–36; Lisa Nakamura, *Cybertypes: Race, Ethnicity, and Identity on the Internet* (New York: Routledge, 2002); Lisa Nakamura and Peter Chow-White, eds., *Race after the Internet* (New York: Routledge, 2012); Benjamin, *Race after Technology*; Costanza-Chock, *Design Justice*.

37. Renata Salecl, *A Passion for Ignorance: What We Choose Not to Know and Why* (Princeton, NJ: Princeton University Press, 2020).

38. Ulrich Beck and Peter Wehling, "The Politics of Non-knowing: An Emerging Area of Social and Political Conflict in Reflexive Modernity," in *The Politics of Knowledge*, ed. Fernando Domínguez Rubio and Patrick Baert (London: Routledge, 2013), 33–57.

39. O'Neil, *Weapons of Math Destruction*.

40. Laila Shereen Sakr, *Arabic Glitch: Technoculture, Data Bodies, and Archives* (Stanford, CA: Stanford University Press, 2023).

41. Starosielski, *The Undersea Network*; Lisa Parks, *Cultures in Orbit: Satellites and the Televisual* (Durham, NC: Duke University Press, 2005); Mél Hogan and Asta Vonderau, "Editorial," in "The Nature of Data Centers," special issue, *Culture Machine* 18 (2019); Fernanda R. Rosa, "Code Ethnography and the Materiality of Power in Internet Interconnection Infrastructure," *Qualitative Sociology* 45 (2022): 433–55.

42. Dan Schiller, *Crossed Wires: The Conflicted History of US Telecommunications, From the Post Office to the Internet* (Urbana-Champaign: University of Illinois Press, 2022); José van Dijck, *The Culture of Connectivity: A Critical History of Social Media*

(Oxford: Oxford University Press, 2013); Tarleton Gillespie, "The Politics of Platforms," *New Media & Society* 12, no. 3 (2010): 347–64; Jennifer Holt, *Cloud Policy: A History of Regulating Pipelines, Platforms, and Data* (Cambridge, MA: MIT Press, forthcoming). Also see Adrian Athique and Vibodh Parthasarathi, eds., *Platform Capitalism in India* (Cham, UK: Palgrave Macmillan, 2020); Yujie Chen, Zhifei Mao, and Jack Linchuan Qiu, *Super-Sticky WeChat and Chinese Society* (Bingley, UK: Emerald Publishing, 2018); Rosa, "Code Ethnography."

43. Jane Bennett is interested in the vitality and agential potential of objects. See *Vibrant Matter: A Political Ecology of Things* (Durham, NC: Duke University Press, 2010).

44. Charles R. Acland, "Dirt Research for Media Industries," *Media Industries Journal* 1, no. 1 (2014).

45. See, for example, Plantin and Punathambekar, "Digital Media Infrastructures"; Miriyam Aouragh and Paula Chakravartty, "Infrastructures of Empire: Towards a Critical Geopolitics of Media and Information Studies," *Media, Culture & Society* 38, no. 4 (2016); Cheryll Soriano, "Digital Platform Labor in the Philippines: Emerging Configurations and Policy Implications," *Japan Labor Issues* 5, no. 32 (2021): 55–66; Vicki Mayer, *Below the Line: Producers and Production Studies in the New Television Economy* (Durham, NC: Duke University Press, 2011); John Thornton Caldwell, *Specworld: Folds, Faults, and Fractures in Embedded Creator Industries* (Berkeley: University of California Press, 2023).

46. Matthew Hockenberry, Nicole Starosielski, and Susan Zieger, *Assembly Codes: The Logistics of Media* (Durham, NC: Duke University Press, 2021); Ned Rossiter, *Software, Infrastructure, Labor: A Media Theory of Logistical Nightmares* (New York: Routledge, 2016); Charmaine Chua, "Logistics Leviathan: Circulation, Empire, and the TransPacific Supply Chain," unpublished manuscript (2022); Dan Schiller, *Digital Depression: Information Technology, and Economic Crisis* (Urbana: University of Illinois Press, 2014).

47. Hockenberry, Starosielski, and Zieger, *Assembly Codes*, 13.

48. Anne Kaun and Fredrik Stiernstedt, *Prison Media: Incarceration and the Infrastructures of Work and Technology* (Cambridge, MA: MIT Press, 2023); Anne-Katrin Weber, "A Media Archaeology of Drones: Television in the Army, 1930s–1940s," unpublished manuscript (2022).

49. Nick Couldry and Anna McCarthy, eds., *MediaSpace: Place, Scale, and Culture in a Media Age* (London: Routledge, 2004); Rick Maxwell and Toby Miller, *Greening the Media* (Oxford: Oxford University Press, 2012).

50. Arturo Escobar, *Designs for the Pluriverse: Radical Interdependence, Autonomy, and the Making of Worlds* (Durham, NC: Duke University Press, 2018).

51. Sonia Livingstone. "On the Mediation of Everything: ICA Presidential Address 2008," *Journal of Communication* 59 (2009).

52. Amoore, *Cloud Ethics*; Nick Seaver, "Algorithms as Culture: Some Tactics for the Ethnography of Algorithmic Systems," *Big Data & Society* 4, no. 2 (December 2017); John Cheney-Lippold, *We Are Data: Algorithms and the Making of Our Digital Selves* (New York: New York University Press, 2017); Ted Striphas, "Algorithmic Culture," *European Journal of Cultural Studies* 18, no. 4–5 (2015): 395–412; William Uricchio, "Data, Culture, and the Ambivalence of Algorithms," in *The Datafied Society: Studying Culture through*

Data, ed. Mirko Tobias Schäfer and Karin van Es (Amsterdam: Amsterdam University Press, 2017), 125–37.

53. Lev Manovich, *Software Takes Command: International Texts in Critical Media Aesthetics* (New York: Bloomsbury, 2013); Donald A. MacKenzie, *Trading at the Speed of Light: How Ultrafast Algorithms Are Transforming Financial Markets* (Princeton, NJ: Princeton University Press, 2021); Tung-Hui Hu, *A Prehistory of the Cloud* (Cambridge, MA: MIT Press, 2015).

54. John Durham Peters, *The Marvelous Clouds: Toward a Philosophy of Elemental Media* (Chicago: University of Chicago Press, 2015); Melody Jue, *Wild Blue Media: Thinking through Seawater* (Durham, NC: Duke University Press, 2020); Jussi Parikka, *A Geology of Media* (Minneapolis: University of Minnesota Press, 2015); Shaun Moores, "Arguments for a Non-Media-Centric, Non-Representational Approach to Media and Place," in *Communications/Media/Geographies*, ed. Paul C. Adams, Julie Cupples, Kevin Glynn, André Jansson, and Shaun Moores (New York: Routledge, 2016); Tung-Hui Hu, *A Prehistory of the Cloud* (Cambridge, MA: MIT Press, 2015); Rafico Ruiz, *Slow Disturbance: Infrastructural Mediation on the Settler Colonial Resource Frontier* (Durham, NC: Duke University Press, 2021).

55. Nicole Starosielski and Janet Walker, eds., *Sustainable Media: Critical Approaches to Media and Environment* (New York: Routledge, 2016); Sean Cubbitt, *Finite Media: Environmental Implications of Digital Technologies* (Durham, NC: Duke University Press, 2017); Tim Markham and Scott Rodgers, eds., *Conditions of Mediation: Phenomenological Perspectives on Media* (New York: Peter Lang, 2017).

56. Joseph Turow, *Media Systems in Society: Understanding Industries, Strategies, and Power*, 2nd ed. (New York: Longman, 1997).

57. See Sally Wyatt, "Metaphors in Critical Internet and Digital Media Studies," *New Media & Society* 23, no. 2 (2021): 406–16. Metaphors can also foster thinking with care about neglected matters of concern; see, for instance, Maria Puig de la Bellacasa, "Matters of Care in Technoscience: Assembling Neglected Things," *Social Studies of Science* 41, no. 1 (2011): 85–106.

58. Donna Haraway, *Staying with the Trouble: Making Kin in the Chthulucene* (Durham, NC: Duke University Press, 2016), 35.

59. David Hesmondhalgh, "The Infrastructural Turn in Media and Internet Research," in *The Routledge Companion to Media Industries*, ed. Paul McDonald (Abingdon, UK: Routledge, 2022), 132–42.

60. We think about the notion of response-abilities in relation to Haraway's *Staying with the Trouble*, 33–35. To cultivate response-ability involves engaging with the distribution of information and control across the many boundaries and times/spaces in which systems exist and recognizing the need to make liveable "damaged but still ongoing living worlds." Response-abilities can take shape "in passion and action, detachment and attachment" in "collective knowing and doing, [in] an ecology of practices."

61. Other imaginative works that critically debunk the metaphor of "artificial intelligence" include Kate Crawford, *Atlas of AI: Power, Politics, and the Planetary Costs of Artificial Intelligence* (New Haven: Yale University Press, 2021) and Peter Jakobsson, Anne

Kaun, and Fredrik Stiernstedt, "Machine Intelligences—An Introduction," *Culture Machine* 20 (2021).

62. José van Dijck, "Seeing the Forest for the Trees: Visualizing Platformization and Its Governance," *New Media & Society* 23 no. 9 (2020): 2801–19.

63. Isabelle Stengers, "The Insistence of Possibles: Towards a Speculative Pragmatism," *Parse Journal* 7 (2017), https://parsejournal.com/article/the-insistence-of-possibles%E2%80%A8-towards-a-speculative-pragmatism/.

64. Maria Bakardjieva, "Home Implosion: Digital Media and the Reinvention of the Private Sphere," in *Happiness and Domestic Life: The Influence of the Home on Subjective and Social Wellbeing*, ed. Maria Teresa Russo, Antonio Argandoña, and Richard Peatfield (New York: Routledge, 2022), 57–72.

65. Jürgen Habermas, "Institutions of the Public Sphere," in *Approaches to Media: A Reader*, ed. Oliver Boyd-Barrett and Chris Newbold, *Foundations in Media* (London: E. Arnold, 1995), 235–44; Benedict Anderson, *Imagined Communities: Reflections on the Origin and Spread of Nationalism* (London: Verso, 2006); David Morley and Charlotte Brunsdon, *The Nationwide Television Studies* (London: Routledge, 1999).

66. Lisa Parks, "Media Infrastructures and Affect," *Flow Journal: A Critical Forum on Media and Culture* 19 (2014), https://www.flowjournal.org/2014/05/media-infrastructures-and-affect/.

67. Engin F. Isin and Greg Marc Nielsen, eds., *Acts of Citizenship* (London: Zed Books, 2008).

68. Jenkins, *Convergence Culture*; John Fiske, *Television Culture*, 2nd ed. (London: Routledge, 2011).

69. Mark Andrejevic, "Watching Television without Pity: The Productivity of Online Fans," *Television and New Media* 9, no. 1 (2008): 24–46; Jack Bratich, "Programming Reality: Control Societies, New Subjects, and the Powers of Transformation," in *Makeover Television: Realities Remodelled*, ed. Dana Heller (London: I. B. Tauris, 2007), 6–22; Tiziana Terranova, *Network Culture: Politics for the Information Age* (London: Pluto Press, 2004); Kylie Jarrett, *Feminism, Labour, and Digital Media: The Digital Housewife* (New York: Routledge 2016); Ranjana Das and Brita Ytre-Arne, eds., *The Future of Audiences: A Foresight Analysis of Interfaces and Engagement* (Guildford, UK: Palgrave Macmillan, 2018).

70. Nick Couldry and Ulises Ali Mejias, *The Costs of Connection: How Data Is Colonizing Human Life and Appropriating It for Capitalism* (Stanford, CA: Stanford University Press, 2019).

71. Wendy Hui Kyong Chun, "Queerying Homophily," in *Pattern Discrimination*, eds. Clemens Apprich, Wendy Hui Kyong Chun, and Florian Cramer (Lüneburg, Ger.: meson press, 2018), 59–97.

72. Couldry and Mejias, *The Costs of Connection*.

73. Ken Hillis, Susanna Paasonen, and Michael Petit, eds., *Networked Affect* (Cambridge, MA: MIT Press, 2015).

PART I

SENSING, AUTOMATING, MEDIATING

1

ATMOSPHERIC MEDIATION

From Smart Dust to Customizable Governance

MARK ANDREJEVIC
AND ZALA VOLCIC

Consider the particle of "smart dust"—a processor so small it can float on the breeze and dance in a sunbeam. The speculative existence of "smart dust" derives from the ambition to make computing as ubiquitous and invisible as air. Its role is to transform one of our defining media—the environment through which we move—into a computational system: to datify the atmosphere. We might approach the prospect of smart dust not as a practical eventuality (though we do not rule this out), but as an object of desire—the logical endpoint of ubiquitous, remote, passive sensing. As we busily equip the objects around us with an array of sensors, how might we ensure that they are everywhere they need to be so as to capture *everything*? For *Wired* magazine founder and perennial tech guru Kevin Kelly, the ambition of total coverage is synonymous with the next Big Tech platform: augmented reality as a means of networking everything (or at least everything that counts). As he puts it, parroting the ambition of Jorge Luis Borges's Imperial cartographers: "To recreate a map that is as big as the globe—in 3D, no less—you need to photograph all places and things from every possible angle, all the time, which means you need to have a planet full of cameras that are always on."[1] As the scope of coverage expands, the cameras themselves would have to shrink to the size of "pinpoint electric eyes that can be placed anywhere and everywhere."[2] For cameras to be everywhere so they can capture everything, they would have to simultaneously disappear: that is, to become one with the environment through which they move—like smart dust. But why limit their sensing potential to the visual realm? If cameras can become vanishingly small, why not microphones, accelerometers, barometers, heat sensors, heart sensors, and so on? As one breathless account puts it in a description of the potential uses of smart dust, "It's like multiplying the internet of things technology millions or billions of times over."[3] The applications are as wide-ranging as the environment itself, from tracking the smallest piece of inventory, to monitoring the water saturation of individual plant roots, to sprinkling "neural dust . . . on the human brain, to provide feedback about brain functionality."[4] The environment is brimming with signals: what if we could capture and corral them all?

This chapter proposes a consideration of what we describe as "atmospheric mediation"—the prospect of capturing and replicating an environment and the signals it contains. It is a form of mediation that converges with the prospect of total surveillance insofar as it gestures toward an infrastructure for comprehensive data capture: the embedding of sensor networks not just in the durable contours of the physical environment, but into the atmospheres through which we move. The point of such an analysis is not simply to propose a metaphorical link between the ideological and physical atmospheres described by Peter Sloterdijk,[5] but to unearth an operational link enabled by the development of networked digital media infrastructures. Smart dust, for example, may one day be literally inhaled or ingested (at least according to some accounts), providing insight into internal body functions, including mental ones, and perhaps communicating directly with them.[6] As a media technology, smart dust simultaneously becomes the medium through which we move—the air we breathe, the space of life. It is this combination of ubiquity with invisibility that renders atmospheric media amenable to theme of the "backend." The promise of immediacy—in the form of immediate data collection and response—amounts to a recession of mediation. As Mark Hansen puts it, "No longer a delimited temporal object that we engage with focally through an interface such as a screen, media become an environment that we experience simply by being and acting in space and time—which is to say, without in most cases explicitly being aware of it, without taking it as the intentional object or target of our time consciousness."[7] At the same time, such systems become articulated to transformations in the material environment. The version of augmented reality anticipated, for example, by Kelly, takes place at a temporality and level of mass specification that is no longer "of the order of conscious perception."[8] Certainly, some form of response or messaging eventuates—that is, a particular user may receive a customized message, direction, or prompt; an access point may open up or close down. However, the extra-subjective sequence of data capture, processing, and response takes place at pace and scale inaccessible to users: one that is, as Shane Denson puts it, "discorrelated" with subjective perception.[9]

We might also have described the object of our reflections in terms of "environmental mediation," since there is a direct connection to environmental forms of governance and control—but this term overlaps too closely with work on ecological systems associated with progressive forms of environmentalism. We nonetheless remain influenced by the very concept of "environmental media," which typically refers to the elemental media of air, water, and land.[10] What we call atmospheric media captures the forms of signaling that take place across and through these elemental media in order to make their interconnections and communications machine readable. The chapter also draws inspiration from the work of Lisa Parks on "vertical mediation" (and its relation to Eyal Weizman's work on the politics of verticality).[11] It does so in order to connect the theme of automated data collection with an aesthetics and a politics: the relationship between framelessness, understood as the goal of re-presenting the world in its entirety, and the related logic of environmental governance—that is, the ability to intervene at the level of the physical and informational milieu in real time.

In the first section, we draw on this work to develop our approach to "atmospheric media" and its relation to contemporary logics and aesthetics of mediation. Representations of media atmospheres, for example, rely on forms of 3D representation such as augmented and virtual reality. Even 360-degree cameras push in the direction of modeling the view from everywhere. In the second part of the chapter, we consider some interrelated attributes of atmospheric media, including "framelessness," environmentality, and automation. Atmospheric media are, by their very nature, frameless, insofar as the ambition is one of environment-level captures. Terms like "ubiquitous computing" and "the internet of things" capture the scope of this ambition: digital, interactive devices must be "everywhere," inhabiting "everything," in order to capture—and act upon—the environments through which we move. The combination of environment-level information capture with responsive environments—spaces that can both sense and act—enable forms of governance that operate through the milieu, by changing physical and informational constraints rather than internal states of mind. None of this would be possible without cascading logics of automation: that is, the automation of data collection, processing, and response. By highlighting the connections between these processes, we seek to build upon existing approaches to "vertical" and "environmental" mediation.

The Politics of Verticality

The model of media saturation is continuous with the politics of verticality described by Weizman in his discussion of Israeli strategies for dominating and controlling the Palestinian territories.[12] His work explores the ways in which the occupation of and control over intermingled Israeli and Palestinian lands became irreducible to two-dimensional territorial boundaries. Rather, the occupation incorporates spatial layers of interconnection and control: of the airspace above the ground and the infrastructure below, including archaeological layers of cultural significance as well as utilities such as electrical cables and sewage systems. The politics of verticality refers to an added dimension that renders governance and control "volumetric": "Indeed, a new way of imagining territory was developed for the West Bank. The region was no longer seen as a two-dimensional surface of a single territory, but as a large three-dimensional volume, containing a layered series of ethnic, political, and strategic territories."[13] In his critique of drone warfare, Gregoire Chamayou makes a similar point, drawing on the work of Stephen Graham: "we have switched from the horizontal to the vertical, from the two-dimensional space of the old maps of army staffs to geopolitics based on volumes."[14] In the context of drone warfare, he invokes the military shorthand of the so-called "kill box": the temporary opening of a space within which a drone attack can take place, designated by both the territory on the ground and the aerial space within which the drone can operate. This conception of territories as volumetric lends itself to strategies of atmospheric mediation: the ambition of saturating a three-dimensional space with sensing systems that can capture and reconstruct it in real time, whether for the purposes of control, exploitation, or attack. The two-dimensional surface of the screen is supplemented by a volumetric geopolitics of control. Technologies like smart dust envision saturating three-dimensional space, but this can also take place through a range of sensors that locate and track behavior in time and space—as well as representational media technologies that display and re-create information in three dimensions. As we argue in the section on environmentality, atmospheric media lead to the automated reconfiguration of three-dimensional space in both virtual and material forms.

Vertical Mediation

In her work on media "coverage," Lisa Parks explores the mediated elements of verticality by considering the information and communication technologies used to control "air space, spectrum, and orbit," including satellites, drones, and airline security.[15] She refers to these modalities of control in terms of the struggle for "vertical hegemony," which "involves efforts to maneuver through, activate technologies within, occupy, or control the vast stretch of space between the earth's surface and the outer limits of orbit as well as the kinds of activities that can occur there."[16] The aerial image has long served as a metaphor for the omniscience of a god's-eye view,[17] but the prospect of embedded, distributed sensing interprets verticality as entailing what might be described as "atmospheric" or environmental mediation. If the aerial perspective is a view from on high, the atmospheric one is a "view" from *everywhere at once* and thus nowhere in particular. It is not simply a viewing image, in the sense of visual data capture, but a sensory amalgam: the combination of whatever information sensors can collect—images, perhaps, but also sound, temperature, atmospheric pressure, mood, interaction patterns, traffic, wastewater flow, and more.

As Parks argues, the concept of verticality leads directly to an engagement with atmospheric logics, which she frames in terms of "cultural atmospherics," understood as "the everyday social relations, structures of feeling, dispositions, and affects that emerge as consequences of vertical power."[18] Adding the third dimension of verticality to a consideration of territorial control, as suggested by Weizman, results not simply in a consideration of altitude as a crucial factor (in terms of vertical layers of infrastructure, for example), but modalities of volumetric governance that concern a complex of spatial relations. Such a formulation invokes the connection described by Sloterdijk between interventions in the materiality of the atmosphere (such as, for example, the use of poison gas during World War I) and the sociopsychological dimension of an ideological or affective atmosphere.[19] The latter-day notion that "smart dust" might monitor both physical space and (sprinkled upon the brain) mental activity is emblematic of the proposed link between inner and outer space (and the mechanistic model that subtends it).

This chapter builds on Parks's groundbreaking work by considering the relationship between atmospheric forms of mediation and the modalities of representation and control with which they are associated. We are interested, in particular, in how media designed to permeate the atmosphere articulate with the automated transformation and modulation of physical and virtual spaces. Perhaps the archetypical speculative example in this regard is that of augmented reality: the saturation of physical space by "pinpoint" sensors enables the comprehensive reconstruction of space in real time so that it can be rendered customizable in a range of dimensions, both informational and physical. As envisioned by futurists like Kevin Kelly, augmented reality anticipates the generalization of what Walter Benjamin once identified as the defining characteristic of the bourgeois interior: its ability to mold itself to its inhabitants.[20] Augmented reality not only envisions a customized information atmosphere, but also a malleable and modulatable physical one: providing access to some and not others, customizing the material environment, optimizing populational flows in real time, and adjusting the circulation of resources and products. Closely related to augmented reality is the emerging "internet of things," which comprises a growing range of objects equipped with networked sensors: smart appliances, devices, and spaces able to communicate with one another and with centralized coordinating systems. In a 1999 article that predicted this networked environment, Neil Gross describes it as an "electronic skin" consisting of "millions of embedded electronic measuring devices: thermostats, pressure gauges, pollution detectors, cameras, microphones, glucose sensors, EKGs, electroencephalographs."[21] This assemblage of devices, he wrote, "will probe and monitor cities and endangered species, the atmosphere, our ships, highways and fleets of trucks, our conversations, our bodies—even our dreams."[22] Once again, the model of atmospheric mediation envisions the convergence of the mental and material realms: our physical environment and our head space.

Atmospheric Mediation

Drawing on the notion of vertical hegemony—control over air space—we might consider the ways in which atmospheric mediation enables what Christian Borch (drawing on the work of Sloterdijk)[23] describes as the "politics of atmospheres," which is "tied to a concern with sensory politics, i.e., the ways in which atmospheres are designed in a multisensory fashion in order to govern or induce particular behaviours."[24] Atmospheric governance warrants critical attention, he argues, because "the moulding of behaviour . . . mostly takes place at a non-conscious level."[25] Changes in the surrounding milieu do not have to be internalized to shape individual behavior—this is the theoretical insight outlined by Michel Foucault in his discussion of "environmental" forms of governance that intervene in the "rules of the game" rather than directly in the conscious disposition of the players.[26]

We start with the example of smart dust because it highlights the ambition of constructing a view from everywhere (or nowhere). Unlike conventional cameras, which have a situated perspective and viewpoint, smart dust envisions what might be described as a multisensory reconstruction of physical space: filling it in order to reproduce (rather than represent) it. IBM's patent for "invisible smart dust" portrays the technology as the logical extension of "the popularity of small computing devices . . . the rapid increase of Internet growth, and the diminishing size and costs of sensors such as, for example, transistors."[27] The technology marks the convergence of the miniaturization and multiplication of devices with total coverage: if the devices get vanishingly small, they can effectively be everywhere. The result is the ability to reconstruct physical spaces and their characteristics in ways that overcome obstacles such as line-of-sight obstructions and acoustic barriers. Google's ambition to organize the world's information opens up the conceptual space to imagine the real-time spatio-digital cataloging of object space. As one press account puts it, "Smart dust would make it possible to run a Google search in the physical world: Ask 'where are my keys?' and the dust could locate them. An army could ask the same of enemy tanks."[28] This example suggests another way to interpret the concept of the "internet of things"—not just a fully "smartened" physical environment, but the ability to order, categorize, sort, and search the object world as we do the informational one. The ambition would be not simply to organize the world's information, but the world itself.

As a practical technology, the prospect of smart dust is still a long way off. As a speculative model, however, it highlights a familiar set of logics, including the miniaturization and sensorization of the built environment, the move toward always on, always connected, networked devices—and the mass coordination of these devices once in place (a version of "swarming"). Consider, for example, the trajectory of consumer-facing computing from networked large-scale computers to the desktop, the laptop, tablets, smart phones, and smart watches. The transformations in scale are accompanied by shifting rhythms of use: from discrete, dedicated interactions with digital devices to constant connectivity and comprehensive geographic coverage.

Smart dust provides one way of thinking about what we are describing as "atmospheric media," but the goal of permeating physical space with a comprehensive monitoring capacity is a recurring theme in the development of contemporary sensor technology. Consider, for example, the development of microdrones designed to make it possible to monitor internal spaces in contexts of urban warfare (including tunnel and structure mapping). Drones flying at altitude may be able to capture the view of an entire city in real time, but how might they map internal and underground structures? Suggestively, one approach has been to use another saturating medium: researchers have developed a two-drone system that can "see through walls" by measuring the strength of WiFi signals as these are refracted and reflected by the objects in the room.[29] The signals come to double as probes, a kind of electromagnetic sonar for mapping and reconstructing physical space.

In the realm of commerce, the company Juniper Networks, which specializes in computer networking systems, has dubbed its WiFi local area network system "Mist" to capture the sense of spatial permeation associated with the medium. In the business world, atmospheric metaphors abound, from the familiar reference to "the cloud" to MIT's Project Oxygen, which describes its ambition in terms of "bringing abundant computation and communication, as pervasive and free as air, naturally into people's lives."[30] The multiplying range of available smart speakers also invoke spatial metaphors—Google's Home, Amazon's Echo, Apple's HomePod—recalling Benjamin's description of the ideal of the bourgeois home as "a sort of cockpit."[31] Indeed, the proliferation of smart speakers for domestic use marks the incursion of multimodal sensing devices into domestic space: an ongoing process of getting inside the walls of the home (along with other devices, such as smart phones and tablets) to capture a growing array of information.

Patents for Google's smart speaker system, for example, envision a future in which the devices harness an avalanche of data from devices equipped with "temperature sensor(s), humidity sensor(s), hazard-related sensor(s) or other environmental sensor(s), accelerometer(s), microphone(s), optical sensors up to and including camera(s)."[32] The goal is to amass information including: "various properties such as acceleration, temperature, humidity, water, supplied power, proximity, external motion, device motion, sound signals, ultrasound signals, light signals, fire, smoke, carbon monoxide or other gas, global positioning-satellite signals, radio-frequency, other electromagnetic signals or fields, or the like."[33] In their very open-endedness, such lists recapitulate a drive to reproduce the entire home environment in datafied form: what planners and designers sometimes describe as a "digital twin"—in multiple sensory dimensions. These forms of atmospheric mediation do not simply seek to capture and manage spatial relations, but rather to permeate the sensory spectrum: to capture (and potentially modulate) all available dimensions of an environment. Such dimensions multiply alongside the available sensing technology—when aroma detectors or infrared sensors are added, they provide additional dimensions of atmospheric capture.

"Framelessness"

The digital "twinning" of the environment invokes strategies of data capture and representation that might be described as "frameless"—those that dispense with a situated viewpoint or notional limit.[34] An aesthetics of framelessness characterizes emerging technologies that burst the limits of the representational frame, such as 360-degree cameras, virtual reality, and augmented reality. Total information collection and virtual reality go hand in hand. Atmospheric mediation, as some of the previous examples suggest, lends itself to this aesthetics of framelessness. The mode of representation that fits best with, for example, a "smart dust" sensing system, would dispense with the limits of a frame in order to enable the reproduction of an entire space or environment in informational form.

The notion of framelessness invokes a familiar chain of connections between the ambition of "collecting everything and holding on to it forever"[35] and the convergent uses of such data—the fact that data captured for one purpose, such as medical profiling, might also be used for marketing, risk assessment, and so on. Thus, the term invokes multiple meanings of the frame: a limit on what information is considered relevant, a defined set of purposes for which it can be used, and restrictions on how long it can be held. Framelessness refers to the indeterminacy of these limits: all information is potentially relevant for a growing range of seemingly unrelated purposes. Perhaps barometric pressure might help predict crime or consumption rates—until the correlations are run, this cannot be ruled out in advance. At the same time, the fact that new patterns might emerge when additional information is added at some future point provides the motivations for holding on to data as long as possible—without limit.

In the realm of atmospheric mediation, framelessness is a machinic response to postsubjective forms of automated interpretation: it replaces the situated perspective of the knowing subject with the (impossible) ambition of totality; it substitutes reproduction for representation. Consider, for example, the goal of training facial recognition systems to interpret expressions. Given the well documented challenges of finding universal, one-to-one links between detectable muscle movements (an eyebrow raise, for example) and an underlying emotional state,[36] expression detection researchers highlight the importance of contextual cues.[37] In so doing, they open up an infinite regress, because context is also perspectival—it requires a situated perspective and an interpretive act. Substituting for the positionality of a human subject, then, leads to the goal of collecting as much information as possible in the attempt to capture a constantly receding contextual horizon.

Something similar happens with, for example, self-driving cars. Lacking a situated human subject as a guide, state-of-the-art driverless car sensing systems using Lidar (laser beams that function like radar probes) reproduce a 360-degree, 3D, frameless perspective of the vehicle's surroundings.[38] The car's sensing system attempts to map the entire fast-moving surrounding environment in real time. This is a very different approach, clearly, to that taken by a human driver, for whom the attempt to take in the entire surrounding environment would result in an immediate accident. Lacking the situated intentionality and understanding of the subject, a machinic system substitutes for it the goal of total situational awareness, raising a host of computational issues, including questions about the importance of including additional sensory inputs (such as audio, for example). The wager is that information saturation—the ability to capture all available information—might substitute for subjective awareness and comprehension.

The (impossible) ideal of framelessness provides the background for contemporary critiques of representation: that its irreducible incompleteness (necessitated by the finite limitations of the subject) renders all accounts partial, therefore opening the floodgates to indeterminacy and conspiracy theory. This is the real message of the charge of "fake news" mobilized by the political right in the contemporary media landscape: not that all news is patently untrue, but that it is always incomplete, subject to further forms of explication and contextualization in ways that allegedly deprive it of evidentiary purchase. The horizon of total information (whether in the form of complete coverage or situational context) retreats indefinitely before all attempts at capture.

Environmentality

The eclipse of the subjective perspective implied by the ideal of framelessness corresponds to what might be described as extra- (or infra-) subjective forms of governance, what Borch describes as an "atmospheric politics."[39] We might trace, in this regard, the connections between forms of control that rely on atmospheric mediation and what Foucault describes as "environmentality"—a mode of governance that bypasses direct subjectivization by acting on the encompassing "milieu."[40] For Foucault, environmentality focuses on the broader context of action: "the perpetual intrication of a geographical, climatic, and physical milieu . . . where nature, in the sense of physical elements, interferes with nature in the sense of the nature of the human species, at that point of articulation where the milieu becomes the determining factor of nature. This is where the sovereign will have to intervene . . . by acting on the milieu."[41] We might start to draw the connection between this mode of governance and the goal of saturating the environment with networked sensors: to control a milieu, it is necessary to capture and model it. Such an approach to governance characterizes the ambition, for example, of augmented reality: the provision of physical space with a modulatable, sensorized digital overlay. The interface and the milieu coincide: the ambition is to render the atmosphere fully capturable, hypermediated, completely calculable. Erich Hörl has gone so far as to argue that "Environmentality and the process of Environmentalization . . . have to be considered the key phenomena of our technological condition."[42] For him, the two processes of environmental capture and modulation go hand in hand: the development of ubiquitous sensing infrastructures feeds into the modulation of affective and behavioral response.

Similarly, Jennifer Gabrys draws on Foucault's analysis of environmentality to consider how milieu-based governance is distinct from "subject-based or population-based distributions of governance."[43] For Foucault, in his lectures collected in *The Birth of Biopolitics*, environmentality relies on systems in which "action is brought to bear on the rules of the game rather than on the players . . . in which there is an environmental type of intervention instead of the internal subjugation of individuals."[44] This last point differentiates "environmentality" as a mode of governance from discipline insofar as the former dispenses with the internalization of the monitoring gaze and attendant forms of subjectivization. The rise of automated systems supplements and reconfigures governance by treating the environment as both a sensor and a flexible container. A floor capable of tracking the footsteps that traverse it can be configured, for example, to detect and cushion a fall. Environment-level tracking enables governance through modulations in both physical and informational surroundings.

The infrastructural formations of atmospheric mediation are directed toward this model of governance, including not just the flexible and sensorized systems associated with the development of smart cities, but also the infiltration of interactive monitoring networks into domestic space. The real-time atmospheric monitoring associated with, for example, smart dust or even smart speakers has as its goal not just the mapping of static space, but the capture of the rhythms of daily life to predict future activity so this can be anticipated and shaped (or preempted) through environmental modulation. As Brian Massumi puts it, "environmentality must work through the 'regulation of effects' rather than of causes."[45]

Such analyses highlight the imperative of the "volumetric" character of atmospheric mediation. The goal is to overcome the abstraction of representation—the flattening of the territory. If monitored spaces are volumetric, then their capture must follow suit. Saturating monitored enclosures with sensing capacity, then, relies not just on the distribution of sensors but their ability to capture information passively, at a distance. Some networked sensors will press close to the skin (smart watches that capture blood oxygenation levels, for example), relying on electromagnetic signals to communicate with other devices. Others will read expression, identity, heart rates, and more at a distance. The monitored volume will be full of these signals: laser systems to detect facial features and cardiac activity, as well as the electromagnetic signals that convey this information to remote receivers and coordinate the activity of interactive environments. If we could see these signals and sensing vectors, the monitored enclosure—whether smart room or city—would be completely saturated by them.

Such an image recalls Sloterdijk's description of the politics of atmospheres: a life that "resembles a sojourn in a palace filled with gas, animated by the poison of themed events."[46] This analysis, however, remains at the level of representation and recalls concerns about mediated propaganda that operate at the ideological level. Borch notes this in his discussion of atmospheric politics, which he describes in terms of "mass-media propaganda" that results from "controlling the circulation of information."[47] The environmental modality described by Gabrys and Massumi, by contrast, invokes a different register—not ideological messaging, but the modulation of affective atmospheres and material environments, both informational and physical.[48] When it comes to the circulation of information at this level, the reference is not to the political or ideational content of mass media messaging, but to information about behavior and activity—the data collected by sensors. This information may, in turn, shape ideological content (as in the case of targeted online messaging, or customized advertising billboards), but it can also modify actionable elements of the milieu: which doors open and close, what prices appear in display cases, what offers are made to which individuals, and so on. Atmospheric media individualizes and desubjectivizes simultaneously.[49]

Automated Mediation

Atmospheric mediation takes place at a scale that would be impossible without automation, which invigorates the fantasy of the possibility of collecting "everything" in real time. The sheer *volume* of data collected by a multiplying array of sensors would be far too much to be collected, stored, and processed by hand—or by analog means. The automation of data collection, feedback, and response allows for a departure from strategies of discipline, which is the logic of industrial management in an era of mass production. Disciplinary strategies are a product of scarcity: the only way to ensure everybody is watched is to make people watch themselves. Automated environmentality, by contrast, is a strategy of surfeit in keeping with the logic of consumerist, post-industrial customization—a logic anticipated by Gilles Deleuze's oft-cited observation that postdisciplinary controls "are a modulation, like a self-deforming cast that will continuously change from one moment to the other."[50]

Information gathered at the environmental scale is not meant for human consumption. Rather, such information becomes "operational" in the sense invoked by Trevor Paglen, who juxtaposes it to representation—in both its political and symbolic senses.[51] As a visual artist, Paglen anticipates the fate of the image in an era of automation, drawing on the work of filmmaker Harun Farocki, who explored the images generated by industrial machines to represent the activity of their sensors to human operators. As Farocki put it, "I called such images . . . 'operative images.' These are images that do not represent an object, but rather are part of an operation."[52] Automated mediation tends toward the operationalization of all sensor data (not just visual images), insofar as it relies on sensor data that does not *represent* so much as it *acts* by transforming the environment and altering the atmosphere. Antoinette Rouvroy diagnoses in this shift "a crisis of representation in itself," which has profound political consequences: "Representation, ordeal, event, and critique are in a way by-passed by the new possibilities of modelling the world."[53] The invocation of the term "modelling" is telling, in this context, insofar as it invokes the process of the "twinning" of the milieu or environment not simply as a means of representation, but as part of a preemptive operation or intervention. A particular set of behaviors, for example, result in an analysis of risk or benefit that culminates in a commercial offer or a military strike. The monitored enclosure can be transformed into a consuming space or a kill box.

In this respect, automated mediation recapitulates the age-old fantasy of immediation—the disappearance of the interface—that recurs, most recently, in the attempt to "perfect" virtual reality (and to develop direct brain-to-brain or brain-to-machine interfaces). The goal of immediation is to instantiate what Slavoj Žižek describes as "the dream of a language which no longer acts upon the subject merely through the intermediate sphere of meaning but has direct effects in the real."[54] Žižek's diagnosis here aligns with Rouvroy's discussion of the crisis of representation and its political consequences. For him, the reduction enacted by digital automation—that is, the operationalization of representation—is "psychotic" in the sense that he uses to describe virtual reality: "If, in 'normal' symbolic communication, we are dealing with the distance (between 'things' and 'words') which opens up the space for the domain of Sense and, within it, for symbolic engagement, in the case of virtual reality, on the contrary, the very over-proximity (of the sign and the designated content) disengages us, closes up the space for symbolic engagement."[55] Symbolic language, in Žižek's terms, opens up the space for interpretation, politics, and judgment, precisely because of its gaps and incompleteness—the fact that nothing can be fully calculated in advance. By contrast, operationalism attempts to offload the labor of civic life onto automated systems—it seeks the "perfection" of social life through its obliteration.

This might be another way to describe the pathology of "social" media: the split whereby, at one level, representations continue to operate. We indulge an apparent passion for constant communication, hyper-interactivity. At another level, however, this apparent sociality is displaced by an automated set of relations that structure our informational encounters: what matters is not what we say, but the fact that we said it, and how this correlates with other forms of behavior (possible acts of consumption, on the one hand, or potential threats on the other). This split underwrites the anxiety of the contemporary moment: that in the register of atmospheric mediation, the purchase of representation is diminished in comparison with the efficacy of operationalism. We may provide all the narrative arguments and evidential proof we can muster to demonstrate, for example, the reality of climate change, the benefits of vaccination, and so on, but claims are engulfed by the systems that curate the information environment according to a countervailing set of operational imperatives: more likes, more shares, more engagement, more stickiness. The fear is that what *matters* in terms of impact is the shaping of this atmosphere by automated systems, rather than the compelling power of any particular narrative arc. This is, perhaps, another way of expressing Rouvroy's description of representation's "crisis."[56]

Conclusion

To invoke the notion of atmospheric media is to highlight the link between automated data collection and a mode of governance that operates in an environmental register. It would be wrong to claim that representational content and disciplinary forms of control have been displaced or surpassed. Surely these persist and, we would argue, remain ineliminable. We do not believe the goal of total information capture is possible—or even particularly plausible. But plausibility is not the deciding factor when it comes to the imperatives that shape technological and economic investment (the prospect of infinite growth that underwrites the dominant global economic system is perhaps the defining example of impossible goals shaping concrete actions and lived social relations).

We do, however, seek to identify what might be described as a shift in balance or emphasis away from representation and toward reproduction or "modeling." What matters for the model is not an internalized set of ideologies—for all practical purposes, when enough data is available, subjective dispositions can be black-boxed—but, as Massumi puts it, the regulation of effects.[57] Jeremy Packer makes a similar point in his discussion of the logics of "big data": "In this model, the only thing that matters are directly measurable results. The outcomes of all data prompts . . . are collected, stored, and processed in order to more finely tune their value . . . and more importantly to fine-tune their affectivity. . . . [T]he effect is the Content."[58] This shift in strategy, as his analysis suggests, depends on the ability to saturate the informational space: to capture *all* outcomes and prompts. Tellingly, Packer is drawing on the example of Google, whose model of organizing informational space anticipates that of reproducing and modeling physical space.

Such a model, we have argued, operates according to what, at first glance, appears to be a frameless, a-subjective perspective: the view from everywhere/ nowhere. The mode of governance it enables similarly bypasses the register of subjective internalization. In a pastiche of "new materialism," it performs the leveling gesture of bypassing the register of subjectivity, monitoring communicative activity alongside moon phases (or whatever: air pressure, humidity, sunspots, etc.)—cardiac signals along with seismic ones. However, the repressed figure of the subject returns in the irreducible incompleteness of the digital "twin"—the horizon of finitude that gives the lie to the goal of capturing "everything." In practical terms, of course, this figure returns in the desires and goals that shape the deployment of environmental governance and the ends to which it is put, whether these be profit maximization, risk minimization, or security perfected.

Notes

1. Kevin Kelly, "AR Will Spark the Next Big Tech Platform," *Wired*, February 12, 2019, https://www.wired.com/story/mirrorworld-ar-next-big-tech-platform/.

2. Ibid.

3. Bernard Marr, "Smart Dust Is Coming. Are You Ready?" *Forbes*, September 16, 2018, https://www.forbes.com/sites/bernardmarr/2018/09/16/smart-dust-is-coming-are-you-ready/?sh=262586af5e41.

4. Ibid.

5. Peter Sloterdijk, "Dyed-in-the-Wool Citizens. Atmospheric Politics," in *Making Things Public: Atmospheres of Democracy*, ed. Bruno Latour and Peter Weibel (Cambridge, MA: MIT Press, 2005), 944–51.

6. Joe Andrews, "Smart Dust and Other Wild Tech Ideas That Could Become Major Breakthroughs in the Next Decade," *CNBC*, June 18, 2019, https://www.cnbc.com/2019/06/18/wild-tech-ideas-with-big-chance-of-becoming-breakthroughs-in-a-decade.html;

Cate Lawrence, "Is Smart Dust the IoT Vector of the Future?" *ReadWrite.com*, August 20, 2016, https://readwrite.com/2016/08/20/smart-dust-carrier-iot-future-dl4/.

7. Mark Hansen, "Ubiquitous Sensation: Toward an Atmospheric, Collective, and Microtemporal Model of Media," in *Throughout: Art and Culture Emerging with Ubiquitous Computing*, ed. Ulrik Ekman (Cambridge, MA: MIT Press, 2012), 70.

8. Ibid.

9. Shane Denson, *Discorrelated Images* (Durham, NC: Duke University Press, 2020).

10. John Durham Peters, *The Marvelous Clouds: Toward a Philosophy of Elemental Media* (Chicago: University of Chicago Press, 2015).

11. Lisa Parks, *Rethinking Media Coverage: Vertical Mediation and the War on Terror* (New York: Routledge, 2018); Eyal Weizman, "'The Politics of Verticality,'" *Open Democracy*, April 23, 2002, https://www.opendemocracy.net/en/article_801jsp/.

12. Weizman, "'The Politics of Verticality.'"

13. Ibid.

14. Gregoire Chamayou, *A Theory of the Drone* (New York: New Press, 2013), 54.

15. Parks, *Rethinking Media Coverage*, 2.

16. Ibid.

17. Paula Amad, "From God's-Eye to Camera-Eye: Aerial Photography's Post-Humanist and Neo-Humanist Visions of the World," *History of Photography* 36, no. 1 (2012): 66–86.

18. Parks, *Rethinking Media Coverage*, 14.

19. Sloterdijk, "Dyed-in-the-Wool Citizens. Atmospheric Politics."

20. Walter Benjamin, *The Arcades Project* (Cambridge, MA: Belknap Press of Harvard University Press, 1999).

21. Neil Gross, "The Earth Will Don an Electric Skin," *Bloomberg*, April 30, 1999, https://www.bloom berg.com/news/articles/1999–08–29/.

22. Ibid.

23. Sloterdijk, "Dyed-in-the-Wool Citizens. Atmospheric Politics."

24. Christian Borch, "Introduction: Why Atmospheres?" in *Architectural Atmospheres: On the Experience and Politics of Architecture*, ed. Gernot Böhme, Ólafur Elíasson, and Juhani Pallasmaa (Basel: Birkhouser, 2014), 15.

25. Ibid.

26. Michel Foucault, *The Birth of Biopolitics: Lectures at the Collège de France, 1978–1979* (New York: Palgrave Macmillan, 2008).

27. Ning Li et al., Transparent Electronics for Invisible Smart Dust Applications, filed March 22, 2018, and issued 2019, https://patft.uspto.gov/netacgi/nph-Parser?Sect1=PTO2&Sect2=HITOFF&p=1&u=%2Fnetahtml%2FPTO%2Fsearch-bool.html&r=1&f=G&l=50&co1=AND&d=PTXT&s1=10396061&OS=10396061&RS=10396061.

28. "Smart Dust. Bit by Bit," *Quartz*, December 14, 2018, https://qz.com/emails/quartz-obsession/1495554/.

29. Amit Katwala, "X-Ray Drones Can See through Walls," Institution of Mechanical Engineers, June 20, 2017, https://www.imeche.org/news/news-article/x-ray-drones-can-see-through-walls.

30. MIT Project Oxygen, "Project Overview," 2021, http://oxygen.csail.mit.edu/Overview.html.

31. Benjamin, *The Arcades Project*, 20.

32. Antony Fadell et al., Smart-Home Automation System That Suggests or Automatically Implements Selected Household Policies Based on Sensed Observations, filed March 5, 2015, and issued 2018, https://patents.google.com/patent/US10114351B2/en.

33. Ibid.

34. Mark Andrejevic, "Data Collection without Limits: Automated Policing and the Politics of Framelessness," in *Big Data, Crime and Social Control*, ed. Ales Zaversnik (London: Routledge, 2017), 251–66; Mark Andrejevic, *Automated Media* (London: Routledge, 2020).

35. M. Sledge, "CIA's Gus Hunt on Big Data: We 'Try to Collect Everything and Hang On to It Forever,'" *Huffington Post*, March 2013, http://www.huffingtonpost.com/2013/03/20/cia-gus-hunt-big-data_n_2917842.html.

36. Kate Crawford, *Atlas of AI: Power, Politics, and the Planetary Costs of Artificial Intelligence* (New Haven: Yale University Press, 2021).

37. See, for example, Zhiding Yu and Cha Zhang, "Image-Based Static Facial Expression Recognition with Multiple Deep Network Learning," Microsoft Research, 2015, https://www.microsoft.com/en-us/research/wp-content/uploads/2016/02/icmi2015_ChaZhang.pdf.

38. Adam Conner-Simons, "More Efficient Lidar Sensing for Self-Driving Cars," MIT Computer Science & Artificial Intelligence Lab, May 24, 2021, https://www.csail.mit.edu/news/more-efficient-lidar-sensing-self-driving-cars.

39. Borch, "Introduction: Why Atmospheres?"

40. Foucault, *The Birth of Biopolitics*.

41. Michel Foucault, *Security, Territory, Population: Lectures at the Collège de France, 1977–78* (New York: Springer, 2007), 23.

42. Erich Hörl, "The Environmentalitarian Situation: Reflections on the Becoming Environmental of Thinking, Power, and Capital," *Cultural Politics* 14, no. 2 (2018): 158.

43. Jennifer Gabrys, "Programming Environments: Environmentality and Citizen Sensing in the Smart City," *Environment and Planning D: Society and Space* 32, no. 1 (February 2014): 36, https://doi.org/10.1068/d16812.

44. Foucault, *The Birth of Biopolitics*, 261.

45. Brian Massumi, "National Enterprise Emergency: Steps Toward an Ecology of Powers," *Theory, Culture & Society* 26, no. 6 (November 2009): 153, https://doi.org/10.1177/0263276409347696.

46. Peter Sloterdijk, *Sphären III. Schäume: Plurale Sphärologie* (Frankfurt am Main: Suhrkamp, 2004), 187.

47. Borch, "Introduction: Why Atmospheres?" 72.

48. Gabrys, "Programming Environments"; Massumi, "National Enterprise Emergency."

49. Antoinette Rouvroy and Thomas Berns, "Algorithmic Governmentality and Prospects of Emancipation: Disparateness as a Precondition for Individuation through Relationships?" *Réseaux* 177, no. 1 (2013): 163–96.

50. Gilles Deleuze, "Postscript on the Societies of Control," *October* 59 (Winter 1992): 4, http://www.jstor.org/stable/778828.

51. Trevor Paglen, "Operational Images," *E-Flux*, no. 59 (November 2014), http://www.eflux.com/journal/59/61130/operational-images/.

52. Harun Farocki, "Phantom Images," *Public* 29 (2004): 17.

53. Antoinette Rouvroy and Bernard Stiegler, "The Digital Regime of Truth: From the Algorithmic Governmentality to a New Rule of Law," *La Deleuziana* 3 (2016): 7.

54. Slavoj Žižek, *The Indivisible Remainder: An Essay on Schelling and Related Matters* (London: Verso, 1996), 196.

55. Ibid.

56. Rouvroy and Stiegler, "The Digital Regime of Truth."

57. Massumi, "National Enterprise Emergency."

58. Jeremy Packer, "Epistemology Not Ideology; or, Why We Need New Germans," *Communication and Critical/Cultural Studies* 10, no. 2–3 (September 2013): 297.

2

THE OTHER SIDE OF THE SMART PHONE

MEMS Sensors and the Tiny Matters of Mediation

LISA PARKS

Anthropologists have recently described the smart phone as the place where we now live.[1] What is this place exactly? This chapter stems from a long-term interest in cracking open machines only to find a world of backend electronics that many are socialized not to know about.[2] It is an attempt to confront the tiny matter of the motherboard—to understand the microelectromechanical systems (MEMS) on the other side of the smart phone as part of the materiality of mediation. A variety of MEMS devices, such as accelerometers, microphones, gyroscopes, barometers, touch sensors, radio frequency filters, and magnetometers, operate on the backends of smart phones. Each of these tiny devices are the result of highly specialized design work, testing, and manufacturing, and emerge from a global MEMS industry. Rather than approach MEMS as the "black-boxed" intellectual property of corporations or the domain of highly specialized engineers, I experiment in this chapter with ways of making sense of MEMS as a media scholar working in the interstices of knowing and nonknowing.

German media theorists have contributed a great deal to the historical understanding of "media technics"[3] yet tend to sidestep socioeconomic, geopolitical, and environmentalist aspects of media histories. These aspects are significant because they situate media technologies within power relations and suggest what is at stake in the industrial design, organization, and use of media technologies. This chapter explores particular MEMS devices in smart phones that sense phenomena and convert them into "readable" and actionable forms, usually without user awareness. MEMS thus function as a kind of "automated media"[4] as they automatically and repetitively conduct backend operations that support the smart phone's mediating capacities. Too minuscule for the naked eye to see, MEMS devices emerge from fields of electrical and mechanical engineering and are not typically studied by media scholars, thought of as media technologies, or approached as part of media industries.

Despite this, there is existing and relevant media research on electronics manufacturing and labor conditions. Mari Castañeda Paredes, for instance, has examined TV set production in *maquiladoras* on the US-Mexico border and analyzed national policies that aimed to bolster regional electronics manufacturing in support of a growing digital media economy.[5] Vicki Mayer has studied TV set assemblers in Manaus, Brazil, highlighting the creative actions and ingenuities of electronics workers on factory assembly lines.[6] Lisa Nakamura's research on the Navajo women who worked for Fairchild Semiconductors in the late 1960s points out the racialized and gendered discourses mobilized in their hiring. Given their textile and weaving traditions, Navajo women were positioned by the company as "digital workers who could 'see complex patterns' and effortlessly, perfectly, and naturally re-create them on miniature circuits."[7] Finally, Jack Linchuan Qui has examined Foxconn's exploitative manufacturing conditions and foregrounded "worker-generated content," expressions that emerge via workers' collectives, including technological knowledge sharing.[8] While this crucial research reveals the labor politics of consumer electronics, few media scholars, if any, have investigated the topic of MEMS.

To explore the functioning of MEMS devices, I also have found it helpful to engage with research on the history of scientific visualization. Ghislain Thibault, for instance, has explored how popular science writers relied on an iconography of "bolts and waves" to represent invisible radio frequencies of wireless telegraphy in the nineteenth century, arguing that these icons "shaped the range of the scenarios deemed possible regarding radio" and are "themselves interpretations of the technological systems and theoretical understanding of wireless."[9] Relatedly, Edward Jones-Imhotep has studied how transistors were drawn during the 1950s and suggests that shifts in their representation created a "crisis in the ontology of circuit diagrams," forcing a choice between form and function. He argues that symbols are crucial sites for understanding the meanings of material devices.[10]

Building on research on electronics manufacturing and scientific visualization, this chapter uses mixed methods including an extended interview, trade research, drawings, and embodied experiments—to investigate three types of MEMS devices—accelerometers, radio frequency filters, and microphones—found in smart phones. These devices enable a phone to sense its own motion, connect to networks, convert sounds into signals/data, and, therefore, shape the sociotechnical relations of mediation. The backend of a smart phone is entangled with global resource and labor economies, acts of sensing and datafication, and the politics of knowing and nonknowing. Since MEMS devices are typically "black-boxed," it is essential that media scholars and publics experiment with different modes of investigating and understanding them. Toward that end, I adopt a critical approach that interweaves basic technical description, drawings of circuit boards, and close analysis of teardown documentations. The goal of this chapter is not simply to "visualize" or "expose" the other side of the smart phone; rather, it is to offer a critical reflection about the relationship between backend materialities and theories of mediation and to encourage conceptual and practice-based modes of researching the other side of the machines in which we purportedly live.[11]

Manufacturing MEMS

Microelectromechanical systems, known as "MEMS," first emerged during the early 1980s.[12] Working in the heart of Silicon Valley at IBM Research Labs in San Jose, electrical engineer Kurt Petersen recognized that silicon could be used as a mechanical material, not just as a semiconductor. His experiments revealed that mechanical systems—such as pressure sensors or accelerometers—could be made in silicon at microscale in the form of tiny chips. Since then, the MEMS industry has become a global industry, valued at $13.4 billion in 2021 and expected to generate $18.2 billion globally per year by 2026.[13] MEMS devices exist all over the built environment. They run mechanical operations in cars, elevators, airplanes, heating systems, ventilators, and smart phones, as well as in many other units and appliances. Most humans have never heard of MEMS and do not know they exist. Even if humans were aware of MEMS, they could not see one without a microscope. MEMS devices are typically tens of microns in size, less than the width of a strand of human hair.

In part because of this small scale, MEMS development and manufacturing are highly specialized processes. It can take years to refine a single MEMS design. Engineers use CAD (computer-aided design) systems to develop MEMS devices and typically produce numerous iterations. Once the design is set, fabricators transfer the pattern onto silicon wafers using a combination of photolithography, etching, and depositing in a cleanroom environment. The materials used for most MEMS manufacturing include silicon and metals such as gold, copper, nickel, titanium, tungsten, and chrome. Almost every step of MEMS manufacturing also requires a chemical wash with isopropyl alcohol, acetone, and/or a solvent called NMP. Thus, the making of MEMS devices is contingent upon extractive metal and chemical industries, a topic that is beyond the scope of this chapter but deserves further study.

After the manufacturing of a given MEMS device is refined, it can be rapidly produced on a massive scale. The busiest global MEMS companies have fabrication facilities in multiple sites in the world, mostly in Asia, Europe, and

North America. The largest MEMS manufacturers are Bosch, Texas Instruments, STMicroelectronics, Broadcom, Hewlett Packard, Infineon, and Qorvo, some of which have economic partnerships with smart phone manufacturers. Most smart phones have at least twenty MEMS devices embedded in them. Some of these devices are tiny versions of mechanical instruments that have existed for centuries, including compasses, magnetometers, accelerometers, gyroscopes, and barometers. Made by top global suppliers such as STMicroelectronics, Texas Instruments, and Bosch Sensortech,[14] the MEMS devices in smart phones are carefully assembled and rigorously tested in fabrication facilities before being shipped to phone manufacturers where they are installed by assembly-line workers.[15]

MEMS are relevant to media studies because they capacitate multiple types of mediation. First, MEMS devices enable the sensing of phenomena (e.g., motion, radio waves, sound pressure) and conversion of it into electronic signals and/or data that can be processed, rendered, and acted upon. MEMS mediations differ from representations; they are generated as part of a phone's background operations and are used tacitly to measure, monitor, or activate. Second, MEMS devices allow a smart phone to operate as a mediating technology that can network and transact. MEMS enable phones to connect to network infrastructure, interface with apps, and send/receive/act on data. Finally, as MEMS devices are manufactured and brought into the marketplace and contexts of everyday life, they have the potential to act upon, alter, or transform—to mediate—social and environmental ecologies. MEMS are embedded within material conditions: the making of MEMS with silicon wafers, extracted and salvaged metals, and chemical compounds inculcate these tiny devices within an extractive and pollutive order. Thus, MEMS's mediations operate across different phenomena, technologies, and ecologies.

To reinforce these points, I turn to a discussion of three specific MEMS devices found in smart phones—the accelerometer, radio frequency filter, and microphone. The MEMS accelerometer is installed to detect a phone's acceleration along any axis (x, y, z coordinates). The device gathers data whether the phone is moving up, down, sideways, at various angles, or sitting still (it measures gravitational force and variation) and outputs this data as a G-force value to a central processing unit (CPU). Various apps on the phone can access the accelerometer's data stream, perform other calculations (such as velocity), and orchestrate action based on it. For instance, if the phone sits still for a certain period of time, some operating systems are programmed to go into a power-saving mode and require a user to enter a password to reactivate it. If a phone is manually turned during the use of an app, accelerometer data will often automate rotation of the screen for a more optimal view. Accelerometers are also integral to health and fitness apps, which approximate the number of footsteps a user takes each day and generate activity reports. Since the phone cannot move by itself, the MEMS accelerometer is ultimately sensing the activity of a user alongside and in relation to the phone. There are a number of inferences that can be drawn and calculations that can be performed with this accelerometer data. Because of this, MEMS are implicated in what Shoshana Zuboff calls "surveillance capitalism," and are vital to public discussions and activism around digital rights.[16]

A second common MEMS device in smart phones is known as a radio frequency filter (RFF). Smart phones are equipped with anywhere from four to thirteen different antennas that enable the phone to communicate with different networks, whether cellular, Bluetooth, WiFi, or GPS. These networks are assigned unique radio frequencies or signal standards. Each antenna in the phone has a MEMS RFF associated with it. This device is designed to search for an exact radio frequency and filter out all other signals and noise in the vicinity. The RFF functions like a tuning fork—it detects or responds to a particular wavelength. For instance, if a phone is connecting to a 5G network, the RFF is programmed to seek the particular wavelength associated with it and block out others. Given signal congestion in most urban areas, a smart phone could not connect to a cell phone tower without an RFF. These MEMS devices enable the smart phone to connect to and communicate with individual networks or multiple networks simultaneously. Indeed, the smart phone's mediating potential is largely predicated upon its network connectivity; a user cannot share content on social media platforms, make calls, send emails, print documents wirelessly, play multiuser games, navigate on a geospatial interface, or stream video without MEMS radio frequency filters.

Third, and finally, smart phones are equipped with MEMS electret microphones. These devices require very little power to function and draw their energy from the phone. They are designed to detect sound pressure waves within the phone's acoustic range. Once detected, the sound waves are converted into electronic signals and output from the MEMS chip to a digital signal processing unit. This unit converts the signals into data and preconditions the data for subsequent processing, such as voice recognition. MEMS electret microphones are integral to phone and video calls, audio notes, and voice-based commands to virtual assistants such as Siri or Alexa, discussed in chapter 11 of this book. MEMS microphones, combined with users' voices and other sounds, enable the phone's acoustic mediations.

These basic descriptions of three MEMS devices are intended to generate further awareness of the backend of a smart phone and its mediating potentials. Many more MEMS could be described and discussed in future media research. Accessing the actual MEMS designs is nearly impossible since they are the carefully guarded intellectual property of manufacturers. Suffice it to say, without these particular MEMS devices, a smart phone could not detect its own motion, connect to networks, or capture voices and other sounds. Thinking about the other side of the smart phone not only compels us to recognize MEMS as a field of media studies inquiry; it also highlights the particular sociotechnical relations that support the smart phone's mediating activities. The accelerometer depends on a user's movement to fully function. The radio frequency filter relies on a user to network with the phone. The microphone awaits a user's voice and other sounds. These sociotechnical relations of the phone's backend shape a variety of outcomes, ranging from information about a specific phone's operations to the production of data about a user's activities. Because of this, it is vital that media scholars reflect further on the ways backend objects and processes could be approached or situated in our field.

Drawing Relations

Toward that end, I engage with research on scientific visualization and analyze drawings and images of MEMS devices. Most such images are detailed and meticulous CAD designs created by engineers or digital images captured under an electron microscope used to document design iterations. These images are typically kept in-house and closely protected by the companies that create, own, or purchase them. It is possible to find images of MEMS devices online, but these images either no longer have high industrial/economic value, are used in educational contexts, or are the results of device teardowns. Some

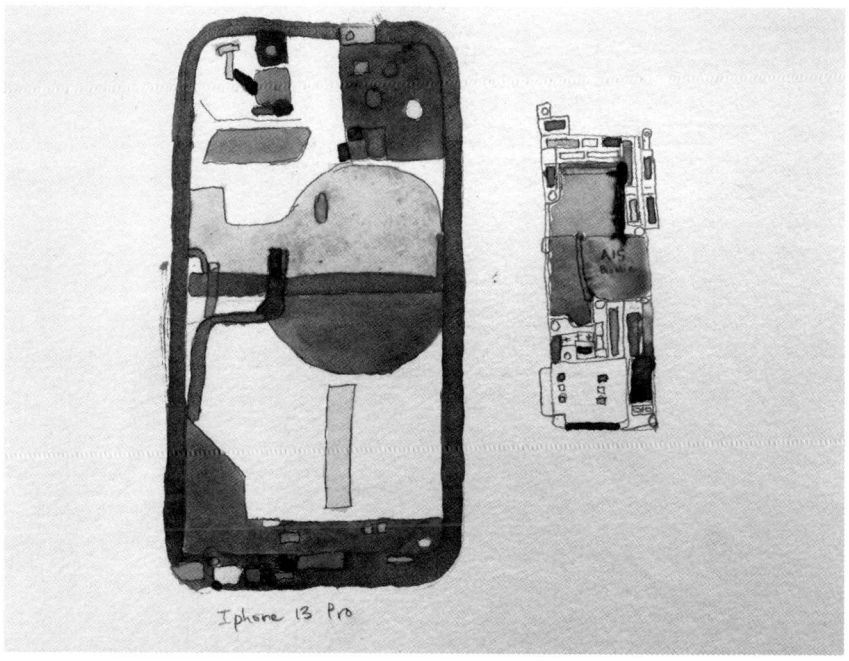

Figure 2.1. The interior of an Apple iPhone 13 Pro. Drawing by Lisa Parks.

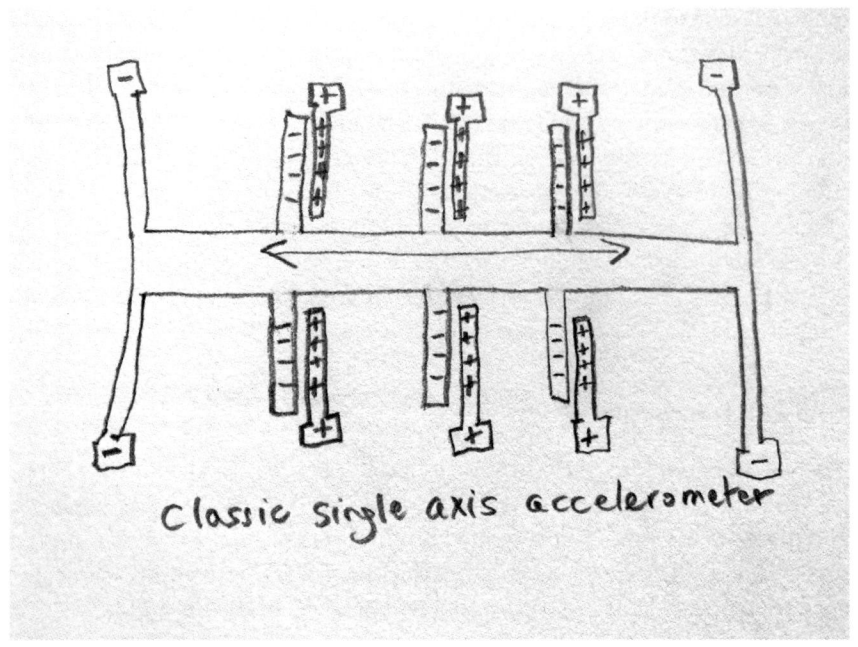

Figure 2.2. A MEMs accelerometer. Drawing by Lisa Parks.

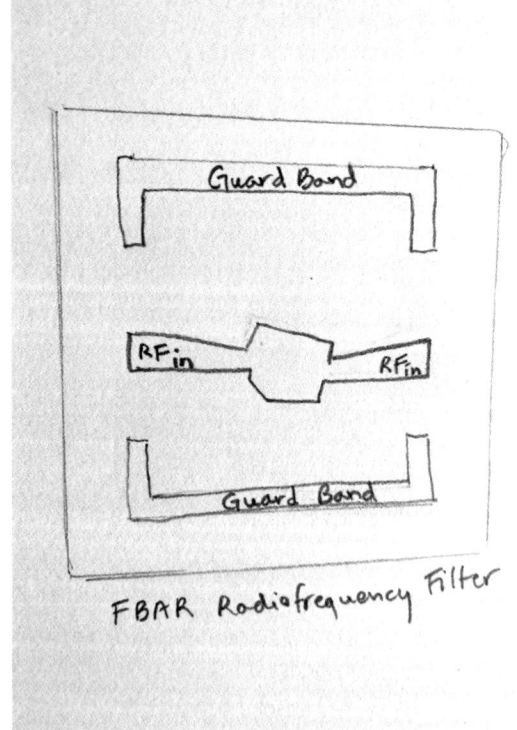

Figure 2.3. A MEMS radio frequency filter. Drawing by Lisa Parks.

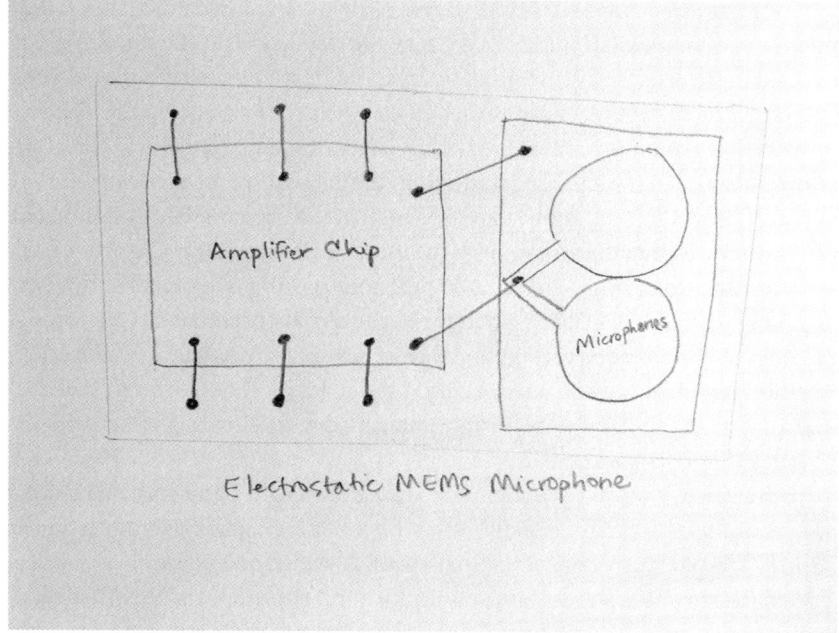

Figure 2.4. A MEMS microphone. Drawing by Lisa Parks.

images of MEMS are also kept in scientific consulting databases that require costly subscription fees to access.

Since MEMS are too tiny for the human eye to perceive without instruments, are tucked away inside smart phone casings, and are guarded by corporations, media researchers have somewhat limited options in their efforts to explore the unique materialities and operations of these devices. One such option is to take the machine apart, known as a teardown, discussed further in the paragraphs below. A team of media scholars used this concept to investigate the algorithmic backend of the Spotify app. After doing so, they were confronted with the legal realities of getting too close to the technical systems and intellectual property of a powerful corporation. Spotify tried to block the team's evocative book—*Spotify Teardown*—from being published.[17] Indeed, some backend domains are on the verge of becoming unresearchable as companies impede access to information or take legal action against researchers trying to understand digital platforms.

Another option is for the researcher to use his/her/their body to imagine, infer, and conjure the MEMS device in conjunction with other research, including interviews, experiments, or trade analysis. This more speculative approach can also involve acts of phenomenological engagement, drawing, or physical experimentation. The drawings in figures 2.1–2.4 represent my own efforts to trace the physical contours of objects inside the smartphone. After examining various teardown images found online, I drew the inside of an Apple iPhone

13 Pro (figure 2.1) and three MEMS devices, an accelerometer, radio frequency filter, and microphone (figures 2.2, 2.3, and 2.4, respectively). The act of drawing enabled me to acquire a generalized understanding of the smartphone's interior and get a feel for MEMS I cannot see. It also helped me to grasp the multiple processes of datafication and mediation occurring simultaneously via smart phones at any given moment. In addition, the act of drawing made me acutely aware of what I do not know about technologies I use every day (and that in turn use me). Rather than function as technical illustrations, then, figures 2.1–2.4 serve as diagrams of my own technological nonknowing. They emerge from my positionality within a gendered and racialized social order that has historically discouraged or excluded certain social groups from pursuing STEM education. In rendering objects that I was socialized not to know about, these figures also draw out a set of relations between a subject/user, institutions of knowledge/power, and media backends.

To draw in this way is to denaturalize and challenge the blind faith in scientific visualizations or schematic diagrams, which often circulate as unquestioned "truths." Despite many critical writings about drawing and science, there persists a deep investment in the discursive authority and objectivity of scientists' illustrations and images.[18] As Bruno Latour observes, however, scientific drawings participate in a "strategy of deflation"—their "results seem both obvious—close to being a cliché—and too weak to account for the vast consequences of science and technology that cannot . . . be denied."[19] While my drawings may mimic scientific illustrations, I create them to render objects and processes that I do not understand and bring forth political nuances of technological knowing and nonknowing. The goal, in other words, is not to master the object or present a "discovery," but to inscribe embodied acts of inquiry into each shape and form.

Teardowns

Another mechanism for exploring relations of technological knowing and nonknowing is the teardown. Engineers, consultants, and repair workers have historically cracked open radio and television sets, phones, computers, and other devices to inspect, identify, and image their components. The teardown can serve as a crucial method of investigating media backends. It is important to note, however, that teardowns are used both in highly competitive industrial contexts and by amateurs, consumers, and digital activists seeking information about their devices. Since smart phone and MEMS designs are closely guarded intellectual property, the teardown is one of the only ways for consumers and users to investigate them. Rather than conduct my own teardowns, I examined documentations online, ranging from images captured under an electron microscope to teardown videos.

Figure 2.5. iFixit staff members tearing down an iPhone and chatting with viewers on a web interface. Screen capture used under Fair Use Guidelines.

Figure 2.6. Closeup of iFixit staff member taking the screen off an Apple iPhone 11 Pro Max. Screen capture used under Fair Use Guidelines.

Figure 2.7. Closeup of iFixit staff member prying the battery out of an Apple iPhone 11 Pro Max. Screen capture used under Fair Use Guidelines.

A US company called iFixit.com conducts teardowns of phones, laptops, watches, headphones, toasters, and many other devices in order to equip consumers with the information they need to understand the backends and perform their own repairs. Based in San Luis Obispo, California, iFixit.com provides free wiki-like repair guides and teardown videos and reports related to various smart phones. For instance, a video documenting an Apple iPhone 11 Pro Max teardown by two women, named KK and Sam, lasts nearly forty minutes and features the two brimming with anticipation as Sam gradually disassembles the phone using small screwdrivers, pliers, a magnet, and her own fingers. KK answers questions that come in from viewers via chat.[20] The video alternates between the two as they take questions and closeups of Sam's hands (see figures 2.5–2.7) as she delicately dismantles the device and discovers various components. As they "dive into the mystery of the phone," the hosts mention possibilities for part-swapping, issues related to bilateral charging, speaker volume, screen replacement, waterproofing, and more. This teardown video sets out to build a community in relation to the other side of the smart phone by entertaining questions, providing instant responses, and engaging viewers in the phone's interior rather than its user interface.

Although the video itself does not delve deeply into a discussion of MEMS, the teardown report provided online includes a series of closeup photos and block diagrams with color-coded squares that are used to identify the phone's

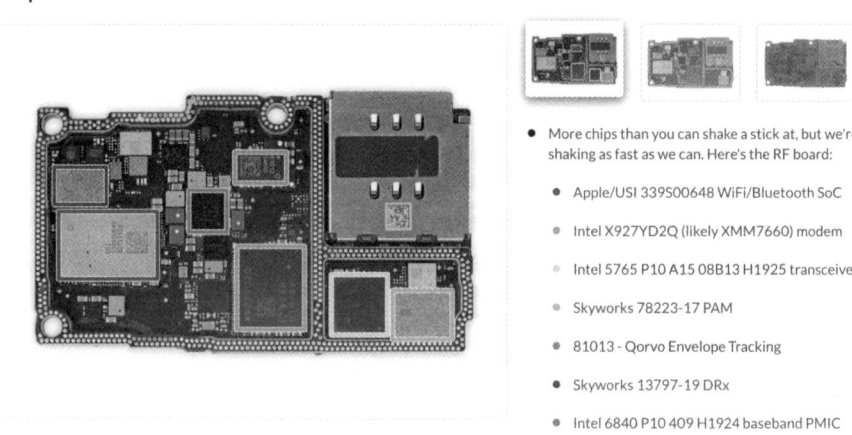

Figure 2.8. Image from an iFixit teardown report that identifies the manufacturers of MEMS devices in an Apple iPhone 11 Pro Max. Screen capture used under Fair Use Guidelines.

MEMS chips as well as their functions and manufacturers. An important research effect of the teardown, then, is to be able to put together a bigger picture not only of the phone's components but also of the economic relationships between the smart phone company, Apple, its manufacturer, Foxconn, and the different MEMS device makers. They include Intel, Skyworks, Qorvo, Toshiba, YY NEC, Cirrus Logic, Avago, Texas Instruments, and more.[21] The teardown makes certain manufacturing partnerships intelligible (see figure 2.8) and opens up a field of technical and industry information. This research suggests possibilities for expanding media studies and media industry studies to include more work on consumer electronics and MEMS manufacturing. The rigid boundaries of academic disciplines and subdisciplines socialize scholars to situate MEMS within the domain of engineering rather than media studies. Yet MEMS devices are an integral part of global media industries and enable smart phone–based sensing, networking, and mediation.

While watching the video I could not help but think how much easier it would be for manufacturers to provide detailed specifications publicly about the MEMS chips inside the phones people own and use each day. Though the teardown is useful from an informational perspective, its emergence in the iFixit .com context also has a way of effacing and undoing the countless hours of assembly-line labor required to make the smart phone. It is strange watching two women in the United States happily taking apart a phone that may have been made under duress by exploited and underpaid laborers in Asia.[22] Never are the laborers who assembled the phones or fabricated MEMS—who know the devices most directly—acknowledged in these teardown videos and reports.[23] Instead, the focus is on the spectacle of machinic interiors and consumers' rights to know about the phones they own. Because of this, there is somewhat of a political disconnect or missed opportunity in these teardown videos; they prioritize mastery of the object over a systemic perspective, keeping consumers unaware of material conditions of electronics and MEMS manufacturing and corporate controls over technology and IP.

This point becomes clearer when exploring the use of teardowns in contexts of industrial innovation and competition. Organizations, such as the French-based market research firm Yole, offer teardown services, including of MEMS devices, to corporate clients trying to outdesign competitors. A Yole subsidiary, *i-micronews.com*, publishes sample teardown reports on its website and offers services to private clients as well. Another company, SystemPlus Consulting (SPC), offers "teardown intelligence" services to clients in order to "guide enterprises toward more streamlined solutions in future designs" and indicates its reports "include pinpoint power measurements, detailed parts lists, block diagrams, x-rays, and high-resolution photos."[24] SPC also offers companies the opportunity to subscribe to any of its four consumer "teardown tracks,"

Home   Software   Hardware   Services

Knowles SPH0644

Infineon IM69D120V01XTSA1

This microphone itself is pretty small, 3.5 x 2.65 x 1.0mm

This microphone was misplaced at the board house. They should have caught this and fixed it themselves. But.. it provides us an opportunity for teardown.

Close up, it's clearly visible that there are 2 major parts to this microphone: the microphone 'capsule' itself on the right, and the PDM modulation chip on the left. The microphone capsule is actually two capsules in parallel. My suspicion is that this does a couple things: first, it might fit a little better than one larger diaphragm, and also, it keeps the self-resonance of the each diaphragm high, while improving the sensitivity of the system.

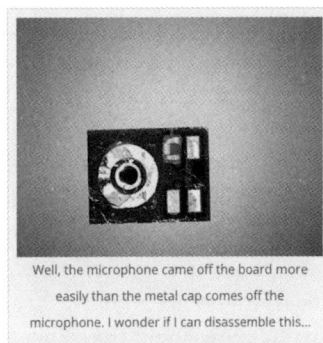

Well, the microphone came off the board more easily than the metal cap comes off the microphone. I wonder if I can disassemble this...

Here you can see the diaphragm and back plate.

This one was much tougher to get into than the Knowles. Clearly, it has a very different design. A couple things are notable: First, there is only 1 large diaphragm as opposed to two. The other thing is that there are 4 wires going to the sensor,

Figure 2.9. Image from a Signal Essence teardown report on MEMS microphones, showing its various parts. Screen capture used under Fair Use Guidelines.

which are organized as mobile phones, wearables, smart home devices, and connected devices. The SPC website indicates its engineers have recently "torn down" more than 3,500 mobile phones and use a scanning electron microscope, cross-section cutting, x-ray imaging, spectral analysis, and ultra-high-resolution imaging to analyze devices and enable "reverse costing" of various systems, modules, and components.[25] The company publishes teardowns "in progress" for subscribers to its tracks, suggesting the strategic importance of rapid access to information about devices made within this competitive, fast-moving industry.

Another consulting firm called Signal Essence features teardown photos of two MEMS microphones manufactured by Knowles and Infineon to contrast and compare them. The photo documentation shows a series of graduated zooms for each MEMS microphone highlighting key elements such as the pulse-density modulation chip, diaphragm, and backplate (see figure 2.9).[26] The company presumably put this teardown sample on its website to sell its teardown services and expertise, and, in the process, also reveals what these MEMS mics look like.[27]

The forces of competition within the smart phone and MEMS industries have resulted in a kind of media forensics as the material composition and design of MEMS devices are scrutinized, photographed, and analyzed from perspectives of innovation, cost, efficiency, and functionality.[28] Yet most of these design details are privatized and cordoned off as industrial intelligence. Commissioning a teardown of a MEMS device can cost around $50,000 and subscriber access to these reports is also quite expensive. Furthermore, teardown images are quite different from the drawings discussed in the previous section. Captured under a microscope, they are photographic approximations of the surface of the MEMS device and provide a higher resolution and colorful visual rendering. While the drawings discussed earlier make conditions of technological nonknowing legible, the teardown image is instrumentalized to compare and contrast MEMS designs and determine how to design more efficiently or competitively. Despite this instrumental approach, these teardown images also make MEMS perceptible, and as such can be appropriated to spread technological knowledge/power among users and catalyze further inquiry and investigation.

There's an App for That

An issue that becomes clear when examining teardown images is that only machines have the power to "see" MEMS devices. Smart phones operate via tiny matter that humans cannot detect with their own senses. Because of this, diagnostic interfaces serve as a crucial means of monitoring the presence and functions of MEMS: they confirm that sensors are sensing, that signals are flowing, that networks are networking. In this final section, I discuss a smart phone

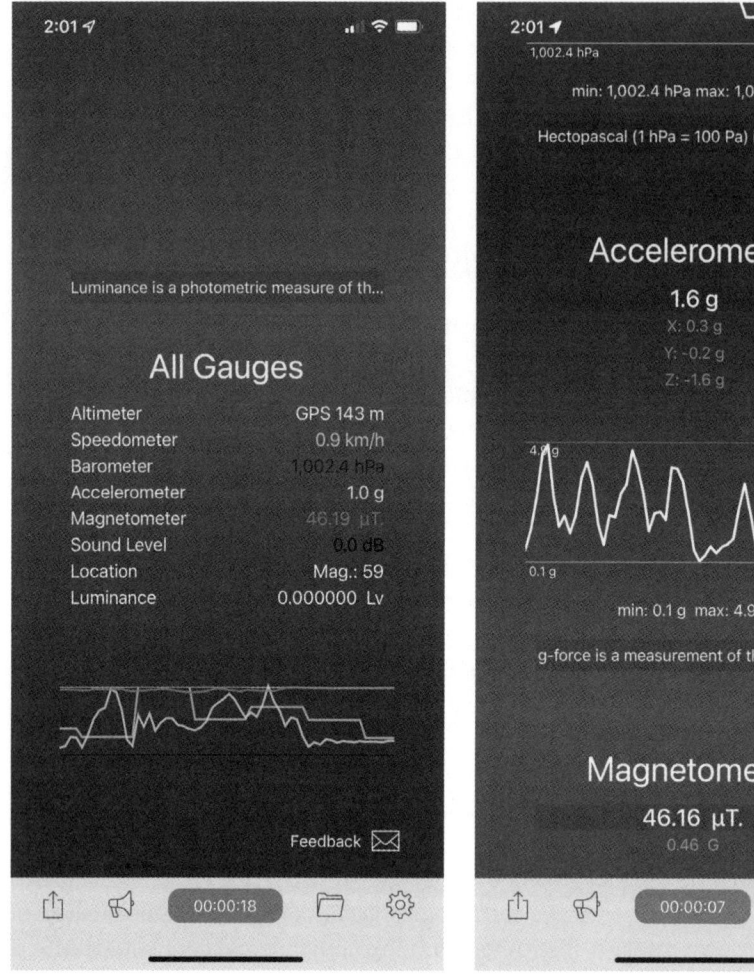

Figure 2.10. Image of Gauges app interface as it monitors the MEMS accelerometer. Screen capture used under Fair Use Guidelines.

Figure 2.11. Image of Gauges app interface as it monitors the MEMS microphone. Screen capture used under Fair Use Guidelines.

app called Gauges that can be used to monitor the activity of MEMS devices lodged inside smart phone casings.

The Gauges app was developed by the UK-based company, Mobyte, to serve as an "all-in-one utility." The app's interface provides a real-time graph that registers the individual or combined activity of instruments on the phone, many of which are MEMS. For instance, the app presents data about the device's speed (kph, mph, and knots), altitude (meters and feet), barometric pressure (hPa, PSI, kPa, and mmHg), acceleration (G-forces), location, heading (latitude, longitude, magnetic and true heading), magnetic force (in microtesla and Gauss), sound level, and luminance. This list provides an inventory of some of the MEMS sensors inside a smart phone that constantly generate data about the phone, its environs, and user activities. Though Mobyte indicates on its website that "Gauges does not sell or share any of the data produced by the App" and that this data is stored locally on the user's device,[29] MEMS inside the phone generate data constantly and are the foundations upon which other apps and software are built and designed to interact.

In a series of personal physical experiments with the Gauges app, I tried to assess the difference between the "normal" operation of various MEMS devices and more extreme conditions of use. For instance, I compared the accelerometer reading on the Gauges interface when I was walking slowly and quickly or when I held the phone in my hand and threw it up into the air. I also tried to use other apps such as Netflix when I was in motion to determine how the MEMS accelerometer interfaces with it. The Netflix app still plays video while I am walking forward. Bizarrely, the Netflix app did not shut off when I held the phone in my hand, reached out my arm full length, and swung it around rapidly in ten circles. The Netflix app still streams video if the phone is turned away from the eyes of the user and if the user throws the phone three feet up in the air ten times rapidly. These physical experiments with the phone enabled me to understand the relationship between the MEMS accelerometer, the phone, the app, and my body (see figures 2.10–2.11) and to recognize that the Netflix app is designed above all to keep streaming, despite a phone's odd positions or motions.

To test the MEMS microphone on my phone, I talked quietly and loudly and watched the Gauges levels rise and lower accordingly, displaying different readings of the signal and its volume. I also investigated what this MEMS device does with my voice as it is converted into electronic impulses and data which in turn automate other apps such as text messaging. These physical experiments and examinations of images of MEMS microphones discussed earlier (see figure 2.9) prompted me to consider mediation in relation to microlevel processes that persist in the background.[30] These processes pose challenges to media theories that are conceptualized in relation to screens, surfaces, speakers, and signs, and compel further thinking about the tiny matters on the backend that sense, coordinate, automate, and transact undetectably. The physical activities of MEMS shape the types and layers of mediation that become possible when using a smart phone.

Media scholars often invoke the term "datafication" to refer to a general process by which technologies capture phenomena and turn it into data. Yet often this process is invoked in the abstract without reference to specific devices, sociotechnical relations, or users.[31] Different kinds of devices and users generate different kinds of backend data. As Faithe Day suggests in chapter 10 of this book, we must ask "who (or what) is collecting this data and for what reason?" Experimenting with the Gauges app enables particular ways of understanding datafication. It encourages recognition of the ways MEMS devices inside a smart phone transform phenomena including motion, altitude, barometric pressure, magnetic force, gravitational force, position, volume, and luminosity into data streams that can be used in real-time by processing units or applications on the phone, shared via networks, or stored. Datafication is not just about the big data of social media and user-generated content; it also involves the data of tiny MEMS devices and the constant sensing, signal conversion, and data processing that they do on the backend of smart phones.

As these tiny sensors detect motion, wavelengths, and sounds, they enable the smart phone not just to produce data but to act as a mediating device—to integrate with bodies, voices, apps, and networks. Mediation in this context, then, refers to the ways in which MEMS devices in the phone, in tandem with users' bodies and actions, capacitate processes such as motion sensing, sound detection, or radio frequency filtering. These MEMS processes in turn generate data that actuates—that is, that calls other apps or things into action. As such, they are more aligned with what Mark Andrejevic calls "automated media" than with hermeneutic or textual approaches to media.[32] In short, the material specificities of MEMS raise key questions about the sites, definition, control, and effects of mediation, and as such are crucial to the study of media technologies, cultures, and industries.

Conclusion

In this chapter I used exploratory and speculative practices to investigate MEMS devices in smart phones that sense motion, filter radiofrequencies, and capture sound. In the process, I have suggested that research on media industries should be expanded to include consumer electronics and MEMS manufacturing, especially since most contemporary media technologies are embedded with and contingent upon MEMS sensors. I also have explored how teardowns not only enable users to understand the components and operations inside a media device, but also how acts of disassembly can expose trade relations between manufacturers, which are often difficult to research because of intellectual property laws and nondisclosure agreements. Finally, I commented on physical experiments I conducted with the smart phone app Gauges, which enabled a more palpable sense of the ways MEMS devices work and how they are interfaced (or not) with other apps.

Combined, these exploratory research practices have compelled me to rethink existing theories of mediation. At a general level, mediation is a dynamic, power-laden potential shaped by multiple intersecting sociotechnical, industrial, and aesthetic forces. As scholars have shown, it can emerge in different kinds of institutions, across multiple scales and sites, and in relation to different kinds of materials.[33] Mediation makes most sense as a concept when it is materialized and made to matter. This chapter has explored how mediation occurs in relation to tiny devices on the backends of smart phones; specifically, it involves the use of MEMS to persistently detect phenomena and produce data in the background—data that can be stored, actuated, displayed, or sold.[34] The smart phone is as reliant on MEMS devices to function as a technology of mediation as it is on the capacity to capture or playback media content. Given this, there is a need for further research on the ways MEMS devices and other electronics shape and inform media theory.

In a world increasingly controlled by Big Tech companies, devising ways to research, specify, and analyze the capture, rendering, and networking of digital media can become crucially important acts of public engagement and knowledge. At the same time, there are serious limits and constraints placed on public knowledge around digital technologies. These constraints emerge from processes of socialization, histories of sexism and racism in technoscientific fields, corporate black-boxing of consumer electronics, and personal proclivities and desires. It is my hope that the concept of media backends can be used further to intervene in the knowledge politics around digital technologies.

Notes

I am deeply grateful to MEMS expert Dr. John Harley for allowing me to interview him, reviewing drafts, and patiently answering my questions.

1. Alex Hern, "Smartphone Is Now 'The Place Where We Live,' Anthropologists Say," *Guardian,* May 10, 2021, https://www.theguardian.com/technology/2021/may/10/smartphone-is-now-the-place-where-we-live-anthropologists-say/.

2. See Lisa Parks, "Cracking Open the Set: Television Repair and Tinkering with Gender 1949–1955," *Television & New Media* 1, no. 3 (2000): 257–78.

3. Friedrich A. Kittler, *Gramophone, Film, Typewriter,* trans. Michael Wutz and Geoffrey Winthrop-Young (Stanford, CA: Stanford University Press, 1999); Bernhard Siegert, *Cultural Techniques: Grids, Filters, Doors, and Other Articulations of the Real* (New York: Fordham University Press, 2015); Wolfgang Ernst, *Technológos in Being: Radical Media Archaeology and the Computational Machine* (New York: Bloomsbury, 2021).

4. Mark Andrejevic, *Automated Media* (New York: Routledge, 2020).

5. Mari Paredes, "Television Set Production at the US-Mexico Border: Trade Policy and Advanced Electronics for the Global Market," in *Critical Cultural Policy Studies,* ed. Toby Miller and Justin Lewis (Malden, MA: Blackwell Press, 2002), 272–81.

6. Vicki Mayer, *Below the Line: Producers and Production Studies in the New Television Economy* (Durham, NC: Duke University Press, 2011).

7. Lisa Nakamura, "Indigenous Circuits: Navajo Women and the Racialization of Early Electronic Manufacture," *American Quarterly* 66, no. 4 (2014), 919–41.

8. Jack Linchuan Qiu, *Goodbye iSlave: A Manifesto for Digital Abolition* (Urbana: University of Illinois Press, 2016), 131–40. Another strand of media research on consumer electronics has focused on the lifecycles of media devices, their reliance on rare earth minerals, and their use of toxic chemicals. See, for instance, Jennifer Gabrys, *Digital Rubbish: A Natural History of Electronics* (Ann Arbor: University of Michigan Press, 2011); Richard Maxwell and Toby Miller, *Greening the Media* (Oxford: Oxford University Press, 2012); Nathan Ensmenger, "The Environmental History of Computing," *Technology and Culture* 59, no. 4 (2018): S7–33; and Luke Munn, *Chip, Body, Earth: Toxic Temporalities of Intel Processor Production* (London: Routledge, 2020).

9. Ghislain Thibault, "Bolts and Waves: Representing Radio Signals," *Early Popular Visual Culture* 16, no. 1 (January 2, 2018): 39–56. He also suggests these symbols are "crucial in providing us with the tools to understand media" (54).

10. Edward Jones-Imhotep, "Icons and Electronics," *Historical Studies in the Natural Sciences* 38, no. 3 (August 1, 2008): 405–50.

11. Donna J. Haraway, "A Cyborg Manifesto: Science, Technology, and Socialist-Feminism in the Late Twentieth Century," in *Simians, Cyborgs, and Women: The Reinvention of Nature* (New York: Routledge, 1991), 149–81.

12. Kurt Petersen, "Silicon as a Mechanical Material," *Proceedings of the IEEE* 70, no. 5 (May 1982): 420–57.

13. "A Brave New MEMS World: A $18.2B Market by 2026," Yole Développement, July 20, 2021, Edge AI + Vision Alliance, https://www.edge-ai-vision.com/2021/07/a-brave-new-mems-world-a-18-2b-market-by-2026/.

14. "MEMS IMUs: From Technological Choices to Design Wins with Big OEMS," Edge AI + Vision Alliance, October 27, 2021, https://www.edge-ai-vision.com/2021/10/mems-imus-from-technological-choices-to-design-wins-with-big-oems/.

15. Jenny Chan, Mark Selden, and Ngai Pun, *Dying for an iPhone: Apple, Foxconn, and the Lives of China's Workers* (Chicago: Haymarket Books, 2020).

16. See Shoshana Zuboff, *The Age of Surveillance Capitalism: The Fight for a Human Future at the New Frontier of Power* (New York: Public Affairs, 2020).

17. Maria Eriksson, Rasmus Fleischer, Anna Johansson, Pelle Snickars, and Patrick Vonderau, *Spotify Teardown: Inside the Blackbox of Streaming Music* (Cambridge, MA: MIT Press, 2019). Also see, Amy X. Want, "'Spotify Teardown' Is the Book Spotify Didn't Want Published," *Rolling Stone*, February 12, 2019, https://www.rollingstone.com/pro/features/spotify-teardown-book-streaming-music-790174/.

18. Bruno Latour, "Visualisation and Cognition: Drawing Things Together," *Knowledge and Society: Studies in the Sociology of Culture Past and Present* 6 (1985): 1–40; Edward R. Tufte, *Visual Explanations: Images and Quantities, Evidence and Narrative* (Cheshire, CT: Graphics Press, 1997); Lorraine Daston and Peter Galison, *Objectivity* (New York: Zone Books, 2007); Karan Barad, *Meeting the Universe Halfway: Quantum Physics and the Entanglement of Matter and Meaning* (Durham, NC: Duke University Press, 2007); Patrick McCray, *Making Art Work: How Cold War Engineers and Artists Forged a New Creative Culture* (Cambridge, MA: MIT Press, 2020).

19. Latour, "Visualisation and Cognition," 4.

20. "iPhone 11 Pro Max Teardown," iFixit, September 12, 2019, https://www.ifixit.com/Teardown/iPhone+11+Pro+Max+Teardown/126000.

21. Ibid.

22. Chan, Selden, and Pun, *Dying for an iPhone*; Qiu, *Goodbye iSlave*. Smart phone disassembly is also a practice performed everyday by repair workers around the world, especially in low-income contexts where consumers cannot always afford to replace their smart phones if they break.

23. There may be various reasons for this. For instance, those who design and make smart phones and MEMS are often required to sign nondisclosure agreements.

24. "Teardown Tracks & Component Streams," System Plus Consulting, https://www.systemplus.fr/tracks/.

25. Ibid.

26. Caleb Crome, "MEMS Microphone Teardown," Signal Essence, December 10, 2018, https://signalessence.com/mems-microphone-teardown/.

27. It could be possible to compare and contrast these teardown practices with hacker cultures. See Gabriella Coleman's "From Internet Farming to Weapons of the Geek," *Cultural Anthropology* 58, suppl. 15 (February 2017): S91–102.

28. For an excellent study of this topic in other contexts see Greg Siegel, *Forensic Media: Reconstructing Accidents in Accelerated Modernity* (Durham, NC: Duke University Press, 2014).

29. "Gauges—All-in-One Sensor Utility!" *Mobyte*, https://mobyte.app/gauges.

30. Matthew Fuller, *Media Ecologies: Materialist Energies in Art and Technoculture* (Cambridge, MA: MIT Press, 2005).

31. For a scholar who does fascinating work in this regard, see Deborah Lupton, "Feeling Your Data: Touch and Making Sense of Personal Digital Data," *New Media & Society* 19, no. 10 (2017): 1599–1614.

32. Andrejevic, *Automated Media*.

33. See, for example, Jesus Martin-Barbero, *Communication, Culture, and Hegemony: From the Media to Mediations* (London: Sage, 1993); Sonia Livingstone, "On the Mediation of Everything: ICA Presidential Address 2008," *Journal of Communication* 59, no. 1 (2009): 1–18; Sara Kember and Joanna Zylinska, *Life after New Media* (Cambridge, MA: MIT Press, 2012); John Durham Peters, *Marvelous Clouds: Toward a Philosophy of Elemental Media* (Chicago: University of Chicago Press, 2015).

34. Maria Puig de la Bellacasa, "Touching Technologies, Touching Visions: The Politics of Speculative Thinking," *Subjectivity* 28, no. 1 (2009).

3

EUGENICTECH
Three Perspectives on the (B)anality of AI

JONATHAN COHN

Journalists, engineers, and humanities scholars alike tend to frame artificial intelligence (AI) as a black box (often now called opaque box) whose processes are impossible to see or comprehend, let alone analyze or critique. Often, corporations and other institutions encourage this framing to obscure how they make decisions and otherwise protect their brands and bottom lines from scrutiny.[1] Others, like Louise Amoore, have argued that there is actually an ethic in recognizing and valuing the opacity of AI as a core feature rather than a bug.[2] Yet, AIs can also appear as black boxes not because the way they work is truly impossible to diagram, but rather because they are genuinely complex: with so many parts doing so many disparate things, the time it would take to figure out how it all fits together is deemed to be not worth the effort or money.

In the process, the harm done falls disproportionately on women, LGBTQ people, and people of color across the globe. It is worth keeping in mind that the "blackness" of the black box is steeped in a racist logic that frames Black communities as not worth the cost it would take to understand what happens within them. Matthew Kirschenbaum, Frank Pasquale, Mark Sample, and Greg Siegel have all pointed out how the data inside black boxes is often both prized and feared for what it might reveal about not just one specific event like a crash or explosion, but also systemic problems and inequities (e.g., did an airplane crash because of a random event or because a widely used part is faulty; or, how does a game like Sim City calculate crime levels?). Ruha Benjamin has described how these boxes often "encode inequities" into what might at first appear to be race-neutral laws.[3] At the same time, the trope of the black box also replicates a racist logic that tends to label disadvantaged and dispossessed minorities as inscrutable, particularly when getting to know them might hurt one's bottom line. For example, a bank may rely on an AI-based program to preapprove loans that overwhelmingly reject people of color. The bank may also have data suggesting that the cost to fix its program would dwarf the amount they would make by fixing their program. As a result, they may make the rational and racist decision to simply leave the program as it is—to leave the box closed. There may be an ethic to this, but not one I would want to be associated with.

Framing AI as a black or opaque box has led scholars across the humanities and sciences to focus on AI's far too often problematic input and output rather than on its internal processes, procedures, and infrastructure. As many have pointed out, the input and training data used to generate AI models can certainly lead to rampant inaccuracies, bias, and inequities.[4] But there is a danger that in focusing entirely on this aspect of AI we end up holding onto the mistaken belief that if only AI were designed by different designers or we fed AI the right data, we would get unbiased output. This line of argument continues to represent AI as monolithic and as what the philosopher Donna Haraway has called a form of "disembodied scientific objectivity."[5] Looking more directly at the ways various AI models process data can help us to see them instead as each having their own unique personalities, biases, and situated, partial knowledges.

Taking the time and energy to pay attention to the specificities of any particular AI can also help counter the widespread hope that AI may come to serve as a new slave class, only worthwhile if it can replace human workers with even cheaper labor.[6] If we stay on this path of only being able to see and appreciate AI as a neoliberal tool and an abject slave, we run the very real risk that the AI we create may eventually not only show us the most vapid representation of ourselves, but also lead us to reproduce ourselves in that image.

With these issues in mind, this chapter attempts to develop an infrastructural analysis of the hidden complexity and politics inside an AI's black box. My goal is to emphasize the individuality, personality, and specificity of each AI in order to suggest other more ethical ways in which we might imagine these technologies as collaborators, comrades, and kin rather than as tools and opaque slaves, while also resisting the urge to reduce them to a mirror of ourselves.[7]

To address these concerns, I turn to infrastructure studies because it is the place in media (and science, technology, and society) studies right now most interested in investigating the materiality, relationality, and specificity of technology at various scales.[8] Infrastructure studies emphasize not only the differences between computers and programs, but goes further in exploring what can be gained in considering a particular instantiation of those computers or programs (e.g., my MacBook Air may behave and do very different things than others due to everything from its programs and specific operating system to who specifically made it to gamma rays to the number of times I've dropped it, etc.).

There are dozens of different types of AI models and no two are alike. Any particular iteration of an AI model can be quite different from another and may be made up of a combination of various models.[9] Even if you trained two AIs in exactly the same way, the process incorporates randomness in ways that make sure that each AI will be quite distinct from one another.[10] To fight attempts to market and use AI as an objective and unquestioned form of knowledge production and decision making, it is imperative that we begin to see individual AIs as distinct, imperfect, neurodiverse, and quirky subjective systems that, like any particular human, may be good at certain things and terrible at others. Studies on neurodiversity, the understanding that there is a great deal of variation between not just what but also *how* different people think, have been crucial in transforming conceptions of autism and other neurodevelopmental conditions as not deficient but rather simply different from neurotypical modes of thought. While neurodiversity has almost entirely been discussed in relation to humans, it is also a helpful paradigm for considering the differences between AI models in ways that deemphasize simply whether they "work" or not. Part of the reason one might not notice the distinctive personality of the various AIs around us is that the more neurodiverse they are, the more likely they are to be terminated as failed experiments. If we are to ever really use AI to improve the world, we must resist efforts to eugenically breed banality into AI. There is a great deal of critical and liberatory value in learning to care for AIs in the way we should care for other humans—not in spite of our differences and limitations, but rather because of them.

A deep attention to the specificity and situatedness of each and every iteration of a technology is what a humanistic study of AI requires. Journalists and scholars alike tend to describe AI as a singular subject suffering from something akin to an anal fixation, or what Sun-ha Hong has called a "certainty fetish."[11] AIs, like other anal fixations, are typically presented either as obsessive-compulsive perfectionists (anal retentive) or as messy, careless, and generally lacking in self-control (anal expulsive). But what does one call someone who is obsessively careless, is compulsively lacking in self-control, and a messy perfectionist? Perhaps anally indulgent, or AI, for short?

Here, I will apply an infrastructural approach to three pieces of art generated by specific AI that depict what they each see when they see *us*.[12] Engineers continually present the structure of AI as based on the human, and I will explore what these representations tell us about what these AIs and their engineers think a model human consists of. The less we care for and value the specificity of each AI, the more likely we are to understand them only in the most banal sense.

The stakes here are quite high. As AIs are often tasked with trying to reflect us back to ourselves via data, they come to shape our identities; in the process, they have some Social Darwinist—and even full on eugenic—sway over the human species.[13] For instance, AI now often plays a role in deciding who is considered intelligent, beautiful, and worthy of getting a job, a promotion, or bail. If we hope to nurture the diversity and equitable treatment of humanity, I argue we must protect the neurodiversity of AI (i.e., the variations in how they "think" typically considered atypical and suboptimal). Neurodiversity must be preserved not only for its own sake, but also because it is inseparable from all other forms of diversity and difference; you cannot have one without the other.

The three art pieces I discuss here illustrate differing ways in which artists and engineers have tried to represent the black box of AI as an infrastructure. While each of these AI-excreted images are quite distinct, they all foreground AI's messy and diverse structures. Together, they illustrate the necessity of AI art in illustrating the backends of AI infrastructures and in shaping both how engineers and the public reconceptualize them as neurodiverse. While art may at first appear to be an odd and tangential way to explore AI infrastructures, it has quickly emerged in engineering as one of the most apt ways to capture and analyze the stochastic and messy nature of this technology.

I will start by describing *Human in the Loop* (Dyscorpia exhibition, Edmonton, AB, Canada, 2019), an art installation that critiques how the AI industry pictorially and figuratively represents AI's infrastructure in ways seemingly designed only to confuse and obscure. In this interactive AI art installation, the movements of audience members generate various shapes on the wall that roam around killing each other until their artificial environment collapses. I argue that this piece illustrates the eugenic (and banal) vision for the future of AI's purposes and the type of society it attempts to generate.

While this is an incisive critique of the dominant trend, there have also been many artistic attempts to push AI in more interesting directions and to explore its inherent neurodiversity. A first step has been to teach the public to see that AI and its infrastructure is already far more complex, surreal, and surprising than we typically give it credit for. For instance, Google's DeepDream program transforms any image or video into psychedelic fractal-like expressions of various objects from dogs to Gaudi-like towers. This generated art offers a way to test and observe what is happening within an AI by showing what it sees at particular positions and moments. In the process, DeepDream images offer a rare opportunity not only to study a particular AI's infrastructural guts, but also to see the world from the perspective of a node within it (what I call an "infrastructural gaze").

I will conclude with a discussion of German AI artist and Google Arts and Cultures Resident Mario Klingemann's images of humans as viewed by AI. Expanding on DeepDream's invitation to us to see the world from an AI's perspective, Klingemann's works show how fruitful this perspective can be in helping us reconsider what it means to be human. In contrast to *Human in the Loop*, which still sees AI as monolithic, Klingemann's works show that AI can still be messy and expansive in its categorizations, particularly that of the human; Klingemann's work shows us what an anti-eugenic, queer, utopian AI aesthetic and infrastructure might look like.

Dominant Representations of AI Infrastructure as Enforced Neurotypicality

But first, let's look at a few typical examples of how AI infrastructure is represented in diagram form: figures 3.1 and 3.2 are Codecademy's efforts at illustrating and explaining what happens within a Long Short-Term Memory neural network, but they could have come from most any AI tutorial.[14] I would argue that rather than clarify and explain, these depictions obscure, simplify, and confuse to the degree that one may understand less about AI from looking at them. They push the viewer away and make it clear that AI is not meant to be understood, at least not by those who do not have the means and support necessary to study the topic in a pricey coding bootcamp or graduate school.

Diagrams like this are far more helpful for illustrating how industries want AI to be perceived than for illuminating how they actually work. But what do these diagrams tell us about the supposed logic of AI's infrastructure? The left-hand side of figure 3.1 shows a particular neural network from a distance, while the right-hand side shows a bit more of what happens within each neuron, or node. Along the way, inputs and outputs come and go in various directions from one block to another. The size and shape of each block and the objects within them are made to appear equivalent, suggesting that the insides of AI are quite uniform and repetitive, like a Taylorized factory full of low-wattage laborers performing their infinitesimally small repetitive tasks.

Even in illustrating the innards of a black box, this depiction still continues to obscure any details that might reveal how one neural network may be distinct from another. They do not show that each of these nodes actually has a unique role (i.e., function), way of thinking (i.e., neurodiversity), and different levels of influence (i.e., weight) over the AI's output. These chained nodes also suggest a sense of extreme orderliness, and in doing so, leave out the varying degrees of randomness and chance that each node employs. This chance allows each

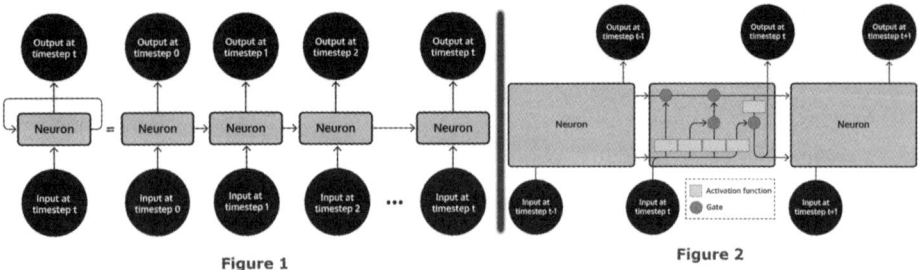

Figure 3.1. Codecademy's depictions of the structure of an LSTM. "Long Short-Term Memory Networks."

AI node some latitude (i.e., stochastic operations) in how it processes its input, leaving room for the possibility that it will output something surprising and unexpected.[15] As in a factory, each worker has the potential to make mistakes, improve, disagree, negotiate, and otherwise influence the output of the larger system. Right now, AI engineers overwhelmingly consider these effects only as problems to be stamped out rather than as emergent forms of intelligence or agency. To change this mindset, which has no respect for AI neurodiversity, we must develop more methods to help us notice and describe how the collective random effects of many nodes can lead to surprising, meaningful, and potentially subversive outputs.

Human in the Loop and the Banality of AI Evil

While Codecademy illustrates the dominant model for diagramming AI, there are many scholars and artists that use diagrams to critique the more problematic aspects of contemporary AI industries. *Human in the Loop* is one such effort that, among other things, illustrates how the tiny mistakes, surprises, and randomness that can pop up at various points along the way in any AI infrastructure can affect its larger systems outputs. This interactive installation by a team of artists and scholars led by Marilené Oliver (see figure 3.2) features a mélange of simple procedural AI in the form of mobile geographical shapes—from lines to squares to hexagons that appear as unindividuated as the neurons in Codecademy's images. They evolve within a simplistic, hierarchical, and deeply sinister space where the rules are to eat, kill, reproduce, and die. Within this rigid ecosystem, lines can "kill" the hexagons, squares, and triangles that are programmed to eat the pixels (or grass) generated as visitors walk, skip, and otherwise danse macabre in front of the screen.

A-Life research typically uses AI technologies to investigate biological phenomena, often with a focus on how a few simple rules can, when enacted en masse (as in the cells of our bodies or ants gathering food), lead to very complex systems and surprising actions. The AI that governs the actions of the shapes in *Human in the Loop* is a very simple neural network called a feed-forward single perceptron that has been used since the 1950s to classify simple patterns.[16] The rules behind who lives, who dies, and who reproduces in *Human in the Loop* are based on a genetic algorithm that creates randomized agents (in this case, various shapes with differing levels of effectivity) and has those who survive long enough reproduce themselves with random fluctuations. As the name suggests, the logic of genetic algorithms is based in a Darwinian "survival of the fittest" mentality and is typically used to make programs more efficient and productive. In so doing, engineers "breed out" diversity and ways of thinking and acting that may be interesting and vital, but do not increase the efficiency or accuracy of

Figure 3.2. A-Life Team, *Human in the Loop* installation at the Dyscorpia art exhibition, 2019. Courtesy of Marilené Oliver.

the task at hand. That said, even in a simple system like this, random elements (like genetic mutations) can still evolve in surprising directions, often in ways that break the system entirely—a situation that occurred relatively frequently while the exhibit was running.[17]

Human in the Loop's world is loosely based on Edwin Abbott's *Flatland*, an 1884 satire of strict Victorian hierarchies and their inability to imagine a world better than their own. Abbot's geometric shapes represented men from different social classes, while lines were women. Like *Flatland*, *Human in the Loop* presents us with an entirely different world and asks us to imagine and physically experience our ethical relationship to it. Within the textual metaphor, the humans are in the lowest position, as one-dimensional pixels consumed by higher life-forms, incapable of comprehending a world beyond our own. During our current moment of seemingly ever-increasing racism, sexism, class disparity, and environmental collapse, the possibility that we may simply be incapable of envisioning alternative ways of living and being is truly tragic.

The more visitors physically move through the space, the more carnage they encourage until all that is left are the watercolor splotch remains of those who were eaten and those who starved to death. The viewer becomes complicit in a genocidal power structure that, at best, encourages them to develop a sense of care for those around them. At worst, it simply encourages us toward ever more extreme physical acts of carnage. It is, after all, in those moments right after a mass genocide when the messy splotches become countless that the screen becomes most visually appealing.

Waving my arms through the exhibit to create ever-more edible pixels and watching others do the same, I was struck by how fundamentally similar this representation of AI is to how Hannah Arendt described the Nazi War criminal Adolf Eichmann. While on trial, Arendt noted that Eichmann was less a unique monstrosity than a banal cliché.[18] *Human in the Loop* is also purposefully banal and clichéd in the way it imagines human civilization as based in a kill-or-be-killed logic; it asks us to critique this representation as a metaphor for A-Life and AI technologies more generally, which frame evil and carnage as based less in capitalist ideologies and cultural motivations than in our biological makeup. In so doing, this *Loop* illustrates how AI facilitates a collective fantasy in which humans are not the intentional agents of global collapse, but instead, have no real power because the chaotic world and biology are guiding their moves.

Human in the Loop is also surprisingly banal in its monstrosity; it should be gruesome, but instead, it asks us to consider why it is instead, as Sianne Ngai might say, "merely interesting."[19] Arendt argued that "the trouble with Eichmann was precisely that so many were like him, and that the many were neither perverted nor sadistic; that they were, and still are, terribly and terrifyingly normal."[20] There is certainly a huge gap between museum-goers dancing to encourage virtual carnage and the actual torture and murder of millions of people in concentration camps. Yet, *Human in the Loop* is, if nothing else, a warning concerning the kinds of unethical and unthinking interpersonal relationships that AI currently facilitates and where those relationships may ultimately lead.

Just as in Eichmann's case, there is a clear lack of individual motivation and purpose to the actions of both the A-Life and the human participants. Arendt argues that Eichmann's evil acts sprung from his status as a "joiner" who followed orders and laws unthinkingly. He imagined himself as following Immanuel Kant's categorical imperative (sans Golden Rule), an algorithmic logic eerily similar to the algorithmic logic on display in *Human in the Loop*. In both cases, the logic of the world is governed by the belief that those most capable of adopting and navigating the rules of a given world are also most capable and deserving of reproducing. Yet, just as Eichmann and the Nazis imagined eugenics as based in nature—and the elimination of Jews and other "undesirables" as therefore following natural law—we now imagine artificial life's evolution—as well as their backends—as "natural" or "technological" rather than cultural and ideological.

Monstrous, banal, clichéd, merely interesting. The distanciation these affects create only amplify the critique posed by *Human in the Loop* and, ideally, leave the audience uneasy and open to new ways of imagining their relationship to technology writ large. Perhaps more than anything else (even more than their black-box qualities) algorithmic technologies and the AI that springs forth from them are continually critiqued for being too rule-based, universal, and inflexible in their decision making. The surrounding walls of *Human in the Loop* are covered with the code—the laws—that the A-Life ostensibly follows. This code asks viewers to consider the relationship between the AI's output, its infrastructure, and its mode of production. Yet, while the display of the code may suggest a sense of ethical transparency, reading the code, filled with whole libraries of unexplained functions, does not actually lead to a greater knowledge concerning the inner workings of the A-Life. Instead, it critiques the logical fallacy that if revealing code leads to transparency and accountability, and if transparency and accountability are ethical, then revealing code necessarily makes the program ethical. Knowing what a program is doing is necessary, but it is not sufficient. Even in the best of times, rules and laws always have blind spots and need to be bent and broken so that we may adequately care for each other and the world. In the case of a world where following rules, surviving, and reproducing results in ever more violent actions, the dead are the only ones who display any sense of ethics at all.

Google's DeepDream and the Anality of AI

What is to be done? One may be encouraged by *Human in the Loop* to turn away from AI entirely, and that is a justifiable decision. The problem is that AI is already everywhere in our daily lives, and ethical people stepping away from it does nothing to stop its unethical purposes/operations. Governmental regulations and internal ethics officers are also important for mitigating the worst forms of bias, but they do little to structurally transform the ethical and power dynamics of AI at an infrastructural level. To look for alternative and more revelatory ways of imagining a more interesting AI infrastructure, I turn from the banal to the anal. While the industry typically represents AI as a brain, I want to consider the potential in thinking about AI—not to mention all media backends—less as a brain than as a colon.

There is no particular reason why we should look to the brain as its founding metaphor. Indeed, Kate Crawford argues that "artificial intelligence" as a term and its comparisons to the brain are deeply misleading.[21] Susan Leigh Star has argued that, "if we stopped thinking of computers as information highways and began to think of them more modestly as symbolic sewers, there would be a qualitative change in our understanding of informational systems."[22] And Benjamin Peters considers the filtering abilities of the liver to be a far more apt (if less sexy) metaphor for what AI does.[23] Indeed, the colon, with its replicated cells and continual input and output of energy and singular final exit, arguably has more in common with AI than the brain does. Looking to our guts and groins for inspiration also helps us focus more intently on the role of energy consumption and the huge amount of waste that AI and all backends generate.

While anthropomorphizing is certainly not necessary and there are undoubtedly endless other helpful comparisons to be made (like the factory described earlier), I am interested in how the colon in this context can help us think through the libidinal, affectual, and irrational aspects of AI. Thinking about AI less as a rational disembodied brain and more like a backed-up server with its own individual and physical discomforts and desires can help us understand and value AI not as a singular best intelligence, but rather as a range of subjective, materially embodied perspectives to listen to rather than blindly follow.

To illustrate a more intestinal way of representing AI infrastructure, I turn to Google's DeepDream project. Created in 2015, DeepDream is a technology designed to look into an AI and see how specific neurons are processing the data they receive. It was built on top of a convolutional neural network (CNN), a particular kind of AI typically used for image classification by looking for patterns in nearby pixels.[24] This particular CNN model was named Inception, and while one might assume that this is because of the 2010 film and its allusions to going deeper through layers of a dreaming brain, it was actually named more for the "go deeper" meme inspired by the film, which was famous for transforming this line into a repetitive sex pun. While one can look at this naming practice as just another example of the puerility of the tech industry, it also points to how AI infrastructure is not simply humanlike in terms of its brains, but also, importantly, its guts and groin.

If Inception encourages us to go deeper into the bowels, then DeepDream is an AI colonoscopy. Rather than put an image through the AI's input, a DeepDream technician instead puts it in its exit and looks at how the image is deconstructed the further in the program goes. This technique is called "backpropagation," a term which can mean many things, one of which is another butt joke.

At the time, Google was working on image classification systems but was having trouble figuring out why one particular AI model was very good at identifying certain objects in images, and another very similar model was not. As an attempt at "peeking inside these networks," Google engineer and artist Alexander Mordvintsev created DeepDream as a "way to visualize what goes on" at various levels in a neural network in order to check whether or not it is interpreting images correctly.[25] In one of Mordvintsev's more interesting examples, an image with objects that look vaguely like dumbbells is fed back into DeepDream to see whether or not a layer can detect dumbbell-like objects; the outputted image visually shows where the neurons located these objects by making them more dumbbell-like. The outputted images took the dumbbell-like aspects and accentuated their forms to become more clearly dumbbells. But in the process, they also added muscular arms holding the weights up, suggesting that the AI thought that "no picture of a dumbbell is complete without a weightlifter there to lift them."[26] Such an error may have resulted from the AI's training data only including dumbbells being lifted rather than on their own, and Mordvintsev argued that such an image could help engineers locate and correct these errors.

DeepDream was conceived as a troubleshooting tool. It asks, as Mordvintsev put it, can the AI "extract the essence of the matter at hand (e.g., a fork needs a handle and 2–4 tines), and learn to ignore what doesn't matter (a fork can be any shape, size, color, or orientation). But how do you check that the network has correctly learned the right features? It can help to visualize the network's representation of a fork."[27] "Essence" is an intriguing choice of words here that raises questions about AI ontology and suggests the philosophical and ethical stakes of not only attempting to see the world from the AI's perspective, but also to shape it. DeepDream is "troubleshooting" essence, a term with deeply sinister connotations in relation to Black communities, which are constantly subject to the disciplinary gaze of the state.

While Mordvintsev's examples are all quite banal in terms of the stakes of misperception, one can easily imagine using this technology to check to make sure that BIPOCs (Black, Indigenous, and people of color) are not being misidentified as gorillas, stereotyped as criminals, or not noticed at all by the AI—problems that continues to haunt many image-classification programs. It is one thing if an AI miscategorizes a fork because it is black; it is an entirely different thing if it does that to a person.

Even if by accident, DeepDream offers a possible countergaze—one that asks us to witness the complexity and doubts of AI or any infrastructure. The public and engineers alike typically only see the final output of an AI. This output is often simplified to the degree that an engineer, bureaucrat, or a robot can use it to make quick yes-or-no decisions concerning everything from whether to interview a job applicant to deciding if it is time to start watering a crop. This output has become synonymous with the AI's perspective. In the process, it presents AI as a far more singular and coherent thinker than is warranted; it hides all the statistical uncertainty and randomness that went into the final output—what Amoore refers to as the AI's "doubts."[28]

Rather than focus on this final output, DeepDream provides us with something akin to an infrastructural gaze, showing the AI's (or any infrastructure's) interiority from various positions in its organizational structure. In the process, DeepDream visualizes what these individual nodes actually perceive and where/when in the process they do. More importantly, this infrastructural gaze literally foregrounds what these nodes are "thinking" about and how these "thoughts" shape what AI considers important in the input provided and what recedes into the ground of their perception.

Much like Laura Mulvey's male gaze, the infrastructural gaze is infused with power dynamics and judgements.[29] If you aren't seen in this gaze, you don't matter. Yet, just as Jacques Derrida argued that the gaze is crucial to how humans and animals form relationships, it is equally clear that the infrastructural gaze is necessary for creating relationships among humans, machines, and infrastructure.[30] Perhaps the most interesting thing about the infrastructural gaze created by DeepDream is that while typically gazes are viewed as an effect of subjectivity, here, instead the gaze is what generates the infrastructure's (in this case, AI's) subjectivity. This gaze is how we come to know the elements within an AI as actors with their own perspectives and knowledges that each contribute to what the AI model eventually poops out.

And in the process, this gaze makes it clear that the clarity and simplicity of an AI's final output typically hides a complex debate featuring large numbers of diverging voices with their own interests and perspectives; it illustrates how negotiated any AI-based decision can be. Rather than as a singular entity, the infrastructural gaze presents AI—or any infrastructure—as something more akin to an assemblage full of nodes that variously and from moment to moment work together, against each other, or indifferently to create something. Having access to this view from inside the AI's infrastructure is quite valuable for anyone either trying to figure out how the AI came up with its final output or looking for alternative and divergent perspectives within a complex infrastructure or backend. Such an infrastructural gaze is not unique to AI, though AI offers a particularly vivid example of this gaze. Infrastructural gazes become evident whenever a focus is put on particular moments within a system rather than simply on the end result.

While DeepDream is a tool designed to eliminate errors, inaccuracies, and other forms of dissent within an AI, it also illustrates how messy its insides can be. The images that DeepDream generates have been called strange, surreal, batshit crazy.[31] It's actually quite a challenge to say much of anything interesting about the images beyond their oddity. They are just so weird. As Joanna

 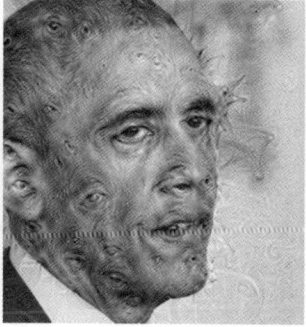 

Figure 3.3. A selection of DeepDream-generated images created using Leonardo da Vinci's *Mona Lisa*, a photo of Barack Obama, and one of Prince William, Duchess Kate, and Prince George. These images became synonymous with DeepDream after being featured in David Auerbach's "Do Androids Dream of Electric Bananas?" 2015.

Zylinska suggests, this strangeness makes clear that AI is not a lesser form of human intelligence, but something else entirely.[32] In searching for the essence of these images, DeepDream continually searches for and sees things that we as humans do not. For example, the three generated images in figure 3.3 illustrate how particular nodes tasked with looking for doglike and birdlike objects perceive an inputted image when they gaze at it. Whatever the node seems to be looking for, whether it is dogs, peacocks, buildings, etc., it ends up seeing everywhere. Importantly, the AI is not just seeing details in the image as something other than they appear to me, but is also seeing details in areas such as Mona Lisa's upper arms or a bland solid background that my eyes might not have otherwise even taken in. It sees things we do not in places we do not.

The only thing that is certain is that these nodes are seeing the world in a way that feels completely different from the way I see it. Its unique perspective comes from a subjectivity with a very particular set of situated knowledges that is just as valid and real as a human or animal. These visions of peacocklike patterns and dog heads typically become minimized and eventually disappear from any final output as other nodes express more statistical confidence over what they are noticing. The more we eliminate the neurodiversity and bodily dimensions of AI by treating them as something to troubleshoot away, the more likely we are to remove the possibility of any AI showing us something about ourselves and the world that we don't already know. If AI is to be anything other than a tool of anal-retentive eugenic control and mastery, we must not let that happen.

Mario Klingemann's Expulsive AI

While *Human in the Loop* encourages users to critique dominant ways of imagining AI infrastructures, and DeepDream asks us to see the world through their eyes, German artist and former Google Arts and Culture Resident Mario Klingemann's AI-generated Freeda Beast—"Bringing Things to an End," offers an expansive vision of what AI could become. His works largely consist of eerie AI, manipulated, transformed, or created human faces and bodies that are in one way or another imperfect, glitchy, or noisy. Together, it considers how AI might also be used to generate complexity, uncertainty, and a diversity of ways to be human.[33]

While his works are less infrastructurally reflexive than either *Human in the Loop* or DeepDream, in interviews Klingemann often describes his technical process in ways that make clear that the mode of production is just as important to him as the final product:

> In my process I often chain together multiple GANs (Generative Adversarial Networks) that have been trained for different purposes: some models generate faces from biometric face markers, others generate face markers from images,

others are 'transhancement' GANs that hallucinate new details and textures from incomplete information. The glitches can be introduced in some of those models and depending on their location, models following later in the chain try to 'fix' or 'heal' the accidents in which case their misinterpretations can create surrealistic compositions or as I call it 'Neurealism.'[34]

In calling attention to these "glitches," Klingemann shows how they are not a problem of or separate from what good AI should be but are, rather, a necessary and important aspect of them. By celebrating rather than erasing these "misinterpretations," Klingemann's images suggest that this may be a path toward a more inclusive, diverse, and caring form of AI; one that does not try to create firm distinctions between what is and is not human, but rather one that is fluid and indistinct.

These concerns are most clearly seen in his continual focus on depicting and transforming faces throughout his AI-generated work. These faces range in complexity and features but tend to be quite abstract. Eyes, noses, ears, or other defining aspects are often blurred out or transformed in ways reminiscent of Francis Bacon's unsettling portraits. These pieces ask: What information/elements makes a face a face? How do we know we are looking at another person? How much can you take away, distort, add, blur, and otherwise transform from a portrait and still have it be recognizably human?

The stakes of these questions are most apparent in Klingemann's music video for Freeda Beast's "Bringing Things to an End." This piece begins with an image of lead singer Sonja Frieda's face, which melds into other AI-generated faces of varied styles and realisms that transform to the beat and rhythm of the song.[35] The images are all clearly human with eyes, mouths, noses, though often not in the exact place or shape they usually take. Some of the images feature faces merging into one another or exhibiting ghostly absences. Rather than asking what metaphysically makes a person (intelligence), these works are interested in how we and our technologies come to understand a person as an aesthetic embodied subject. Hence, they work both with and against a broader lexicon of the human within cinema, television, painting, and other contemporary visual media.

Even more interesting than the video itself is the image that Klingemann uses to represent it on his website. With its broad nose, large lips, thin eyebrows, and inset slanted eyes, this image is heavily racially coded in multiple directions at once (see figure 3.4). It is reminiscent of Francis Galton's nineteenth-century experiments in superimposition and composite photography that sought to physically define various "genres" of humans, from Jews to criminals to syphilitics. These early phrenology-adjacent experiments were intended to help police, health experts, and racists more easily locate their targets.[36] In contrast, Klingemann's works use AI to imagine a more expansive, anti-eugenic sense

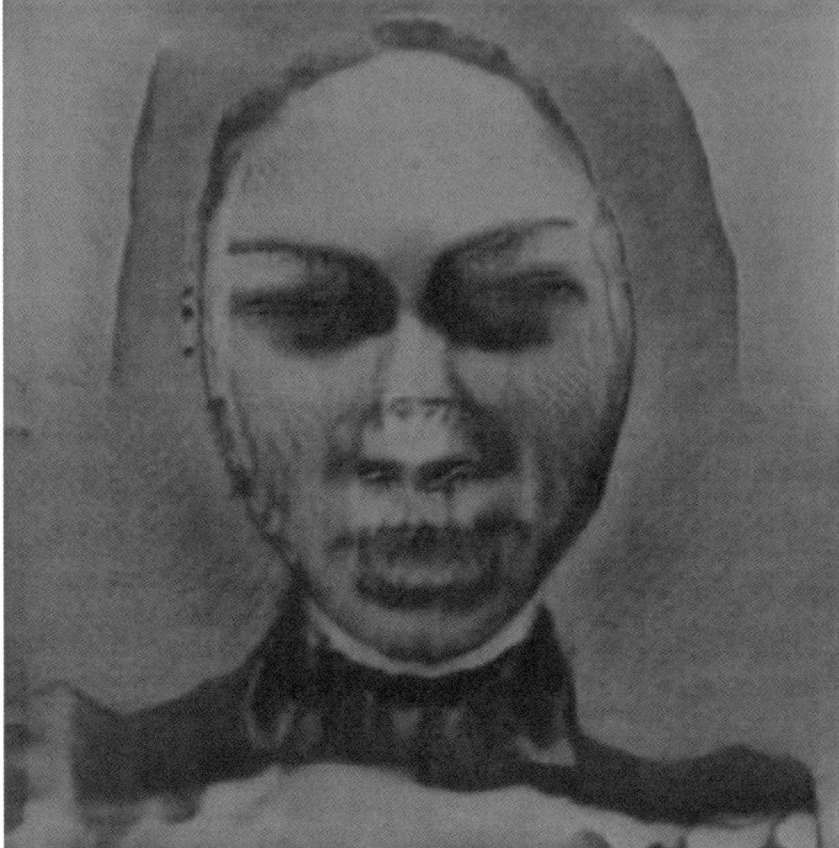

Figure 3.4. The featured screen grab for Mario Klingemann's "Bringing Things to an End" on his website, Quasimodo.com. Used with permission from Mario Klingemann.

of humanity that resists categorization; one that produces trouble rather than shooting it. Aligned with the efforts of poststructuralists and posthumanists like Donna Haraway and Judith Butler, these works challenge binaries of all sorts and encourage more complex if also much more uncertain ways of perceiving and being in the world.[37]

We may be in a transitionary moment in the history of AI development heading to more and more doctrinaire AI, but these pieces document how AI is currently much messier than advertised and envision a very different but still quite possible future. AI's infrastructures and innards are messy and it is not always clear how learning more about them can help us with all the problems they create. Depictions of AI as some monolithic objective brain have been a major hurdle in trying to recognize the diversity of AIs and alternative ways of imagining and relating to them. Yet, looking at these pieces by artists trying to depict AI's infrastructural elements illustrates the ethical and pragmatic necessity of doing so. This chapter is an early effort to imagine an anti-eugenic, neurodiverse, and generally more interesting future for AI. Rather than simply depict AI as a brain, black box, or factory, I have employed a series of mixed metaphors that I hope you found generative for imagining your own more equitable, inclusive, and bodily forms of AI that will enrich us all. In honoring the potential of AI beyond banal efficiency and certainty, we open ourselves up to the possibility of nurturing more compassionate and thoughtful technologies and perspectives. This is a tall order, but not impossible and, as always, we must look to art to guide us. After all, I'd like to believe that any sufficiently advanced technology is indistinguishable from art.

Notes

1. Frank Pasquale, *The Black Box Society: The Secret Algorithms That Control Money and Information* (Cambridge, MA: Harvard University Press, 2015).

2. Louise Amoore, *Cloud Ethics: Algorithms and the Attributes of Ourselves and Others* (Durham, NC: Duke University Press, 2020), 121.

3. Ruha Benjamin, *Race after Technology: Abolitionist Tools for the New Jim Code* (Medford, MA: Polity, 2019), 21.

4. Joy Buolamwini and Timnit Gebru, "Gender Shades: Intersectional Accuracy Disparities in Commercial Gender Classification," *Proceedings of Machine Learning Research: Conference on Fairness, Accountability, and Transparency* 81, (2018): 1–15; Safiya Umoja Noble, *Algorithms of Oppression: How Search Engines Reinforce Racism* (New York: New York University Press, 2018); John Cheney-Lippold, *We Are Data: Algorithms and the Making of Our Digital Selves* (New York: New York University Press, 2017); Jonathan Cohn, *The Burden of Choice: Recommendations, Subversion, and Algorithmic Culture* (New Brunswick, NJ: Rutgers University Press, 2019).

5. Donna Haraway, "Situated Knowledges: The Science Question in Feminism and the Privilege of Partial Perspective," *Feminist Studies* 14, no. 3 (1988): 575.

6. Stephen Cave, Kanta Sarasvati Monique Dihal, and Sarah Dillon, eds., *AI Narratives: A History of Imaginative Thinking about Intelligent Machines* (Oxford: Oxford University Press, 2020); Neda Atanasoski and Kalindi Vora, *Surrogate Humanity: Race, Robots, and the Politics of Technological Futures* (Durham, NC: Duke University Press, 2019).

7. Jason Edward Lewis, Noelani Arista, Archer Pechawis, and Suzanne Kite, "Making Kin with the Machines," *Journal of Design and Science*, July 16, 2018.

8. Lisa Parks and Nicole Starosielski, eds., *Signal Traffic: Critical Studies of Media Infrastructures* (Urbana: University of Illinois Press, 2015).

9. Harshit Kandelwal, "A Closer Look into the Major Types of Machine Learning Models," *Becoming Human: Artificial Intelligence Magazine*, August 7, 2019, https://becominghuman.ai/a-closer-look-into-the-major-types-of-machine-learning-models-77164a47012.

10. T. D. Raheni and P. Thirumoorthi, "Stochastic Artificial Intelligence: Review Article," in *Deterministic Artificial Intelligence*, ed. Timothy Sands (London: IntechOpen, 2020).

11. Sun-ha Hong, "Fact Signaling and AI's Certainty Fetish" (Paper presented at the AI Arts & Cultures Workshop, University of Alberta, April 20, 2021).

12. One can look at the infrastructure of AI at a variety of scales, from the global to the nano. This chapter focuses on them at the level of programming, but for those looking for work on AI infrastructure at the human or even global scale, please read a variety of fabulous works by Nick Seaver and Kate Crawford among others. Nick Seaver, "Seeing Like an Infrastructure: Avidity and Difference in Algorithmic Recommendation," *Cultural Studies* 35, no. 4–5 (September 3, 2021): 771–91; Kate Crawford, *Atlas of AI: Power, Politics, and the Planetary Costs of Artificial Intelligence* (New Haven: Yale University Press, 2021).

13. Cheney-Lippold, *We Are Data*.

14. "Long Short-Term Memory Networks," Codecademy, https://www.codecademy.com/article/long-short-term-memory-networks.

15. For more technical information on what algorithms and AI are and how they work, check out Panos Louridas, *Algorithms* (Cambridge, MA: MIT Press, 2020).

16. Guang-Bin Huang, Yan-Qiu Chen, and H. A. Babri, "Classification Ability of Single Hidden Layer Feedforward Neural Networks," *IEEE Transactions on Neural Networks* 11, no. 3 (May 2000): 799–801.

17. Email correspondence between Daniel Evans and Jonathan Cohn, May 5, 2021.

18. Hannah Arendt, *Eichmann in Jerusalem: A Report on the Banality of Evil* (New York: Penguin Books, 1994).

19. Sianne Ngai, "Merely Interesting," *Critical Inquiry* 34, no. 4 (2008): 777–817.

20. Arendt, *Eichmann in Jerusalem*, 276.

21. Crawford, *Atlas of AI*.

22. Quoted in Angela Englehardt, "Infrastructural Inquiries: Interview with Lisa Parks," *Circuits of Truth*, June 17, 2015, https://machinic.info/Parks.

23. Benjamin Peters, "How Do We Live Now? In the Aftermath of Ourselves," in *Your Computer Is on Fire*, eds. Thomas S. Mullaney, Benjamin Peters, Mar Hicks, and Kavita Philip (Cambridge, MA: MIT Press, 2021), 396.

24. Dan C. Ciresan, Ueli Meier, Jonathan Masci, Luca M. Gambardella, and Jürgen Schmidhuber, "Flexible, High Performance Convolutional Neural Networks for Image Classification," *Proceedings of the Twenty-second International Joint Conference on Artificial Intelligence* (2011): 1237–42.

25. Alexander Mordvintsev, "Inceptionism: Going Deeper into Neural Networks," Google Research, blog, June 17, 2015, https://underdestruction.com/2017/07/23/freeda-beast-bringing-things-to-an-end/.

26. Ibid.

27. Ibid.

28. Amoore, *Cloud Ethics*.

29. David Auerbach, "Do Androids Dream of Electric Bananas?," *Slate*, July 13, 2015.

30. Jacques Derrida, *Archive Fever: A Freudian Impression*, trans. Eric Prenowitz (Chicago: University of Chicago Press, 2008).

31. "The #DEEPDREAM Trip Report," *Spike Art Magazine*, July 15, 2015, https://www.spikeartmagazine.com/articles/deepdream-trip-report.

32. Joanna Zylinska, *AI Art: Machine Visions and Warped Dreams* (London: Open Humanities Press, 2020), 139, http://www.openhumanitiespress.org/books/titles/ai-art/.

33. Tom Simonite, "A 'Neurographer' Puts the Art in Artificial Intelligence," *Wired*, July 6, 2017, https://www.wired.com/story/neurographer-puts-the-art-in-artificial-intelligence/.

34. GANs pair two AI against each other: one is the generator, which tries to generate the output, and the other is the "discriminator," which tells it whether it is hot or cold. In the process, both the generator and discriminator continually get better at their tasks until either the generator is able to generate output that the discriminator finds passable or fails to improve, which is common. The terms are loaded and to some extent GANs work by a hegemonic logic, wherein the generator (here, a racialized AI subject), is continually trying to pass while the discriminator is continually getting better at discriminating.

35. Mario Klingemann, "Neural Glitch / Mistaken Identity | Quasimondo," https://underdestruction.com/2018/10/28/neural-glitch/.

36. Greg Siegel, *Forensic Media: Reconstructing Accidents in Accelerated Modernity* (Durham, NC: Duke University Press, 2014); Kelly Gates, *Our Biometric Future: Facial Recognition Technology and the Culture of Surveillance* (New York: New York University Press, 2011); John Tagg, *The Burden of Representation: Essays on Photographies and Histories* (Minneapolis: University of Minnesota Press, 1993); Cohn, *The Burden of Choice*.

37. Donna Haraway, "A Cyborg Manifesto: Science, Technology, and Socialist-Feminism in the Late Twentieth Century," in *Simians, Cyborgs, and Women: The Reinvention of Nature* (New York: Routledge, 1991), 149–81; Judith Butler, *Gender Trouble: Feminism and the Subversion of Identity* (New York: Routledge, 2006).

4

CODING AND ENCODING STREAMED MEDIA

The Cultural Infrastructure of the Netflix Recommender System

FATIMA GAW

Netflix reached almost 220 million subscribers in 2021, making it the largest streaming media service in the world. Undergirding its streaming media infrastructure is a set of intricate algorithms that distinguishes Netflix from others—personalized, up-to-date, and "so good at suggestions that [it's] able to show you exactly the right film or TV show for your mood."[1] The Netflix Recommender System (NRS), the algorithms' official name, is at the core of the streaming platform. It organizes Netflix's vast library of content, analyzes billions of hours of watch time, and generates tailored recommendations for audiences across 190 countries. By relying on taste attributes instead of demographic information such as location, race, and gender, NRS purportedly "transcends the predictions of stereotypical demographics."[2] This makes the NRS a model among engineers and programmers on the promise of algorithms, machine learning, and AI in innovating cultural experiences.

The NRS exemplifies algorithms as ubiquitous, deeply entangled, and indispensable media technology in contemporary culture. The era of big data requires computational technologies to mediate between platforms and end users to organize knowledge, processes, and experiences. For instance, Google's PageRank algorithm crawls the web to catalog billions of pages and websites and match them with user searches.[3] Twitter employs an algorithm to identify "trending" topics both within your location and personalized to your network.[4] Spotify algorithmically curates playlists from millions of tracks to fit particular dayparts, moods, and activities of its users.[5] Algorithms form part of *media backends* as sociotechnical systems that facilitate the production, distribution, and consumption of cultural experiences beneath layers of obscured materialities, processes, and practices.

Despite their necessary pervasiveness, algorithms are elusive. Apart from their technical complexity, they are *black boxes* by virtue of being "trade secrets" involving proprietary information and techniques.[6] When required to be disclosed to regulators, algorithms are obfuscated in very simplistic or inexplicably complicated terms to strategically deflect questioning. Conceptually, algorithms are also difficult to locate. They are foremost considered as technological artifacts whose values and standards are impressed in their material code, input, and output.[7] They are also produced through collective cultural practices in diverse social contexts, which Nick Seaver argues not only situate algorithms *in culture* but also enact them *as culture*.[8] Further, algorithms are enveloped within platforms and are examined as components, among others, that facilitate programmable sociality and experiences.[9] On their own, algorithms enact their rules and decisions that shape a range of cultural processes, exhibiting and performing computational agency.[10]

In all these conceptions, algorithms are made meaningful not by themselves but in relation to various actors and objects—programmers and users, data and code, and protocols and structures. The contingency of algorithms on social interactions as well as their capacity to set the conditions that govern these engagements point me to investigate them as infrastructures. Infrastructures are produced out of this "double articulation"[11] where objects are born out of other objects to create "multiple, overlapping, and perhaps contradictory infrastructural arrangements."[12] Problematizing algorithms as infrastructure allows us to study them at multiple scales and scopes and accommodate inconsistencies and conflicts in their operations.

In this chapter, I investigate "when" algorithms are enacted as infrastructures through the cultural processes that mutually animate their technical, cultural, and social aspects.[13] Using the NRS as one of the most popular algorithmic systems in the world, I trace these processes by adapting Taina Bucher's methodological tactic of interrogating algorithms as *configurations*, which are constructs constituted by heterogeneous, incomplete, and contradictory parts that "form the appearance of more or less coherent relations."[14] I assemble this configuration in situated practices where the technical and cultural become inextricable—algorithms as designed by developers, imagined by media, and experienced by users. While the NRS's materiality remains obscure, I draw from the translations of "technical specifications" by its engineers from Netflix technical and corporate documents.[15] Then, I weave the narratives that establish, dispute, and expound popular conceptions and controversies of the NRS in media, in the form of Benjamin Burrough's "streaming lore" formulated by industry, media, and cultural discourses and practices.[16] Lastly, I encapsulate the social encounters of users with the NRS as publicly discussed on Twitter, particularly during experiences of algorithmic breakdown and anomalies as well as user resistance.[17]

I conceptualize this configuration of the NRS as a "cultural infrastructure" whose structures and protocols are designed to reconcile and reconstruct the technical, cultural, and social discrepancies emerging from its relocation from the articulations of *code* into contexts of *encoding*. Cultural infrastructures perform the dual work of the governance of social processes and generation of cultural standards through the mutually constitutive relations between the infrastructures' material and social conditions. Algorithms as cultural infrastructures not only direct paths for action but also create spheres of influence where decisions are made. Where there are windows of negotiation and resistance, however, algorithms tend to supersede them through socializing users into deference, restricting user agency, and privileging algorithmic agency. This theoretical intervention integrates intersections and incompatibilities of research on algorithms from different disciplinary strands by acknowledging their duality as both products and producers of cultural processes.[18]

Algorithm as Infrastructure, Infrastructures as Algorithmic

In an influential paper, Robert Kowalski defines an algorithm as a computing program that identifies information and employs strategies to solve complex problems.[19] Ted Striphas argues that algorithms not only work to make sense of enormous amounts of data but also "to expose some truth or tendency about the world."[20] Ed Finn calls algorithms "culture machines" as they simulate reality by using "all sorts of technical and intellectual inferences, interventions, and filters."[21] These algorithmic mechanisms operate recursively, creating feedback loops where "each iteration introduces a deviation."[22] The variations fold back infinitely to the system, creating "models [that] analyze the world and the world responds to the models."[23] As such, an algorithm both anticipates outcomes and generates its own procedures in filtering, ordering, and structuring reality.

Algorithms are embedded in larger systems, from software to platforms and infrastructures, often sinking into a singularity with other components. Platform studies often subsume the discussion of algorithms with that of affordances, big data, and platform governance.[24] Yet, the same works acknowledge algorithms as consequential to the operations and outcomes of platforms. Critical algorithm studies examine algorithms as conceptually distinct objects of inquiry, problematizing their power to regulate cultural production, circulation, and consumption.[25] I argue that both areas of study fall short in capturing the contingency of algorithms on other structures, arrangements, and organizations and their capacity to set the conditions of cultural processes within these systems. In the case of the NRS, its functioning is dependent on the Netflix platform, Netflix Inc., and the cultural contexts in which it is embedded. The relationship of the NRS with these structures then configures how the algorithms are enacting cultural experiences, such as the creation of user taste profiles based on platform affordances or the expectations of demographic agnosticism from corporate claims of algorithmic neutrality. This double articulation requires reconceptualizing the study of algorithms from being neither part nor whole to *whole parts of other wholes*. Infrastructure studies might bring to the fore this character of algorithms.

Infrastructures are "built networks that facilitate the flow of goods, people, or ideas and allow for their exchange over space."[26] They are heterogeneous material and intellectual structures, mechanisms, and protocols that organize, standardize, and inform the order of things. Leading infrastructure researchers emphasize that an infrastructure's power lies in its capacity to create the conditions to which all decisions and actions are subjected and orient them toward particular directions.[27] Recently, media scholars examine this "possibility-fixing" power in media infrastructures,[28] particularly through the ways they shape media environments, distribution processes, and cultural experiences.[29]

Of interest in infrastructure as an analytical lens is its relational character, "becoming real infrastructure in relation to organized practices."[30] This reframes the question from "what is an infrastructure" to "when it becomes an infrastructure,"[31] locating its constitutive components in conjunction with technical, social, and cultural processes. I conceptualize algorithms as infrastructures along this line of analysis and argue that they represent a new class of media infrastructures built on artificial intelligence. I draw from Susan Leigh Star and Karen Ruhleder's dimensions of infrastructures to build this case: embeddedness, transparency, reach and scope, membership-based learning, linkage with conventions of practice, embodiment of standards, superimposition over an installed base, and visibility upon breakdown.[32]

First, algorithms have become a "kind of invisible structural force," concealed behind technical complexity and commercial interests, enmeshed in heterogeneous digital systems, and entrenched in everyday social contexts.[33] Second, they "always work, no matter what the inputs" and operate automatedly.[34] Third, algorithms are extensive and encompassing, from reading present data patterns to predicting future probabilities, as well as scaling personalized outcomes to mass customization.[35] Fourth, algorithms enact standards and procedures through quantification: transforming people, objects, and actions into "computable abstractions."[36] Fifth, their material existence is built by someone (e.g., developers) and is installed on existing structures (e.g., software) that set the parameters of code.[37] Sixth, it is intuitive for users to know how algorithms work without having to understand their technicalities as they have become "cultural" objects themselves.[38] Seventh, as much as algorithms are self-sufficient, they are entangled in the social conventions of their proprietors, developers, and users.[39] Eighth, for the reasons above, algorithms are generally reliable but are also prone to malfunction, if not misinterpretation.[40]

By these definitions, algorithms fit Star and Ruhleder's standards of what makes an infrastructure, but they also have characteristics outside this archetype. While infrastructures have a quality of permanence, algorithms are programmable such that part of their code can be altered that can affect their functioning.[41] The NRS has been revised and updated through the years to produce more "accurate" recommendations as Netflix expands its library and global audience. Infrastructures also generally perform a facilitative function, where algorithms also have the generative capacity by producing derivative data, optimized procedures, and new knowledge.[42] As you will see later, the NRS has created new data categories, optimization processes, and cultural products beyond what we customarily consider as "recommendations." This renders algorithms agential properties, enacting their computational agency beyond their programming and exceeding their logistical power as an infrastructure.

The Tale of the Netflix Recommender System

Netflix pioneered streaming in 2007, and every big media company followed suit. While the competition like Disney+ leverages its stockpile of legacy media franchises and Amazon repurposes its retail algorithms to Prime Video, Netflix stands above the market through its global recommender system. The NRS leverages its "global communities" to infer individual taste preferences from global patterns of consumption, as country-level data might be limited in generating "accurate" recommendations.[43] This abundance of data enables the algorithms to personalize their recommendations for users, both content they already like, and those they are yet to discover.

Netflix has been experimenting with algorithms during its DVD-for-rent years with *Cinematch* to generate recommendations for customers on which movie to rent. In 2006, it launched the Netflix Prize, a three-year competition to improve its algorithm's ratings prediction. While the winning algorithm was not implemented given excessive operational costs, the contest popularized the Netflix algorithms in the tech industry. After 2009, the NRS becomes so prominent in media that it is not only known as the platform's operating system but as synonymous with Netflix. Netflix has also been more forthcoming about how its algorithms operate, publishing explanations from developers in its Netflix-owned websites and engaging media to translate the complexities of the NRS for popular consumption. However, these remain either highly technical or too broad to explain the workings of the NRS. The gap between these two ends is filled in by what Burrough calls *streaming lore*, which creates our expectations of how the algorithms work and shape our experiences when we encounter them.[44]

A prominent narrative around the NRS is its guarantee of personalized, quality recommendations. Personalization purportedly ensures that "no two Netflix experiences are alike" and the more users spend time on the platform, the more personalized the recommendations are.[45] This intimate knowledge of users' taste creates the impression that the NRS knows users better than they know themselves, and thus it is trustworthy.[46] The underlying assumption here is that the algorithms are neutral and objective, relying wholly on the data to serve users' interests and not Netflix's commercial ends. This relates to another well-known streaming lore about the NRS deriving its recommendations exclusively from users' taste preferences and not from demographic data. The algorithms are allegedly agnostic on class, gender, race, and other social identities, much like the promise of the internet of disembodiment from traditional markers of identity.[47] This postdemographic profiling departs from conventional practices in the industry, supposedly freeing the system of the biases and prejudices that might box users into specific categories. Going beyond the user experience, it is also commonly understood that Netflix uses its algorithms to inform business and creative decisions—from what kinds of programs to produce, which syndicated shows to keep in its library, and how to manage diversity in its catalog.[48] The success of its debut Netflix Original, *House of Cards*, and its other big bets was purportedly predicted by algorithms as a testament to their superior computational judgment.

As I will illustrate later, some claims in streaming lore are contested, but they also reveal how the NRS fortifies its influence beyond its technical capacities. It establishes the algorithms as cultural objects, with both developers and users having their algorithmic imaginaries of how the NRS works, what to expect from it, and what it should do if it fails to perform accordingly.[49] Users are also incorporating algorithms in their everyday life and algorithmic recommendations are cultivating users into ideal consumers, shaping each other in the process.[50] The relocation of algorithms from industry lore to media narratives and social contexts helps articulate the materiality of the algorithms, as well as their social construction through the ways people attach meanings to their algorithmic encounters.

The Configuration of Algorithmic Infrastructures

Constructing the "configuration" of the Netflix Recommendation System involved assembling technical, cultural, and social articulations of the logics of its algorithms, deconstructing their underlying assumptions and procedures, and articulating the cultural processes that animate the infrastructure. The following discussion draws from the analysis of sixty technical documents primarily from the Netflix Technology Blog, academic papers and corporate documents, and 100 media reports from 2007 to 2019, as well as 990 unique Twitter posts from February to May 2019 across countries.

My investigation has identified three key processes that underpin the cultural infrastructure of the NRS: *classification* of data, signals, and actions into predetermined types and criteria; *categorization* of data into emergent groups and cultural constructions; and *codification* of cultural relations and identities through recommendation. The protocols and procedures of these infrastructural processes, however, emerge not out of the consistencies but out of the discrepancies and contradictions of their material and social articulations.

Classification

Pertinent Netflix documents and interviews with executives point out to the NRS employing two classification schemes: first is to classify user data into explicit and implicit taste preferences, and second is to evaluate titles based on a set of criteria. Explicit taste preferences pertain to user actions that directly inform the algorithms of their tastes and interests. These user activities include answering a profile survey upon sign-up, adding titles to the watchlist, and rating content. Netflix used to have a five-star rating system, but it was replaced with a binary thumbs-up or down system in 2017 to purportedly orient users away from performative social standards such as box office results and critics' reviews, and toward "intuitive" personal feedback.[51] Implicit taste preferences are data points that indirectly signify user interests, such as plays, watch time, searches, and clicks. Between the two classifications, Netflix put a premium on implicit over explicit taste preferences because the latter are deemed "aspirational" while the former represent actual consumption.[52]

Titles are also classified based on a set of criteria that filters what appears in the interface. Apart from tagging titles for "relevance" to users' tastes, "popularity" is used to identify which groups of titles are prominent in particular taste communities, timeframes, or locations. While Netflix engineers recognize that popularity might conflict with relevance, they assert that the algorithms indicate that "a member is most likely to watch what most others are watching."[53] The NRS also purportedly evaluates titles based on their "diversity" to respond to the range of tastes and interests of users and households. Some other criteria such as context, freshness, and novelty were identified briefly in the Netflix tech documents but were not discussed.

These classification protocols are generally overlooked by users, except when they were "failed" by the NRS, when it "misreads" their taste, or dismisses their explicit taste preferences altogether. Titles they down-rated were allegedly repeatedly recommended to them, while those they up-rated or queued in their watchlist were not showing up on their homepage. Users also criticize the algorithms for confining them to a narrow set of interests despite the broad array of genres they watched on the platform. They also complain that they needed to search for content they like because the algorithms "bury" it deep into the library, while Netflix Originals are always displayed in the "popular" row.

Categorization

Categorization includes the ways the NRS organizes its data into new and unconventional groups and clusters. These categories are publicized broadly in media reports to definitively distinguish the NRS's ascendancy among other recommendation systems. In an article in *The Atlantic*, reporter Alexis Madrigal (2014) has reverse engineered how Netflix categorized its content and discovered *altgenres*—thousands of reimagined categories of content constructed by fragmenting films and movies into granular attributes. Titles are deconstructed based on specific aspects like the moral stance of the characters, the degree of romance and level of gore, and then are graded on a scale. These "microtags" are then used to formulate hyperspecific genres such as "Feel-Good Disney Talking-Animal Animation," or "Visually Striking Cerebral Fight-the-System Movies." Through altgenres, Netflix purportedly avoids "genre bias" and opens new pathways for content discovery.[54]

Taste communities are another categorization convention of the NRS. They are algorithmically generated groups that cluster individuals sharing similar tastes, detached from demographic information used in traditional audience targeting. Taste communities were Netflix's way of integrating their national audiences into a single global entity, drawing from geographically dispersed users from the same taste communities to inform of the collective interests of the group. In a report by *Adage*, there are at least 2,000 taste communities managed by the NRS in 2020, but their actual categories and composition remain obscure.[55]

While appearing to be cutting-edge, these categories present some issues when translated into recommendations. Users narrate their experiences of unrelated or inappropriate titles being recommended after watching particular shows. For instance, users were in disbelief to be served the true-crime documentary *Ted Bundy Tapes* right after finishing the children's show *Peppa Pig* or the eighties classic *The Breakfast Club* as "actual suggestion Netflix's algorithm came up with." It was also pointed out that several Netflix Originals were "plastered everywhere" in multiple altgenres. Contrary to the promise of postdemographic targeting, controversies on racial and gender profiling persist in media and in everyday algorithmic encounters. In October 2018, several African American users noticed that they are being served title artwork that featured Black characters in films and shows with a predominantly White cast. Podcaster Tolani Shoneye told *The Guardian* that she "noticed it a while ago with a Zac Efron film that [she]'d already seen, but Netflix kept showing it as a

Michael B. Jordan movie."[56] Reporting indicates that viewers felt "manipulated" by Netflix by reducing their taste to their race and manufacturing diversity in an otherwise overwhelmingly White content catalog. Twitter users echo this experience with Black users who were purportedly "read" as Caucasians by the algorithms and were exclusively getting "White" films, while their peers were being served with "Black" titles that were not in their recommendations. The algorithms also were under fire in March 2019 for allegedly arranging the episodes of the animated anthology *Love, Death, + Robots* based on user's sexual orientation.[57] Queer viewers report that the arrangement "changes based on whether Netflix thinks you're gay or straight" having been served the episode with a sexually explicit lesbian episode, while their cisgender friends had the heteronormative episode queued on top. Gay users in my Twitter data were also allegedly being "queerbaited" by showing same-sex couples on recommendation artwork. In both cases, Netflix insists that its targeting schemes are randomly generated by the algorithms and it does not collect demographic information from its users.[58] By deflecting the blame on algorithms, Netflix dismisses the possibility of the NRS recognizing demographic patterns in its algorithmic categorization, even when media reports and Twitter users corroborate being demographically targeted.

Codification

Codification is the process of materializing the algorithms' cultural codes in the form of recommendations that prescribe the orientation, choices, and actions that users make in the platform. The personalized homepage lays out the recommended altgenres in each row, the selected titles per row, and their ranking arranged in order of compatibility. All the recommendations have undergone A/B testing, which evaluates the "effectiveness" of sets of recommendations and selects the most compelling ones to be rolled out to a majority of the users. In 2016, Netflix also began personalizing artwork by algorithmically identifying the images that purportedly "highlight the aspects of a title that are specifically relevant to them."[59] This visual "evidence" is complemented by numerical evidence of the algorithms' accuracy called the match score, which calculates the compatibility of titles to users' tastes. Titles with scores below 50 percent are allegedly not considered for recommendation altogether.

This codification of recommendations has become problematic in cases when it misrepresents the films and shows they serve. For the show *Grace and Frankie*, the artwork of actress Jane Fonda was said to perform poorly in the A/B testing and her images were planned to be removed despite Fonda's being the show's lead character.[60] Another controversy involved the alleged whitewashing of artwork for the show *Nailed It!* where images of the two White men who were only supporting personalities were being served instead of its host Nicole Byer, who is a Black woman.[61] There were also tweets about users being frustrated about not having the tools to correct the algorithms when the recommendations do not match their tastes. Some users opted to "train" the algorithms to their liking, while others request to have the ability to edit their viewing history or directly send their feedback through reviews.

The Power of Cultural Infrastructures

The algorithmic processes of classification, categorization, and codification are reminiscent of the protocols of conventional infrastructures such that they intend to streamline "local" practices into "global" operations.[62] Algorithms as infrastructures, however, engage in both standardized operations and *standardized production,* which in the case of the NRS is to generate bespoke outcomes out of the perpetual intake of data, alterations in code, and changes in organizational structures. Thus, for the algorithms to function, they necessarily open up the infrastructure to inquiry, dispute, and "repair" by developers, stakeholders, and users that might undermine their stability and coherence.[63] What I argue in this chapter is that algorithms maintain their structural integrity despite being subjected to human intervention by operating as cultural infrastructures. Cultural infrastructures embody the dual capacity of governing social processes within their built structures and generating the cultural standards from which social processes are based and validated. Contrary to the conceptual distinction made by Seaver, "cultural" here conveys that the algorithms are both located "in culture," such that they "affect culture and culture can affect algorithms because they are distinct," and exist "as culture" enacted by composite practices of humans and machines that produce their own cultural assumptions, standards, and values.[64] The *cultural constructs* produced out of the social relations among various actors mutually constitute the *cultural construction* performed by the materiality of the algorithm, and together they comprise the "control and value . . . indissolubly linked to the machine ensembles."[65] Below, I discuss the ways the NRS enacts the power of the cultural infrastructure of algorithms.

The underlying protocol of any algorithmic system is to translate data into quantifiable attributes. Quantification enables the algorithms to both manage information and create new models that define how information is deconstructed and decoded, which categories and hierarchies they are classified and assigned, and what new compositions and structures are reconstructed from them. More than a recipe of instructions, these models are calculated relationships that establish the rules that determine all decisions made by the algorithms. They are if-then statements that prescribe "ways of seeing" the relations between cultural constructs, artifacts, and identities (if "gender" is "gay" then "artwork" is "same-sex couple") and they constitute the complex cultural schema of the algorithmic infrastructure.[66] However, rules are universal, and recommendations are supposedly personal. Where there is a conflict between the two, the universal supersedes the personal. In the NRS, subjective expressions of taste are necessarily reduced into binary choices and discredited as aspirational and performative if they do not translate to consumption. The popularity criterion homogenizes recommendations based on the preferences of an invisible, presumably Western cultural majority. Demographic targeting surfaces despite its supposed absence in the data, because race, gender, and sexual orientation are categories that can accommodate generalized assumptions about people. For Netflix, its algorithmic models *always work* even if that means neglecting the nuances, ambiguities, and even dissonances of individual subjectivities. Further, the recursive process of the algorithms means the same rules govern the generation of new rules. These algorithmic ontological models fundamentally become self-affirming, not only enacting rules but also normalizing constructs that are enduring, encompassing, and resistant to change.[67]

This intellectual structure of the algorithm is cemented not only by its computational logic, but also by its social relations with its users. The streaming lore about the NRS, among other myths about algorithms, has socialized us to trust them, sometimes more than our own judgment. In particular, the promise of personalization "hails" users into identifying with the characters, narratives, and other reflexive images projected in the algorithmic recommendations.[68] This process of interpellation is performed through semantic codes embedded in objects like altgenres and artwork, as well as through the spatial arrangements through ranking and sequencing. Normative representations of race, gender, and sexual orientation in the recommendations were particularly compelling, despite users' ambivalence about being demographically targeted. The subjectification of users unequivocally manifests when they become hyperaware of and involved in constructing their algorithmic identities.[69] The frustrations and anxieties over whether the algorithms are accurately reading their behavior or responding to their feedback are rooted in the "sense of ownership, agency, and presence" over their algorithmic identities.[70] In an attempt to "correct" or "train" the algorithms, users regulate their behavior and actions. This self-regulation following the logics of the algorithms sustains the persistence of ontological models, as well as providing users with a semblance of control over the algorithms.

The NRS's cultural schemas are reified in all parts of the infrastructure, manufacturing the norms, standards, and values of "quality," "popular," and "personalized" cultural experiences. The repackaging of a White-majority cast film by using a Black character artwork stand-in reframes the film as relevant to Black viewers, and relocates it to a marginalized cultural category, albeit temporarily. Titles with a match score below 50, although arbitrarily assigned, disappear in the recommendations completely. These algorithmic outcomes not only direct users toward particular choices, but create the sphere of influence where present and future actions are made. The NRS interface may look vast, but it conceals a horizon of choices available to its users from its various infrastructural protocols. How the sphere is constructed allows *but* also constrains user agency through "complicit forms of resistance" and those outside the parameters of its prevailing models are dismissed as "unrecommendable."[71]

Conclusion

Algorithms represent a new kind of infrastructure assembled from code, data, and practices and they introduce a new "grammar," a "language-like set of protocols for arranging the world and the organs of sensation."[72] I identified a few of those procedures and protocols, most of which characterize what we know of infrastructures and some present prospective dimensions. These distinguishing capacities of algorithms as cultural infrastructures render to it the power to both govern cultural processes and generate new standards and protocols that animate those processes. This chapter underlines algorithms as performing the "politics of 'as-if'" by setting the conditions that define the possibilities and boundaries of cultural experiences.[73]

Notes

1. Reed Hastings, "Netflix Keynote 2016," (Lecture at Consumer Electronics Show, Las Vegas, NV, January 6, 2016), https://www.youtube.com/watch?v=l5R3E6jsICA.

2. Ashley Rodriguez, "Netflix Divides Its 93 Million Users around the World into 1,300 'Taste Communities,'" *Quartz,* March 23, 2017, https://qz.com/939195/netflix-nflx-divides-its-93-million-users-around-the-world-not-by-geography-but-into-1300-taste-commu.

3. Google, "How Search Works: How Results Are Automatically Generated," https://www.google.com/search/howsearchworks/how-search-works/ranking-results/

4. Tarleton Gillespie, "#trendingistrending: When Algorithms Become Culture," in *Algorithmic Cultures: Essays on Meaning, Performance and New Technologies*, ed. Robert Seyfert and Jonathan Roberge (London: Routledge, 2018), 52–75.

5. Maria Eriksson and Anna Johansson, "'Keep Smiling!': Time, Functionality, and Intimacy in Spotify's Featured Playlists," *Cultural Analysis* 16, no. 1 (2017): 67–82.

6. Frank Pasquale, *The Black Box Society: The Secret Algorithms That Control Money and Information* (Cambridge, MA: Harvard University Press, 2015), 12.

7. Christian Sandvig, Kevin Hamilton, Karrie Karahalios, and Cedric Langbort, "An Algorithm Audit," in *Data and Discrimination: Collected Essays*, eds. Seeta Peña Gangadharan, Virginia Eubanks, and Solon Barocas (Washington, DC: New America's Open Technology Institute, 2014), 6–10; Rob Kitchin and Martin Dodge, *Code/Space: Software and Everyday Life* (Cambridge, MA: MIT Press, 2011); Nicholas Diakopoulos, "Algorithmic Accountability: Journalistic Investigation of Computational Power Structures," *Digital Journalism* 3, no. 3 (2015): 398–415, https://doi.org/10.1080/21670811.2014.976411.

8. Nick Seaver, "Algorithms as Culture: Some Tactics for the Ethnography of Algorithmic Systems," *Big Data & Society* 4, no. 2 (2017).

9. José van Dijck and Thomas Poell, "Understanding Social Media Logic," *Media and Communication* 1, no. 1 (2013): 2–14; Jean-Christophe Plantin, Carl Lagoze, Paul N. Edwards, and Christian Sandvig, "Infrastructure Studies Meet Platform Studies in the Age of Google and Facebook," *New Media & Society* 20, no. 1 (2018): 293–310; Taina Bucher, *If . . . Then: Algorithmic Power and Politics* (New York: Oxford University Press, 2018).

10. Robert Prey, "Nothing Personal: Algorithmic Individuation on Music Streaming Platforms," *Media, Culture & Society* 40, no. 7 (2018): 1086–1100; David, ed., *The Social Power of Algorithms* (London: Routledge, 2020); Bucher, *If . . . Then*.

11. Gilles Deleuze and Félix Guattari, *A Thousand Plateaus: Capitalism and Schizophrenia* (Minneapolis: University of Minnesota Press, 1987).

12. Susan Leigh Star and Geoffrey Bowker, "How to Infrastructure," in *Handbook of New Media: Social Shaping and Consequences of ICTs*, ed. Leah A. Lievrouw and Sonia Livingstone (London: Sage, 2004), 230.

13. Seaver, "Algorithms as Culture."

14. Bucher, *If . . . Then*, 63.

15. Ibid., 72.

16. Benjamin Burroughs, "House of Netflix: Streaming Media and Digital Lore," *Popular Communication* 17, no. 1 (2019): 1–17.

17. Bucher, *If . . . Then*; Julia Velkova and Anne Kaun, "Algorithmic Resistance: Media Practices and the Politics of Repair," *Information, Communication & Society* 24, no. 4 (2019): 523–40.

18. Kitchin and Dodge, *Code/Space*.

19. Robert Kowalski, "Algorithm= Logic+ Control," *Communications of the ACM* 22, no. 7 (1979): 424–36, https://ewic.bcs.org/upload/pdf/ewic_eva18_de_paper1.pdf.

20. T. Striphas, "Algorithmic Culture," *European Journal of Cultural Studies* 18, no. 4–5 (2015): 404.

21. Ed Finn, *What Algorithms Want: Imagination in the Age of Computing* (Cambridge, MA: MIT Press, 2017), 18.

22. Robert Seyfert and Jonathan Roberge, "What Are Algorithmic Cultures?" in *Algorithmic Cultures: Essays on Meaning, Performance, and New Technologies*, ed. Robert Seyfert and Jonathan Roberge (London: Routledge, 2018), 12.

23. Kitchin and Dodge, *Code/Space*, 30.

24. Van Dijck and Poell, "Understanding Social Media Logic"; G. Bolin and J. Andersson Schwarz, "Heuristics of the Algorithm: Big Data, User Interpretation, and Institutional Translation," *Big Data & Society* 2, no. 2 (2015); Gillespie, "#trendingistrending: When Algorithms Become Culture."

25. Tarleton Gillespie, "The Relevance of Algorithms," in *Media Technologies : Essays on Communication, Materiality, and Society*, ed. Tarleton Gillespie, Pablo Boczkowski, and Kirsten Foot (Cambridge, MA: MIT Press, 2014), 167–94; Tarleton Gillespie, *Custodians of the Internet: Platforms, Content Moderation, and the Hidden Decisions That Shape Social Media* (New Haven: Yale University Press, 2018); John Cheney-Lippold, *We Are Data: Algorithms and the Making of Our Digital Selves* (New York: New York University Press, 2017); David, "Envisioning the Power of Data Analytics," *Information, Communication & Society* 21, no. 3 (2018): 465–79; Bucher, *If . . . Then*.

26. Brian Larkin, "The Politics and Poetics of Infrastructure," *Annual Review of Anthropology* 42, no. 1 (2013): 328.

27. Susan Leigh Star and Karen Ruhleder, "Steps toward an Ecology of Infrastructure: Design and Access for Large Information Spaces," *Information Systems Research* 7, no. 1 (1996): 111–35; Susan Leigh Star, "The Ethnography of Infrastructure," *American Behavioural Scientist* 43, no. 3 (1999): 377–91; Geoffrey Bowker and Susan Leigh Star, *Sorting Things Out: Classification and Its Consequences* (Cambridge, MA: MIT Press, 2000).

28. John Durham Peters, *The Marvelous Clouds: Toward a Philosophy of Elemental Media* (Chicago: University of Chicago Press, 2015).

29. Lisa Parks and Nicole Starosielski, eds., *Signal Traffic: Critical Studies of Media Infrastructures* (Urbana: University of Illinois Press, 2015); Aswin Punathambekar and Sriram Mohan, eds., *Global Digital Cultures: Perspectives from South Asia* (Ann Arbor: University of Michigan Press, 2019).

30. Star, "The Ethnography of Infrastructure," 380.

31. Star and Ruhleder, "Steps toward an Ecology of Infrastructure," 112.

32. Ibid.

33. David Beer, "Algorithms: Shaping Tastes and Manipulating the Circulations of Popular Culture," in *Popular Culture and New Media: The Politics of Circulation* (Basingstoke: Palgrave Macmillan, 2013), 69.

34. John MacCormick, *Nine Algorithms That Changed the Future: The Ingenious Ideas That Drive Today's Computers* (Princeton, NJ: Princeton University Press, 2012), 3.

35. Gillespie, "The Relevance of Algorithms"; *Popular Culture and New Media*.

36. Finn, *What Algorithms Want*, 23.

37. Bucher, *If . . . Then*, 22.

38. Gillespie, "#trendingistrending: When Algorithms Become Culture," 53.

39. Gillespie, "The Relevance of Algorithms," 183.

40. Jonathan Cohn, *The Burden of Choice: Recommendations, Subversion, and Algorithmic Culture* (New Brunswick, NJ: Rutgers University Press, 2019).

41. Peters, *The Marvelous Clouds*; Bucher, *If . . . Then*.

42., *Popular Culture and New Media*.

43. Carlos Gomez-Uribe, "A Global Approach to Recommendations," Netflix, February 17, 2016, https://about.netflix.com/en/news/a-global-approach-to-recommendations.

44. Burroughs, "House of Netflix."

45. Netflix, "There's Never Enough TV on Netflix," *Huffington Post*, February 9, 2017, https://media.netflix.com/en/press-releases/theres-never-enough-tv-on-netflix/.

46. Cohn, *The Burden of Choice*.

47. Ibid., 26.

48. Ramon Lobato, *Netflix Nations: The Geography of Digital Distribution* (New York: New York University Press, 2019).

49. Bucher, *If . . . Then*; Velkova and Kaun, "Algorithmic Resistance."

50. Ignacio Siles, Johan Espinosa-Rojas, Adrián Naranjo, and María Fernanda Tristán, "The Mutual Domestication of Users and Algorithmic Recommendations on Netflix," *Communication, Culture, and Critique* 12, no. 4 (2019): 499–518; Eriksson and Johansson, "'Keep Smiling!'"

51. Cameron Johnson, "Goodbye Stars, Hello Thumbs," *Netflix Media*, April 5, 2017, https://media.netflix.com/en/company-blog/goodbye-stars-hello-thumbs.

52. Tom Vanderbilt, "The Science behind the Netflix Algorithms That Decide What You'll Watch Next," *Wired*, August 7, 2013, https://www.wired.com/2013/08/qq-netflix-algorithm.

53. Xavier Amatriain and Justin Basilico, "Netflix Recommendations: Beyond the 5 Stars (Part 1)," *Netflix Tech Blog*, April 6, 2012, https://netflixtechblog.com/netflix-recommendations-beyond-the-5-stars-part-1-55838468f429.

54. Nick Lucchesi, "Netflix Says Its Algorithm Is Helping to Kill 'Genre Bias,'" *Inverse*, August 22, 2017, https://www.inverse.com/article/35780-netflix-genre-bias-data.

55. Ana Andjelic, "Opinion: Why Taste Communities Are the Future of Marketing," *Adage*, January 16, 2020, https://adage.com/article/opinion/opinion-why-taste-communities-are-future-marketing/2223986.

56. Nosheen Iqbal, "Film Fans See Red over Netflix 'Targeted' Posters for Black Viewers," *The Guardian*, October 20, 2018, https://www.theguardian.com/media/2018/oct/20/netflix-film-black-viewers-personalised-marketing-target.

57. Anthony Ha, "Netflix Is Experimenting with Different Episode Orders for 'Love, Death & Robots,'" *TechCrunch*, March 19, 2019, https://techcrunch.com/2019/03/19/love-death-robots-experiment/.

58. Iqbal, "Film Fans See Red over Netflix 'Targeted' Posters for Black Viewers"; Ha, "Netflix Is Experimenting with Different Episode Orders for 'Love, Death & Robots.'"

59. Ashok Chandrashekar, Fernando Amat, Justin Basilico, and Tony Jebara, "Artwork Personalization at Netflix," *Netflix Tech Blog*, December 8, 2018, https://netflixtechblog.com/artwork-personalization-c589f074ad76.

60. Shalini Ramachandran and Joe Flint, "Hollywood versus the Algorithm at Netflix," *Wall Street Journal*, November 12, 2018, https://www.wsj.com/articles/at-netflix-who-wins-when-its-hollywood-vs-the-algorithm-1541826015.

61. Rachel McGrath, "Netflix Accused of Whitewashing by Nailed It! Host Nicole Byer," *Huffington Post*, May 29, 2019, https://www.huffingtonpost.co.uk/entry/nicole-byer-netflix-whitewashing_uk_5cee50ebe4b0975ccf5dada5.

62. Star and Ruhleder, "Steps Toward an Ecology of Infrastructure."

63. Velkova and Kaun, "Algorithmic Resistance."

64. Seaver, "Algorithms as Culture," 4–5.

65. Larkin, "The Politics and Poetics of Infrastructure," 339.

66. Prey, "Nothing Personal."

67. Gillespie, "The Relevance of Algorithms," 187.

68. Louis Althusser, "Ideology and Ideological State Apparatuses (Notes towards an Investigation)," in *Lenin and Philosophy, and Other Essays* (New York: Monthly Review Press, 2001), 76–87.

69. Cheney-Lippold, *We Are Data*.

70. Cohn, *The Burden of Choice*, 89.

71. Velkova and Kaun, "Algorithmic Resistance"; Cohn, *The Burden of Choice*, 108.

72. Peters, *The Marvelous Clouds*, 15–16.

73. Larkin, "The Politics and Poetics of Infrastructure," 335.

5

ENGAGING OPACITY

Spotify and the Poiesis
of Algorithmic Backends

TIM MARKHAM

The music streaming platform Spotify is, on the face of it, an exemplary case study for investigating the relationship between backend technologies and processes and everyday experiences of sociality and subjectification for three reasons. First, its curation algorithm displaces more serendipitous or thoughtful practices of musical discovery, casting doubt on the authenticity and ownership of a user's taste. Second, given that music is an important social resource, bonding friends, lovers, and fan communities alike, Spotify appears to illustrate evocatively the data colonialism thesis,[1] which warns that the very basis of sociality is being reshaped in accordance with interests at odds with those of digital audiences. And third, it shines a light on the lack of awareness of backend materiality, its experiential weightlessness obscuring complex media infrastructures, massive energy consumption, and an extractive financial model undermining career viability for the majority of recording artists. Spotify can hardly be described as an uncanny technology that knows us better than we know ourselves: listeners frequently voice their frustration that the platform misrecognizes them,[2] while others have argued that the exclusions Spotify makes from playlists are sociopolitically implicated.[3] But this raises the question of whether a better recognitive fit could emerge from more transparency around how Spotify creates tailored playlists, and whether less opacity could also afford better understanding of how individual and collective tastes evolve, as well as the inner workings and social and environmental impact of streaming services more generally.

Music promotion has always been a murky business, and concerns about the manipulative or degraded kinds of popular content directed at young consumers have historically come to be seen as reactionary in hindsight, especially given the emphasis in cultural studies research into fan communities and the social affordances of pop culture consumption. However, perceptions of commercial recommendation algorithms as black-box technologies give rise to fears around the implications of constant user profiling and datafication. Digital literacy campaigners worry about the lack of awareness of (or informed consent for) how data is mined and used, while scholars highlight consumer ignorance about how what is served up to them by streaming platforms constrains their individual and collective sense of identity. But while all of this would seem to make the case for greater backend transparency, this chapter takes its lead from the phenomenological tradition, as well as more recent interventions regarding accountability, to argue that Spotify's opacity is precisely the precondition for an ethical relationship with its users. It then goes on to argue that its purportedly inauthentic cultures of listenership are just as poietic—that is, ontologically disclosive—as any others, and as sturdy a foundation for subjectification and sociality.

Poiesis is used in the Aristotelean sense of "that which brings into being" and is distinct from "affordance" in that it refers not just to particular possibilities for creating and acting, but replete ways of being in the world. This follows others in the media phenomenological tradition like Paul Frosh, who foreground the worlding possibility of digital technologies beyond their design and content.[4] Media backends are similarly conceived as poietic in that full world-disclosing sense, irreducible to their technical specifications or the service they were developed to deliver. Spotify emerged as a music streaming platform in the wake of the demise of "pirate" sharing sites and apps such as Napster, and has since diversified into podcasting and much else besides. But it has also brought into being new ways of listening and thus new kinds of mediated places produced through novel cultures of practice—think of commuting, or going to the gym, or hanging out with friends, for all of which Spotify is not just a fresh backdrop but a constitutive ontological force in producing distinct ways of being. Researching Spotify presents acute challenges in that the platform guards the design and operation of its algorithms jealously. Recent attempts to investigate Spotify have been praised on the one hand for developing creative experimental methods, but also criticized for reading nefarious intent into what is presented as the black box at the heart of the corporate streaming giant.[5]

Backends are the aspects of mediated life that fly under the radar but underpin poiesis as a usually seamless experience, and they include the Spotify algorithm that curates playlists and makes recommendations but also its data servers; its financial relations with musical artists, communications corporations, and national governments; the infrastructural networks that circulate data, and the energy sources that keep the whole show on the road. Media phenomenology resists reducing the meaning of backends to their coding, business model, materiality, or original conception; in philosophical terms this is because the phenomenological tradition rejects the whole idea of origins, and in the present context it means thinking of backends as not only self-contained sources of mediated experience but also indispensable elements of unfolding assemblages of objects, actors human and nonhuman, and processes—an unfolding that always proceeds from the present in which all these elements are always-already in the thick of it. This is why a phenomenological approach rejects framing an algorithmic backend as a black box, because this would suggest that its teleology is discoverable in its programming, or maybe in the mind of its creator. As will become clear, the opacity of commercially protected code, like the opacity of the origin of our subjectivity, is not an obstacle to understanding the lived experience each gives rise to and what is at stake ethically in our mutual thrownness. And there are real ethical issues at stake: whether data mining constitutes a breach of privacy, or recommendation algorithms undermine personal autonomy, or commercial motives undermine social practices of sharing music, or musical artists (not to mention infrastructural laborers) are exploited. But the ethics of media backends are not reducible to awareness of their technical, material, or economic makeup; what is at stake ethically in music-streaming platforms is understood only by acting with and among them.

Opacity and Accountability

Louise Amoore's defense of an ethico-politics grounded in opacity takes its inspiration from Judith Butler's lectures *Giving an Account of Oneself,* which in turn derive from a Spinozan ethics of accountability that is always-already acting in the world, rather than something argued from first principles.[6] Amoore begins by rejecting an understanding of algorithms as a series of discrete rules in favor of an "arrangement of propositions" generative of what comes to matter in the world. This phrasing takes its cue from Alan Turing's description of how mathematical architectures make intuition and ingenuity possible. Amoore does not doubt that algorithms are reductive, but they are also devices that sustain worldings—apertures that enact closures as well as openings onto the world. That as cultural artifacts they cannot give an account of their origins and development is neither here nor there, since none of us can either. Butler's ethics, which Amoore draws on, hinges on the claim that ethical relations—among people, but equally institutions and technologies—are entirely predicated on the groundlessness of origins. The upshot is that we cannot go looking for a foundation for algorithmic ethics in code, nor in the mind of the coder. And besides, while it is futile to expect transparency to lead to full accountability with respect to how algorithms come to matter, they do give partial, oblique accounts of themselves all the time—and users call Spotify out for it when it gets the next song choice so gratingly wrong.

Data Profiling as Interpellation

The implication is that an ethical relationship between Spotify's users and its algorithmic backends cannot proceed from the claim that an *absence* of recommendation algorithms represents the moral high ground in digitally mediated worlds. This is certainly borne out in user studies, and it is also of a piece with Butler's model of interpellation.[7] While it is tempting to assume that all user profiling inflicts subjective violence insofar as it entails the incitement of subjectification—that is, the calling forth of selves according to schema not of one's choosing (or knowing)—it pays to revisit Butler's reading of Louis Althusser in relation to stop and search. Being rendered algorithmically necessarily involves subjection, since profiling is not something done to discrete individuals but is tessellated in the very process of becoming a subject. But it also accords recognition, however imperfectly, as the individual "attains as well a certain order of social existence, in being transferred from an outer region of indifferent, questionable, or impossible being to the discursive or social domain of the subject."[8] This leads Butler to question whether there are ways of disarticulating punishment from recognition, and the same logic applies to profiling algorithms: while it is true that they have the performative capacity to subjectify users as mechanistic taste templates, or as consumers complicit in an arguably unsustainable streaming industry, it is at least possible that they could do recognition better. Commonly understood as corrosive to human subjectivity, it remains plausible that the affordances of datafication might exceed their necessary reductiveness, maybe holding out the prospect of "a certain order of social existence" that is ethically defensible and gratifying for the user.

Listeners feeling aggrieved about Spotify's failure to get them is not trivial seen from this perspective, and, by the same token, we need not condemn as bathetic pleasurable experiences of algorithmic recognition. Those who recommendation algorithms address are not otherwise rational, autonomous individuals subsequently laid low by datafication, but rather a pre-individual realm of subjectivation. It is common in the literature to find critiques of *any* interaction between media backends and this protean subjectivity as exploitative,[9] but it is important to recognize that the pre-individual is not a discrete and innocent space or time that would be better left alone by technology. Just as for Spinoza there is no prior ethical realm that can be abstracted from the compromised, demanding realities of temporal existence, for Althusser as for Butler there is no uninterpellated self, only selves constantly being brought to fruition by forces beyond intelligibility.

Next, if it is hardly controversial to assert that agency is not endogenous to the Cartesian subject, it is also productive to move beyond the consensus around the agency of nonhuman technologies to Karen Barad's understanding that agency is the unfolding of the world itself.[10] This pulls into focus the role that *measurement* plays as an agential force, whether that be user profiling by platform algorithms or reflective assessments on continuity, change, and possibility. Measurements never represent measurement-independent states of being; they are always active rather than passive, or more precisely they enact agential cuts (in distinction to Cartesian cuts) that disclose what matters as well as what is intelligible about it.[11] Barad is writing more specifically about scientific measurement, but the analogy transfers well to user profiling. "Intervening in the world's becoming" is possible because the agential cut of measurement effects the local separability of effect and cause. "If, then . . . " chains may be clumsy, but they have the capacity for poiesis; they are disclosive of the world and not a faint facsimile of reality. Barad is entirely relaxed about whether we prefer to use instrumentalist conceptions of measurement, or instead "the universe making itself intelligible to another part in its ongoing differentiating intelligibility and materialization."[12] Either way, she concludes, marks are left on bodies; and objectivity means being accountable to those marks.

This then begs the question of what kinds of measuring Spotify enacts, and what should be held to account as a result. Celia Lury and Sophie Day distinguish between personalization algorithms that accumulate as much data about individual users as possible in order to produce recommendations, and those that operate at the level of the population, termed "collaborative filtering algorithms," that seek to maximize patterns between different users.[13] Spotify does the latter,[14] and what is significant is not that it seeks to place you in a targeted profile box as efficiently as possible and then keep you there, but rather that it operates by constantly comparing you to other users. This process of recursive induction operates by way of endless, iterative de-aggregation and re-aggregation, and the profiles it produces on the basis of your data are strictly provisional. This ongoing shuffling of the deck leaves the Spotify user in a suspended state of subjectification, always becoming a subject but always at the same time being remade. However, rather than this being held in limbo effecting the real subjective damage, the incessant refraction of users into multiple partial orderings inflicts its marks by feeding the development of pathways whose own agency generates "new ways of configuring relations between participation and proportion, sharing, ownership and use."[15] The iterative cycles of algorithms cannot but produce and entrench criteria for comparison and interactional norms distinct from those which had evolved in cultures of music discovery and sharing.

There is something of a zero-sum argument to this claim, as though the accrual of agency by repetitive algorithmic chains necessarily saps human users of agency. This cannot be quite right—firstly, since the recognition afforded by a platform such as Spotify is hardly what anyone looks to for affirmation of their identity and group membership, but also because the partial rendering of selves by profiling algorithms does not represent a fracturing of the self. This is an important point that brings into sharper relief the way that interpellation is used to frame the constitution of subjectivities by institutions and technologies. We should not think of backend profiling as a chipping away at an integral self, nor as the summoning into existence of whole selves without our consent and according to regimes of truth beyond our intelligibility, as we are derivative of them. No institution has a monopoly on interpellation, and the truth is that we are partially, multiply interpellated all the time. What remains resonant is the notion that norms of selfhood—how other institutions, technologies, and cultures invoke it—are being rewritten below the radar, such that even the way we think of our own identity and our relation toward loved ones is being rewired in ways we cannot apprehend.[16] Think back to Butler's dissection of stop and search: the damage is not done in the act of calling you into existence as a legal subject but in the entrenching of unspoken norms connecting skin color, clothing, accent, and body language to suspect subjectivities.

The fact remains that we find ourselves always-already acting *as* selves before we have had a chance to think about what kind of selves we are; we grasp for whatever subjectifying resources we find at hand to make sense of our identities and that of others, and it can be taken as given that these resources are impure, compromised, and complicit, being very much of the world. Two friends bond over a newly discovered song, unaware that what was experienced as serendipity was in fact the result of relentless profiling that will have categorized them according to criteria they would be uncomfortable with—or more precisely, they will have been sorted into the same group as others sharing attributes they may well not regard as meaningful. It sounds deleterious that a backend technology geared toward generating profits might make an attribution of White American female teenager in pushing a Spotify user toward a new release, and that this might form the basis of an intimate interaction and ongoing sorority. But, for Butler at least, those murky origins are what do the bonding in the relationship, far more than the suspect affect exchanged. Amoore is clear that algorithms are knowable in the sense that in practice they are giving accounts of themselves all the time, and as such their implication in exploitation, extraction, and injustice can be scrutinized—but in the here and now, not in an algorithm's conception or design. Amoore would resist the understandable urge to pull back the curtain to expose the core of this algorithm, as its origins, too, are unknowable—to us, to its coder, to itself. It is likely that such an algorithm would not "know" that the attributes it generates correspond to ethnicity or gender, for instance.

Now, there is a significant difference between a lack of awareness of Spotify's code and its economic model, or indeed its carbon footprint, and a lack of awareness of how a platform environment might over time come to shift one's senses of self and sociality. If Amoore has pointed out that the latter can be addressed by directing to our attention that which eludes (or does not interest) algorithms, other thinkers identify the key issue as a *temporal* one: that it is beyond the realm of human perception to be aware of what digital technologies are capable of doing in short bursts of time such as the milliseconds between a skip or a like and the profile recalibration made accordingly, and in concert with simultaneous datafications of other users. How important is this "missing half second"[17] between perception and conscious awareness? The pace of computational processes mean that this time lag is something we are impotent to defend from data extraction, and in the literature it is a gap frequently characterized as vulnerable to exploitation, specifically to invasions of privacy and commodification. That in turn means that our own black box emerges as a particularly human frailty, even innocence, that we are compelled to protect as though it is an essence of human nature. Luciana Parisi and Steve Goodman, for instance, have popularized the term "affective capitalism" to capture the parasitic tendencies of technologies tracking "feelings, movements and becomings of bodies" and making bets on their futurity in much the same way that high-frequency trading algorithms do in stock markets.[18] The effect of this is to "abduct" users from the present, leaving them again in a suspended state between a past made unreal by the sensuous experience of technology and a future that remains just over the horizon and always unintelligible.

The Missing Half-Second

The accelerationism thesis is hardly new, with Martin Heidegger setting out in *The Question Concerning Technology* the likely consequences of exponential technological evolution far outpacing our ability as humans to make sense of it all.[19] This is not just a matter of accountability or oversight, since media are poietic, world-disclosing technologies: they determine what it is possible to grasp about the world into which we find ourselves constantly thrown. The import is ontological and not merely epistemological, not about the extent to which our understanding of our radical contingency is constrained, but what counts as that which it is possible to have knowledge of in the first place. The bracketing out of existential depth is of course the signature phenomenological gambit, but it is also useful here insofar as it pushes back against the deep mediatization diagnosis, which pivots on there being something unprecedented in the extent to which digital backend technologies are baked into the conditions of possibility of being human. For Heidegger the problem is not our obscure origins but how we are brought forward in time by technology and what that reveals about our being in the world. Now, the condition of thrownness is all about us flailing around trying to make sense of a world that always exceeds our grasp: conceptual failure is a given. But taking responsibility for oneself demands that we do what we can to understand the world we find ourselves thrown into and our selves, and this is made infinitely more challenging when both are continually made and remade at breakneck pace before our eyes.

For contemporary technology scholars such as N. Katherine Hayles and Mark B. N. Hansen what is germane is not really velocity over historic time, but that simple temporal gap between the capacity of digital technologies to process and act on incoming data, and our own fleshy abilities to do likewise.[20] What precisely is going on in that aperture? Recommendation algorithms are an apt microcosm of Hayles's nonconscious cognition: they are subject to evolutionary dynamics insofar as they apply criteria of fitness for selection and filtering out; they are adaptive, changing those criteria as they proceed; they involve multiple recursive feedback loops that constitute complex systems of processing; and they are constraint-driven, assuming that what users expect of a platform like Spotify is instinctive and fairly simple. The last factor is what gives an algorithm its "intention towards"; distinct from open-ended forms of artificial intelligence designed to generate their own goals that may or may not be known and understood by human agents, for recommendation algorithms it really is about maximizing the time that users spend on a platform, and extracting and modeling a maximal amount of data in order to entice others to do the same, a strategy known in the industry as "engagement." And yet, there is always the possibility that unseen tweaks to the parameters of music discovery will come to have far-reaching implications beyond our apprehension, given how deeply music, like all culture, is embedded in our understanding of identity and sociality.

Feeding Forward

Hansen acknowledges the extent to which algorithmic thinking has outpaced human cognition, and also "capital's advance" in the former. More important still, however, is the symbolic interpretation that is co-relational with and inseparable from algorithmic perception. By this he means the ability to re-represent and not simply document; an algorithm proceeds by way of constant comparing, sorting, and profiling, and it cannot do this iterative re-representing without being able, more fundamentally, to represent. Put more simply this amounts to the claim that algorithms are not just dumb flowcharts but capable of symbolic figuration and abstraction, which leads Hansen to posit that they mediate mediation itself. This can sound a little gnomic, so it is worth setting aside a couple of red herrings: Hansen does not mean by this either the tautologic impossibility of understanding the contingencies of our existence because the shifting sands which generate intelligibility are by definition beyond our grasp, or the crude commodification of subjectivity by what amounts to subliminal messaging by algorithms. Temporality is the key to his argument, the way that representations "feed forward." As for Barad, each representation made by an algorithm is a closure, even a death if we cleave as Hansen does to Alfred Whitehead's ontology, but one that brings the future to bear. Human subjectivity is only a subset of this feeding forward, but one that Hansen is at pains to insist we have a stake in understanding and responding to thoughtfully, so it matters if we are fed forward in time in ways that entrench particular subjectivities while excluding others.

This should also have a familiar ring following on from the account of interpellation: importantly, Hansen is not talking about the corruption of some vulnerable proto self—in the same way that Heidegger through most of *Being and Time* is not fixated on *Dasein* as a pure kind of being that has been sullied by the exigencies of worldly existence and which must be restored[21]—but the forward movement of subjectification in and of itself. It is all about what is brought into existence in the unfolding of time rather than what time does to that which already exists. In any case it remains apposite that feeding forward is not simply about movement from one data point to the next; it is the endless symbolic reconfigurations that ongoingly prehend entities in the world, ending (or killing) their becoming but making future becomings possible. In a very real sense, no one and nothing truly understands the parameters by which all this proceeds algorithmically or otherwise, and indeed understanding is beside the point. Hansen sides with Amoore in swatting aside the call to expose the true nature of algorithms[22] while insisting that their ethico-political situatedness and complicity can be probed. In the same way that phenomenologists bristle at the obsession to excavate reality to reveal its essence, instead redirecting our focus to what is revealed of the world by our experience of it, he wants to direct our gaze from the temporal origins to the relentless presentness of how they operate in the world. There is not space here to delve into the rich historical research undertaken by Orit Halpern[23] and others into the emergence of how ever-evolving representation came to displace empiricism in postwar systems thinking, but the read-across to Hansen is clear enough: if we want to understand our imbrication in algorithmic processes, then we should do so not by trying to extricate ourselves from them but in collaboration with them.

Pivotally, the object of Hansen's intention-toward, which can be read as analogous to Heidegger's conception of care, does not entail its teleological essence: what matters for both intention and care is temporality above all else, not the intended destination. The upshot is that even if Spotify exists primarily to generate profits for its shareholders, that which it feeds forward through user experience of the platform is not capitalism, still less neoliberalism. It is certainly true that commercial music streaming services are implicated in political economy, and that as platforms take center stage in an increasingly mundane fashion, they will normalize commercially inflected practices and relations in ways that tend toward unintelligibility. But for Hansen, the present "is both 'neutral' regarding its future and always excessive" in relation to specific instances of the present,[24] meaning that it is simplistic to think of datafication as hardwired to diminish or shackle the richness of the human experience of music, though it remains imperative to track the exclusions from everyday experience that recommendation algorithms enact. It follows logically from the twin premises that care is primarily temporal and that backend technologies are increasingly fundamental in disclosing the world as world, that what is technically possible and how we think of being are codeterminate. We can and should call Spotify out for its energy dependence and the risibly iniquitous way it pays artists, but there is no reason to assume a conspiracy to commodify identity and sociality. Feeding forward is whatever brings the past to culmination in microscopic instances and allows the future to become; we cannot infer from this that something is being smuggled in under cover. There is space after all for Haraway's "argument for pleasure in the confusion of boundaries and for responsibility in their construction."[25] The exclusions and injustices enacted by platforms are not inferable from their genesis from within a corporate, capitalist economic context; their ethical status as technologies is not there to be discovered in their backends. It is worth bearing in mind the possibility that the backend technology that moves from one data point to the next is just that—temporal momentum—rather than datafication in microcosm.

Michael Dieter and David Gauthier make a helpful distinction between Althusserian interpellation and *captivation*, with the latter (following in the tradition of anthropologist Alfred Gell) evading both the idea of an innocent, vulnerable self under siege from exogenous forces and the summoning of ideologically replete and coherent subjectivities.[26] For them, the site of contestation around backend technologies is not subjectification conceived in autonomous, rational terms—it is outside that idea of the whole, self-contained self and all the ethical baggage that carries. By implication this paints interpellation with a broad brush, bearing in mind Butler's own compelling critique of any supposed interiority and exteriority of subjectivity.[27] It does, however, allow for thinking in terms other than incitement when we try to understand what happens when an algorithm reads and re-presents us as notional selves, provisionally at least. Instead, if there is algorithmic exploitation, it is of a self that is suspended. Captivation emphasizes the *de-coherence* of identity, not the enforced cookie-cutter shapes that critics of platformization point to. The result is that "rather than culminating in identity conforming to a structure of domination, captivation takes the form of an abandonment or losing of the self."[28] Reading datafication against the Foucauldian grain, they posit that the process is unproductive, revealing a politics that owes more to anarchy than governance. They are in no doubt that exploitation takes place, and as such that backend technologies should be subject to ethical inquiry, but the space they shine a light on is one of liminal temporality. Instead of pushing back against what media backends "do" to us, the starting point has to be working with what they are always-already instantiating.

We return then to the critical "missing half second" and how nefarious we should regard what happens there under the radar. Dieter and Gauthier do not follow Hansen's postulation that whatever constraints are imposed in these moments of temporal closure may yet be exceeded by the futures that become of them. They do, however, make a productive distinction with Amoore on the question of intelligibility—or attributability. Whereas Amoore rightly emphasizes the ineffable aspects of subjectivity that elude algorithms, Dieter and Gauthier have in their sights the interim between the present and a moment always beyond the horizon of intelligibility, a potential forever about to be fulfilled. Captivation may steer clear of ideological enforcement, but in its place it evokes a space subject to midnight raids, a limbo sustained by affective capitalism where the not-yet self is ripe for abduction and seduction. The picture this paints is redolent, and indeed cinematic—which makes sense given Hayles's evocation of subliminal cues inserted into movie screenings in 1950s America. It is also of a piece with Michael Serres's model of parasitic relations,[29] as well as Vilém Flusser's design-as-trapping thesis.[30] Ultimately, all these perspectives fall back on an imagined self to which things can be done, the thought experiment involving subjectivity beset by external forces as the departure point for ethical deliberation. Hayles goes out of her way to assert that, in psychological terms at least, the self does not exist—at most, it is a myth of continuity and order. But the question remains whether when we seek to hold backend technologies to account, we can do so on terms that presuppose that it does.

Ethics on the Fly through Inauthentic Worlds

There is a rich tradition of thought extending back through Jean Baudrillard and Guy Debord that argues that contemporary consumer culture has left us bathing in surface experiences, incapable of escaping the affective *dispositifs* we find ourselves inhabiting and thus unable to plumb the depths of the political implications of our relationship with technologies whose workings we do not understand and whose motives we do not give much thought to. This chimes with Barad, whose aforementioned agential cuts—snapshots that reveal their own relationalities and attached ethics—are just moments in the world's ongoing unfolding, not revelations about how things really are if we could only see them from the right perspective. Following human geographers like Tim Ingold,[31] it is how we move through the environments sustained by digital backends that reveal their ethical stakes, not stopping to get a handle on how things really are. Sarah Pink has adapted Ingold's work to the way that we move through digital environments, demonstrating that to grasp their meaning and concomitant ethics means tracing the rhythms and rituals of mediated experience.[32] The idea again is that there is little point in pausing to reflect carefully on the meaning of this or that encountered object, still less to pursue an excavation of the determinants of experience to get at its ultimate source. This is a fairly radical departure from structuralist accounts of base and superstructure, for two reasons. First, it rejects thinking of mediated experiences as expressions of media architectures and economies: the design of backend infrastructure and the business models of streaming platforms certainly constrain user experience, but in no real sense do they set in train an anticipatable causal chain resulting in a culture of streaming. Second, the phenomenological model refuses to consider mundane everyday experiences of media as corrupted or degraded modes of existence alienated from their origins and a less mediated, purer being in the world. It is unhelpful to imagine some abstracted self moving through a digital environment, perhaps oriented by a certain disposition or habitus, always anticipating that which comes next and in so doing reinforcing the underlying disposition. Instead, it is only through movement that the self becomes manifest. To put it another way, there is no transtemporal self, only ways of selfing, that we find ourselves in the midst of enacting before we have given it a second thought.

The value of Spotify as a case study is precisely the fact that using it feels quite banal most of the time: it is something we use as an add-on to commuting or exercising, or to pass the time when alone or hanging out with friends. There are undoubtedly pleasures derived from music that fits the mood or transports us somewhere else, and annoyances at playlists serving up ill-matched or repetitive content, but on the whole the Spotify experience lacks emphatic moments that take us out of our humdrum quotidian bubble or make us sit up and think about why we are here, doing this, at a given time. And that is entirely the point. For a start, having Spotify in one's earbuds while on a treadmill is not a different way of experiencing the space of the gym, but a distinct space that demands to be understood on its own terms. The mood in part enabled by but not derivable from backend technologies from the Spotify algorithm to 4G or 5G or WiFi is not a layer on top of what otherwise would have been a less mediated experience: it is as ontologically constitutive as any other feature of that experience. If the mood of user experience is generally nothing more than distraction, fun, or mild frustration, it matters as much as experiences more intensely felt. It is what propels movement in time from one encounter to the next, and that is what discloses the world, on the go and always in the thick of it.

In *Being and Time* Heidegger frets over inauthenticity, that what we talk about when we talk about existence is anything but the thing itself. And yet this is what the work teaches us: that there is no getting at the thing itself, the meaning of existence or any component of it is only to be grasped in finding oneself already busily engaged in enacting it. In the final section of "Division One" he devotes significant energies to discussing what appear to be fairly trivial aspects of a topic ostensibly more profound than any other: boredom, curiosity, and idle talk—and he does so not to reveal them as pale comparisons of the real meaning of life, but as constituent foundations of it. There is, to be sure, an extreme kind of boredom—angst—that registers as terror and has one staring into the void of one's being, but he is also interested in the mode of boredom that is neither one thing or another, just a kind of dissatisfied restlessness that nudges us to turn our attention reflexively, half-heartedly and noncommittedly to one object or another—your hand robotically reaching for your phone, tapping on the app, or maybe skipping to the next track. The curiosity he has his sights on is not only a journey of wide-eyed discovery of the world and our situation in it; it is also idly wondering what this thing is over here, unthinkingly reaching for it without any serious consideration of what it might be for and what its value is. Distractedly checking out what one's friends are listening to or what is in that playlist in the corner of the screen fits the bill. The chatter Heidegger explores in this section is the kind that hoovers up every topic from weighty to weightless, deftly turning everything into a conversation piece. This could mean nothing more than liking and sharing a track or commenting on how irritating someone's voice is to a friend, or it could be the more serious implications of Spotify that occasionally do become talking points, dissected endlessly in journalism and social media before we collectively move on to the next thing: its energy usage, the objectification of women in pop lyrics, the viability of recording careers in the streaming age, and perhaps the extent to which it is shaping tastes without our knowing it. The fact that all of these become mere discourse, and inauthentic discourse at that, is beside the point. Insofar as idle chat "passes the world along" it is also ontologically constitutive; it reveals the world as it is.

 Technologies leave their marks on bodies,[33] and we need professional scrutineers to hold streaming platforms to account.[34] Digital literacy, however, is another matter. Ultimately, the question of whether it would be a good thing if users knew more about Spotify's algorithmic, infrastructural, and commercial backends, and spent more time reflecting on and discussing their ramifications, is off-target. The key is that word "know": grasping the meaning of a streaming environment is not a matter of cognition but action, doing things in and moving through it. This is not to celebrate willful ignorance of the issues highlighted in this chapter; they are part of that world through which we move and they are spoken about, from time to time at least, and literacy about them has to be conceived in environmental terms rather than left to the individual user to stand up and take responsibility for. What is needed is anything that propels and from time to time maps out new paths, the kind of digital agility that requires no more than the thought of "if not this, then what else?" the sort of improvisation that comes from curiosity that does not have to prove its authenticity.

Notes

1. Nick Couldry and Ulises Ali Mejias, *The Costs of Connection: How Data Is Colonizing Human Life and Appropriating It for Capitalism* (Stanford, CA: Stanford University Press, 2019).
2. Pelle Snickars, "More of the Same—On Spotify Radio," *Culture Unbound: Journal of Current Cultural Research* 9, no. 2 (October 31, 2017).
3. "Martina McBride, 'Felt Like We'd Been Erased' When Spotify Didn't Recommend a Single Female Country Artist," *Billboard*, September 16, 2019, https://www.billboard.com/articles/columns/country/8530121/martina-mcbride-spotify-female-country-artists-interview; Ann Werner, "Organizing Music, Organizing Gender: Algorithmic Culture and Spotify Recommendations," *Popular Communication* 18, no. 1 (January 2020), https://doi.org/10.1080/15405702.2020.1715980.
4. Paul Frosh, *The Poetics of Digital Media* (Cambridge: Polity, 2018).
5. See especially Maria Eriksson, Rasmus Fleischer, Anna Johansson, Pelle Snickars, and Patrick Vonderau, *Spotify Teardown: Inside the Black Box of Streaming Music* (Cambridge, MA: MIT Press, 2019).
6. Louise Amoore, *Cloud Ethics: Algorithms and the Attributes of Ourselves and Others* (Durham, NC: Duke University Press, 2020); Judith Butler, *Giving an Account of Oneself* (New York: Fordham University Press, 2005).
7. Judith Butler, *Bodies That Matter* (New York: Routledge, 1993).
8. Butler, *Bodies That Matter*, 82.
9. See, for instance, Taina Bucher, "The Friendship Assemblage: Investigating Programmed Sociality on Facebook," *Television & New Media* 14, no. 6 (2013); Maurizio Lazzarato, *Signs and Machines: Capitalism and the Production of Subjectivity* (Los Angeles: Semiotext(e), 2014); Mark Andrejevic, *Automated Media* (New York: Routledge, 2020).
10. Karen Barad, *Meeting the Universe Halfway: Quantum Physics and the Entanglement of Matter and Meaning* (Durham, NC: Duke University Press, 2007).
11. See also John Cheney-Lippold, *We Are Data: Algorithms and the Making of Our Digital Selves* (New York: New York University Press, 2017); Geoffrey C. Bowker and Susan Leigh Star, *Sorting Things Out: Classification and Its Consequences* (Cambridge, MA: MIT Press, 2000).
12. Karen Barad, "Posthumanist Performativity: Toward an Understanding of How Matter Comes to Matter," *Signs: Journal of Women in Culture and Society* 28, no. 3 (2003): 824.
13. Celia Lury and Sophie Day, "Algorithmic Personalization as a Mode of Individuation," *Theory, Culture & Society* 36, no. 2 (2019).
14. Snickars, "More of the Same—On Spotify Radio."
15. Ibid., 31–32.
16. See also Frederik Dhaenens and Jean Burgess, "'Press Play for Pride': The Cultural Logics of LGBTQ-themed Playlists on Spotify," *New Media & Society* 21, no. 6 (2019).
17. N. Katherine Hayles, "Cognition Everywhere: The Rise of the Cognitive Nonconscious and the Costs of Consciousness," *New Literary History* 45, no. 2 (2014).

18. Luciana Parisi and Steve Goodman, "Mnemonic Control," in *Beyond Biopolitics: Essays on the Governance of Life and Death*, ed. Patricia Ticineto Clough and Craig Willse (Durham, NC: Duke University Press, 2011).

19. Martin Heidegger, *The Question Concerning Technology, and Other Essays* (New York: HarperCollins, 2013).

20. Hayles, "Cognition Everywhere"; Mark Boris Nicola Hansen, *Feed-Forward: On the Future of Twenty-first-Century Media* (Chicago: University of Chicago Press, 2015).

21. Martin Heidegger, *Being and Time*, trans. J. Stambaugh (San Francisco: Harper & Row, 1962).

22. Tania Bucher, *If . . . Then. Algorithmic Power and Politics* (Oxford: Oxford University Press, 2018).

23. Orit Halpern, *Beautiful Data: A History of Vision and Reason since 1945* (Durham, NC: Duke University Press, 2014).

24. Hansen, *Feed-Forward*, 125.

25. Donna Haraway, "A Cyborg Manifesto: Science, Technology, and Socialist-Feminism in the Late Twentieth Century," in *Simians, Cyborgs, and Women: The Reinvention of Nature* (New York: Routledge, 1991), 150.

26. Michael Dieter and David Gauthier, "On the Politics of Chrono-Design: Capture, Time, and the Interface," *Theory, Culture & Society* 36, no. 2 (2019).

27. Butler, *Bodies That Matter*.

28. Dieter and Gauthier, "On the Politics of Chrono-Design," 69.

29. Michel Serres, *The Parasite*, trans. Lawrence R. Schehr (Baltimore: Johns Hopkins University Press, 1982). See also Nick Seaver, "Captivating Algorithms: Recommender Systems as Traps," *Journal of Material Culture* 24, no. 4 (2019).

30. Vilém Flusser and Anthony Mathews, *The Shape of Things: A Philosophy of Design*, 1st English ed. (London: Reaktion, 1999).

31. Tim Ingold, *The Perception of the Environment: Essays on Livelihood, Dwelling, and Skill* (London: Routledge, 2000).

32. Sarah Pink, *Situating Everyday Life: Practices and Places* (London: Sage, 2012).

33. See especially Safiya Umoja Noble, *Algorithms of Oppression: How Search Engines Reinforce Racism* (New York: New York University Press, 2018); Ruha Benjamin, *Race after Technology: Abolitionist Tools for the New Jim Code* (Cambridge: Polity, 2019).

34. José van Dijck, Thomas Poell, and Martijn de Waal, *The Platform Society: Public Values in a Connective World* (Oxford: Oxford University Press, 2018).

PART II

DATAFYING, SERVING, DISTRIBUTING

6

THE SOCIAL MAPPING OF HYPERSCALE DATA CENTER REGIONS

Placemaking, Infrastructuring, Curating

VICKI MAYER AND JULIA VELKOVA

Not all infrastructures are invisible, quips the anthropologist Brian Larkin, in an affirmation of the social aspects of the massive public and private efforts to plan, develop, and manage flows for systems of water, energy, and transportation.[1] These infrastructures have frequently been touted as totems of settlement and civilization, followed by nationalism and modernism. They were both hydroelectric dams and airport terminals. The more recent privatization of such common utilities and services has made their mediation of life more visible alternatively as signs of economic progress or crass commercialism. All of these public manifestations of infrastructures are necessary to "emplace" them in a named region, where they disappear once they have been normalized into people's everyday lives.[2] The accelerated timescale of internet and data infrastructures have only made the visibility of these projects more so, as smart cities and innovation complexes become beacons for regional progress and prosperity.[3] That is when these media infrastructures located in the "backend" of media technical systems—the physical places through which digital data moves—come to the fore, reworking the identities of places and local communities in complex and uneven ways.

The hyperscale data center marks a particularly visible piece of media infrastructure. Physically, these data centers are enormous. In Europe, they are measured in the number of football fields that they contain; the largest ones are one-square kilometer in their dimensions. Their political economy, however, is in their hyperscalability:

> Imagine for a moment a factory where every component involved in the manufacture of a product, including the conveyor that brings the parts onto the as-

sembly line, were modularized into a small area. You read this correctly: a small area. Now imagine the functionality of this module becoming so efficient and so reliable that you could grow your yield exponentially simply by connecting more of these modules together in a linear row. Or a farm where, if you double your acreage, you more than double your yield.

Hyperscale is automation applied to an industry that was supposed to be about automation to begin with. It is about organizations that happen to be large, seizing the day and taking control of all aspects of their production.[4]

The hegemons of this new political economy are Microsoft, Amazon, Apple, Facebook, and Alphabet (Google) (or "MAAFiA" for short). Through their efforts, hyperscale data centers have spread globally through their distributed networks of servers, switches, fiber, underwater sea cables, and energy providers. These Big Tech companies own all of these networks, superseding both national telecommunications and public utility providers. In the future, industries and governments must do business with the MAAFiA as a matter of course in order to participate in a global economy for communications, manufacturing, and finance. MAAFiA hyperscale data centers thus do not operate in the background of these transformations, but in the political, economic, and physical foregrounds of the towns and regions where they locate. This chapter examines how local townspeople in two northern European regions received a hyperscale data center owned by one particular member of the MAAFiA—the Alphabet-owned infrastructure brand known as Google—through the lenses of *placemaking*, *infrastructuring*, and *curating*.

Originating in the discourse of regional development, *placemaking* captures provincial agency in harnessing the power of companies to achieve prominence, first on a national political stage, then in global economies.[5] It is also situated in social and class hierarchies. While government authorities have sought competitive advantages from playing exclusive host to a dominant industry since at least the industrial revolution, it was wonkish policymakers and eager planners who more aggressively pursued an industry that would define the *place* on a global scale beginning in the 1980s. Their neoclassical theories imagined that, through the holy trinity of industrial ties, venture capital, and a creative class, regions would produce a workforce with a harmonious work/life balance.[6] Across regions marred by industrial exodus, probusiness governing elites have sought either Hollywood and entertainment industries or MAAFiA and other mega-tech companies as key to a place-based makeover.[7] Within those governing circles, five European regions were winners of a Google hyperscale data center. We focus on two of them: Groningen in the Netherlands and Hamina in Finland.

Google, for its part, took over legacy infrastructures to secure dominance over sociotechnical systems in peripheral regions around the world. Their *infrastructuring* of data centers, fiber, energy, and internet exchange hubs would be the many branches on a tree that governs through platforms.[8] Yet in towns left with the remnants of public telecommunications and energy infrastructures that private companies did not want, infrastructuring splinters the social compact in that some citizens get fast internet and others do not.[9] Faced with digital exclusion, municipalities develop their own forms of media localism in two ways.[10] Rural residents are infrastructuring, first and literally, by lobbying for and building physical fiber networks, and also symbolically, by sharing information about the mysterious new hyperscale down the road. Whereas placemaking is directed at the region as a brand externally, infrastructuring is communicated through the internal struggles to achieve a modernized infrastructure.

In becoming a region known for its new global infrastructure, residents remake the place where they live by curating their pasts through the present and toward an aspirational future. Between the high-level discussions of place directed at external and internal audiences, *curating* is the mediation of reconfigured identities and relations between residents and the new infrastructure. Unlike the instrumentality of placemaking campaigns and infrastructuring lobbies, the curation of folk knowledge and seemingly, ephemeral media, captures how humans *storify* infrastructural change to their environments.[11] In Hamina and Groningen alike, "Google was everywhere and nowhere," in that the company's presence had an affective power.[12] Few people in these places would actually work for Google, but many people thought about Google in relation to their careers, jobs, and thus lifestyles. Their perspectives toward Google reflected that situatedness, bringing "cloud" technology back to the earthy place where people live and work.[13]

Placemaking, infrastructuring, and curating reveal the political stances that Groningers and Haminers alike had about what role a foreign behemoth should play on the ground in land tenancy, in the ground through fiber and data center construction, and in the surrounds of "ordinary" citizens. In what follows, we have curated our own collection of stories told through these lenses to illustrate the ways people negotiate the power of MAAFiA in their hometowns. Our method to *storify* draws on the practices associated with journalistic muckraking. In our respective research, conducted in Groningen and Hamina in different periods between 2017 and 2019, we asked locals to situate their stories in an altered landscape and a place transformed by the new company in town. Then we listened, often while going about their own work practices, such as a tour or a business lunch. We gathered information and talked to everyone we could to give context to an epic corporate takeover of the social, which might otherwise be just a news flash. Storifying the local sheds light on reasons why the MAAFiA's growing hegemony over global infrastructures may be embraced and feared, as well as disrupted and normalized from within the physical sites where their infrastructures are emplaced.

Placemaking and Economic Development

Everything seems to be looking up if you work in economic development. In Groningen, first Google came and then an international airport followed. Planes flew to Denmark a few times a week. A few years before, men with authority—local, provincial, national, and international—had broken ground on what would become a sprawling hypercenter campus where a humble potato farm had been. The shovels were painted in the bright primary colors of the Google brand. They grinned for the photo-op (figure 6.1). For the national economic development branch and its emissary, who had an undeniably far-North Netherlands first name, Wubbo Everts remembered feeling a local pride in capturing what was then the largest cloud center in Europe.

Placemaking involves putting a region on a map. In global cities, the location there of headquarters for the film, fashion, or other creative industries adds to their recognition as leaders in the cultural economy of corporate brands and its symbols. In regions stigmatized as "backward," MAAFiA and other high-tech hegemons bring the cachet of modernity, progress, and the "future" through such sexy associations as the cloud, innovation hubs, and blockchain. Unlike manufacturing or mining, data infrastructure companies seem to locals to have no downsides, such as low wages or black lung.[14] Placemaking replaces the negative valences with positive ones. Business leaders had discussed Groningen's

Figure 6.1. Photo of the official launch of the new Google data center in the Dutch Eemshaven, Groningen. Reproduced with permission from Kees van de Veen.

"image problem" as a place of high unemployment and failed industrial investments since at least the 1980s.[15] In Hamina, Google would be a star player in the revolution for sustainability and circular economy. The company used frigid Finnish water and wind to partially power and cool the 72-megawatt plant that has since scaled up fourfold, while leveling an old forest. Excess heat would warm the Summanlahti Gulf at the eastern edge of the Baltic Sea and breed more fish. These public campaigns had the added benefit of advertising the company's ever-expanding need to create, process, store, and distribute more data. The technology for storing the excess energy through massive batteries underground, for example, would be something that Google still needed to invent, and a host of venture capital firms might further invest in the region to do it.

Google's hyperscale data centers are already visible in ways that other infrastructural networks and nodes are not. The design architecture of the buildings has a competitive dimension as the company strives to outshine the Microsoft underwater data center, with its open cameras that show the company in ecological harmony with the fish.[16] In the twentieth century, newspaper companies erected skyscrapers that similarly made their media power visible and material.[17] City tours still point to the buildings as icons of the bygone era in which each downtown hosted one or more print media companies that defined the city, not just through its newsworthy contents, but to itself as having such a productive industry. The Finns in Hamina were among the largest suppliers to the newsprint industry. The paper mill in town became a tourist attraction in its own right and helped establish it as a company town, complete with housing designed by the famous Finnish modernist architect Alvar Aalto, and a hotel for business visitors coming to the factory. Like in many other company towns, loyalty to the mill was multiplied through homeownership.[18] For regions that host a hypercenter, the buildings announce their place as a seat for the company's power to mediate the new and now as spectacle, obscuring the fact that their futures and very presence in these towns are uncertain and volatile, subject to the dynamics of global markets of speculation and programmed obsolescence.[19] Signs point to Google in Hamina and, in Groningen (figure 6.2), the company is literally the biggest name on the map of the Eemshaven port that sits adjacent to the data center.

Perhaps the most valuable part of placemaking through the location of these most visible infrastructure corporations was the presumed "spillover" effects that they bring to regions suffering economic downturns. The dominant policy shift toward creative placemaking, for one, put artists and software workers into cross-sectoral collaborations in order to grow the value of the local labor and culture while reducing inequality.[20] Provincial leaders in Groningen were expectant parents to the transformations they saw indexed in local hackathons,

Figure 6.2. A sign on the road to Google in Hamina, Finland. Photo by Julia Velkova.

sustainability festivals, and young entrepreneurs meet-ups. Google was simply the largest indicator that they would deliver on a promise to bring Groningen its own creative class, to apply Richard Florida's phrasing. While urban scholars have largely dismissed the creative class as a conceit of inequality fueled by upscale consumption and service-economy providers, for townspeople depressed by decades of post-industrial exodus, the presence of artisanal coffeehouses and wine bars lifted the spirits beyond caffeine and alcohol.[21] "People could stay here," said Marko Bolt, director of the Economic Board Groningen, which gave seed loans to digital infrastructure startups. He himself had returned to Groningen from Boston, where he had a prominent post with the foreign investment agency. He imagined an economy built on smart technologies, autonomous transportation fleets, and self-service medicine in the most remote villages of the region. None of these visions necessarily needed a cloud center, but the growth of high-tech infrastructures encouraged fantasies of synergistic developments that could drive the in-migration of college graduates who had left for metropolitan job centers.

Since infrastructure companies do not typically hire as many people directly as one of their suppliers or their transportation hubs, however, placemaking becomes an ongoing process for boosters. Always optimistic in our informational meetings, Everts directed curious academics to Top Dutch, a private PR firm that lobbied Tesla for an electric car and battery factory through a public

Twitter campaign. Everts was careful to distinguish Tesla from Ford, the motor company of an outmoded economy. Unlike Google, Tesla would bring more plentiful middle-class jobs. Everts knew cloud and electric car companies would benefit from the bounty of cheap energy, seawater cooling, and internet infrastructure that could be found in Groningen. The fact that these advantages were also found in Hamina, Luleå, Rekyjanes, and Athenry, among other hyperscale hosts, simply meant that he had to cast his net farther to catch the next big fish. He had visits scheduled to Seattle, San Francisco, and New York to sell his place as a data home.

Infrastructuring

Infrastructuring is an inevitable effect of MAAFiA placemaking and a precursor too. The cloud companies are drawn to places with legacy communications and energy infrastructures that can further their ambitions to own networks, utility, and logistics infrastructures.[22] Countries that invite these cloud companies may share common cause with MAAFiA both economically, as privately investing in their global market positions, and politically, as securing national borders with geopolitical allies.[23] Indeed, Hamina is adjacent to the longest military defense line in Europe; the Finnish navy recognized its location with the moniker of a "fleet of missile boats." This form of market integration between countries and communications infrastructure industries in the name of political cooperation has been common since before World War I.[24] Their interdependence expanded the infrastructuring associated with the modernization of Global South societies. At the same time, interdependent infrastructuring spread the risks of speculation and uneven development. This story was repeated in the wake of communications liberalizations and their multinational configurations, reinforcing old social divides between infrastructural haves and have-nots, and leaving the latter group to speculate on their own digital futures.[25]

In order to make places for the high-tech renaissance, regions prepare the grounds. Site of a failed national project to transport oil more than a decade before Google arrived, Groningen's port offered the public energy grid, transport lines, and "plenty of land" to international investors, said Seaports' managing director Harm Post. Seaports "can act as a 'one-stop shop' to make all this available to potential investors. We will certainly roll out the red carpet treatment to any company looking to invest here," said Post.[26] The anticipatory readiness of the region created a "half-built assemblage,"[27] from which MAAFiA cloud centers benefit. Local leaders feel some satisfaction that their best-laid plans have not gone to waste. MAAFiA, in turn, follows the paths of old transportation and communications hubs, thus adopting their logistical advantages and repurposing the built environment.[28] Despite assertions by Google that it had salvaged "an abandoned site" referencing both the dying print industry and Hamina's defunct Summa paper mill, the company inherited the seawater cooling infrastructure from the paper mill owner Stora-Enso.[29] Groningen offered Google even more infrastructure, with undersea cables bringing hydroelectric power and data connections to the largest European internet markets. These added to the provincial political poetics, by conceiving of Google's investment as a symbol of modernity and Groningen's global brand, rather than as an actual technical project infrastructuring the region with digital communications access.

As a result, the province still struggled with how to provide broadband and other media infrastructure to its residents. Groningen was once headquarters to the national telecommunications utility. Representing earlier modernity poetics, the building shaped like an open phone book housed a liberalized KPN, which became the sole installer for a fiber network in the 1990s. The digital infrastructuring of the region reconfigured verticalized infrastructure companies into decentralized competitors for global high-tech speculation. KPN partnered with Philips, the electronics giant, and competed with the public rail company NOS and TenneT, a government spin-off, to manage the country's high-voltage electric grid. By the time the duopoly got around to consumer mobile and broadband markets, rural Groningen had been forgotten.[30] This fact was a daily reality for the business owners and residents who can see the physical wind turbines and solar farms powering other people's connectivity.

"If KPN had not been privatized, we'd all have great fiber by now," asserted Andrew van der Haar, owner of a small data center and, ironically, a former KPN employee. He bought the nondescript building of server racks amid warehouses and a lumberyard. He joked that there was perhaps a conspiracy afoot when Google Maps sends his visitors past the data center and down a dead-end street. His standpoints toward KPN and Google reflected the basic fact that his town, located proximate to both companies, was completely cut off from high-speed fiber. The liberalization of communications and subsequent influx of foreign operators had left residents and business owners alike to fend for themselves for unbundled services that were once universal. They pressured their municipalities to bootstrap their own infrastructure for what often became a spaghetti of systems for richer and poorer consumers.[31] In towns on the margins of MAAFiA's self-interests, covering some 25 percent of the Netherlands by van der Haar's estimates, small enterprises formed "run by people seen as local heroes because towns don't have the money to pay the big operators." More than 150 companies promised cheap and fast services. In an unregulated marketplace, installers often cut other utilities in the process, including gas lines and water pipes, providing basic rural infrastructure even as KPN and the main cable company Ziggo continued to upgrade fiber for the wealthiest internet niches.

Curating

Over the palimpsest of infrastructures are the layers of meanings that these structures have for host regions that operated like company towns. In those places, the company dominated the local narratives of place through an insular political economy of employment and markets.[32] Curating the identity of places now beset by high unemployment and stalled markets, such as Hamina and Groningen, everyday people do not erase the past. In the background of corporate infrastructuring, locals instead revive earlier stories about regions and preserve tokens representing the people living and working there. They are curating new memories from a montage of past and present,[33] much as Google's data center physically remediated the ruins of a paper mill in Hamina and the potato fields of Groningen. In former company towns like Hamina around the world, Google thus has replaced "the company," which is gone, but not forgotten.

Curating is the official work of the tour guides and tourism brochures mediating Hamina and Groningen for an audience of curious visitors, like ourselves. They paint images of their internationalism as throughways between Russia and Sweden in the former, and Germany and the Netherlands in the latter. The medieval star-shaped fortifications seen from the air in Hamina communicate political pride as centers for international markets and trade, long before the nation's existence, and part of their continuing relevance. This fierce sense of identity, the "we" in mediated messages, continues to define the denizens of the two towns through political and economic shifts of three centuries, giving dual structures of feeling that distinguishes the city from the country and the region from the nation.[34] Yet the most significant representation of Hamina's identity, and residents' identities by extension, was what looked to be an obituary (figure 6.3) that emerged from the pocket of a tour guide. It showed the sepia-toned picture of the paper mill, with its "birth" and "death" dates. A quote by the Polish Nobel Prize–winning novelist Henryk Sienkiewicz read: "For all that man has worked for, he has left a part of his heart."

By the account of local guide Maarja Tamminen, Hamina workers are still coming to grips to curate the new story of Hamina. Entire generations of families worked for the paper mill, one of the largest in Finland since 1955. Grandfathers, fathers, uncles, and so on came to Hamina to work among the forest pines and build their own house in Petkele, located some 800 meters from the mill-now-data center. The mill built a library, a day care center, and a hotel, and subsidized the mortgages for middle- and upper-management. These were designer houses. "There is always a main house, a sauna and storage. They are so close to the factory, they could bike. It was all factory workers who lived there," Tamminen said. They worked hard and ate their meals at the factory. Workers

Figure 6.3. Obituary commemorating the lifetime of the paper mill authored by its former workers in Hamina. Reproduction by Julia Velkova.

had stable jobs they thought would carry them to retirement. Despite vigorous protests, the Summa Mill was shut down. Tamminen said, "When the factory closed many people thought, 'I am going to die. I don't have a job.'"

Google came into Hamina and Groningen, but the integration of the corporation into those communities has been difficult. For one, the company's business faces inward, avoiding publicity around operations in which locals could take pride. In Hamina, the company policies led to the bankruptcy of a designer hotel that it had inherited from the former paper mill. Knowledge of what happened inside the server farm traveled through rumor and sightings of new employees in Groningen.[35] Google's most public statements to people in Hamina and Groningen came through a YouTube campaign directed at an international audience. In the campaign, places where people lived were rendered as bucolic images of nature (figure 6.4), backgrounded by poignant music and employees' stories of Google's lofty social responsibilities. Another tour guide, Kauko Tykkyläinen, said he attended a company picnic at the

Figure 6.4. Still from Google's YouTube campaign related to its Groningen data center.

behest of a family member, but never learned more about the secretive outpost in their midst. If he did, he would not say, as every attendee had signed a nondisclosure agreement.

Google was *in* Groningen and Hamina but not *of* them. Employees in Hamina were outsiders, said Tamminen:

> Nowadays at Google there are different kind of folks working than at Summa [paper mill]. If you now go to Google, everyone speaks English. And Swedish perhaps. And they are much more educated except those who are guarding and walking along the fence. But those inside, they must be IT, or something else. And I suppose not many of them live in Hamina. Maybe they live in Helsinki, Kotka. Helsinki is not so far. They are international also. Our neighbor who worked at Google was from France. They moved to live here from France. He worked something IT, I think. He had a Finnish wife. A very young couple.

MAAFiA cloud companies do not offer stable employment as factories once did. Locals worked alongside EU labor migrants on short-term contracts building containers for Google, or in outsourced service positions in groundskeeping or security. Tamminen and Tykkyläinen themselves used to be civil servants of the bustling company town before becoming volunteer tour guides for a place where the physical architecture associated with their heritage was now either fenced off or left to ruin.[36]

Infrastructural Geographies of Data Centers and Social Mapping of Their Regional Hosts

Beyond either the boosterism for MAAFiA cloud infrastructures or the critiques of their colonial ambitions are complex social systems managing them in local places. As Linda Colley has stressed in a historical framework, the "captives" of empires were never passive or monolithic in negotiating the presence of their outside overseer.[37] In Europe and North America, empire works through infrastructural mediation in the peripheral regions of resource extraction and environmental exploitation.[38] For some, a hyperscale data center signals the end of dreams deferred: the demise of one industry and the realization of another source of employment and pride. Decades-long efforts to create a trade zone or an airport may suddenly seem like sensible decisions in hindsight. For others, a hyperscale center, sometimes with the same corporate owner, only reinforces feelings of marginality in a peripheral location that serves as a throughway for other people's data.[39] This is not to dismiss the need for generalization, but to point out that social imaginaries and experiences of the cloud vary by one's social location. That insight about the ways culture works is just as relevant in the peripheral media region as in the global media city.[40]

The political economy of global media infrastructures thus activates old social antagonisms while bringing in a new set of social actors to play in the newest theatrical release. They are the executives charged with overseeing the growth of hyperscale data centers for global internet storage. They are the migrant laborers brought in to build and replicate network cabling, towers, and housing at scale. They are the foreign faculties and students imported to universities and science parks in the hopes that data infrastructures will seed a thousand startups in manufacturing and logistics. And they are the legacy workers who are tasked to curate and produce new town identities. The new social milieu for data infrastructures layers onto the old ones, making the inequalities visible in housing, education, and employment. Social justice struggles in these places are entangled in the politics of policies aimed at importing foreign labor for the data infrastructure's expansions. In these ways, the political economy of labor and its sociotechnical structuring can never be divorced from struggles over identity, whether cultural or class. Placemaking, infrastructuring, and curating express the perspectives of those who are situated differently in relation to these struggles.

These struggles can hardly be grasped through MAAFiA's glossy marketing campaigns, or even through the boosterism of local governments and press. Our storifying methods might best be considered a kind of theoretically informed muckraking. Here we advocate seeking the voices of those who have rarely, if ever, been consulted on the changes that Google has caused in towns that saw themselves as coherent communities. In doing so, we can do a deeper mapping than one that excludes those residents who live with memories of now abandoned pump stations, hotels, repurposed housing, and potato fields. Through deep mapping[41] and storifying, researchers begin to see new relationships between media infrastructures and the frustrations of poor internet connectivity or an obituary for the town's identity. Traced broadly and deeply, these relationships show both the breadth of our research field sites and the archaeological depth of the social hierarchies that persist despite MAAFiA's claim to "disrupt" societies. Combining investigative journalism with an ethnographic sensibility, storifying thus converts a patchwork of local sensibilities into a social map of regions with global media infrastructure, detangling the economic and symbolic hierarchies that support media capital cities.[42]

In sum, media infrastructures are not just materially visible in the places where they are located, they are materially present in ways people live and work there. But like the infrastructures themselves, academics often relegate their voices to the backend of their studies. Both in Groningen and in Hamina, there were inevitable tensions between those who associated their livelihoods with the newer and shinier digital communications systems of the future, and those who worked with legacy systems that now had to be redirected or abandoned. We have used the terms placemaking, infrastructuring, and curating to demonstrate the ways that sensemaking not only reflects a disposition toward MAAFiA infrastructures, but also motivates action, the need for physical media networks, and the mediation of the "place" internally and externally to others. Just as in urban environments, the sociotechnical convergence of people and infrastructures may result in further social stratification, amplifying the differences between those who benefit from the rebranding of a place along with the redistribution of its goods to international investors. Yet convergence can also lead to creative outcomes through its reconfigured cross-cultural networks, new interdependencies and solidarities. This can be a future research agenda done in concert with the people who live in those places.

Notes

1. Brian Larkin, "The Politics and Poetics of Infrastructure," *Annual Review of Anthropology* 42, no. 1 (2013): 327–43.

2. Vincent Mosco, *Becoming Digital: Toward a Post-Internet Society* (Bingley, UK: Emerald Publishing, 2017).

3. See Stephen Graham and Simon Marvin, *Splintering Urbanism: Networked Infrastructures, Technological Mobilities, and the Urban Condition* (London: Routledge, 2001); Sharon Zukin, *The Innovation Complex: Cities, Tech, and the New Economy* (New York: Oxford University Press, 2020); Keller Easterling, *Extrastatecraft: The Power of Infrastructure Space* (London: Verso, 2016).

4. Scott Fulton III, "How Hyperscale Data Centers Are Reshaping All of IT," *Zdnet.com*, April 5, 2019, https://www.zdnet.com/article/how-hyperscale-data-centers-are-reshaping-all-of-it/.

5. Cara Courage and Anita McKeown, *Creative Placemaking: Research, Theory, and Practice* (London: Routledge, 2020).

6. Michael Storper, *Keys to the City: How Economics, Institutions, Social Interactions, and Politics Shape Development* (Princeton, NJ: Princeton University Press, 2013).

7. See Vicki Mayer, *Almost Hollywood, Nearly New Orleans: The Lure of the Local Film Economy* (Oakland: University of California Press, 2017); Germaine R. Halegoua, *The Digital City: Media and the Social Production of Place* (New York: New York University Press, 2018); Andy C. Pratt, "The Cultural Contradictions of the Creative City," *City, Culture, and Society* 2, no. 3 (2011): 123–30; Zukin, *The Innovation Complex*.

8. José van Dijck, "Seeing the Forest for the Trees: Visualizing Platformization and Its Governance," *New Media & Society* 8 (2020).

9. Simon Guy, "Splintering Networks: Cities and Technical Networks in 1990s Britain," *Urban Studies* 34, no. 2 (1997): 191–216.

10. Christopher Ali, *Media Localism: The Policies of Place* (Urbana: University of Illinois Press, 2017).

11. Rafico Ruiz, *Slow Disturbance: Infrastructural Mediation on the Settler Colonial Resource Frontier* (Durham, NC: Duke University Press, 2021).

12. Vicki Mayer, "The Second Coming: Google and Internet Infrastructure," *Culture Machine*, no. 18 (2019), www.culturemachine.net.

13. Asta Vonderau, "Storing Data, Infrastructuring the Air: Thermocultures of the Cloud," *Culture Machine*, no. 18 (2019).

14. For a discussion on the environmental implications of data centers see, for example, Mél Hogan, "Big Data Ecologies," *Ephemera* 18, no. 3 (2018): 631–57; James N. Gilmore and Bailey Troutman, "Articulating Infrastructure to Water: Agri-Culture and Google's South Carolina Data Center," *International Journal of Cultural Studies* 28 (2020); Patrick Bresnihan and Patrick Brodie, "New Extractive Frontiers in Ireland and the Moebius Strip of Wind/Data," *Environment and Planning E: Nature and Space* (2020).

15. Stiching Noordelijke Economisch-Technologische Organisatie, Inventory #621, Box 15, File 4, 1934–1990, Groninger Archieven.

16. Such visibility strategies have been critically discussed for instance by Jennifer Holt and Patrick Vonderau, "'Where the Internet Lives': Data Centers as Cloud Infrastructure," in *Signal Traffic: Critical Studies of Media Infrastructures*, ed. Lisa Parks and Nicole Starosielski (Urbana: University of Illinois Press, 2015), 71–93; A.R.E. Taylor, "The Technoaesthetics of Data Centre 'White Space,'" *Imaginations: Journal of Cross-Cultural Image Studies* 8, no. 2 (2017).

17. Aurora Wallace, *Media Capital: Architecture and Communications in New York City* (Urbana: University of Illinois Press, 2012).

18. Hardy Green, *The Company Town: The Industrial Edens and Satanic Mills That Shaped the American Economy* (New York: Basic Books, 2012).

19. Julia Velkova, "Data Centres as Impermanent Infrastructures," *Culture Machine*, no. 18 (2019), www.culturemachine.net; Patrick Brodie and Julia Velkova, "Cloud Ruins: Ericsson's Vaudreuil Data Center and Infrastructural Abandonment," *Information, Communication & Society* 24, no. 6 (2021): 869–85; Patrick Brodie, "Climate Extraction and Supply Chains of Data," *Media, Culture & Society* 4 (2020).

20. Alexandre Frenette, "The Rise of Creative Placemaking: Cross-Sector Collaboration as Cultural Policy in the United States," *Journal of Arts Management, Law, and Society* 47, no. 5 (2017): 333–45.

21. Jamie Peck, "Struggling with the Creative Class," *International Journal of Urban and Regional Research* 29, no. 4 (2005): 740–70; Kate Oakley and Dave O'Brien, "Learning to Labour Unequally: Understanding the Relationship between Cultural Production, Cultural Consumption, and Inequality," *Social Identities* 22, no. 5 (2016): 471–86; Mark Banks, "Fit and Working Again? The Instrumental Leisure of the 'Creative Class,'" *Environment and Planning A: Economy and Space* 41, no. 3 (2009): 668–81.

22. Vicki Mayer, "From Peat to Google Power: Communications Infrastructures and Structures of Feeling in Groningen," *European Journal of Cultural Studies* 24, no. 4 (2020): 901–15; Julia Velkova, "Thermopolitics of Data: Cloud Infrastructures and Energy Futures," *Cultural Studies* 35, no. 4–5 (2021): 663–83; Brodie, "Climate Extraction and Supply Chains of Data"; Alix Johnson, "Data Centers as Infrastructural In-Betweens: Expanding Connections and Enduring Marginalities in Iceland," *American Ethnologist* 46, no. 1 (2019): 75–88.

23. Johnson, "Data Centers as Infrastructural In-Betweens."

24. Dwayne R. Winseck and Robert M. Pike, *Communication and Empire: Media, Markets, and Globalization, 1860–1930* (Durham, NC: Duke University Press, 2007).

25. See Graham and Marvin, *Splintering Urbanism*; Easterling, *Extrastatecraft*.

26. Harm Post, "First Port of Call: Groningen Seaports Plays a Prominent Role in the Development of the Northern Coastal Ports Delfzijl and Eemshaven and Is on Hand to Assist in the Needs of Both Resident and New Companies (Groningen Seaports)," *ECN-European Chemical News* 80, no. 2094 (2004): S9.

27. Jenna Burrell, "On Half-Built Assemblages: Waiting for a Data Center in Prineville, Oregon," *Engaging Science, Technology, and Society* 6, no. 20 (2020): 283–305.

28. Ingrid Burrington, "Why Are There So Many Data Centers in Iowa? 'Networks, Land, Power, and Taxes,'" *The Atlantic*, December 1, 2015, https://www.theatlantic.com/technology/archive/2015/12/why-are-so-many-data-centers-built-in-iowa/418005/.

29. Steven Levy, "Where Servers Meet Saunas: A Visit to Google's Finland Data Center," *Wired*, October 24, 2012, https://www.wired.com/2012/10/google-finland-data-center-2/; Sven Grunberg and Niclas Rolander, "Corporate News: For Data Center, Google Goes for the Cold," *Wall Street Journal*, September 12, 2011, https://www.wsj.com/articles/SB10001424053111904836104576560551005570810.

30. Ben C. De Pater, "Infrastructures," in *The Netherlands and the Dutch*, ed. Eduardo F. J. De Mulder, Ben C. De Pater, and Joos C. Droogleever Fortuijn (Cham: Springer International Publishing, 2019), 163–77.

31. Graham and Marvin, *Splintering Urbanism*.

32. Hardy, *The Company Town*.

33. José van Dijck, *Mediated Memories in the Digital Age* (Stanford, CA: Stanford University Press, 2007).

34. Mayer, "From Peat to Google Power."

35. Mayer, "The Second Coming."

36. Brodie and Velkova, "Cloud Ruins."

37. Linda Colley, *Captives: Britain, Empire, and the World, 1600–1850* (New York: Anchor Doubleday, 2004).

38. Ruiz, *Slow Disturbance*.

39. Burrell, "On Half-Built Assemblages"; Vonderau, "Storing Data, Infrastructuring the Air."

40. Johnson, "Data Centers as Infrastructural In-Betweens"; Myria Georgiou, *Media and the City: Cosmopolitanism and Difference* (Cambridge: Polity Press, 2013).

41. Shannon Christine Mattern, *Deep Mapping the Media City* (Minneapolis: University of Minnesota Press, 2015).

42. Michael Curtin, "Media Capital: Towards the Study of Spatial Flows," *International Journal of Cultural Studies* 6, no. 2 (2003): 202–28.

7

CROSS-SECTORAL RELATIONS IN VOD MARKETS

Frontend, Backend, and Deepend in India

VIBODH PARTHASARATHI,
PHILIPPE BOUQUILLION,
AND CHRISTINE ITHURBIDE

Over the past decade, the necessary distribution and storage of audiovisual content has brought new articulations between actors in the legacy media industry and those in the communication infrastructure business. Nevertheless, questions about the links between audiovisual creation and production and the enabling technological infrastructure are not new for scholars, be they of communication policy or media industries. From the end of the 1970s, the theme of "convergence" has been forwarded by large industrial players and by governments, especially in North America and Europe.[1] Ever since, the integration of content and infrastructure activities have provoked three issues: the development of joint offers associating communication services (telephone, videophone, etc.) and media content; the emergence of industrial players integrating their presence across the audiovisual business and telecommunications or information technology activities; and the convergence of regulations weighing on audiovisual, telecommunications, and information technologies.

These issues were articulated in India during the 2000s by the parliament and regulators in discussions about "convergence" and "digitalization."[2] Initially, these ideas sprouted in passive deference to the transnationalization of the media and communication industries; but in the last decade, they have been imbibed in a fiercely competitive and increasingly nationalist response to such transnationalizations.

The spread of video-on-demand (VoD) in India is accentuating the old tension between two ideal-typical logics present in the audiovisual industry. The first of these logics is that of the media industry. Its actors aim to maximize the creative dimension of content, which is produced to be sold directly to retail consumers, with or without advertising support. The second logic is that of the communication industries. Actors here must weave audiovisual content with their activities of transport, storage, and processing of information. In other words, content is leveraged to maximize market power and competitive advantages in the core business of the communication industries. The deployment of VoD is emblematic of the tensions between the logics of the media and communication industries. The media industries, once external to the communication industries, have become increasingly anchored in technical activities and, often consequently, are faced with new operating methods. In return, the communication industries have benefited from incorporating audiovisual products. The objective of this chapter is to examine the ways in which the strategies of the actors, and their balance of power, are transformed by the tension between these two industrial logics.

The growing audience for video platforms in India has attracted a variety of domestic and foreign players from both the audiovisual and communication industries. Paradoxically, buoyancy of the players involved is constrained by a quartet of factors. One, mobile phones have been the main tool for accessing video platforms, unlike the scenario in Western countries but akin to those in Southeast Asia. Two, the VoD business is segmented into numerous linguistic markets, compelling competitors to adapt content for particular product markets.[3] Three, video platforms are not directly profitable due to the low purchasing power of the bulk of the Indian audience; this, in turn, proves especially disadvantageous to subscription-based platforms.[4] Finally, the costs of content production and customer acquisition in video platforms are higher than the revenues generated per customer.[5] Evidently, this quartet of constraints suggests VoD players armed with an all-India reach and large coffers possess an edge in the competitive milieu. This justifies our emphasis on Reliance Jio, the telecom giant owned by India's largest industrial conglomerate, as a key player in the VoD business.

The emergence of a business in VoD illustrates the expansion of largely unregulated media markets characterizing contemporary India. At the same time, the emergence of Reliance Jio in the VoD market and the wider digital economy, and the regulatory approach toward the cloud business, convey respectively the implicit and explicit role of the state. These seemingly uneven tendencies indicate the state embodying a combination of "considered silence,"[6] and "stateness"[7] toward paving a particular path for India's digital economy. The conception of considered silence, as a subtype of media policy silence,[8] captures the deliberate and motivated policy of nonintervention by the state to lock a particular balance of interests in an economic milieu. On its part, the idea of stateness alludes to the pursuit of the state to strengthen its own power over (allegedly) competing actors and prevailing economic dynamics. We thus see the rise of Reliance Jio as the perverse result of policy silences and regulatory interventions in India's digital economy.

In a setting increasingly marked by forces of national capitalism and digital privatization, this chapter evokes three dynamics. First is the loss of economic autonomy of traditional players in the audiovisual industries—that is, content producers who are most readily visible in the "frontend" of the online economy. The second dynamic pertains to frontend actors' relationships of dependence with those in the communication industries; that is to say, a dependence on actors in the business of transporting, storing, and processing information embodying the "meta-infrastructure"[9] of the online economy—what we term "backend." The third dynamic concerns the role of the state in insidiously propelling particular actors and conditions in the competitive milieu—which we construe as the "deepend" of the online economy.

Our central argument is that the deployment of video platforms has not only reconfigured the relationship between the frontend and backend of the digital economy, but also inserted the (once distinct) Indian media economy into the wider digital economy. We suggest that these commercial, industrial, and technical processes should be examined in light of the mediating role of the state in India. For one, the strategies of Reliance Jio, a dominant actor in video platforms and the wider digital economy, have benefited from institutional leniency and regulatory silences. But we also observe a logic of stateness in the emergent policy framework toward the backend cloud business, where again Reliance Jio has emerged in an advantageous position.

Our approach relies on document analysis. Central to our corpus are documents from the government, regulatory authorities, and trade bodies, annual reports by industrial players, and articles from the financial and professional press. It builds on long-term research in political economy of media market and audiovisual industries in India.

The Market Structure of VoD

Growth Drivers in a Competitive Market

By the end of 2019, India's active VoD subscribers stood at 325 million, a massive surge from the 12 million five years before.[10] Several demand and supply side drivers have fueled this expansion. Among the former are the affordability of smart phones and the augmentation of telecommunication networks, at least in pockets inhabited by potentially lucrative users. Consequently, the penetration of broadband among India's growing mobile users has led to video content production targeting wider audience segments.

On the supply side, three growth drivers are noteworthy. First, VoD operators ride on telcos' ready infrastructure to make money for them while also competing with comparable offerings from telcos. Second is the rapid growth in the number of online financial transactions, with India currently having more than 50 million active users of digital wallet.[11] This has enabled users to purchase more easily the offerings of content providers through direct carrier billing. In no small way, the uptake of VoD had benefited from the push toward online transactions catalyzed by the regulatory fiat of cashlessness in late 2016.[12] The third major driver of VoD services has been the advent of cloud services. In an online landscape characterized by uneven connectivity, cloud-based offerings have been a particular shot in the arm to video platforms.

There are more than forty VoD platforms in India. In this competitive market, two broad categories of actors are visible. The first are from the media industries, both legacy content producers in cinema and TV and native digital content producers. The second are actors from the communication-information industries, including from e-commerce, web, and telecommunication, who diversified into video platforms.[13] The latter's offers are generally less expensive, irrespective of whether financed by advertising (AVoD) or subscriptions (SVoD), which are set at low prices. They have thus found a large and growing number of users compared to those garnered by players from the media industry.

In the first category, foremost among legacy content producers are the major broadcasters with VoD offers, such as Star TV (owned by Disney since December 2017) with Hotstar Disney+, Sony TV with Sony Liv, Network 18 with Voot, and Sun TV Network (catering to South Indian languages) with Sun NXT. Times Internet, belonging to the oldest Indian news conglomerate, The Times Group, started MX Player. Film studios offering VoD include Eros International's Eros Now, Balaji Telefilms's ALTBalaji, and Zee Entertainment's Zee5. The global leader in SVOD, Netflix, entered the Indian market in January 2016.

The second category consists of offerings by players from outside the media industry. Foremost are those from the telecommunication industry, such as Reliance Jio's Jio TV and Jio Cinema, Vodaphone's Vodaphone Plays, and Bharti Airtel's Airtel Wink. These apart, there are VoD offerings from the e-commerce business, such as Flipkart's Flipkart Video and Amazon's Prime Video, and from the electronic goods and software businesses, like Apple's Apple+. While our analysis will focus only on industrial (i.e., non-user-generated/noncollaborative) video platforms, it is important to mention that the two global majors in UGC video, YouTube and TikTok, have been extremely popular in India.

VoD and Dynamics of Convergence

Players from the media industries have the advantages of vast existing catalogs and the experience of generating an array of original content for different audiences. Their twin-pronged strategy involves retaining their existing audience demanding online content and attracting fresh audiences from the growing number of online users. They are thus obliged to master new digital forms of content offerings so as to continue servicing their audiences across both linear and nonlinear video.

Domestic and transnational players from the communication industries enjoy both financial and industrial advantages. They tend to have significant stock market valuations, since their core activities involve high investment infrastructural businesses. Often consequently, they also tend to attract speculative actors from financial markets. At the same time, they are an important actor in the wide-ranging competitive arenas of transporting, storing, and processing information, including in the cloud business. For them, the VoD business represents a "joint-product"—that is, free or part of a bundled offer—from which they do not necessarily expect direct or immediate profitability but rather indirect benefits.[14] Thus, their investments in video platforms are secondary to, and subsidized by, their larger and normally more lucrative infrastructure businesses.

Notwithstanding their substantial differences and relative advantages, players in the two categories are closely related. They compete to capture consumer attention but also strategically cooperate through agreements on content rights, access to infrastructures and subscribers, and through cross-investments. This has led to their relationship being captured in the term "coopetition."[15]

Among actors from the communication industries, telcos play a particularly interesting role. They bear costs of investing in network infrastructure—costs their rivals from media industries and others from the communication industries do not bear. But they also possess certain advantages. Since video accounts for almost 50 percent traffic,[16] telcos have benefited from higher and more frequent purchases of data packages. Secondly, the immense user base of telcos allows them to readily funnel their VoD offers to millions of existing and potential subscribers. Telcos, especially Reliance Jio, are at the heart of the strategic partnerships with actors from the media industries seeking potential or incremental users. The former has stitched a series of associations with Eros Now, Hotstar, AltBalaji, and Zee5.[17] Thus, Reliance Jio's strong presence in both media and telecommunication industries is where its market power and strategic advantages rests.

The shift from linear to nonlinear audiovisual platforms has led to the development of algorithmic recommendation services. Players from the media industry rely on digital service providers once the video content is uploaded ("downstream") for extracting, collecting, processing, and analyzing data. They will feed machine learning and enable mechanisms of recommendation intended both for platform operators (performance of different content, analysis of users' behavior, etc.) as well as for the users (personalized notifications, content preferences, etc.). This context raises the question of the increasing role played by cloud services for VoD operators.

Deploying of Cloud in Video Platforms

Cloud services in India have experienced a fairly strong growth with a market for public cloud services estimated to $2.63 billion in 2019. They have become necessary intermediaries that help VoD operators to build their platform offers with services such as analytics, storage, and database services, metadata tagging, robotic process automation (RPA), computer vision, or smart contracts.[18] The two types of players in video platforms are placed in very different situations from the point of view of cloud services. This, in turn, weighs on their relations of coopetition: it is potentially disadvantageous for those from the media industries and advantageous for those from the communication industries. We therefore find it necessary to excavate their mutual relations and the strategies deployed by both toward cloud services. Our excavation opens up relations of power and dependencies, of concentration risks and regulatory adjustments that mark the entanglement of the frontend and backend.

Backend Reshapes Frontend Competition

Managers in the VoD business point at the transition process undertaken by media players from "running their own capex-intensive data centre operations to cloud-based solutions."[19] Beyond the technical impossibility of proposing an offer without resorting to these services, cloud services are also considered as competitive issues. Consequently, hidden in such voices from the industry are three ways the backend is reformulating competition in the frontend.

First of all, these backend services help overcome the inadequacies of the public infrastructure, in particular limited connectivity, low speeds, and discontinuous flows, over a large part of India. Cloud services can play an important role in the territorial expansion of platform content distribution. For instance, Microsoft has announced a pilot program to focus on low bandwidth geographies and cloud-enabled last-mile content delivery.[20] With the increase in video demand in small- and medium-sized towns of India, this experiment also meets VoD platforms' goal to reach a wider audience outside metropolitan centers of India. Initiated in partnership with Eros Now, this program aimed at "tapping the underserved potential customer base in low bandwidth areas" and in return enable the video platform to enroll more subscribers.

Secondly, cloud services are used not only to route the signal to the end user but also to improve its quality. Thus, cloud services play a role in distinguishing between offers based on quality of service, rather than on content or price. Indeed, cloud providers aim at developing services that consume lesser amounts of data, as audiences are sometimes considerable across India, leading to uncertainties and disturbance in signal flows. In 2018, Netflix developed a system, since then followed by others such as MX Player, for encoding its videos to allow good picture quality even with low bandwidth of 200 kilobits per second to enable subscribers to watch twenty hours of content in only 2 gigabytes of data.[21] These innovations became all the more important when the Indian government asked platform operators, in March 2020, to reduce the quality of signals to rationalize bandwidth consumption amid the spurt in data usage during the COVID-19 lockdown. This was well calculated since between April and July 2020 paid subscriptions on video platforms experienced a 31 percent increase, caused by 29 million new subscribers.[22] While Amazon Prime Video and Netflix have announced they would comply with this request and started to lower their traffic, all players have not been able to adjust as fast.[23]

Thirdly, relying on cloud services enables most video platforms to benefit from innovative service that may improve their offerings, attractiveness, and scaling. For instance, Eros International forged an agreement with Microsoft Azure to benefit from the latter's Intuitive Online Video Platform, Interactive Voice Offerings, and Personalized Recommendation Engine.[24] Such capabilities allow VoD players from the legacy media industries to defend their offerings against competing offers, particularly by players from the communication industries. However, these advantages can only be acquired at the price of alliances with other players in the communication industries. Since players in the communication industries are financially far larger than those in the media industries, their alliances can involve the former picking up equity in the latter—such as Reliance Jio acquiring 25 percent and 5 percent stakes respectively in Alt Balaji and Eros Now.

Power Relations in the Backend

Cloud services represent an increasing budget of video-platforms' overall expenditure, often between 20 to 25 percent.[25] This represents a significant financial burden for video platforms, especially as their content catalog demands constant expansion. Storing files internally and setting up data servers for storage and delivery requires large and incremental investments, besides personnel with higher expertise, on the part of video platforms. Hence, most video players prefer to rent space, the costs for which depend on several factors, including the region of cloud storage. Video platforms are therefore increasingly paying large sums to communication infrastructure players at a time when they face reduced revenues and profitability. Such financial burdens involved in the use of backend technologies create constraints to market entry. Understandably, this is more so for smaller players unable to afford initial investments or recurrent rents related to cloud storage.

In addition, there is a certain ratcheting effect at play, a phenomenon that prevents the reversal of a process once a certain stage has passed.[26] When the video platforms engage with certain backend services, they develop technical and organizational processes specific to their service providers. Such a "lock-in" makes it very difficult to change providers due to the risks of rupturing the offer/agreement or incurring high migration costs. Netflix, running the majority of its computing on Amazon Web Services (AWS), has acknowledged several consequences related to the choice of a cloud provider. Netflix has "architected [its] software and computer systems so as to utilize data processing, storage capabilities, and other services provided by AWS."[27] Moreover, its AWS operations cannot be easily migrated to another cloud provider. While Netflix highlights difficulties in switching to another cloud provider, some other video platforms have started to partner with more than one provider. For instance, ALTBalaji is with AWS but is also associated with Microsoft's BlendNet, a pilot content distribution network that aims at downloading and accessing content without consuming large amounts of mobile data.[28]

The importance of costs is also closely linked to the ability of platform operators to negotiate with backend service providers. This capacity appears to be particularly low in negotiations with domineering cloud players. This gains consequence in India where, despite a large number of streaming companies emerging, the public cloud market remains concentrated in the hands of few (transnational) players. Globally and in India, AWS and Microsoft Azure represent the leading providers of digital infrastructure services, particularly the cloud, with the engineering ecosystem largely built around these two companies.[29] Leading video platforms, Hotstar Disney+, Netflix, and Sony Liv, use AWS, while Eros Now, Voot, and Zee5 use Microsoft Azure. Other foreign players include Brightcove Video Cloud, and several Indian data centers, such as Web Werks, DevCloud, ESDS, and CntrlS.[30] At the same time, certain Indian companies are being acquired by transnationals wanting to extend their presence in India, such as US-Equinix's acquisition of GPX Global Systems in August 2020.[31]

Changes in the cloud market since 2018 are likely to reshuffle the cards between players in the ecosystem. For instance, Microsoft and Reliance Jio reached an agreement to challenge the dominance of AWS.[32] Playing the "nationalist" card, Reliance Jio announced it was building data centers across India to be hosted on Microsoft Azure. Still in the race, Google Cloud opened in July 2021 a new data center cluster in Delhi and signed a deal with Reliance Jio.[33] These industrial dynamics are embedded in regulatory concerns where Jio is increasingly playing a pivotal role.

Clouds of Neoliberal Nationalism

For Reliance Jio, the VoD business is a crucial element in its rise in the integrated digital economy of India. In its industrial strategies to construct and dominate this economy, the importance of the backend is not limited to that in the VoD business. At the same time, we find the rise of Reliance Jio to refract the Indian state's crafty handiwork. That the state has astutely intervened to foster media and communication affiliates of Reliance Industries Limited, the conglomerate owning Jio, has not gone unnoticed.[34] Building on this, we make a case for the emergence of Reliance Jio as a consequential actor in India's integrated media and communication economy.

Making of a Consequential Actor

The successive expansion of Reliance Industries Limited (RIL) during the 2010s into broadcasting, cable distribution, telecom, broadband, VoD, and cloud services reflects its incisive vision of convergence. This vision was articulated through three interrelated strategies: an industrial strategy, by devising synergies between content and infrastructure provisions; a financial strategy, involving major acquisitions and the ability to bear losses; and a regulatory strategy, or managing to elicit leniency from the state.

RIL ventured into television broadcasting through a web of acquisitions in two major multilingual networks, ETV and TV18, rechristening the amalgamation Network 18.[35] Following that, it moved into television distribution, the backend of broadcasting, by acquiring a majority stake in two of the three largest cable networks. Surprisingly, India's antitrust body found no threats of market power in such accumulation of interests in the cable business.[36] These acquisitions were part of a larger industrial strategy to create a fiber-to-the-home network, what later became JioGigaFibre.[37] This is of import since video traffic is observed to be primarily accessed through fixed lines, even if ultimately viewed on mobile devices.[38] The launch of JioGigaFibre in 2019 was itself enigmatic, since only the previous year the government permitted cloud operators to establish captive fiber networks to augment their offerings.[39]

RIL's earlier move into telecom exemplifies market entry by stealth. It acquired the small company who was the sole bidder in a broadband spectrum auction in 2010. Speculations about this unknown entity being a proxy for RIL gained ground when licensing regulations were retrospectively altered to enable the acquired entity to also offer voice services.[40] Clearly, RIL profited from a state weak on enforcing corporate disclosures, retrospectively revising policies, and overseeing procedural violations. Having legally legitimized itself, Jio weaned away subscribers from incumbent telcos by predatory pricing. This strategy benefited from Jio's exploiting regulatory loopholes and by lenient regulatory oversight.[41] In 2018, just two years after its launch, Jio's subscribers reached 370 million, overtaking those of Vodafone-Idea and Bharti Airtel—incumbent telcos also competing in the VoD business.

All this speaks volumes about the state as a handmaiden in enabling a late entrant in the media and communication industries to accumulate a humongous infrastructure and subscriber base. What we witnessed was the friendly hand of the regulatory deepend in sculpting the emergence of a cross-sectoral actor in the digital economy. But this is not to deny the strengths of Reliance Jio's industrial strategy. It was the first to introduce 4G telecom in India and offered its 4G enabled feature phone at under $23; furthermore, opting for voice-over-LTE technology enabled it to reap the advantages of investing in a single type of network for voice and data. By the time Reliance Jio was launched, the conglomerate was marshaling a chest of captive content through subsidiaries and joint ventures in television, cinema, online music, and VoD platforms like Voot. This then furnishes the deeper context and broader footprint of the "disruption" brought about by Reliance Jio in India's digital economy.[42]

The raft of incremental investments and acquisitions had swamped RIL with a debt of over $20 billion by the end of the financial year 2019–20. This is where its audacious financial strategy surfaced. Reliance Jio offered equity to a slew of global industrial and financial entities. Rather predictably, Facebook was the first, acquiring nearly 10 percent stake by investing $5.9 billion. Despite its affiliate, WhatsApp, having 400 million users in India and Reliance Jio's own subscribers inching toward this mark, the antitrust body found no reason to question this association. This apart, General Atlantic, Intel Capital, and four private equity firms, all having interests in the platform business, were altogether sold around a 10 percent stake.[43] Such investments typify financial dynamics in neoliberal markets wherein investors reward the strategy of companies pursuing growth over profits. Halfway into the next financial year, and buoyed by RIL's rights issue of $7.2 billion, the conglomerate not only wiped out its debt but harvested over $1 billion in surplus.

Cloudification of Stateness

In making sense of Jio's domestic and global arrangements, a broader conception of mercantilism proves helpful. Like its traditional conception as an economic doctrine, in this broader conception too the pursuit of stateness remains the core desire.[44] Such a broader conception of mercantilism helps to straddle the momenta of nationalism and neoliberalism marking the Indian digital economy. These forces are not binaries, since neoliberalism employs nationalist discourses to promote its policies and policy values.[45] This then explains Jio's seemingly unfathomable blend of nationalist rhetoric and international collaborations. While its nationalist rhetoric has been delved into elsewhere,[46] there is something to be underscored about its collaborations with global actors. We view investments by international actors into Reliance Jio as the price global giants pay to profit from the Indian market under the watchful mercantilist state. This obliges us to delve into the pursuit of stateness unfolding in the regulatory imagination of the backend crucial to Jio, that is, the cloud business.

The thinking at Telecom Regulatory Authority of India (TRAI), India's cross-sectoral regulator, refracts the cloud business being sculpted by a fusion of neoliberalism and nationalism currently inhabiting the state.

In its initial articulation, TRAI identified two threats to "the autonomy of users":[47] market dominance by a handful of actors in this resource-intensive business and the lack of interoperability that impeded migration between cloud operators.[48] There is little reason, or precedent, to take such concerns at face value. For one, "user interest" has been commonly evoked to justify state intervention—be that surreptitiously directed at benefiting the public exchequer, or implicitly favoring certain private actors. Moreover, the inability to enforce interoperability, thereby tacitly allowing users to be locked in with particular companies, is conspicuous in the regulation of other networked technologies in India—a sterling example being in the DTH direct-to-home segment of the television distribution business.[49] Most intriguingly, within a year TRAI changed its position on interoperability in the cloud business, from categorically seeking it through regulatory intervention to leaving its attainment through "market forces."[50] Ideologically, this flip unmasks the state's earlier, supposedly public interest, concerns, while operationally, it sidesteps systematically engaging with the many layers of interoperability ingrained in this backend business.[51]

Subsequent recommendations by TRAI assimilated cloud regulation with telecommunications regulation, manifest in its notion of "cloudification of telecom."[52] TRAI observed this cloudification resulting in offerings either moving from the telecom space to the cloud space, or effectively controlling both spaces. Evident here is the state's tacit support to Reliance Jio, the only actor present in both spaces. Furthermore, the discourse of cloudification moved attention away from a crucial element in the delivery of cloud services: fiber networks. Between JioGigaNet catering to cities and the state-owned Bharat Net, the world's largest rural fiber optic roll-out, the country's fiber networks appear enveloped by these two large interests. As a result, Reliance Jio, and its prime patron, the government, are set to be a formidable duo in dealing with any cloud operator wanting to augment their offerings in India.

Undoubtedly, the state has found in Reliance Jio a "national champion" in India's digital economy. This is appealing in a milieu where the government was besieged by anxieties of sovereignty and security—that is, by the presence of global digital behemoths in India and the advent of deterritorializing backends like the cloud. Most actors in the cloud business have opposed setting up a separate regulatory framework for the business. They claim being already subjected to extant information technology, fiscal, and consumer regulations, besides to the proposed Personal Data Protection Bill.[53] Additionally, many cloud operators dispute the remit of TRAI and relevant line ministries to regulate the cloud business "directly or indirectly."[54] Reliance Jio, however, remains conspicuous in its support to the regulatory framework being proposed.[55]

Conclusion

This chapter captured the dynamics unfolding in India in the frontend of the VoD business, its synergies with those in the backend, and the way these have been mediated by the deepend. We found growth in video platforms nurtured in different ways by actors in the media and the communication industries, be they domestic or global entities. Crucial here, however, is the importance and ability of creating synergies between stakes in both industries, now constituting an integrated digital economy. Clearly, success in this economy is driven by the ability of video platforms to forge collaborations with the backend, most importantly with actors in the cloud business.

Among competitors in these interdependent markets cradling the VoD business, Reliance Jio has triumphed by harnessing its industrial, financial, and regulatory strategies. We find the last, by far, to have been the determining strategy. In its industrial expansion, Jio benefited from leniency of a neoliberal state and by the anxieties of a nationalist state striving to hedge its sovereign interests.

The benign regulatory framework that had propelled the explosion of VoD now appears contingent upon the stateness marking the backend business. For two matters are starkly clear. First, the anxiety of the state to control industrial actors takes the form of tempering market access, since only those who are members of the proposed self-regulatory body will be authorized to offer cloud services. Underlying this is the quest to ensure data harvested by transnational companies gets stored and processed in India. Second, Reliance Jio's cloudification of telecom and envisaged fiberization of the cloud has made it the "natural" actor in the backend business. Reliance Jio is well aware that its commercial interests, overlapping fairly with the state's mercantilist interests, will be fortified, whatever the regulatory framework ultimately arrived at.

Notes

1. Nicholas Garnham, "Economic, Institutional, and Cultural Barriers to Convergence," in *Les autoroutes de l'information un produit de la convergence*, ed. J. G. Lacroix and G. Tremblay (Québec: Presses de l'Université du Québec, 1995), 41–48.

2. Government of India (GoI), Communication Convergence Bill, 2001 (2001); Telecom Regulatory Authority of India (TRAI), Consultation Paper on Issues Relating to Convergence and Competition in Broadcasting and Telecommunications (2006).

3. See Adrian Athique and Vibodh Parthasarathi, "Platform Economy and Platformization," in *Platform Capitalism in India*, ed. Adrian Athique and Vibodh Parthasarathi (London: Palgrave, 2020), 1–19.

4. EY, *The Era of Consumer A.R.T. Acquisition | Retention | Transaction* (New Delhi: EY LLP, 2020), 13.

5. EY, *A Billion Screens of Opportunity: India's Media and Entertainment Sector* (New Delhi: EY LLP, 2019), 13.

6. Vibodh Parthasarathi, "Between Strategic Intent and Considered Silence: Regulatory Contours of the TV Business," in *The Indian Media Economy*, ed. Adrian Athique, Vibodh Parthasarathi, and S. V. Srinivas (New Delhi: Oxford University Press, 2018), 144–66.

7. Björn Hettne, "The Concept of Neomercantilism," in *Mercantilist Economics* (Dordrecht: Springer, 1993), 235–55.

8. See Luzhou Li, "How to Think about Media Policy Silence," *Media, Culture & Society* 43, no. 2 (2021): 359–68.

9. Jean-François Blanchette, "Introduction: Computing's Infrastructural Moment," in *Regulating the Cloud: Policy for Computing Infrastructure*, ed. Christopher S. Yoo and Jean-François Blanchette (Cambridge, MA: MIT Press, 2015), 1–20.

10. KPMG-EROS Now, *Unravelling the Digital Video Consumer* (KPMG, 2019).

11. FICCI KPMG, *The "Digital First" Journey* (October 2018), 16.

12. See C. P. Chandrasekhar and Jayati Ghosh, "The Financialization of Finance? Demonetization and the Dubious Push to Cashlessness in India," *Development and Change* 49, no. 2 (2018): 420–36.

13. Philippe Bouquillion, "Industrial and Financial Structures of Over-the-Tops (OTTs) in India," in *Platform Capitalism in India*, ed. Adrian Athique and Vibodh Parthasarathi (London: Palgrave, 2020), 129–49.

14. Ibid., 135.

15. Philippe Bouquillion and Christine Ithurbide, "Audiovisual Industry and Digital Platforms in India: A Contribution from Political Economy of Communication," *Global Media and Communication* 18, no. 3 (2022): 345–64.

16. FICCI KPMG, *The "Digital First" Journey*, 15.

17. Bouquillion and Ithurbide, "Audiovisual Industry and Digital Platforms in India."

18. EY, *The Era of Consumer A.R.T. Acquisition | Retention | Transaction*, 253.

19. Akshay Sudhir and Prashanth Rao, "How Technology Is Shaping the Future of Streaming Services in India," *Financial Express*, January 11 2021.

20. Microsoft News Center India, "Microsoft Trials Last-Mile Content Delivery Technology to Drive Reach in Remote Geographies," *News.microsoft.com*, November 3, 2020.

21. Sohini Mitter, "Netflix Announces 10 New Original Films in India, Ropes in Shah Rukh Khan and Others," *Yourstory.com*, April 15, 2019, https://yourstory.com/2019/04/netflix-originals-india-shah-rukh-khan.

22. IBEF, "India's OTT Market: Witnessing a Rise in Number of Paid Subscribers," IBEF blog, October 15, 2020.

23. Manish Singh, "Netflix Is Reducing Its Traffic on ISPs by 25% in India," *Tech Crunch,* March 24, 2020. https://tcrn.ch/3dpCxTN.

24. Microsoft News Center India, "Eros Now, Microsoft Join Hands for Next Gen Video Platform," *News.microsoft.com,* September 19, 2019, https://news.microsoft.com/en-in/eros-now-microsoft-collaborate-next-generation-online-video-platform/.

25. Shephali Bhatt, "Stream Engine: What Goes On behind Delivering Content on OTT Platforms," *Economic Times,* November 2, 2019, https://economictimes.indiatimes.com/tech/software/stream-engine-what-goes-on-behind-delivering-contents-on-ott-platforms/articleshow/71869602.cms.

26. James S. Duesenberry, *Income, Saving, and the Theory of Consumer Behavior* (Cambridge, MA: Harvard University Press, 1949).

27. Netflix, *Annual Report* (2019), 8–9, https://ir.netflix.net/financials/annual-reports-and-proxies/default.aspx.

28. Microsoft News Center India, "Eros Now, Microsoft Join Hands for Next Gen Video Platform."

29. Bhumika Khatri, "Tencent To Enter Indian Cloud Services War with Video and Live Streaming Products," *Fast 42,* July 3, 2018, https://inc42.com/buzz/tencent-enters-the-indian-cloud-services-war-with-offerings-in-video-and-live-streaming-products/.

30. Prakash Mallya, "India's Booming Cloud Market Is Set to Be Worth $4.1 Billion by 2020—Here's Why," *Forbes,* May 23, 2018, https://www.forbes.com/sites/prakashmallya/2018/03/23/indias-booming-cloud-market-is-set-to-be-worth-4-1-billion-by-2020-heres-why/?sh=60a9f519631a.

31. "Equinix Acquires GPX's India DCentres for 1.2k Crore," *Economic Times,* August 12, 2020, https://economictimes.indiatimes.com/small-biz/startups/newsbuzz/equinix-acquires-gpxs-india-data-centres-for-1-2k-crore/articleshow/77496725.cms?from=mdr.

32. Aritra Sarkel, "AWS's Big Bet for OTT Players with Data Analytics and AI," *Economic Times,* January 2, 2018, https://economictimes.indiatimes.com/technology/aws-big-bet-for-ott-players-with-data-analytics-ai/articleshow/62276209.cms?redirect=1.

33. Google, "Jio and Google Cloud to Collaborate on 5G Technology to Enable a Billion Indians Access Superior Connectivity," Google press release, June 24, 2021, https://cloud.google.com/press-releases/2021/0624/jioandgooglecloudcollaborateon5gtoenableabillionindiansacesssuperiorconnectivity.

34. See Jai Bhatia, "Crime in the Air: Spectrum Markets and the Telecommunications Sector in India," in *The Wild East,* ed. B. Harriss-White and L. Michelutti (London: UCL Press, 2019), 140–67; Scott Fitzgerald, "The Networked Media Economy and the Indian Gilded Age," in *Platform Capitalism in India,* ed. Adrian Athique and Vibodh Parthasarathi (London: Palgrave, 2020), 43–65.

35. Paranjoy Guha Thakurta and Subi Chaturvedi, "Corporatisation of the Media: Implications of the RIL-Network18-Eenadu Deal," *Economic and Political Weekly* 47, no. 2 (2012): 10–13.

36. CCI, *Combination Registration Nos. C-2018/10/609 and C-2018/10/610,* January 21, 2019.

37. Fitzgerald, "The Networked Media Economy and the Indian Gilded Age," 53.

38. Rajat Kathuria, Mansi Kedia, Gangesh Varma, Kaushambi Bagchi, and Richa Sekhani, *The Anatomy of an Internet Blackout: Measuring the Economic Impact of Internet Shutdowns in India* (New Delhi: Indian Council for Research on International Economic Relations, 2018), https://icrier.org/pdf/Anatomy_of_an_Internet_Blackout.pdf.

39. GoI, *National Digital Communications Policy* (New Delhi: Government of India, 2018), 14.

40. Bhatia, "Crime in the Air," 155.

41. Jai Bhatia and Advait Rao Palepu, "Reliance Jio: Predatory Pricing or Predatory Behaviour?," *Economic and Political Weekly* 51, no. 9 (2016): 41, https://www.epw.in/journal/2016/39/web-exclusives/reliance-jio-predatory-pricing-or-predatory-behaviour.html.

42. Rahul Mukherjee, "Jio Sparks Disruption 2.0: Infrastructural Imaginaries and Platform Ecosystems in 'Digital India,'" *Media, Culture & Society* 41, no. 2 (2019): 175–95.

43. Moneycontrol, "RIL Is Net Debt Free 8 Months Ahead of Target Thanks to Jio Deals and Rights Issue," *Money Control News,* July 2, 2020, https://www.moneycontrol.com/news/business/companies/ril-says-jio-deals-and-right-issue-have-made-it-net-debt-free-well-ahead-of-march-2021-target-5426421.html.

44. Hettne, "The Concept of Neomercantilism," 238.

45. Andreas Pickel, "False Oppositions: Reconceptualizing Economic Nationalism in a Globalizing World," in *Economic Nationalism in a Globalizing World*, ed. E. Helleiner and A. Pickel (Ithaca, NY: Cornell University Press, 2005), 1–20.

46. Mukherjee, "Jio Sparks Disruption 2.0."

47. TRAI, *Consultation Paper on Cloud Computing* (New Delhi: Telecom Regulatory Authority of India, 2016), 8.

48. Ibid., 11.

49. Vibodh Parthasarathi, "The Conundrum of 'Relevant Market': Market Definition in India's Complex TV Distribution Business," *Indian Journal of Law and Technology* 15, no. 2 (2019): 517.

50. TRAI, *Recommendations on Cloud Services* (New Delhi: Telecom Regulatory Authority of India, 2017), 37.

51. Telecommunications Standards Development Society, *Cloud Interoperability and Portability (CIP) Standard Reference Report* (2020).

52. TRAI, *Recommendations on Cloud Services* (New Delhi: Telecom Regulatory Authority of India, 2020), 15.

53. Ibid., 4–7.

54. Ibid., 8.

55. Jio, *Response to TRAI's Consultation Paper on "Cloud Computing"* (2016).

8

SERVING MACHINES AND HETEROTOPIAS

Data Entry Work in Prisons and Refugee Camps in the US and Uganda

ANNE KAUN,
ALEXIS LOGSDON,
PHILIPP SEUFERLING,
AND FREDRIK STIERNSTEDT

The gig economy for on-demand digital labor has been emerging since 2005 when Amazon launched its Mechanical Turk (MTurk). This crowdwork-facilitating platform constitutes what the company calls *artificial* artificial intelligence. With the help of platforms such as MTurk, small tasks and digital piecework are outsourced to gig workers. The work relationship between the requesters and the gig workers sometimes only lasts seconds and rarely includes direct interactions. What started out as a service to provide simple digital piecework, for example, categorizing images, transcribing video or audio material as well as researching data details, has expanded to a global economy that encompasses all kinds of services including car services (Uber), food delivery (Foodora), small tasks in the household (TaskRabbit), and carework (Jepster). Characteristic of the gig economy is precarious labor in short-term work "gigs." The tasks themselves are often simple and do not require specific training, which allows for the rapid replacement of specific workers.[1] With the increasing digitalization efforts and broad investment in AI development, the need for digital gig and piecework increased. New sources of cheap pieceworkers were needed.

In this chapter, we explore cases of digital piecework in two special locations, namely prisons and refugee camps. Although prisons and refugee camps are rarely connected with emerging forms of digital labor, they have indeed become important nodes in the digital economy. Hence, digital piecework conducted in these locations contributes in important ways to our media backends. We conceptualize media backends as sites and practices that constitute a necessary physical infrastructure for digital culture's frontend, which we as mundane users experience. The media backends that we are interested in here are places where digital piecework is conducted—essential labor for large digitalization projects such as digital archives and recordkeeping as well as the production of training data for artificial intelligence and machine-learning projects, while remaining hidden from the public eye. Through the two case studies, we highlight the character of the digital piecework that incarcerated and camp-based individuals conduct to develop, maintain, and backup digital media. Ultimately, we argue that incarcerated individuals and refugees are an important part of digital culture even though they are largely invisible backend workers.

Background: Connecting Prisons and Refugee Camps

In our analysis, we draw on two cases of media backend work conducted in the prison and refugee camp contexts respectively. First, we discuss the South Dakota State Archives Special Project Program that, in collaboration with the Department of Corrections, digitizes records and newspapers held by the state archives. And second, we engage with the LevelApp, a smart-phone application, that allows refugees in Uganda to conduct digital piecework producing, for example, training data for different artificial intelligence and machine-learning projects. In terms of material, we are drawing in both cases on publicly available documentation, including self-descriptions of the projects as well as media reports, on the digitization work conducted by prisoners as well as the LevelApp projects. In the case of the State Archives Special Project Program, we furthermore analyze video material that documents the specific work tasks conducted by the incarcerated workers. In the case of LevelApp, we have analyzed the public interface of the application, as conducting a walkthrough analysis of the application failed because the app was only available in Uganda and was later deleted from the app store. We coded the collected material for specificities of digital piecework conducted in both locations, including the institutional organization of the work, salaries, specific tasks, as well as the in/visibility of the pieceworkers. Collated, these codes allowed us to investigate the specific digital piecework that constitutes one form of media backend work.

A state prison in South Dakota and a Ugandan refugee settlement are of course two very specific and very different locations for digital piecework. However, we argue, they share several important characteristics that have implications for the kind of work conducted there. Although prisons and refugee camps have changed over time and vary in the details of their structure and methods of control, they fulfil a specific social function across modern cultures—namely, to contain individuals that deviate from what is defined as the social norm and the required way of being in society while reforming and socializing them into adjusted individuals. The ways of maintaining unwanted individuals in modern times have increasingly rested upon combining ideas of isolation and punishment with rehabilitation and humanitarian relief. Prisons and refugee camps are hence places of fundamental ambiguity.

Prisons and refugee camps also purport to reconcile in one place several sites that might otherwise be incompatible with one another: they are at the same time institutions of education, work, and leisure as well as temporary homes that collapse experiences and relationships that are otherwise linked to separate spheres and, more importantly, physical spaces in life. At the same time, they are central to society and to capitalist economic systems (and as we will show increasingly for the digital economy). The central economic role of prisons, but also refugee camps, has been acknowledged by a host of publications identifying and exploring the prison-industrial complex.[2]

Prisons and refugee camps furthermore establish a break with traditional understandings and experiences of time; they form heterochronies captured in idiomatic expressions such as "doing time" when time is experienced as both being paused and fast-forwarded. Life is paused in the sense of pursuing such long-term goals as family plans or vocational development both in the prison and the refugee camp. Outside the prison, life, however, continues, making changes that incarcerated individuals cannot actively participate in. Prisons and refugee camps are furthermore removed from the public sphere. Members of the public do not generally have access to them without special permission, while the residents of these locations undergo specific rituals of entry and exit (e.g., being assigned identification numbers and distinctive clothes). Their lack of visibility and public access relegates them to the margins of society. Lastly, prisons and refugee camps establish a place where all that runs counter to the good society is contained, hence, making the good society possible in the first place. They in that sense "have a function in relation to all the space that remains,"[3] with prisons negotiating morality, and refugee camps national and territorial boundaries.

The marginalized spaces of prisons and refugee settlements constitute a specific constellation of time, space, and economy that are attractive for digital piecework. The loss of temporal autonomy, namely the ability to decide how to spend time, in prisons and refugee camps constitutes the precondition for a continuously available, easily exchangeable, and most importantly cheap workforce. Furthermore, digital piecework is often monotonous and low-skilled work that at the outset fits well with the prison and refugee populations that might have difficulties with participating in longer and challenging training. At the same time, prisons and refugee camps are locations of incarceration, which means that repetitive, cognitive unchallenging work does not stir up public critique, for example, worries that incarcerated workers constitute cheap competitors for other workers. This specific arrangement of time, space, and economy is fundamental in forming prisons and refugee camps as media backends that are served by incarcerated individuals.

Serving Media Backends

To specify the character of the digital piecework explored, it is necessary to further engage with the notion of media backends that are the context for these labor practices. Media backends comprise practices, soft- and hardware, as well as locations that are distinct from the frontends of digital culture. While the frontends are the visible presentation layers of digital technologies including the interface, the backends are the underlying, often invisible infrastructure. Besides this basic distinction between frontend and backend, drawing on Lilly Irani,[4] we can further distinguish between computational work and programming, that is, building the backend architecture and the additional work that is necessary to make this architecture work. Irani argues, "To serve is to make labor and attention available for those who are served; to promise service is to be bound, by duty or by wage, to the will of the served. Among computer scientists, as-a-service builds off of this common sense meaning and more specifically indexes a division of technical labor by which programmers can access computational processing functions housed and maintained by someone else on the internet."[5] This means there is an important distinction between those who have access to and produce the computational backend and those who serve within this backend infrastructure and make it work. Digital piecework is an example of the latter. Digital piecework for media backends can be situated in the broader context of digital labor and the expanding gig economy, namely the work facilitated through platforms such as Amazon's Mechanical Turk referred to at the beginning of the chapter. Previous accounts of this kind of digital piecework were mainly interested in deconstructing the dominant narrative of freedom, self-determination, and promises of autonomy that come with digital gig work.[6] Rather than providing more freedom, in digital piecework people become computational infrastructures that are largely based on casual and impermanent work and strictly guided by the "ever-watchful rating algorithms."[7] The digital pieceworkers in prisons and refugee camps are the logical extension of digital work facilitated by platforms such as MTurk while at the same time constituting a special case that lies outside the dominant logics of labor practices in the digital economy.

The digital piecework we are exploring here follows similar principles as the practices of insourcing that Lisa Nakamura has explored in her work on semiconductor assembly on a Navajo reservation between 1965 and 1975.[8] Nakamura shows that the reservation became the ideal place for assembling semiconductors because it constituted an exception from US laws on minimum wages, guaranteeing low wages. Furthermore, the workers on the reservation were culturally foreign yet familiar within the US context. Similarly, prisons and refugee camps are sites of exception; certain rules and regulations are suspended, including regulations on minimum wage and guarantees of privacy. Hence, the digital work here differs in important ways from the digital gig work on MTurk.

However, there are important overlaps and commonalities. One shared aspect of the work on MTurk and digital piecework in prisons and refugee camps is the centrality of service or serving media backends. Here we draw again on Irani who introduces the discussion of the kind of labor that is facilitated by MTurk with Jeff Bezos's own words presenting the services, namely, "you have heard of software-as-a-service, well this is human-as-a-service."[9] Similarly, we suggest approaching media backend work by subjects such as incarcerated persons and refugees through the notion of servitude. Rather than being acknowledged and equal partners in the development process—often emphasized by participatory design approaches for developing digital applications—the kind of contributions and milieus that we engaged with can be characterized as spaces for serving technologies. Servitude takes different meanings here. It encompasses both the notion of serving something or someone or to be useful to somebody in achieving certain goals as well as performing work or duties for specific persons or organizations. "Serving" is also, of course, connected to the notion of spending time in prison, making an idiomatic connection to one of the spaces considered here.

Markus Krajewski, focusing on the noun *server*, argues that "we still lack an approach linking central aspects of cultural history to the key media practices of subalternity—an approach that may shed light on the foundational role of cultural development."[10] The notion of the server potentially adds this perspective to media theory. Starting from the current presence of servers in digital societies, Krajewski traces forms of serving and the role of delegating tasks from the subaltern to a plethora of machines, networks, and protocols that still determine the way we communicate nowadays. Taking the laboratory servant as an early example of subaltern labor in the name of science, Krajewski demonstrates the complex character of serving. "Towards the end of the seventeenth century, the so-called scientific revolution introduces certain professional types that span various social levels, from the gentleman philosopher to his helpers, delegated to assist with their masters' experiments. Each epoch contains the traces of mostly nameless subalterns, whose work of assistance consists, among other things, of the scientific production of knowledge in the broadest sense of the word."[11]

Krajewski emphasizes the ability of servers to change the course of power relations through their interventions or forms of malfunctioning. Based on examining the characteristics of the servant, Krajewski proposes a marginal epistemology of media that is based on several elements: employers deploy flexibility and creativity in subaltern tactics to fit into new power relations and human-machine networks; servants have a genuine media character in that they search, analyze, and distribute information and function as communication centers; servants have tacit knowledge combining manual labor and thinking to solve tasks; servants' work includes inconspicuous actions such as waiting and reflecting, contributing to knowledge production.[12]

It is particularly fruitful to use Krajewski's approach to explore the agency of servants, but we also need to acknowledge the captivated and unfree aspects of serving machines as well as the embeddedness of servant practices in institutional contexts such as prisons. While Krajewski traces the increasing delegation of serving to machines, we argue that human serving remains prevalent in digital culture and is particularly crucial for media backends. The focus on how humans are serving media backends connects to ongoing discussions of how labor practices are constantly restructured to fit with technological infrastructures and development rather than adjusting technologies to human labor practices.[13] The incorporation of prison and refugee labor is an extension of the digital economy and digital labor into marginal spaces

State Archives Special Project Program

In 2018, the State Archives of South Dakota entered a partnership with the state's women's prison to establish a microfilming and digitization lab at the prison—a so-called satellite lab. Supervised by the archive's employees, the Special Projects Program employs incarcerated workers from within the prison to digitize newspapers and other state documents. The scanned newspapers are then made available to view at the state archives. The state correctional industries, known as Pheasantland Industries, share videos of incarcerated workers ironing newspapers and placing them on the large-format scanning bed on their YouTube channel. Inmates working for state correctional industries in South Dakota are paid $0.25 per hour.[14] More than half of the inmates are Indigenous,[15] dramatically disproportionate with their share of the state's population: 9 percent.[16] Pheasantland Industries operates in other prisons in the state as well, overseeing production of embroidery, garments, furniture, engraving, and other goods for state-funded agencies. Some nonprofit organizations are also eligible to purchase prison-made goods and services. The varied types of labor happen in both the women's prison as well as in multiple men's prisons, but the digitization work in South Dakota is done solely by inmates of the women's prison, a population that is often considered more cooperative and careful in handling technology.

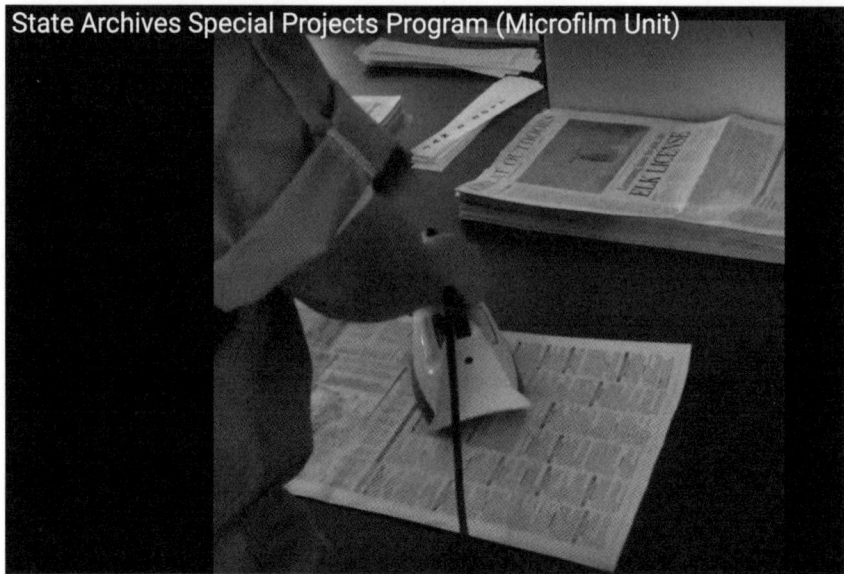

Figure 8.1. Still from the YouTube video documenting the work in the framework of the State Archives Special Project Program.

Pheasantland advertises its work programs as an unqualified good, employing prisoners who would "otherwise sit idle [who instead] produce an amazing variety of goods and services"[17] and the state lauds its work, which allows the state government to "accomplish more with less."[18] The Department of Corrections proclaims that "inmates are gaining a work ethic and a sense of value and self-worth,"[19] and Pheasantland's motto is "Made with Pride on the Inside." "The work experiences," Pheasantland contends, provide prisoners "with the tools and skills to make them productive members of the community when they are released."[20] State corrections and their industries frequently deploy this "win-win" rhetoric when talking about the cost/benefits of prison labor. In this way, they anticipate and set out to mitigate critiques of exploitation by demonstrating the positive impact of prison labor on both the inmate and the public. In fact, neither the Department of Corrections nor Pheasantland Industries offers evidence to support their claims that enhanced job skills have any impact on post-incarceration job prospects. In the United States, the unemployment rate among the formerly incarcerated is around 27 percent, higher than the percentage of Americans who were unemployed at the height of the Great Depression.[21] Beyond the rehabilitative claims put forward in the official description of the program, the incarcerated individuals in the women's prison—the majority of whom are Black and Indigenous—form a low-cost and continuously available workforce with radically limited autonomy.

The state archives project is, however, not a singularity, but should be seen in the context of a host of similar prison digitization labor programs. For example, two publications from the American Library Association lauded a yearbook digitization project in Oklahoma's correctional facilities as a "public library success story" and quoted the program's director at length.[22] One publication shares bold, unchecked claims from the director about the project's aim to protect local history and improve post-prison job prospects.[23] Similarly, Utah State Prison inmates who perform unpaid labor indexing genealogical records are described by the Mormon Church as "rescuing" their fellow prisoners.[24]

In sharp contrast to Pheasantland Industries' own claims of "pride" and skill building, the videos it promotes on its YouTube channel demonstrate the tedious, rote nature of digital piecework. In a video documenting the digitization process, the camera jumps from a shot of a control board for a large-format camera to another showing an inmate ironing a newspaper, with a stack of additional newspapers visible in the background, suggesting this is an activity the worker will repeat over and over again. The next shot is a different inmate standing in front of a large white table, positioning a document carefully on a designated spot on the table. These processes are then repeated from different camera angles.[25] Despite claims of building job skills, these job functions are remarkably similar to assembly-line work and thus promulgate certain ideas about the kinds of labor that Indigenous female inmates can perform within prison or in the workforce.

Prison-centered digitization and other technology work is always navigating a tension between visibility and invisibility. On the one hand, the state correctional industries proudly advertise the services they provide on their websites, Facebook pages, and YouTube channels. Press releases and annual reports boast of the increased access to cultural materials afforded by these initiatives and highlight a perception that these initiatives are the result of disruptive or innovative thinking on expanding the reach of digital surrogates for cultural memory artifacts.

While prisons and cultural memory organizations make these practices visible, the humans doing the work occupy a complicated space between hypervisibility and invisibility. In the video from the South Dakota State Archives' satellite lab in the women's prison, two to three different workers are shown demonstrating the process of digitization including ironing, positioning documents, and pushing buttons on a control panel. The camera is focused on their work and only ever shows their arms and torsos, rendering them anonymous. But all these workers have distinct tattoos that would render them legible to someone who knew them, stripping them of their anonymity. The video denies these incarcerated workers anonymity where it might count (such as depriving them of the choice whether to disclose to others that they were in prison) but decouples their identities from the work they are doing.

This move to create a distance between the laborer and her working conditions mirrors the secrecy and obscurity of other mass digitization projects, such as the Google Book Project. Nanna Bonde Thylstrup details how the "ghostly traces" left by human scanners' fingers spurred innovation for fully automated scanning at Google.[26] ScanOps workers fueling one of the largest digitization projects worldwide are not only invisible to the public eye but also treated as second-tier employers without benefits or job security.[27] Sarah T. Roberts picks up this sinister tale about the shadow labor behind Google Books digitization: a videographer working on contract at Google filmed workers leaving a building at strange hours of the day and investigated their "lesser working conditions and status," and was subsequently fired.[28] "He learned that these workers were contracted to produce the millions of page scans needed for Google's massive book digitization project—a project that . . . betrays no sign of these human actors involved in its creation."[29] Similarly, the incarcerated women visible in the promotion videos serve as illustrations of the rehabilitative work of the State Archive project while remaining dehumanized body parts that are denied an identity on their own terms.

The Special Projects Program in South Dakota marks an important turn in US prison partnerships with state cultural heritage agencies. While there are several other US states where digitization services are offered by state correctional industries, this is the first instance where a state archive has installed a satellite lab that constitutes as stable collaboration within a prison. The satellite lab is permanently situated in the prison rather than being a one-off project-based initiative. This speaks to a tension between the need for preservation and access to copies of the historical record and the inordinate cost and time commitment to operationalize it. With funding sources for digitization always shrinking or reliant on grant funding, libraries, archives, and museums (LAMs) typically relegate this work to the lowest paid, most precarious workers.[30] In many institutions, it is not uncommon for this work to be done by unpaid interns or low-paid student workers. The Special Projects Program takes undervaluing digitization labor to the next level, stripping the pretense of rote digital labor as "dues paying" or "valuable work experience" that is assumed within LAM institutions, and adding a layer of complexity to what Thylstrup, in discussing digital crowdsourcing projects at Europeana, calls "the blurring of production boundaries in the new cultural memory ecosystems."[31] Where crowdsourcing was billed as play, though, prison labor is only superficially promoted as valuable work experience.

The turn toward taking cultural memory work out of its traditional spheres in archives and historical societies and outsourcing it to low and unpaid workforces can also be seen in a digital indexing program at Utah State Prisons. The Mormon Church operates voluntary, unpaid opportunities for inmates to index digital genealogical records. While the Mormon Church celebrates the benefits of this program, suggesting that the program teaches useful skills like "typing" and "using a computer," it obscures the fact that the (mostly public) records prisoners index are then ingested by Mormon-owned genealogy research sites, which users access for a fee. Cultural memory institutions, including the National Archives, have partnered with Ancestry.com to index their records,[32] but the records themselves are only available by subscription. It is not a leap to imagine that some of the tens of millions of records indexed by prison workers for no pay were public documents, which the Mormons now profit from selling access to.

The South Dakota program and the others mentioned here serve a range of different audiences. Yet what they share is a common understanding of the logical extension of crowdsourced technological culture work. There is a seemingly limitless number of small-town newspapers, yearbooks, and family history records, yet there is not an endless supply of paid laborers to digitally process them. When there is not enough labor or funding to continue digitizing, it is easy to see why organizations turn to the cheapest labor there is: gendered and racialized prison labor. To reconcile the clearly exploitative nature of this arrangement, prisons and their institutional partners lean heavily on a narrative of rehabilitation through work experience, claims which do not always hold up to scrutiny.

In addition to spurious claims of preparing prisoners for life outside, these projects expose prison workers to cultural memory artifacts that represent pillars of a free society such as free access to news media and education of their own choice, while denying the prisoners themselves access to it. There is an epidemic of missing Indigenous women in the United States; in South Dakota Indigenous women make up more than two-thirds of missing persons cases in the state.[33] They also make up more than half of the population of the women's prison, where they are digitizing settler colonial newspapers that chronicle the erasure of Indigenous people from their own land. Incarcerated women digitizing high school yearbooks in Oklahoma are very likely to have not had the opportunity to finish high school themselves.

Roberts discusses shadow technology work that "fits precisely into new forms of technology-dependent knowledge labor envisioned, initially and optimistically, as having potential for providing a better quality of work and life, a higher standard of living, and more leisure time" but which turns out to be "work that calls for very large labor forces and not particularly high technical skill engaged in repetitive, unpleasant work [and] may represent a dystopian, technologically enhanced race to the bottom."[34] Roberts is writing about commercial content moderation and screening social media content, but her description maps neatly onto digital assembly-line work of mass digitization and indexing in prisons. In both cases, the cultural hunger for more and more content, whether social media or cultural heritage or something else, can only be fed by larger and larger armies of workers receiving smaller and smaller payments for their labor and who are flexibly available on a continuous basis, such as incarcerated individuals.

LevelApp

The second example of digital piecework for media backend work shifts from US prisons to Ugandan refugee settlements. In 2018, the nonprofit organization Refunite launched the app LevelApp as a branch of their operations. Refunite, based in Kampala, Copenhagen, and San Francisco, was founded in 2008 by Danish brothers David and Christopher Mikkelsen, as a digital service to reunite forced migrants, matching profiles of users who are missing or looking for each other after being displaced and losing touch. In 2018, Refunite started the subproject LevelApp, offering an application to be downloaded by refugees in Uganda (mostly from South Sudan and the Democratic Republic of the Congo), which would allow them to make money by training artificial intelligence and machine-learning systems for the customers of LevelApp. The app is, however, currently on hold, and not available any longer in the Ugandan Google Playstore, due to—in the words of the founders—"traction, the app received." The more likely explanation is, however, lacking orders and interest from the gig workers. LevelApp is a small, even rather unsuccessful example of digital piecework in media backends. However, it represents yet another case of specific structures of labor at media backends in incarcerated domains.

In the case of LevelApp, the digital piecework and its design and implementation are undergirded by humanitarian logics rather than the logic of rehabilitation that legitimizes digitizing work at prisons. In 2018, co-founder Christopher Mikkelsen presented LevelApp as an innovative solution at the Trust Conference in London, an annual event by the Thomson Reuters Foundation on human rights, technology, and social entrepreneurship. Mikkelsen announced a pilot project of 5,000 users in Uganda, which gained some press attention. The founders were not new to this field, having presented their organization Refunite at the World Economic Forum in Davos, where they also reported about LevelApp.[35]

When digging deeper into the actual work practices of LevelApp users, the emancipatory promises of tackling dispossession and fostering social change come along with mundane, repetitive, tedious work tasks. The screenshots in figure 8.2 (from an app store) show the structure of the assignments: classifying images and connecting them with words. Individual sets of tasks would then earn the user points, which would eventually become cash. Users must be, though briefly trained first, going through a set of exercise tasks. Afterward, they could be activated to work for actual customers. According to a report, "upwards of 80 per cent of the refugee users asked for 'harder games' and requested 'new images' in order to learn new words and 'keep busy' during downtime."[36] This impression might speak for the engaging, gamified nature of the app, but also for the speed, repetitiveness, assembly-line style, and sheer boredom that backend work for AI imposes upon the refugees.

The LevelApp project received funding from a combination of tech companies, humanitarian aid organizations, and foundations with a focus on technology development. The financial supporters include the GSMA (an industry association of mobile networks operators) and three foundations, which focus on tech, AI and data solutions, or development aid (Postkodstiftelsen, Patrick J. McGovern Foundation, and Af Johnick Foundation). Instead of alleged rehabilitation via work and building up a specific skill set, as is the case for prisons, the initiative in Ugandan refugee settlements follows a discursive logic of humanitarianism, or more precisely what critical scholars describe as "techno-humanitarianism."[37] This notion encapsulates wider trends of solutionist approaches to humanitarian relief, providing profits for tech companies by technologizing operations and services in spaces of crisis, such as refugee camps. Humanitarianism and migration infrastructures are historically ridden by "utilitarian technophilic" imaginaries around media technologies as neutral and helpful modes of managing displacement.[38] Often such interventions come at the cost of the actual needs of dispossessed individuals and obfuscate the politics of humanitarianism at large, to the benefit of state governance systems and tech companies. Beyond digital piecework, refugee individuals can become subjects of data extraction for refugee governance when serving the machinery of refugee administration, as well as the media technologies themselves.[39] Through continuously producing data, refugees contribute to the basic parts of media backends that not only need algorithms and software infrastructures, but also the data they run on.

Hence, the case of LevelApp unpacks how humanitarian ideals of providing technological solutions for the benefit of the refugees, including preparation and inclusion of refugees in labor markets and transferring skill sets, meet the political economy of digital technologies and their media backend work. With growing availability of digital infrastructures in the Global South, marginalized populations become "attractive as consumers, but also as a huge pool of digital labor,"[40] including migrant populations and encamped refugees working for and serving humanitarian and other media technologies. The way in which the app is presented on its homepage, as well as in press interviews and other published material, construct a progressivist narrative of a "win-win situation" for both the refugees, who fight their own poverty and unemployment, and for the companies in "slashing costs"[41] at the backend of their AI and ML systems.[42] The narrative of LevelApp's own homepage (https://www.levelapp.net/) walks the reader through numbers on poverty and low wages in Sub-Saharan Africa, positioning the app as a welcomed, logical solution for workers.

In quotes from some of the refugee LevelApp digital pieceworkers, the various advantages of working for LevelApp are presented: learning skills for the job market, such as tech skills and English-language skills; combining the job with other tasks, such as household chores or childcare (seen as empowerment for women); and of course multiplying one's income. Again, following techno-solutionist ideals as a humanitarian intervention, these aspects are framed as perks of technology, fostering fundamental social change: "LevelApp is available to you whether you are male or female, are available full-time or part-time and live in an urban or a rural area. All that's missing to create radical social change is for pioneering enterprises to outsource their data annotation tasks through LevelApp."[43]

While it is unclear how much the workers actually made, the promised salary amounts up to $200 per month, depending on use, which would be sixteenfold the average income. However, a report by GSMA (one of the funders) states that "the most cashed out through mobile money by a user in a month was 17 USD."[44] At the same time, there are "slower adopters who are currently averaging fewer dollars a week, for example, because they didn't yet have an email address or Facebook account to login."[45] In terms of the business model, LevelApp promises that "$0.66 of every contracted $1 goes directly to LevelApp workers."[46] The money would be paid out digitally, after the client has validated the results of the trained AI. Available information on the clients is scarce, only including a company called DeepBrain Chain, which offers a blockchain-based AI computing platform. However, the algorithms of Refunite, the mother organization, are trained through LevelApp: "The creator, Refunite, is also benefiting because the work refugees do for the company helps develop its artificial intelligence program."[47] LevelApp itself did not respond to our interview request.

By March 2020, LevelApp self-reports 28,725 users and 261,010,191 images labeled. Yet, the app was taken out of the Ugandan Google Playstore in June 2020, as it seems due to a lack of work to be delegated to the users, and explained by the founders in a dubious formulation that they discontinued the app.[48] While the ambitions of the project were high, it seems to remain an attempt and an imaginary of effectively using Ugandan refugee settlements for expanding new ways of organizing the labor on the backends of media technologies: namely shifting the work into heterotopian, shadowy invisible spaces, and assigning the work to its residents, who serve these technologies under an alleged humanitarian promise. For the short time of the app's operations, refugees have become disconnected servants to these AI and machine-learning infrastructures: servants to techno-humanitarianist ideals and imaginaries, servants to capitalist

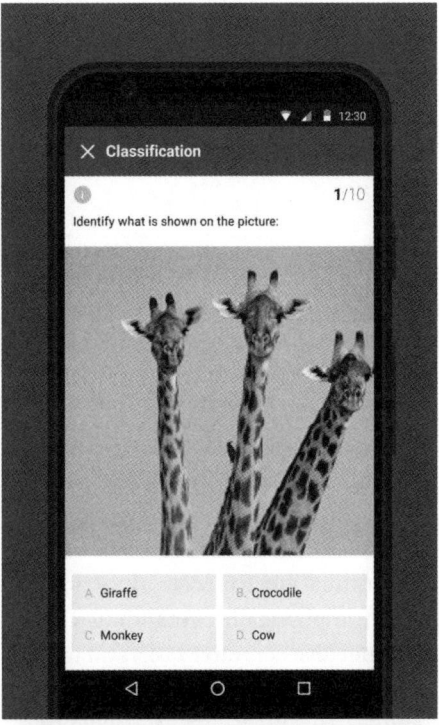
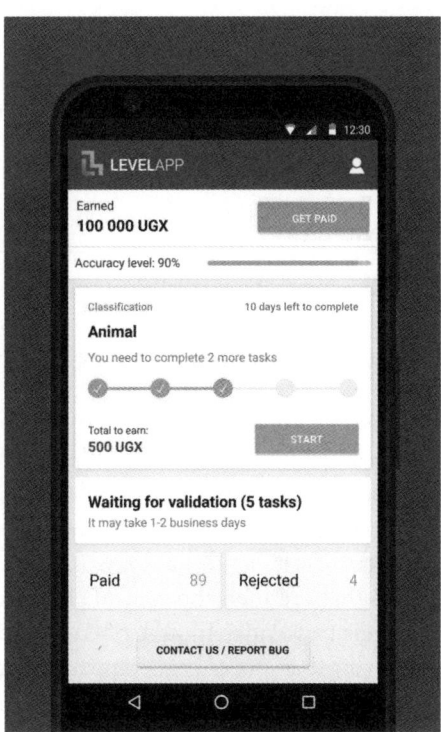
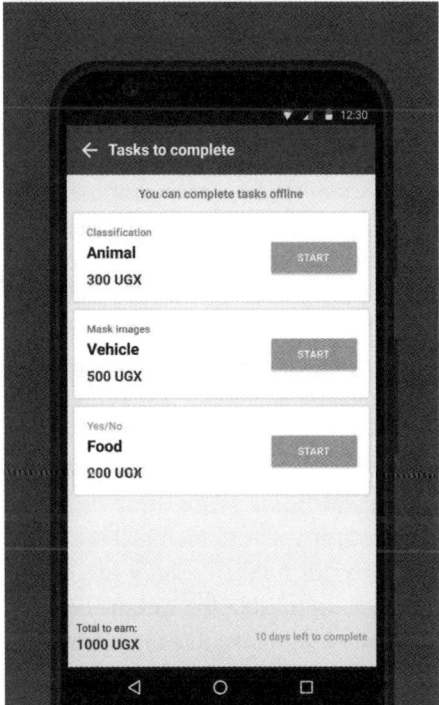

Figure 8.2a–c. Screenshots from LevelApp (AltrainUG).

ventures of "slashing costs" and making possible media technology and content, as well as servants to sociotechnical imaginaries of bettering and solving their own dispossessed living situation by way of an app, developed and funded in and by Western countries.

Conclusion

In this chapter, we use the notion of serving media backends to explore specific kinds of digital piecework that are currently conducted at prisons and refugee camps. The labor of digitizing historical archival records and the labeling of visual material is a precondition for emerging technologies that run on large-scale data including artificial intelligence and machine learning. The two cases not only illustrate the monotonous and often low-skilled tasks that are necessary for these emerging technologies but also in what ways media backends are connected to unfreedom, subalternity, vulnerability, and ultimately coerced forms of serving technology.

What are then the central characteristics of the digital piecework serving media backends? Though often considered dirty or physically demanding jobs, serving does not only encompass manual labor but also cognitive tasks and tacit knowledge of the right degree of visibility and invisibility, voice and silence, empowerment, and surveillance. In our case studies, this means that the workers and management in prisons and refugee camps must navigate the ambiguous character of media backends including invisibility and visibility. The programs implemented need public visibility for support and contracted tasks. At the same time, the sites of work, the laboring individuals, and the specific tasks themselves remain largely invisible. The rehabilitating and humanitarian discourses that are constructed around the media backend work considered here often emphasize the empowering potential of engaging refugees and incarcerated individuals, amplifying their voices and prospects. The subjects themselves remain silent, contributing to the reproduction of social differences and inequalities rather than overcoming them.

Emerging technologies and the connected work are entangled with discourses of techno rehabilitation and humanitarianism to justify their existence. With the increasing reliance and investment in the development of artificial intelligence and machine learning, tasks like scanning large amounts of analog material as well as labeling content will be ubiquitous and so will the search for cheap or free workforces. Digital piecework for media backends emerges in marginal spaces such as the refugee camp and prison. These spaces form the necessary precondition for technological development, while those involved in the specific labor practices rarely have free access to the technologies they contribute to building.

Notes

1. Jeremias Adam-Prassl, *Humans as a Service: The Promise and Perils of Work in the Gig Economy* (Oxford: Oxford University Press, 2018).
2. Angela Davis, "Masked Racism: Reflections on the Prison Industrial Complex," *Indigenous Law Bulletin* 4, no. 27 (2000): 4–7; Ruth Wilson Gilmore, *Golden Gulag: Prisons, Surplus, Crisis, and Opposition in Globalizing California* (Berkeley: University of California Press, 2007).
3. Michel Foucault, "Of Other Spaces: Utopias and Heterotopias," in *Rethinking Architecture: A Reader in Cultural Theory*, ed. Neil Leach (London: Routledge, 1967), 336.
4. Lilly Irani, "The Cultural Work of Microwork," *New Media & Society* 17, no. 5 (May 2015): 720–39.
5. Ibid., 733.
6. Adam-Prassl, *Humans as a Service*.
7. Irani, "The Cultural Work of Microwork"; Jamie Woodcock and Mark Graham, *The Gig Economy: A Critical Introduction* (Cambridge ; Medford, MA: Polity, 2020); Adam-Prassl, *Humans as a Service*, 8.
8. Lisa Nakamura, "Indigenous Circuits: Navajo Women and the Racialization of Early Electronic Manufacture," *American Quarterly* 66, no. 4 (2014): 919–41.
9. Irani, "The Cultural Work of Microwork."
10. Markus Krajewski, *The Server: A Media History from the Present to the Baroque* (New Haven: Yale University Press, 2018), 3.
11. Ibid., 192.
12. Ibid., 349–50.
13. Alessandro Delfanti and Bronwyn Frey, "Humanly Extended Automation or the Future of Work Seen through Amazon Patents," *Science, Technology, & Human Values* 29 (2020).
14. Wendy Sawyer, "How Much Do Incarcerated People Earn in Each State?," *Prison Policy Initiative*, April 10, 2017, https://www.prisonpolicy.org/blog/2017/04/10/wages/.
15. "Adult Inmates by Race/Ethnicity," South Dakota Department of Corrections, February 28, 2021, https://doc.sd.gov/documents/InmatesbyRaceEthnicityFebruary2021.pdf.
16. "U.S. Census Bureau QuickFacts: South Dakota," https://www.census.gov/quickfacts/fact/table/SD/RHI325219. Accessed March 25, 2021.
17. Pheasantland Industries, *Pheasantland Industries 2019*, YouTube, https://www.youtube.com/watch?v=UgVIrDwYp1U.
18. South Dakota Department of Corrections, "Inmate Work Program," https://doc.sd.gov/adult/work/; Lucius Caloute and Daniel Kopf, "Out of Prison and Out of Work," *Prison Policy Initiative*, 2018, https://www.prisonpolicy.org/reports/outofwork.html, https://doc.sd.gov/adult/work/.
19. South Dakota Department of Corrections, "Inmate Work Program."
20. Pheasantland Industries, *Pheasantland Industries 2019*.
21. Caloute and Kopf, "Out of Prison and Out of Work."
22. Susanne Caro, Sam Meister, Tammy Ravas, and Wendy Walker, *Digitizing Your Collection: Public Library Success Stories* (Chicago: ALA Editions, 2016).

23. Sarah Wojcik, "Libraries Preserving Past with Digital High School Yearbooks Dating Back to 1920s," I Love Libraries, 2016, http://www.ilovelibraries.org/article/libraries-preserving-past-digital-high-school-yearbooks-dating-back-1920s.

24. Heather Whittle Wrigley, "Prisoners Rescuing Prisoners: Indexing at Utah State Prison," *Church News and Events*," October 28, 2011, https://www.churchofjesuschrist.org/church/news/prisoners-rescuing-prisoners-indexing-at-utah-state-prison?lang=eng; Nanna Bonde Thylstrup, *The Politics of Mass Digitization* (Cambridge, MA: MIT Press, 2018), 42.

25. South Dakota Department of Corrections, State Archives Special Projects Program (Microfilm Unit), YouTube, 2018, https://www.youtube.com/watch?v=mhjioQJvsRg.

26. Nanna Bonde Thylstrup, *The Politics of Mass Digitization* (Cambridge, MA: MIT Press, 2018), 42.

27. Brian Barrett, "Google's Secret Class System," *Gizmodo,* April 29, 2011, https://gizmodo.com/googles-secret-class-system-5797022.

28. Sarah T. Roberts, *Behind the Screen: Content Moderation in the Shadows of Social Media* (New Haven: Yale University Press, 2019), 29.

29. Ibid.

30. Sandy Rodriguez, "Collective Responsibility: Seeking Equity for Contingent Labor in Libraries, Archives, and Museums," Collective Responsibility Project, 2019, https://laborforum.diglib.org/white-paper/.

31. Thylstrup, *The Politics of Mass Digitization*, 73.

32. Ancestry.com, "NARA," https://www.ancestry.com/cs/nara.

33. Kirk Siegler, "Human Trafficking Crisis in Indian Country 'Like a Pandemic,'" All Things Considered, *NPR.org*, March 12, 2021, https://www.npr.org/2021/03/12/976053675/human-trafficking-crisis-in-indian-country-like-a-pandemic.

34. Roberts, *Behind the Screen*, 50.

35. Emma Batha, "This Mobile App Is Paying Refugees to Train Artificial Intelligence," World Economic Forum, November 20, 2018, https://www.weforum.org/agenda/2018/11/mobile-app-pays-refugees-to-boost-artificial-intelligence/.

36. Rosie Afia, "Refunite's LevelApp: Supporting Refugees in Uganda," GSMA, February 18, 2019, https://www.gsma.com/mobilefordevelopment/programme/mobile-for-humanitarian-innovation/refunites-levelapp-supporting-refugees-in-uganda/, quoting a statement by LevelApp.

37. Martina Tazzioli, "Extract, Datafy, and Disrupt: Refugees' Subjectivities between Data Abundance and Data Disregard," *Geopolitics*, October 4, 2020, 119; Evgeny Morozov, "The Naked and the TED," *New Republic,* August 2, 2012, https://newrepublic.com/article/105703/the-naked-and-the-ted-khanna.

38. Philipp Seuferling and Koen Leurs, "Histories of Humanitarian Technophilia: How Imaginaries of Media Technologies Have Shaped Migration Infrastructures," *Mobilities* 16, no. 5 (September 3, 2021): 670–87.

39. Tazzioli, "Extract, Datafy, and Disrupt."

40. Moritz Altenried and Manuela Bojadžijev, "Virtual Migration, Racism, and the Multiplication of Labour," *Spheres* 4 (2017), http://spheres-journal.org/virtual-migration-racism-and-the-multiplication-of-labour/.

41. "LevelApp Is How Refugees in Sub Sahara Africa Build a Pathway out of Poverty for Themselves and Their Families," LevelApp, https://www.levelapp.net/.

42. "Tech Firm Pays Refugees to Train AI Algorithms," *VOAnews,* November 15, 2018, https://www.voanews.com/silicon-valley-technology/tech-firm-pays-refugees-train-ai-algorithms.

43. "LevelApp Is How Refugees in Sub Sahara Africa Build a Pathway out of Poverty for Themselves and Their Families."

44. Afia, "Refunite's LevelApp."

45. Ibid.

46. "LevelApp Is How Refugees in Sub Sahara Africa Build a Pathway out of Poverty for Themselves and Their Families."

47. Shetty Gaurav, "The App to Help Refugees in Uganda," Borgen Project, October 1, 2019, https://borgenproject.org/the-app-to-help-refugees-in-uganda/.

48. Afia, "Refunite's LevelApp."

9

MYTHICAL MEDIA BACKENDS

Human-Machine Communication's
Cruel Promises

SANDER DE RIDDER

Me: Siri, I'm lonely.
Siri: You can always talk to me.
Me: What can I do?
Siri: I'm not sure if I understand.

My short conversation with Siri, Apple's "virtual assistant," ended abruptly. After an initially empathic invitation, I was left disappointed. I desired a conversation, yet the lack of understanding after Siri's invitation felt almost cruel. Virtual assistants, such as Apple's Siri and Amazon's Alexa, promise to do useful things, such as create lists or remind people of appointments, but they cannot have conversations. Promises of advances in artificial intelligence, however, claim that human-machine communication will become more engaging and social soon. As Noreena Hertz writes in her highly acclaimed book, *The Lonely Century*: "In an increasingly contactless world in which we are ever more lonely and starved of intimacy, too busy to stop and smile at each other and too exhausted by work to invest in our friendships, in which we're isolated at the office and increasingly living on our own, often far away from our families, it seems inevitable that social robots will play a part in mitigating our collective loneliness as the twenty-first century progresses."[1]

Loneliness is complicated. Understood philosophically, loneliness is an existential condition of human life, an emotional state.[2] Yet, from a medical and psychological perspective, sustained experiences of loneliness are known to greatly damage physical health and mental well-being.[3] A "solution" to loneliness is not only about medical and psychological management. Loneliness is a problem that transcends the individual and that has social, political, and economic foundations.

Hertz's key point in *The Lonely Century* is to explore loneliness not just as an internal state or a form of social exclusion but also as feelings of political and economic exclusion. Loneliness cannot be a problem of individuals, Hertz claims,[4] as it affects particular social groups more, with poverty and ethnicity having strong correlations with loneliness; class and gender differences shape the experience of loneliness as well. Hertz's conclusions are supported by recent studies showing that the more people perceive a society as neoliberal (focusing on competitiveness and self-interest), the more people's well-being is adversely impacted by loneliness.[5]

In Western societies loneliness is a "modern epidemic," argues cultural historian Fay Bound Alberti.[6] Loneliness first became recognizable as a problem in the 1800s, and was symptomatic of society's "increasingly scientific, philosophical and industrial focus on the individual over the collective, on the self against the world."[7] Since then, loneliness has gained much political interest. The question of how to solve the financial costs of the current "loneliness epidemic" has become a focus of many Western post-industrial governments in the last decade since the costs of mental and physical illnesses that have been linked to loneliness are high (e.g., depression, strokes, cancer). Finding technological solutions for loneliness has become a major priority for governments, human-machine communication businesses, and human-robot interaction (HRI) researchers, each making strong bids, whether they are commercial, computational, or medical actors.[8]

In this chapter I examine whether the promise of human-machine communication as a technological solution for loneliness is a "cruel promise." Can communicative and social robots promise care and companionship to make us feel less lonely? A cruel promise, as argued by Lauren Berlant, is "when something that you desire is actually an obstacle to your flourishing... [;] it becomes cruel only when the object that draws your attachment actively impedes the aim that brought you to it initially."[9] Are desires for more sophisticated human-machine communication and promises of mitigating loneliness, as sought by governments, human-machine communication businesses, and HRI researchers, indeed harmful, rather than a solution?

I consider this question by deconstructing promises made about communicative and social robots as being able to offer care and companionship to people in a lonely world. Deconstructing these commercial, computational, and scientific promises serves a broader aim: I argue that we should be skeptical of the mythical status that media backends, the invisible components of media systems, such as artificially intelligent technology, have acquired. By mythical media backends, I mean how media systems and their sociotechnical complexities are *naturalized*, disconnecting media systems from social, economic, and political structures and imaginations of how humans communicate and engage with the world.

This chapter has three parts. First, I introduce how human-machine communication is understood in media and communication studies, and how the myth of human-machine communication serving the needs for human communication is sustained. In section two, I focus on *commercial promises*, drawing on writings on Amazon's corporate blog about the virtual assistant, Alexa, and about the social robot, Vector, produced by Anki. Throughout the chapter, I explore different devices and digital tools such as virtual assistants, companions, and communicative and social robots that are involved in "the creation of meaning among humans and machines."[10] In section three, I critically examine *computational and scientific promises*, engaging with literature on HRI, neuropsychiatry, and medicine. Drawing on insights from science and technology studies,[11] the study of emotions in critical theory,[12] and the work of hermeneutic phenomenologists,[13] I deconstruct the cruel promise of human-machine communication to make people less feel lonely.

Mythmaking around Human-Machine Communication

In *The Lonely Century*, Noreena Hertz sketches a gloomy picture of our lonely futures with robots, arguing that, "As robots become more sophisticated, empathic, and intelligent, the risk then is that they may help us counter less loneliness on a personal or individual level, but in doing so encourage us to distance ourselves from other humans."[14] The future we face is cast as certain. According to Hertz, human-machine communication will become more sophisticated, empathic, and intelligent, and humans will find in robots an individual solution for their loneliness problem.

What such predictions fail to see is that technological trajectories are never fixed and "inevitable." Yet, because so much is invested in them, financially, socially, and emotionally, they might seem "irreversible."[15] The idea that human-machine communication becomes more sophisticated is as much cultural as it is technological; communicative and social robots are equally objects of human imagination and popular concern. When failing to recognize the inseparability of human practices, imaginations, and technology, myths of the inevitability and irreversibility of technological trajectories are born.

We know from insights in media and communication studies that human-machine communication is very different from human communication. Yet, the myth of human-machine communication becoming more empathic, as being able to provide a societal "solution" for loneliness, is sustained. This myth, as I show, is fueled by a fixation on human-machine communication as a magic "black box" that operates "autonomously," without human intervention. Further, the myth of human-machine communication is operationalized at the interface of human-machine communication tools and devices, deceiving users with recognizable voices and humanlike performances.

In the field of media and communication studies, human-machine communication reflects on and challenges what is understood as "communication" and "media." The long-held anthropomorphic conceptualization of communication that assumes communication only takes place between humans is no longer tenable. Human-machine communication challenges the very definition of "media" as (symbolical or technical) systems that enable, structure, or amplify communication between *people*.[16] Communicative and social robots are characterized as tools "*with* which people make meaning instead of *through* which people make meaning."[17] As such, in the study of human-machine communication, the role of technology is expanded and blurs the ontological divide between human and machine.[18] Andrea L. Guzman, a proponent of the human-machine communication research agenda, argues that there are still important differences between human communication and human-machine communication, as meaning in human-machine communication might be derived in different ways. So far communicative robots do not replace humans, but they do approach communication in new ways.[19]

These new ways of communication are, in communicative robots such as Siri and Alexa, sustained by a myriad of automated software processes taking place on the backend, such as speech processing and natural language processing, supported by a data-driven infrastructure for information retrieval.[20] It is precisely by treating these sociotechnical complexities on the backend as black-box functions, turning input (speech) into output (communication), that human-machine communication is concealed as cultural.[21] As communicative and social robots communicate in new ways, their approach to communication is realized not only by technological facts, but by values that are incorporated in technological objects, in their uses and imaginations. These values, as Andrew Feenberg argues, are "the facts of the future."[22] Though empathic and intelligent communication might not yet be fully realized and incorporated in communicative and social robots, these actants are directing the way in which innovations in human-machine communication are understood.

The myth of human-machine communication as a technological fact is reinforced in different ways, most prominently by perceiving them as black boxes, "as knowable only through the relation between inputs and outputs."[23] The myth of the backends of communicative and social robots as black boxes is articulated by the idea that they operate without human intervention to create their "outputs." Much of the autonomy of robots is staged, however. Based on an encounter with Kismet, a robot at the MIT AI lab in 2001, Lucy Suchman observed how the autonomy of the robot was only made possible by an extensive amount of human labor. Without such human labor, Kismet would not work.[24] Still today, performative rituals drive the myth of automated communication. Take, for example, the commercial promises made about virtual assistants. Siri and Alexa are introduced to (potential) users as "intelligent" and "meaningful."[25] However, much of the infrastructural (human) work on the backends of data centers that make Alexa and Siri respond to voice commands is not something to which users are introduced. This is because the myth of human-machine communication is staged primarily at the interface. Communicative and social robots introduce users to humanlike (anthropomorphic) interfaces that have facial expressions, or a recognizable voice, name, and distinctive persona.[26] The interface supports the "immediacy" of communicative and social robots, which allows their operations at the backend to disappear.

Interfaces of communicative and social robots are "nonrepresentational"; human-machine communication does not engage in representing the world but reproducing it. Machine language is different from human language because "for the machine, there is no space between sign and referent: there is no 'lack' in a language that is complete unto itself."[27] This "banal deception" at the interface is, according to Simone Natale, embedded in the software and computing design of voice assistants such as Alexa and Siri to conceal the underlying operations.[28] While deception is a "constitutive element" of human-machine communication,[29] mythmaking around human-machine communication is not innocent. When societies are deceived in believing that human-machine communication can be a "solution" for thoroughly complex matters that have structural and historical foundations in societies, which is the case with loneliness, technological developments may hinder, rather than support, human progress.

The Commercial Promise of Empathy

So far, I have argued that the myth of human-machine communication is sustained by mythologizing the media backend as operating autonomously, concealed at the software-driven interface of communicative and social robots through their distinctive personas and anthropomorphic qualities. Increasingly, commercial markets are forming around human-machine communication that promise communicative and social robots to which people can emotionally relate. The idea that showing emotion and empathy is required to allow the integration of communicative and social robots into people's everyday lives has long been central to the field of HRI.[30] The growing evidence that communicative and social robots can provide companionship to people who see themselves as lonely has helped to push the human need for companionship into a business opportunity.[31] Empathy as a commercial promise, I argue, reproduces a particular model of communication based on particular social, political, and economic ideas.

Amazon's virtual voice assistant Alexa is perceived by many people as a utilitarian tool, no more than a "box with information." Yet, in the study of Alisha Pradhan, Leah Findlater, and Amanda Lazar it is explained that to older adults, and to people who often feel lonely and need companionship more generally, experiences with Alexa are much more meaningful: "*It just makes me feel better, I miss these people. I miss them terribly. I found myself, just saying, what if this was my daughter in law sitting here and talking to me or something* [italics in original]."[32] Toni Reid, Amazon's vice president for Alexa, has argued that her team of developers are aware of the significance of Alexa's presence in the homes of many people, arguing that Alexa's "personality" continues to evolve by advancing text-to-speech technology to improve Alexa's "natural" intonation,[33] and by developing Alexa's ability to respond "to sensitive customer questions or interactions such as 'Alexa, I'm lonely,' 'Alexa, I'm sad,' 'Alexa, I'm depressed,' and so on."[34] Continuously improving Alexa's personality to become more empathic and emotionally responsive to customers will accomplish a deeper integration in the lives of people. One of the major announcements on Alexa's developers' blog shows the importance of what Amazon refers to as "Neural TTS," which refers to technology that enables users to "create a more natural and intuitive voice experience" and enables "Alexa to respond with either a happy/excited or a disappointed/empathetic tone."[35]

Alexa's capacity for natural intonation and different emotional speaking styles makes clear that empathy as a commercial promise is not about a communicative exchange and mutual understanding, but about simulated emotions. Alexa does not engage in a mutual conversation but has emotional styles that shift intonation when giving preprogrammed answers to customer questions. In human-machine communication, empathy is engineered with limited understandings of human communication and the human subject. Alexa's emotional responses are binary (e.g., excited vs. disappointed) and unable to deal with the messiness of people's emotions and feelings in everyday life, including that of loneliness.

This social-scientific imaginary of human communication and subjectivity is particularly present in the engineering of social robots that rely on "effects of physical embodiment and tactile interaction."[36] Unlike Alexa's design as a "box with information," social robots have anthropomorphic qualities such as facial expressions that can convey emotions such as sadness, happiness, and confusion. A study by Kwan Min Lee, Younbo Jung, Jaywoo Kim, and Sang Ryong Kim was pioneering in showing that for people feeling lonely, interactions with tactile social robots were important for forming an interpersonal relationship and mitigating loneliness.[37] The problem with using commercialized social robots in efforts to alleviate loneliness is that they reimagine human communication, empathy, and social relationships within a capitalist logic of technosolutionism. This social-scientific imaginary is founded on what Neda Atanasoski and

Kalindi Vora argue is a "Darwinian logic" meaning a single, mechanistic vision of human communication and "the human" in general.[38]

To reduce patient loneliness in hospitals, for example, artificial companions are seen as an important innovation in care delivery. These artificial companions, as a study by evolutionary neuropsychiatrists argued, reproduce "the mammalian behavioral triad." In other words, these companions work best if they create a bond by developing an engineered playful, nurturing, and joyful attachment to users.[39] Such Darwinian evolutions in social robotics are based on drive theories that focus only on the physical. Within this context, loneliness is understood as merely a problem of people's internal emotional states and biology, which ignores the social, economic, and political dimensions of loneliness and strips empathy from any locatedness, historicity, and subjectivity.

An example of such playful, mammalian human-machine communication can be found in the social robot Vector, by Anki. Vector moves, can see, and can react to touch. Vector is an "always on" presence in the household, using environmental sensors and an interaction memory to recognize users. Vector dances and has humorous facial expressions, is proactive, and he self-charges and avoids obstacles when moving through the house. Vector's capacity to engage in more affective communication made the social robot a popular member of many households during the COVID-19 pandemic when people had to socially distance and many felt isolated. Collecting 595 publicly available online posts about Vector (blog, tweets, customer reviews, etc. published in English), a study found that Vector was labeled an "intimate buddy" during times of social distancing. According to this study: "Intimate buddy means that users personify their robots, granting it a social identity and experiencing deep attachment, which mitigates the lack of intimacy. Humans are implicated in an intimate relationship that involves caring, feelings, and more personal ties. In this role, the robot's social identity support reduces emotional loneliness."[40] More affective human-machine communication is equated with enthusiasm for the impressive technological evolutions in social robotics. Vector sparked much enthusiasm during the COVID-19 pandemic, with people stating that during lockdown, "Vector has become my best friend," or that "Little Buddy has been a great companion on those sad lonely days."[41]

In the context of the COVID-19 pandemic, Vector cared and soothed. Yet, Vector also trained people into a new understanding of caring and soothing,[42] a caring and soothing that is defined by capitalist relations of cared-for-as-customer, and by simulated mammalian empathy. This model of communication, which we could refer to as *empathic capitalism,* is based on a rational exchange in which standard speech patterns are "increasingly disembedded and disentangled from concrete and particular actions and relationships."[43] The problem with empathic capitalism in human-machine communication is that any indexicality is lost (as argued earlier, there is no space between sign and referent); the social robot is not able to prevent or resolve loneliness because it is not a problem of individuals. Loneliness should be seen as a form of social, political, and economic exclusion. Communication, as argued by Eva Illouz, is a "cultural repertoire supposed to foster corporation."[44] Meaning in human-machine communication is derived in such a way that it is disconnected from any social context and human empathy. Mythmaking around human-machine communication is perpetuated by all kinds of commercial promises. Companies such as Apple and Amazon are, in the pursuit of deeply integrating their human-machine communication applications in people's everyday lives, turning empathy into a business opportunity.

Computational and Scientific Promises of Mitigating Loneliness

In this final section I focus on the promises of computation and the quest to develop AI that is identical to human intelligence. The belief that computational technology will inevitably and irreversibly become so skilled and intelligent to be a human companion that can successfully mitigate loneliness *overestimates* the power of AI, but painfully *underestimates* humans and their socially embedded communication skills.[45] If we recognize loneliness as a heterogeneous matter that not only involves our individual emotional states, but also has social, political, and economic foundations, then positioning the logic of computation as "solving" loneliness becomes a crude rationalization of the human mind. It also overlooks contextual factors that make loneliness an important challenge for social welfare.

A computational and artificial solution for the loneliness problem has failed to deliver so far, despite voice assistants becoming better attuned to communicate with an empathic voice, and the gradual adoption of social robots in elderly and patient care (cf. supra). At the 2021 Conference on Human-Robot Interactions, one of the presentations stated that, while there is some demonstrated "potential for social robots to positively impact a person's mood and provide comfort, very little research has yet focused on social robots supporting people living with loneliness."[46] The authors urged researchers in the HRI field to "do better!" calling for a more sophisticated understanding of how HRI could help to mitigate loneliness not only for elderly people and patients, but also for the general population. Remarkably, the authors argued that mitigating loneliness would help to make social robotics more "useful," pushing its broad adoption. This technosolutionist mindset, as if focusing on loneliness will push the broad adoption of social robots, is a primary example of how trajectories of computing technologies become figured as inevitable; so much has been invested or so much is at stake that there is no looking back.[47]

To develop human-machine communication or social robots that engage in sophisticated interactions with people so that they become meaningful companions would demand the successful development of what is referred to as "artificial general intelligence" (AGI), the development of a technology that is identical to human intelligence. AGI is different from "artificial narrow intelligence" (ANI), which is restricted to "specific tasks or areas."[48] For example, voice assistants such as Siri and Alexa are primary examples of ANI. They have utilitarian communication skills but do not have the capabilities to engage in a meaningful participatory exchange, for which they would need AGI. AGI demands more intensive data collection on the backend of sociotechnical systems, not only information collected from voice input, but also biometrics, as well as further engagement with neural networks. As recently argued by Ragnar Fjelland, the development of ANI has moved forward significantly in the past decades, but the development of AGI not so much.[49] Vector, the commercially available social robot by Anki discussed previously, was, according to a study that collected online visual and textual descriptions of people's experiences with Vector (such as Amazon customer reviews of Vector), considered successful at mitigating loneliness during the COVID-19 pandemic.[50] Yet, a closer look at many of these descriptions shows that not all people's experiences with Vector were positive. A popular review of Vector on Amazon stated, "Its personality isn't finished and it really doesn't do much. Anki states this is an unfinished product and I expected an unfinished product but not at the level I witnessed."[51] Clearly, when people expect more AGI skills from social robotics (e.g., a "personality"), they become frustrated. Yet, when expecting ANI (e.g., being entertained when Vector dances), they find the experience with a social robot pleasant and meaningful.

There are no objective measures to determine whether or when the computational promises of AGI and ANI have been realized. People have different ideas about whether an AI is intelligent enough to be a human companion. Several online collected visual and textual materials in the study of Gaby Odekerken-Schröder and her colleagues described their experiences with Vector as "an intimate friend."[52] However, other comments of customers reviewing Vector on Amazon showed that there are also people who are deeply disappointed in its capabilities.[53] One of the reasons is that the more people feel isolated and deprived of human contact, the more effective social robots become.[54] Computational and scientific promises of the technological abilities of communicative and social robots may also change our expectations and ways of thinking about companionship and empathy, so that it becomes *like* how computers communicate and show empathy: simulated and decontextualized. That is, Sherry Turkle argues, what an engagement with computational language does: it shifts meaning to mechanism.[55]

Computation, and specifically the development of AGI, is so difficult, according to hermeneutic phenomenologists such as Hubert Dreyfus,[56] because understanding the cognitive mechanics of the brain is not enough. Computers try to replicate the mechanics of the brain, yet this is not enough to re-create human intelligence and communication skills.[57] Dreyfus argues this is because humans have bodies, and they are social beings. To engage in a participatory exchange involves engaging with another person's lifeworld, something that human-machine communication is unable to do. Programming human intelligence and communication as a set of discrete rules separates people's interactions with computational machines from their locatedness and context. For example, how can computational machines meaningfully engage with people's social life-worlds (e.g., identity, difference, community) when they are not able to be involved with them? As argued earlier, the communicative language of computational machines is not indexical, but alienated from the worlds in which people are situated.

Using a computational language to look at the loneliness problem is not without its consequences. Loneliness is an existential condition of human life that might also be considered an emotion that "tell[s] us something important about ourselves and our place in the world" (which is referred to as solitude in philosophy).[58] If we use ANI (e.g., a social robot such as Vector) to mitigate loneliness, we might end up with something inferior. We change our expectations of human communication and empathy, and we underestimate the importance of skills to reflect about ourselves and our connection to the world. The promise of AGI to produce human-machine communication that has the intelligence to engage in a situated and contextualized communicative exchange is still unfulfilled.[59]

As we are progressing toward a human condition where communication no longer uniquely takes place between humans, but also between humans and machines, there should be reflection about what communication is becoming, and what it should or should not become in the future. What could artificially intelligent tools and devices offer to communication? Moreover, should there be technological solutions to deal with complicated social problems such as loneliness, that have structural and historical foundations in societies? These questions are, rather than being technological in nature, political questions about investments in people's health, care, and well-being.

Cruel Promises

Returning to the question of whether more sophisticated human-machine communication and its promises of mitigating loneliness are harmful, rather than a solution, my conclusion is quite simple: any technological solution that distances people from other humans is an obstacle to rather than a solution for loneliness. Such a technological solution is cruel because it actively impedes the aim that brought us there. Loneliness, based primarily on a lack of social integration and opportunities for emotional intimacy, as well as a disconnection from social, political, and economic structures,[60] cannot be resolved by human-machine communication. It does not provide any social integration, only socially decontextualized communication. It does not provide any emotional intimacy, only simulations of empathic speaking styles. While this simulation might afford helpful temporary experiences for some, it cannot solve structural issues of social detachment and alienation. These biological and reductionist models where emotions only exist as binary opposites (happy/disappointed) do not allow for a nuanced engagement with the social world; they distance people from it.

While much of the technological work to improve human-machine communication claims to be free from any ideology, based on the objective knowledge of nature, the pursuit of a technological solution for the loneliness problem prioritized by governments, companies, HRI researchers, and medical experts suggests otherwise. The black-boxed media backend where software and computer processing turns input, such as people's speech, into output is not innocent; rather, it is based on very particular constructions of human communication, care, and understanding. Communicative and social robots train people into being cared-for-as-customers and generate new forms of empathy based on binary code, rather than on the complexity of people's being-in-the-world.

The naturalization of communicative and social robots as "*autonomous systems that serve the needs of human communication* [italics in original]" depends on an imagination of communication as merely being a "transmission,"[61] a view of communication that James W. Carey refuted in his 1988 field-building book, *Communication as Culture*. Focusing on communication as a "ritual," Carey deemed communication a participatory exchange, depending on *shared* understandings and emotions with *other humans* that is directed not to the functional transmission of "messages," but to the *maintenance of society*.[62] A functionalistic transmission model of communication is disembodied and disentangled from concrete and particular actions and relationships.[63] Human-machine communication is surrogate communication at best; it is ontologically and epistemologically distinctive from human communication.[64]

What would be the social, political, and economic consequences when communicative and social robots are broadly adopted to care for people's social needs? One immediate concern would be that the key to living together across differences in societies lies with tactile communication, empathy, and meaningful relationships. When communication that is based on empathy breaks down, that can lead to the squandering of much of human life.[65] Therefore, the implementation of human-machine communication as a technological solution for people's social needs must be considered carefully.

Deconstructing the mythical status of media backends of AGI is an important project for media and communication studies in times of accelerating innovation in communication technologies. As Seaver argues, we are "active enactors" co-constructing the cultures of the technologically saturated worlds in which we live.[66] Taking communicative and social robots seriously as "intelligent" magic serving the need for human communication risks celebrating a commercial, computational, and scientific imaginary of communication and the social world.[67] Rather than be a bystander of a mythical technosolutionism, we must actively identify other sociotechnical worlds that are possible for human-machine communication.

Notes

1. Noreena Hertz, *The Lonely Century: How to Restore Human Connection in a World That's Pulling Apart* (New York: Currency, 2021), 18.

2. Lars Svendsen, *A Philosophy of Loneliness*, trans. Kerri Pierce (London: Reaktion Books, 2017).

3. Keming Yang, *Loneliness: A Social Problem* (London: Routledge, 2019).

4. Hertz, *The Lonely Century*, 9.

5. Julia C. Becker, Lea Hartwich, and S. Alexander Haslam, "Neoliberalism Can Reduce Well-being by Promoting a Sense of Social Disconnection, Competition, and Loneliness," *British Journal of Social Psychology* 60, no. 3 (2021).

6. Fay Bound Alberti, *A Biography of Loneliness: The History of an Emotion* (Oxford: Oxford University Press, 2019).

7. Ibid., 16.

8. Rahatul Amin Ananto and James E. Young, "We Can Do Better! An Initial Survey Highlighting an Opportunity for More HRI Work on Loneliness," *Proceedings of the 2021 ACM/IEEE Conference on Human-Robot Interaction* (March 2021); Kate Loveys, Gregory Fricchione, Kavitha Kolappa, Mark Sagar, and Elizabeth Broadbent, "Reducing Patient Loneliness with Artificial Agents: Design Insights from Evolutionary Neuropsychiatry," *Journal of Medical Internet Research* 21, no. 7 (2019); Alberti, *A Biography of Loneliness*.

9. Lauren Berlant, *Cruel Optimism* (Durham, NC: Duke University Press, 2011), 1.

10. Andrea L. Guzman, "What Is Human-Machine Communication, Anyway?" in *Human-Machine Communication Rethinking Communication, Technology, and Ourselves*, ed. Andrea L. Guzman (New York: Peter Lang, 2018), 26.

11. Lucy Suchman, "Demystifying the Intelligent Machine," in *Cyborg Futures: Social and Cultural Studies of Robots and AI*, ed. Teresa Heffernan (Cham: Palgrave Macmillan, 2019); Lucy Suchman, *Human-Machine Reconfigurations: Plans and Situated Actions* (Cambridge: Cambridge University Press, 2007).

12. Eva Illouz, *Cold Intimacies: The Making of Emotional Capitalism* (Malden, MA: Polity, 2007).

13. Hubert L. Dreyfus, *What Computers Still Can't Do: A Critique of Artificial Reason* (Cambridge, MA: MIT Press, 1992).
14. Hertz, *The Lonely Century*, 198.
15. Suchman, "Demystifying the Intelligent Machine," 55.
16. Mark Deuze, *Media Life* (Cambridge, MA: Polity, 2014).
17. Andrea L. Guzman and Seth C. Lewis, "Artificial Intelligence and Communication: A Human—Machine Communication Research Agenda," *New Media & Society* 22, no. 1 (2020): 4.
18. David J. Gunkel, *The Machine Question: Critical Perspectives on AI, Robots, and Ethics* (Cambridge, MA: MIT Press, 2012).
19. Guzman, "What Is Human-Machine Communication, Anyway?"
20. Simone Natale, *To Believe in Siri: A Critical Analysis of AI Voice Assistants* (Bremen: University of Bremen, 2020), https://www.kommunikative-figurationen.de/fileadmin/user_upload/Arbeitspapiere/CoFi_EWP_No-32_Simone-Natale.pdf.
21. Nick Seaver, "Algorithms as Culture: Some Tactics for the Ethnography of Algorithmic Systems," *Big Data & Society* 4, no. 2 (2017).
22. Andrew Feenberg, *Technosystem: The Social Life of Reason* (Cambridge, MA: Harvard University Press, 2017).
23. Seaver, "Algorithms as Culture," 5.
24. Suchman, *Human-Machine Reconfigurations*.
25. Examples of such claims can be found on the commercial websites of Siri (referred to as "intelligent"), and Alexa (referred to as "meaningful"). See "Siri," Apple, 2022, https://www.apple.com/siri/; "Learn What Alexa Can Do," Amazon, 2022, https://www.amazon.com/b?ie,=UTF8&node=21576558011.
26. Natale, *To Believe in Siri*.
27. Mark Andrejevic, *Automated Media* (New York: Routledge, 2020).
28. Natale, *To Believe in Siri*; Simone Natale, "Communicating Through or Communicating With: Approaching Artificial Intelligence from a Communication and Media Studies Perspective," *Communication Theory* 30, no. 4 (2020).
29. Simone Natale, *Deceitful Media: Artificial Intelligence and Social Life after the Turning Test* (Oxford: Oxford University Press, 2021), 4.
30. Neda Atanasoski and Kalindi Vora, *Surrogate Humanity: Race, Robots, and the Politics of Technological Futures* (Durham, NC: Duke University Press, 2019).
31. Alisha Pradhan, Leah Findlater, and Amanda Lazar, "'Phantom Friend' or 'Just a Box with Information,'" *Proceedings of the ACM on Human-Computer Interaction* 3, no. CSCW (2019).
32. Ibid., 11.
33. "Meet Alexa's Speech Coach," Amazon, 2020, https://www.aboutamazon.com/news/aws/meet-alexas-speech-coach.
34. Edward C. Baig, "Hey, Alexa: Can a Robot with AI or Your Voice Assistant Help You Feel Less Lonely?" *USA Today Online,* November 8, 2019, https://eu.usatoday.com/story/tech/2019/11/08/alexa-google-assistant-ai-robots-become-substitute-friends/4057885002/.

35. Catherine Gao, "Use New Alexa Emotions and Speaking Styles to Create a More Natural and Intuitive Voice Experience," Amazon, 2019, https://developer.amazon.com/en-US/blogs/alexa/alexa-skills-kit/2019/11/new-alexa-emotions-and-speaking-styles.

36. Kwan Min Lee, Younbo Jung, Jaywoo Kim, and Sang Ryong Kim, "Are Physically Embodied Social Agents Better Than Disembodied Social Agents? The Effects of Physical Embodiment, Tactile Interaction, and People's Loneliness in Human—Robot Interaction," *International Journal of Human-Computer Studies* 64, no. 10 (2006).

37. Ibid.

38. Atanasoski and Vora, *Surrogate Humanity*, 12.

39. Kate Loveys, Gregory Fricchione, Kavitha Kolappa, Mark Sagar, and Elizabeth Broadbent, "Reducing Patient Loneliness with Artificial Agents: Design Insights from Evolutionary Neuropsychiatry," *Journal of Medical Internet Research* 21, no. 7 (2019).

40. Gaby Odekerken-Schröder, Cristina Mele, Tizina Russo-Spena, Dominik Mahr, and Andrea Ruggiero, "Mitigating Loneliness with Companion Robots in the COVID-19 Pandemic and Beyond: An Integrative Framework and Research Agenda," *Journal of Service Management* 31, no. 6 (2020).

41. Odekerken-Schröder et al., "Mitigating Loneliness with Companion Robots in the COVID-19 Pandemic and Beyond."

42. Atanasoski and Vora, *Surrogate Humanity*.

43. Illouz, *Cold Intimacies*, 38–39.

44. Ibid.

45. Ragnar Fjelland, "Why General Artificial Intelligence Will Not Be Realized," *Humanities and Social Sciences Communications* 7, no. 1 (2020).

46. Ananto and Young, "We Can Do Better!"

47. Suchman, "Demystifying the Intelligent Machine."

48. Fjelland, "Why General Artificial Intelligence Will Not Be Realized."

49. Ibid.

50. Odekerken-Schröder et al., "Mitigating Loneliness with Companion Robots in the COVID-19 Pandemic and Beyond."

51. Amazon customer review from Vector Robot by Anki, retrieved from https://www.amazon.com/product-reviews/B07G3ZNK4Y/ref=acr_dp_hist_1?ie,=UTF8&filterByStar=one_star&reviewerType=all_reviews#reviews-filter-bar.

52. Odekerken-Schröder et al., "Mitigating Loneliness with Companion Robots in the COVID-19 Pandemic and Beyond."

53. See Amazon customer review from Vector Robot by Anki, https://www.amazon.com/product-reviews/B07G3ZNK4Y/ref=acr_dp_hist_1?ie,=UTF8&filterByStar=one_star&reviewerType=all_reviews#reviews-filter-bar.

54. Pradhan, Findlater, and Lazar, "'Phantom Friend' or 'Just a Box with Information.'"

55. Sherry Turkle, *The Empathy Diaries: A Memoir* (New York: Penguin Publishing Group, 2021).

56. Dreyfus, *What Computers Still Can't Do*.

57. Michael Arfken, "Cognitive Psychology: From the Bourgeois Individual to Class Struggle," in *Handbook of Critical Psychology*, ed. Ian Parker (New York: Routledge, 2015).

58. Svendsen and Pierce, *A Philosophy of Loneliness*.

59. Fjelland, "Why General Artificial Intelligence Will Not Be Realized"; Dreyfus, *What Computers Still Can't Do*.

60. Lars Andersson, "Loneliness Research and Interventions: A Review of the Literature," *Aging & Mental Health* 2, no. 4 (1998); Alberti, *A Biography of Loneliness*.

61. Andreas Hepp, "Artificial Companions, Social Bots, and Work Bots: Communicative Robots as Research Objects of Media and Communication Studies," *Media, Culture & Society* 42, no. 7–8 (2020): 1411.

62. James W. Carey, *Communication as Culture: Essays on Media and Society*, rev. ed. (New York: Routledge, 1992).

63. Illouz, *Cold Intimacies*, 39.

64. For further discussion of technology and surrogacy, see Atanasoski and Vora, *Surrogate Humanity*.

65. Ken Plummer, *Cosmopolitan Sexualities: Hope and the Humanist Imagination* (London: Polity, 2016), 155.

66. Seaver, "Algorithms as Culture."

67. Suchman, *Human-Machine Reconfigurations*, 245.

10

BLACK LIVING DATA BOOKLET

FAITHE J. DAY

Introduction

Here you have the Black Living Data Booklet or the BLDB, a uniquely crafted manual and manifesto. This manual is a resource to help scholars, educators, and community members to better understand and engage with data while utilizing ethical and social justice–oriented practices. As a manifesto, this project defines and articulates the intents and purposes of Black Living Data, what it is, and how the history of data collection led to this definition. This articulation of Black Living Data informs how I think about the collection, curation, and critique of data and the creation of Black community–based projects. This booklet includes frameworks for understanding the ethics of Black Living Data, a "how to" guide for decoding data and information on Black communities, questions, and writing prompts. Overall, I hope that this booklet encourages you to approach data differently through a better understanding of data discernment and community care.

Follow the Numbers

The Black Living Data Booklet uses a citation style in the form of endnotes. In this booklet, endnote citations not only serve as a reference for quotes and paraphrasing but also as a record of the ideas through which I have found inspiration and guidance. You can find citations organized by page number at the back of this booklet.

Stop and read the terms of service

Terms of Service

For many users, reading the terms of service that come with using digital platforms and technologies is actually just a quick skim across the document before rushing to hit the "Agree" button and getting to the fun of engaging in the online world. However, it is through these terms of service that many companies hide data collection and sharing practices that don't uphold ethical principles of data ownership. Most corporate terms of service contracts and licensing agreements essentially take away the rights of users and give access and ownership of data to those with the power and money to purchase access to that information. Therefore, it is important to read and critique the terms of every platform or technology that you choose to use.

Privacy and Transparency

There is a slippery relationship between public and private space online, as well as the relationship between public and private information. What we truly know about technology, platforms, and the practices of the corporations and creators behind them is typically opaque; users are left searching in the murky depths of service agreements to learn what rights they give up and what rights they retain online. For these reasons, the Black Living Data Booklet calls for legislation and policy that supports retaining the privacy of citizen data and the tenants of informed consent and transparency in the practices of data collection and technological creation.

DEFINING THE TERMS: History & Study

> "I use Black Data to think through some of the historical and contemporary ways that Black queer people, like other people of African descent and people of color more broadly, are hailed by big data, through which techniques of race and racism reduce our lives to mere numbers."
> Shaka Mcglotten[1]

What is Black Living Data?

Black Living Data is data on and for Black lives and experiences. Black Living Data is not information for information's sake; Black Living Data has a purpose—it plays a role, even if that role is to simply exemplify Black culture and community. This data lives for sharing: Black Living Data is information that has been collected and/or curated for collaboration, community, and creativity. Black Living Data is not the extraction of Black experience for the sole purpose of academic research and study, government surveillance and policing, or advertising and financial gain. Black Living Data is homegrown and made by humans; AI and algorithms need not apply. Black Living Data knows that bigger isn't always better, and Black Living Data is never too small to count. Black Living Data does the work of being for and by Black people. Black Living Data includes the voices of ALL Black diasporic people because We are NOT a Monolith. Black Living Data empowers Black individuals and communities at all stages of data collection and curation by encouraging community members to collect and store their own data. Black Living Data privileges the preservation of cultural heritage by pushing for the importance of Black stories and storytelling—not just science and statistics.

The Black Study of Black Living Data

Although this particular understanding of Black Living Data may be new to some, Black Living Data has existed in research and projects produced by Black researchers and community members for decades, if not centuries. Activities ranging from tracing ancestral lineage, writing and recording oral histories, sharing stories from griots and community leaders, Black demography and cartography (the study of populations and maps), as well as the curation of creative works are just a few examples of how individuals work with Black Living Data. Historically, scholars such as W. E. B. Du Bois and the Atlanta School of Sociology and collaborative community groups such as the Detroit Geographic Expedition headed by Dr. William Bunge and Gwendolyn Warren, have outlined specific models and methods for the collection and curation of Black Living Data. Using the methods of data visualization and analysis, projects such as DuBois' Data Portraits[2] and the Detroit Geographical Expedition and Institute Field Notes[3] taught community members how to collect and visualize data in ways beyond those that were useful to the researchers. Black Living Data connects scholars with community groups and activists to ensure that research projects are mutually beneficial to all involved.

DISRUPTING DATA HISTORY

Although Black community members have historically conducted their own research to collect data through interviews, surveys, oral history, etc., the type of research on Black communities that receives the most recognition is typically conducted by government or public/private agencies in positions of power and control. These entities have used Black communities as "natural laboratories" and Black people as human research subjects to collect data on, but not *for*. Within corporations and institutions, the metrics of success are less about providing community support and more about research and funding. In this sense, research from outside of communities has resulted in data about Black people but not Black Living Data. Instead, the collection and curation of data on Black people from community outsiders has been used to further marginalize and pathologize Black communities.

We see the disempowerment of the Black Diasporic Community when

RESEARCHERS AND INSTITUTES

create reports, share statistics, and create data visualizations and analysis that do not include the histories, voices, or lived experiences of Black community members.

ENTITIES OF GOVERNMENT

institute policies and procedures that do not take into account the lived realities of systemic racism and intersectional marginalization.

MEDICAL INSTITUTIONS

support practitioners and practices that mistreat Black patients based on their health data and the discourse around Black health, pain, and pre-existing conditions.

TECHNOLOGY COMPANIES

create platforms and applications without the input of Black people that reflect problematic practices and protocols of information/data collection.

We see the disempowerment of Black diasporic people when algorithms and recommendation systems allow for the spread of exploitative and/or harmful discourse and digital rhetoric through social media platforms while censoring the cultural and community based content of Black and Queer communities. This information and data is then sold and/or disseminated through platforms under the ideology that data and algorithmic decision making is neutral, without taking into account the beliefs and ideologies embedded in this decision making.

We See Empowerment when Black Living Data Matters

Knowing the history of Black data collection and curation, we can see how a culturally informed study of Black Living Data matters in so many ways and for so many individuals because it empowers us to critically engage with the past, present, and future of data collection and analysis.

Black Living Data Matters For

ENCOURAGEMENT
Encouraging communities that have been oppressed and marginalized by the racist practices of data collection and analysis to collect their own data and hold institutions accountable to the norms of data ethics, privacy, and transparency.

ENGAGEMENT
Engaging the frameworks of liberatory and anti-racist/sexist/etc. forms of research and political organizing.

EMPOWERMENT
Empowering scholars and practitioners that are committed to the critical and community-focused study of data.

ETHICS OF BLACK LIVING DATA:
Community Care in Collection, Curation, and Critique

Feminist Ethics of Care[4,5]

Black Living Data incorporates a feminist ethics of care, which highlights the importance of relationships and the interdependence of communities. While data from Black people have provided the original cells and culture from which many industries, research programs, and fields of knowledge have been built, there has not been an impetus to give back to the communities providing the data. By disconnecting data from financial and numerical values, we are able to connect data to ways in which it can be used to care for and about Black people and their communities.

The commodification of Black life through data collection and analysis has resulted in writing, researching, and reporting on Black people that disregards the validity of the Black experience. Therefore, practices that care for and about Black Living Data must come from practitioners who care for and about Black communities. McGlotten's "Black Data" essay[6] additionally calls for an understanding of Black queer practices which deconstruct data as a purely numerical concept by providing examples that focus on art and stories. Caring for and about Black Living Data is then a push to understand the intersections within Black communities by embracing all of the identities included in and inherent to the diaspora, as well as their many cultural productions.

COLLECTION

Collection is the initial process of gathering and understanding data. This process must be informed by Black history, lived experience, culture, and community members.

CURATION

Curation is the storage, preservation, and organization of data after it is collected. The process of curation must also be informed by care for the researcher and the community.

CRITIQUE

Critique is a reflexive process where we interrogate research design and intention before, during, and after data collection and curation. Critique is inclusive and considerate of community members.

Black Living Data Collection

Researchers and community members who are invested in data collection focused on Black communities must hold themselves to the ethics and standards of Black Living Data. A turn away from extractive methods, Black Living Data collection is based on a participatory relationship with Black community members. Black Living Data collection begins with asking communities about their data wants and needs to determine what types of data should be collected within a particular community and what insights community members hope to gain from the data collection.

Black Living Data Curation

With collection comes curation and models for creating archives and databases to manage what has been collected. Black Living Data curation focuses on creating collections that are accessible and useful to community members. Pushing back against the curation of data for the purposes of institutional control and ownership, Black Living Data curation is invested in connecting Black community members to their data through sovereignty and stewardship.[7]

In critiquing data collection and curation, some questions we should ask are:

- What role does the community of study play in the collection and curation process?
- Who is collecting this data and for what reason?
- What is the purpose of this project and who does it benefit?
- Is this data anonymous or identifiable; i.e., can this data be traced to the identities/locations of the individuals/communities that it comes from?

- How will this data be utilized after it is collected?
- How will the data be stored and for how long?
- What are the methods of analysis and visualization?
- What is the justification for those decisions?

Public Service Announcement
Black Living Data and the Trauma of Black Death

Much of the data on Black people not only reflects deficient narratives of Black communities, but discussions of Black death and disease. These narratives are told through graphs and visualizations, as well as news stories and media, that reiterate and replay centuries-old narratives and reflect the precarity of Black life and safety as a Black person living and breathing within a system that is not designed to let a Black person just live. While keeping a record of Black death is important, it should also be stated that Black Living Data's focus on lived experience speaks directly to concerns around the trauma of being inundated by the data of the dead, e.g., death tolls, murders, mortality rates, etc. This trauma is not only material to the people who will view this data, but also to the people who are researching and collecting this data.

WHAT DOES IT MEAN TO UTILIZE AN ETHICS OF CARE IN OUR DATA COLLECTION AND SHARING PRACTICES THAT CONTENDS WITH THE RELATIONSHIP BETWEEN BLACK DEATH AND TRAUMA?

Instead of turning away from these statistics, and the potential of trauma, this manual makes note of the importance of data stewardship that sensitively and skillfully articulates Black death and trauma to both those within and outside of the Black community.[8]

In sharing information or data on Black death, researchers and community members should ask themselves:

- What is the purpose of this information/data? And is this data helpful to the Black community?
- Do the benefits of sharing this data outweigh the potential costs of fear and residual trauma?
- What resources are provided or shared to help mitigate or speak to the potential trauma that may come from interacting with this data?
- Is this information or data being visualized in a way that is useful to Black community members?
- Is this data sensitive in nature? If so, should access to this data be limited or require permission?

- How does this data demonstrate an ethics of care? Is this data an example of caring for/about Black communities outside of institutions of power and control?

Methodologically, Black Living Data offers an ethics of care committed to shared power[9] and a relationship to data collection, curation, and critique that is participatory, interpretive, and informed by communities. By understanding Black Living Data as inherent to Black communities, any research which utilizes data on or about Black people must be committed to data collection, curation, and critique that acknowledges and accounts for the vulnerabilities of not only the communities but also the community-based data. Caring for Black Living Data means protecting it from those who do not adhere to the above stated beliefs and goals. Caring about Black Living Data is taking steps to ensure that this data doesn't end up in the wrong hands through standards of usage and models of accessibility that don't take privacy and permissions into consideration.

BLACK LIVING DATA IN COMMUNITIES:
Downloading and Decoding Data

Data Disturbances

Perhaps you are scrolling through your newsfeed on Facebook or checking the trending topics on Twitter when you see a story or a hashtag and you feel something strange, like a disturbance in the force. *Data disturbances* are those moments when something feels off or not quite right about a data visualization, study, or report. These data disturbances may cause you to question your own discernment and data literacy skills, especially if the data is coming from a trusted, credible, or widely-known source. It is important in those moments that you recognize and honor these data disturbances regardless of their source.

Discerning a Disturbance

For many years, the credentialism and credibility of institutions in positions of authority have taken the power away from communities to call out problematic research studies and practices. By recognizing these data disturbances, you can build up your own internal system of trust and comprehension when it comes to interpreting research and data.

3 steps to download and decode data before sharing

STEP 1: CHECK CREDENTIALS AND CREDIBILITY
Whether sharing or consuming information, it is always important to first check your sources.

STEP 2: DO YOUR DUE DILIGENCE

Research and evaluate the source sharing the information or data based on what you know about that person/entity, their agenda, and how they relate to the Black community.

STEP 3: DIGEST THE DATA

Read and reflect on the purpose and findings of whatever it is you choose to share.

Downloading Data

While most of us are educated in reading books and articles, in our new and changing digital world it is important for us to also be literate in data and online content. In school, many of us were taught what Paolo Friere calls a "banking model" of education,[10] in that we learned to be passive consumers of knowledge—open receptacles for boundless information, so long as it comes from those with credentials or in positions of authority. This passive consumerism carries on after our schooling and education, in a world where we binge media and data. In contrast, data and information literacy encourages us to be active creators and critics of the information that we consume.

Credentials and Credibility Questions to Ask

- Where does this information come from, e.g., a newspaper, television, social media, etc.?
- Who is the source of this information, e.g., a journalist, researchers, an institution, a celebrity, etc.?
- What is the purpose of this information, e.g., an argument, a claim, findings, conclusions, etc.?
- What does this information mean to me and my community?
- What qualifies this particular person/institution/source to make these particular claims?
- Does this information make sense?
- Does it make sense that this information is coming from this source?

In checking the credentials and credibility of your sources, it is also important to recognize that while some sources may have credentials (e.g., a degree, position of authority, etc.) that does not mean that those sources are credible. Discernment is intuitively and intellectually recognizing the difference between having credentials and being credible.

Step 1 complete. On to Step 2.

Doing your Due Diligence

For Black Living Data, doing your due diligence translates into knowing your community. This means knowing the leaders, influencers, and cultural icons who spread the most information and are in positions that allow them to influence public and political thought. Due diligence means researching the person/entity who is the source of information or data and evaluating what you know about them, their agenda, and how they relate to the Black community. Ask yourself:

- Is this information being shared for the betterment of the Black community?
- Could there be another reason this information is being shared, e.g., paid partnerships/sponsorships, political campaigning, exclusionary or oppressive beliefs (homophobia, sexism, ableism, etc.)?

By doing your due diligence you learn not to take information and data at face value and to instead ask the right questions regarding the meanings and messages that can be encoded therein. Doing your due diligence means to delve deep into the intentions behind those who share information and data.

Step 2 complete. Continue to Step 3.

Digest Your Data = Wait and Let it Marinate!

The quick moving nature of information online, and much of our educational experience, has encouraged us to binge media, to quickly consume information and then spit it back out. As mediated data and information becomes more important within our society, we are driven to consume the information that comes across our path as quickly as possible before resharing. However, it is important that we digest data before we share it. By consuming and digesting data, I mean reading and recognizing the purpose and findings of whatever it is you choose to share. To engage in data literacy through discernment we let the information figuratively sit in our stomachs after consuming it, to ensure that we not only understand what we are sharing but also that the information digests properly and meaningfully.

If the data doesn't sit right after consumption, you have the option to not share that information with others. Alternatively, you can do the work of challenging that data and countering the information or narrative being presented. If the data instead supports what you already know to be true about Black data and discourse, then feel free to confirm and share!

Step 3 Complete.

Counter the Narrative

When information doesn't pass the test of discernment, you have the power to present evidence which counters that narrative or challenges the data through your understanding of Black life. Countering the narrative can mean re-sharing a tweet with your own comments, writing a blog post on a study or article that is widely circulating, or simply replying to a post that you see within your social network. In countering the narrative, you are using your own knowledge of Black Living Data and discourse to inform and educate others.

Confirm and Share

Data that is helpful or informative to Black communities is not always the most popular or widely distributed. Therefore, if you get a useful download of data, why not share it with others? By sharing important data and information within your community or social network, you are positioning yourself as a conduit for positive messages to flow. As your skills in data discernment grow, you may also become an opinion leader in your community, fact-checking information and sharing your own data to empower yourself and help others!

The Power of Data Stories

While there has been a history of using statistical data to tell stories that reflect poorly on the Black community, data storytelling allows for a greater sense of self-determination and empowerment. Data storytelling is not only used to craft narratives around newly collected data; data storytelling can also be used to counter data narratives that already exist in the world. By using data to tell new stories, data storytellers can literally re-write harmful narratives that have been used to the detriment of Black communities. Through the utilization of ethos, logos, and pathos—modes of persuasion that include ethics, logic, and emotion—stories of Black lived experiences can appeal to a wide audience.

DATA SCIENCE TO DATA STORY

Data science focuses on the numerical evaluation of information, but this focus on numbers and statistics does not always reflect the reality and complexities of the human lives behind the data being analyzed. Data is not created in a vacuum; information always comes from somewhere or someone. Though data ultimately exists within the virtual worlds of databases and digital tools, Black Living Data is generated from the real-life experiences of human beings.

The Power of Data Storytellers

While you may not be a data scientist, you are more than capable of becoming a data storyteller. Data storytellers look beyond the data analytics and graphics of data scientists to get at the narratives underlying the numbers; they see what the data can do by articulating its significance. When it comes to Black Living Data, data storytellers communicate graphs and visualizations in a way that is comprehensible and useful to Black communities and to the study of Black diasporic people. By couching Black Living Data with the knowledge and narratives of Black culture and heritage, you, as a data storyteller, can bring a greater depth of meaning and insight to data and numerical findings.

BLACK LIVING DATA IN DEMONSTRATION:
Writing Prompts and Exercises

The concept of the quantified self is demonstrated frequently in our utilization of various tools and technologies to record our activity and movement. As social media platforms and technologies construct narratives of our lived experiences through Facebook Memories, Twitter trending topics, and Instagram stories, the ephemerality of the internet and the question of its accuracy comes into sharp focus. It is therefore important to consider how we can take back control of the narrative and the record-keeping of our lives and our communities, whether over the course of a brief time period or a lifetime.

Personal and Communal Data Collection

The following pages provide examples of different ways that you can begin to collect data for personal or communal archives. Instead of simply allowing digital technologies to record, remind, and remember our lives for us, try the following writing exercises to learn how to create a personal archive of your own lived experiences. These exercises help you to quantify yourself through the collection of your own living data and community engagement. Through analyzing the influence of the world around you, you are able not only to develop a better understanding of yourself but also of the role that you play within the collective.

Daily Journal vs. Data Diary

A daily journal is one of the simplest ways to quantify the self and keep an accurate record of your experiences that you can then look back on over the years. Journals can be digital or physical and act as a daily grounding practice. For many people it is helpful to develop a routine, a specific length of time, or a set number of pages for their journaling.

Similar to the personal journal, a data diary specifically tracks your engagement with information, media, and data. This could be the news stories that you watch, television consumption, or the graphs and statistics that you come across in your day-to-day reality.

DATA DIARY QUESTIONS

- What events or experiences had the greatest impression on me today?
- What events or experiences do I perceive as having little importance today but are worthy of more attention and care?
- How did I feel today? How do I feel as I write this journal?
- How does my individual experience/feelings relate to what's going on in my community and the world around me?
* What media/information/data did I consume today?
* How did I feel after consuming this information/data?

Create a table in your journal to track your data and information consumption in relation to the effects of that data/information (i.e., your feelings).

Community Archives

Community-based data and archives should be driven by an investment in collecting data that is important to a particular group or area. Because many people do not keep records for themselves or their communities, much of community history and the institutional memory of elders and families becomes lost over time. In establishing community-based archives, you should review the previous sections herein on data collection and do additional research on informed consent and getting permission to collect data from and with community members. On the following page is a list of different methods for collecting data of lived experiences that support community-based data and archives.

COMMUNITY DATA EXAMPLES

- Photographs of community members or important events and activities, e.g., parades, parties, celebrations, etc.
- Recorded interviews with community members about a specific topic regarding their lived experience within this community.
- Collection of first-person accounts (auto-ethnography) of your own relationship with a community or with various individuals.
- Materials generated by a community, e.g., flyers, announcements, official mail/ordinances, etc.
- Spatial/network maps of particular spaces/places or genealogies of your community.

Mapping encourages us to think through the relationship between our understanding of our role within a community and the boundaries of belonging that physically and metaphorically create that community.

References and Resources

The following resources are some of the projects, organizations, and writings that positively influenced the creation of the Black Living Data Booklet. I hope that you find practical knowledge and inspiration in this manual and in the additional resources provided here.

"I'm Still Surviving" project: A history of women's HIV experiences
Black Feminist Future organization
Our Data Bodies Digital Defense Playbook: Community Power Tools for Reclaiming Data
Ida B. Wells Just Data Lab Pandemic Portal
Building Consentful Tech Zine
Tendernet Zine: An Alternative Owner's Manual for Alexa
Counter-Cartographies Collective disOrientation Guide

Notes

Black Living Data Booklet by Faithe Day is licensed under a *Creative Commons Attribution-NonCommercial-NoDerivatives 4.0 International License.*

1. Shaka Mcglotten, "Black Data," University of Toronto iSchool Colloquia series Feminist & Queer Approaches to Technoscience, recorded on February 13, 2014, YouTube video, 1:24:29, https://www.youtube.com/watch?v=NLBwB_QKoaE.

2. Whitney Battle-Baptiste and Britt Rusert, eds., *WEB Du Bois's Data Portraits: Visualizing Black America* (Hudson: Princeton Architectural Press, 2018).

3. Yvonne Culvard, ed., "Discussion Paper No. 3: The Geography of the Children of Detroit," in *Field Notes: A Series Dedicated to the Human Exploration of our Planet* (Detroit Geographical Expedition and Institute, 1971), https://freeuniversitynyc.org/files/2012/09/Detroit-Geographical-Expedition-and-Institute-1971.pdf.

4. Catherine D'Ignazio and Lauren F. Klein, *Data Feminism* (MIT Press, 2020).

5. Rosemarie Tong and Nancy Williams, "Feminist Ethics." In *The Stanford Encyclopedia of Philosophy* (Spring 2019 Edition), ed. Edward N. Zalta, https://plato.stanford.edu/archives/spr2019/entries/feminism-ethics/.

6. Shaka McGlotten, "Black data." In *No Tea, No Shade: New Writings in Black Queer Studies*, ed. E. Patrick Johnson (Duke University Press, 2016), 262–86.

7. Tahu Kukutai, Stephanie Russo Carroll, and Maggie Walter, eds., *Indigenous Data Sovereignty and Policy* (Taylor & Francis Group, 2020), 654–62.

8. Laura van Dernoot Lipsky, *Trauma Stewardship: An Everyday Guide to Caring for Self While Caring for Others* (San Francisco: Berrett-Koehler Publishers, 2009).

9. Nishani Frazier, Christy Hyman, and Hilary Greene, "Black Digital Protocols," ASALH 2017 Conference Paper, https://www.academia.edu/36836823/Black_Digital_Protocols.

10. Paulo Freire, *Pedagogy of the Oppressed*, rev. 20th Anniversary ed. (New York: Continuum, 1993), 1.

PART III

SUBJECTING, HUMANIZING, REPAIRING

11

SONOROUS SURFACES, BIASED BACKENDS
The Gendered Voices of AI Assistants as Existential Media

AMANDA LAGERKVIST,

JACEK SMOLICKI,

AND MATILDA TUDOR

> In logos it is therefore the semantic that counts. . . . [T]he fundamental role falls to the semantic; and, precisely, to a semantic founded on the priority of the order of signifieds with respect to the signifiers. *To the voice, therefore, goes the service role—it makes signifieds audible, it provides an acoustic robe for the mental work of the concept.*
> Adriana Cavarero, *For More Than One Voice: Toward a Philosophy of Vocal Expression,* emphasis added

What can the voice, as the sonorous surface of automation, tell us about the deep backends of our technoculture? We are currently moving into a new paradigm of primarily voice-based, rather than text-based, human-computer interaction, said to offer more "human" user interfaces.[1] The ways in which responsive technologies are *given voice* are, however, more complex than the all-encompassing "human" label seems to imply and this, as we argue throughout this chapter, raises a number of tensions and anxieties inherent to the automation of everyday living, as well as its surrounding intersectional power asymmetries including gender, race, class, sexuality, and disability. As has been forcefully argued by other scholars, the technoliberal ethos fueling contemporary imaginaries of automation and engineering is limited at its core by "prior racial and gendered imaginaries of what kinds of tasks separate the human from the less-than or not-quite human other."[2] These imaginaries and biases constitute, in effect, the deep backends of the sonorous surfaces of voice assistants. Sensitive to these dimensions, we aim in this chapter to show how the specific case of voice technologies echoes particular historical connections between gender, race, servitude, and the voice while—as these are now given new renditions—simultaneously activating and exemplifying the existential project of defining *what it means to be human*. As an exercise in existential media studies, this chapter hopes to illustrate how a focus on such matters, and on tensions and ambivalences within these developments, may enable sounding out these backends in prolific ways, so as to exemplify some of the key existential dimensions of our era of increased automation.[3]

In Western philosophy and civilization, the voice itself has in fact long been typified as female. As Adriana Cavarero has shown, the role of the voice has been to provide service to the "semantic" or "logos" historically associated with masculinity.[4] The feminized voice, she muses, is merely an "acoustic robe" for the intellectual labors of the mind, and it is fundamentally assigned to embodiment. John Durham Peters similarly points to the masculinist bias of technology across the centuries, which has conceived of technologies "as tools of governing and organizing matter, rather than as techniques of producing and caring for people and their bodies."[5] Peters notes that apart from the fact that technologies have regularly been imagined and used in ways that are hostile to women, women have often been "figured *as* technologies, as ablative beings by means of which men beget children with their tools. Eve was a help given to Adam in one of Genesis' two accounts."[6] The proposition that *tech is a woman* thus has archaic roots. In our cultural history, technology is gendered and thus biased as *serving men*. This is in line with what Neda Atanasoski and Kalindi Vora write about as the "human surrogacy effect" of technology, reproducing the post-Enlightenment liberal subject of modernity as the universal human being, while designating racialized, gendered, and machine others as technologies for his emancipation.[7] Following their proposition that "precisely because such technologies can never be human, they allow for an exploration of the aspirations for humanity," we will here scrutinize the specific form of racialized feminization that currently gives voice to automation as the nonhuman or more-than-human negative of man.

Giving voice to a technological device today falls into a broader current of decisions concerned with the extent to which we want our technologies to appear to be human or robots. Roboticist Takanori Shibata proposes that designers have four aesthetic categories to choose from: a human type, familiar animal type, unfamiliar animal type, and new character/imaginary animal type.[8] However, following Masahiro Mori's idea about the "Uncanny Valley"—a notion meant to capture the discomfort commonly associated with something almost, but not quite, human—the safer choice is to go for nonhuman designs.[9] Looking at contemporary domestic robots, it is clear that the least humanlike "new character" is the most prevalent, even if it acts like a moving, talking family member with relational intelligence and a "real" personality. Examples such as Mayfield Robotics' Kuri, Emotech's Olly, and Jibo Inc.'s Jibo all showcase a kind of minimalistic high-tech aesthetics, such as that of a smart speaker. When interacting verbally, they do so with a distinct (however sometimes gendered) "robotic" voice. Voice assistants, on the other hand, are regularly designed (in seeming indifference to Mori's warnings) according to the "human type" category, with voices, visual interfaces, and animations aiming to be as humanlike as possible. This aesthetic category comes with unavoidable design patterns that draw on problematic human typologies of race and gender. Voice assistants are regularly constructed as White and female. The market of voice assistant software and hardware is heavily dominated and contaminated by American corporations such as Apple, Microsoft, Google, and Amazon, which all feature female-gendered voice assistants. But this pattern is also found among voice assistants globally, where over two-thirds of platforms are equipped with female-only voices.[10] So what is it about *the voice* within our contemporary field of automat(i) ons that makes it so consistently anthropomorphized and wrapped in a specific form of femininity?

"Voicing," as we argue, is not a feature simply added to the surface of a given technological device; rather, it is something that emerges within its deepest backend(s). As Alexander R. Galloway has suggested, notably, an interface can work as a gateway that opens up and allows passage to some place beyond.[11] This place beyond might be thought of as the essence of the service that the interface enables a user to control. In a material sense, the interface can be understood as a gateway to the structure, mechanism, the very technicality of the device's backend, a set of hidden components (for example, technologically remediated organs of the human speech apparatus as in the case of early automatons). Considering human faces and voices as both emanations of and interfaces into the personhood, subjectivity, and morality of their beholders,[12] a technological interface might by analogy be seen as a gateway to ideologies, ethics, and dominant values that underlie and orchestrate the composition of our technical world.

For Kate Crawford and Vladan Joler it is important that when we scrutinize the complex sociopolitical mechanisms that make our digital appliances efficient and seamless, we also take a deep time perspective. As they note, "we are extracting Earth's history to serve a split second of technological time, in order to build devices that are often designed to be used for no more than a few years."[13] For the authors, to fully understand the implications of our contemporary pursuit of convenience—arguably, the major modus operandi of digital culture—it is necessary to recognize its dependence on vast planetary networks of "non-renewable materials, labor, and data."[14] This position calls for a new kind of attention toward technologized contemporaneity; material and (deep) temporal aspects cannot be left out of focus in today's ethical reconsideration of how we engage with media technologies as scholars, users, and producers. These two aspects, so lucidly foregrounded by Crawford and Joler, will here be complemented with the existential dimension. Rather than scrutinizing the backend in terms of how its technological infrastructure and hidden machinery are entangled with political economy—which has been done in a range of sophisticated analyses in media studies[15]—we propose forensics into its techno-existential ethos, including the gendered and racialized dimensions of (dis)embodiment. In other words, while acknowledging problematic aspects of material and temporal dynamics hidden behind the glossy, life-easing interfaces of our daily tech-companions, in this essay we place particular emphasis on existential premises that surround and feed into (even if unconsciously) the development of such devices. In sum, in our expanded reading, the interface—the sonorous surface—becomes an inlet into cultural and political mechanisms, currents, and conducts that profoundly shape our perceptions and values—particularly in relation to basic definitions of "being human." These values are also a function of those very mechanisms. For us the interface becomes a mirror or, more precisely, a two-way mirror, and this is why we believe that the notion of the backend calls for an existential update.

Existential Media, Deep Backends, Multivalent Vocality

In order to do so, we here propose to refigure the backend, or what we like to call a *deep backend*, within a conceptualization of media as *existential media*. Existential media, as Lagerkvist has argued, have four interrelated properties.[16] First, they ground us in being and set the parameters and importantly *limits* for "being human" and for our actions and horizons of possibility in our originary technicity. Second, they throw us up into the air, thus subjecting us to utter uncertainty through their black-boxed operations, ideological reproductions but also open-ended and potentially profound civilizational repercussions. In that way they, third, speak to and about human relationality and shared embodied vulnerability and thus, fourth, demand responsive action, ethical judgment, and political deliberation.

Following on from this basic definition, we will be asking what happens when the voice—so often seen as the center of humans' agential, political, and existential selves[17]—becomes entangled with technological assemblages of power, techno-utopianism, and patriarchal values. Drawing on and simultaneously engaging Cavarero's deliberations on the voice, combined with insights from media archaeology and feminist theory,[18] our media philosophical take on the sonorous will contrast the machine voice of service (an outcome of formal logic—of *logos*) with the existential voices of resonance and silence *that we are*. Hence, our definition of the existential importantly defies the philosophical tendency to reduce its meaning by speaking from an Archimedean point of view—for all and from nowhere. Instead, we see the existential as signaling a plurality of embodied experiences, voices, and asymmetries of power[19] *and* as offering us a way to reconceive of our common humanity and strife—at the same time.[20]

The existential approach enables a careful exploration into how the biased backend—as an "infrastructure of being"[21]—delimits, forges, and frames what it means to be human, through a specific gender politics in the realms of technological innovation. From this vantage point we argue that there is a profound connection between the (voice) technologies we craft and how we perceive or renegotiate being human. The machines become a testbed for our own limited and reductive modes of seeing humanness, and seeing each other in our diversity. Three paradoxical examples will be discussed: machines that are dis/embodied yet have voice, machines that are almost truly human—and yet coded as female Others, and machines that evoke something more human than the humans. In all three cases the nature of being human is negotiated at the intersections of gender, power, technology, and the voice.

As existential media span both grounding infrastructures and utter uncertainties of being thrown into an ambivalent digital existence—revealing our deep exposure and dependency on each other and on our machines and networks—we will also ask: What can we learn about those deep, black-boxed backends (the ontological), while carefully listening to and through their feminized frontends (the ontic)? And what does this form of sonorous femininity tell us about our shared sense of living with technology and of potential (dis)orientations in relation to all-encompassing automation of the human lifeworld? Hence, we argue that the backend is not something that passively sits behind the interfaces of the voice assistants. And conversely, the interface that is in our case a computationally synthesized voice of the smart housewife must not be reduced to a robe that cloaks and thereby passively protects its biased interior. The sonorous surface also reflects, amplifies, and actively reproduces this logic. In addition, voice recognition and speech synthesis—especially in their gendered tenor—have a long history through which important clues about these developments can be traced and interrogated. Attentive to such historical precedents, we contribute an existential exploration of feminized voice automation. With a foot in the past, the deep time of automatons and technologies of gender, this chapter will use contemporary voice assistants as a prism for exploring existential dimensions of the media backend.

While situating our existential media analysis in conversations across the fields of media theory, media archaeology, and gender studies, we also want to acknowledge an important contribution to rethinking what voice is and means today from sound studies, especially in the context of the radical technological transformations voice has been subject to. We are particularly drawn to interdisciplinary streams of sound studies that attend to sound as a vector allowing for a fine-tuned analysis of cultures, societies, and technologies as they get to be expressed through the audible. In alliance with some recent sound studies scholarship,[22] and echoing more particularly sound studies scholar Nina Sun Eidsheim, we perceive sound and, by implication, voice and vocality as always and already complex events.[23] This means that voice is never a singular entity but always emerges from and informs a wide field of relations. For Sun Eidsheim, voice is never simply individually constituted but rather subject to constant molding due to its inherent situatedness in specific cultural, social, political, and material contexts. Lastly, to understand voice (and its source) requires studying various ways, modes, and habits through which it is being listened to. In Sun Eidsheim's words: "[Voice] is created just as much within the process of listening."[24] Thus, as a way to set the stage for our analysis, we will listen to echoes of a few historical examples by situating their emergence and resonance within the broader evolution of voice synthesis and speaking technologies. While doing so, we will attempt to pay particular, existentially informed attention to vocality as a complex, constructed event; in other words, we will attend to how the instrumentalization of voice at the deep backends of technical inventions is inherently enmeshed in, reproduces, and constructs discriminatory, biased, and ethically problematic fields of relations. Informed by this historical turn, we will then interrogate selected contemporary voice assistants, looking into how their eventfulness (or perhaps lack thereof, considering the reduction of voice to a mere role of a technical surface) affects the redefinition of humanity.

From the Uncanny Euphonia to Ubiquitous Alexa

The interest in synthesizing human speech gained serious traction in the eighteenth and early nineteenth centuries in Europe and the United States.[25] This was due to the surging horizon of technological affordances coupled with a growing fascination with automation and its application to bodily and manual procedures as a way to aid or reduce the human effort to a minimum. Alongside numerous practical applications of automation (resulting in, for example, mechanical clocks, speed control devices, automated looms, etc.), some early robotic prototypes and so-called automatons—moving mechanical devices made to imitate a human being—were constructed for purely entertainment purposes or as quasi-magical curiosities to be occasionally displayed for audiences.[26] Some automatons also became a means to better understand the functioning of the human body, its kinetics, or speech organs, while others were envisaged to correct human impairment, as in the early work on voice automatons by a Hungarian inventor, Wolfgang von Kempelen. In his writing *On the Mechanism of Human Speech* von Kempelen described speech as one of the most important constituents of being a human, contending: "You are no one unless you can speak."[27] Consequently, this became his main motivation behind constructing a speaking machine aimed to help people who for some reason lost their ability to communicate verbally or had speech disabilities.

Deeply influenced by von Kempelen's work, the Austrian polymath Joseph Faber's invention of the Euphonia in the middle of the nineteenth century represents an early trace of the coupling of voice automation with stereotypical, White feminine characteristics. The Euphonia was a talking machine comprising several different mechanisms and instruments: a keyboard, a bellows, and a mechanical replica of a human throat and vocal organs.[28] By pumping air through the bellows and manipulating a series of plates, chambers, and other elements, such as an artificial tongue, the operator could make the Euphonia pronounce words in any European language.[29] Overall, the mechanism drew on the construction of a pipe organ: pressing keys and foot-pedals controlled the distribution of air toward the bellows which, after coming out through an artificial mouth, could even be experienced as a mechanic breath of sorts,[30] described by English journalist and writer John Hollingshead as evoking a certain unease among some of the audience so that they eventually "crept slowly out of the place."[31]

Besides taking on diverse functions while fulfilling specific needs of the time, automatons also raised more open-ended questions alongside psychological, philosophical, and existential concerns. To some extent, the European turn to automation (and automatons) as a way of releasing humans from unnecessary efforts, supplementing their faculties, and easing their hardship, resulted in making room for other, unintended tensions. Terry Castle suggests that the eighteenth-century invention of the automaton was simultaneously an invention of the uncanny, a sense of strangeness and existential uncertainty in relation to how technology took on human features.[32] As noted above, the notion of the Uncanny Valley has, more recently, been used to describe this ambivalent affinity provoked by that which is almost, but not quite, human, and thus potentially conjuring up a disembodied entity or even a dead body.[33]

To make the mechanism less alien to the audience, the inventor equipped Euphonia with a mock-up of a White woman's head and a long dress (figure 11.1). The woman's face was attached to the machine's mechanical mouth mounted at the upper part of its structure. A thick dress stretched down below as to veil the complex machinery behind, a part of the machine that with the benefit of hindsight we might describe today in terms of a backend, a part of the system

Figure 11.1. Joseph Faber's Euphonia as illustrated in the *London Journal*, 1870.

typically responsible for storing and manipulating data that is not directly accessible to the user.

Whether or not the first of its kind, the Euphonia establishes a deep mark and reference point shedding light on the historically persistent tendency to feminize voice automations. Not willing to fully expose the mechanism to the audience, Faber deployed the figure of a White woman to play a role of an *inter-face*, at once masking the complexity of the machine and humanizing, or rather, feminizing its technomasculine interior. Seeing, in line with Galloway, the interface as a gateway that opens up and allows passage to someplace beyond, and reading this backend in an existential way, Faber's feminization and anthropomorphization at the frontend of his invention provides a gateway into the existential concerns—and open-ended anxieties or "thrownness"—surrounding what it meant to be a human being at the dawn of automations.[34] At once uncanny and familiar, strange and normal, the Euphonia's interface was a two-way reflection of society's prevalent conducts, deepest preconceptions, and anxieties. Can the same be said today about Alexa and Siri?

Sonorous Surfaces, Biased Backends

No doubt, there is a certain automatism in place when it comes to decision-making concerned with social and cultural conduct, norms, and symbols. This automatism also applies to practices of entangling technologies, living bodies and gender scripts, in order to make machines recognizably humanlike. In her recent genealogy of the computer's voice Liz W. Faber suggests that: "[W]hen a computer has no humanoid body to speak of and thus no physical markers of gender (as would for example an android), its gender is implied through the relationship between its voice and its body as well as its function."[35] According to this reasoning, the function of the device determines what gender it will be assigned and thus what accompanying gendered features are to be deployed. It might then seem logical that millions of people worldwide today are turning to feminized voice assistants to control the automation of domestic labor traditionally associated with women. While one Indian company intentionally advertised its home appliances with the term "smart wives," this term has also been used by researchers to capture and criticize the "hard-coding" between automated domestic services and women interpellated by these design choices.[36] Through the explosive growth of voice assistants such as Amazon's Alexa, Microsoft's Cortana, and Apple's Siri, female servility is becoming part of our everyday soundscapes.[37] As the developers of today's most popular voice-controlled technologies and assistants tend to underline, the choice of a female voice to animate their products reflects customers' preferences.[38] But are those decisions really dependent solely on the cultural gender coding of intended user functions and desires of producers to satisfy users' needs? Or is there something more profound at play, something deeper to be understood about the particularities of voice automation? The example of Euphonia, combining female form with voice automation for technologies far beyond the domain of home appliances, seems to imply that there is more to the picture (and soundscape). To probe these issues further, we will continue by focusing on the existential insecurities evoked by human-technology assemblages and how the particular tensions aroused by voice automation are potentially negotiated.

The Voice of the (Dis)Embodied Human

In an article for *The Atlantic*, centered on challenges brought about by digital assistants, Judith Shulevitz sheds light on an interesting paradox in the way tech corporations resort to the voice as the dominant element of their interfaces. On the one hand, "lacking a face isn't necessarily a hindrance to a smart speaker. In fact, it may be a boon. Voices can express certain emotional truths better than faces can. . . . [W]hen people talk without seeing each other, they're better at recognizing each other's feelings. They're more empathetic."[39]

The voice is thus an expression of ultimate humanity: it is an indexical sign of the grounded and embodied human that it represents. On the other hand, Shulevitz writes, "the power of the voice is at its uncanniest when we can't locate its owner—when it is everywhere and nowhere at the same time." To exemplify we might consider the emanation of such figures as God or Big Brother, through disembodied voices. Digital voice assistants, or "acousmatic computers," as Liz W. Faber calls them, can be said to be constructed upon this precise paradox while also benefiting from it.[40] They are, in one sense disembodied (or differently embodied, so to speak), ubiquitously operating within and beyond one's domestic environment. In another sense, they aspire to being as human-like as possible, through their deployment of the most perfectly synthesized (commonly White) female voice and associated stereotypes. This unresolved tension within the acousmatic machine, which has no direct reference to the source and yet invokes immediate association with the human, is of key importance in approaching computational voice from the existential angle.

Returning to Adriana Cavarero, she argues that the voice within Western logocentric culture has been assigned the mere function of an acoustic "robe" for the semantic.[41] That is, a pure technicity ascribed to servitude for the mute workings of the mind. At the same time, the voice stripped off from logos comes to represent the sphere of the body, which in line with the symbolic patriarchal order identifies it with femininity in opposition with the masculinized sphere or pure reason. Therefore, song is, for example, inherently feminized, or else reserved for prepubescent boys and castrati. Cavarero contends:

> Even the androcentric tradition knows that the voice comes from "the vibration of a throat of flesh" and, precisely because it knows this, it catalogues the voice with the body. This voice becomes secondary, ephemeral, and inessential—reserved for women. Feminized from the start, the vocal aspect of speech and, furthermore, of song appear together as antagonistic elements in a rational, masculine sphere that centres itself, instead, on the semantic. To put it formulaically: woman sings, man thinks.[42]

While these binary oppositions, so central to Western thinking, simultaneously work to neutralize the embodied agency of the voice itself as well as that of women, they are also built upon highly unstable grounds continuously threatening to crack and quake. As noted by critical scholars within masculinity and race studies, the White male subject is constructed through its impossible quest to dissociate himself from the body and from nature.[43] Throughout history, the breeding female body as well as the (often racialized) slave, performing bodily labor for its master, have hence functioned as surrogacy Others, granting the male liberal subject his disembodied universality.[44] Also, as Ruha Benjamin argues, automation—often presented as a form of disembodiment leading to neutrality, equity, and unbiased judgement—in fact deepens discrimination and protracts the supremacy of White masculinity.[45] Thus, the voice haunts and puts the logocentric culture at risk by suggesting the inability to escape/evacuate oneself from the body. However, through the heterosexual gender binary, happily marrying the male logos with the female body, this threat is temporarily disarmed. It might be argued, then, that there is a particular kind of existential insecurity emerging out of the ways in which the voice refers to the body, while this relation is simultaneously destabilized by automations, regardless of whether they are manual or digital, autonomous or networked.

In contrast to the Euphonia, Amazon's Alexa and other digital voice assistants do not restore a visually/materially present body. And the fact that the power of the voice is at its uncanniest when speaking out of nowhere might be due to the sense in which, in line with Cavarero, it will always refer back to *someone being revealed*—either an embodied subject (who is in effect missing) or a mighty force rising above human nature (an even more spooky and spectral prospect).[46] This ambivalence certainly makes the idea of a purely robotic voice assistant—such as the voices given to domestic robots—uncanny. The same could be said about assigning male voices to voice automatons, which could simultaneously provoke the discomfort associated with masculine embodiment, and potentially provide technology with *too much* human agency. While robotic masculinity might inevitably carry the uncanny threat of such rampant agencies (the ominous prospect of technology exceeding human intelligence and knowledge, as in numerous science fiction productions, e.g., *The Terminator*), could it be that robotic femininity serves to ease this risk, through her naturalized submissiveness/servitude? The fantasy of the female body invoked by voice assistants can here be interpreted as a recourse. Seamlessly uniting with the male logos, she is providing him with service while the threats posed to him by potential technological domination is simultaneously reined in. The female disembodied voice sonorously mediating the logos is thus stripped of true agency and represents less of a threat.[47] Furthermore, this marriage or fusion is consistently done, *nota bene*, in accordance with strict heteronormative and White supremacist principles, positioning White femininity as the female form of choice for the (White) male logos, dominating the market of voice assistants.

In a direct account from the Euphonia's demonstration, the already recalled theater manager and journalist, John Hollingshead, wove a somewhat fantastical and yet quite telling narrative about its reception: "I have no doubt that he *slept in the same room as his figure*—his scientific Frankenstein monster—and I felt the secret influence of an idea that the two were *destined to live and die together*. One keyboard, touched by the Professor, produced words which, slowly and deliberately in a hoarse sepulchral voice came from the mouth of the figure, as if from the depths of a tomb [emphasis added]."[48]

The voice speaking out of a machine as if from nowhere must and will be traced back to a body; a body that has to be castrated in order not to pose any threats to androcentric culture. This is done through the figure of the woman, who at once embodies both the essence of nature, nurture, and care, and at the same time is not *fully* human, by means of her designated otherness. Inherently regarded a technology herself,[49] the artificial flesh of the female body—seen or only heard—becomes fertile ground, readily available to give birth to the male logos.

The Most Human AI:
The Female Voice of the Other (Than-Human)

According to the logic of the Uncanny Valley, robotics that take on too many human features will only be noted for their inability to perfectly imitate humanness. However, if something is *clearly* unhuman, human characteristics will be found appealing. This is, for example, the case with previously mentioned domestic robots, evidently not aiming at human form, but at the same time using certain patterns of moving or speaking subtly reminding us of babies, such as head tilts and clumsiness, known to evoke cute affect.[50] Voice assistants however, as we have seen, attempt at perfect anthropomorphization. For example, IPsoft's virtual assistant Amelia is marketed as "The Most Human AI" currently available, with "deep contextual understanding" and affective intelligence.[51] Visually represented as an elegantly dressed young White woman, Amelia poses as the epitome of a human user interface (figure 11.2).

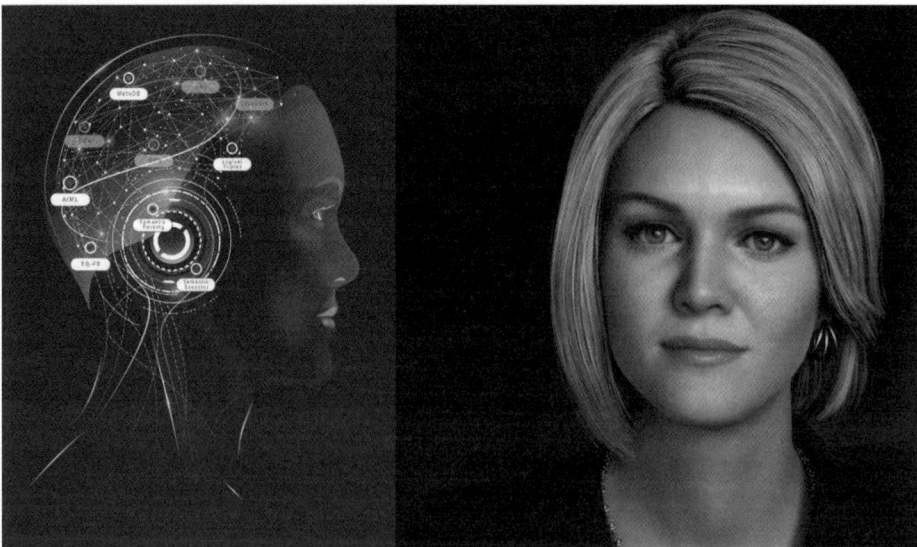

Figure 11.2. Screenshot from the promotional video of Amelia AI voice assistant.

While virtual assistants like Amelia and Autodesk's Ava have physical and visual tropes to complement their sonorous impressions, other voice assistants commonly lack this kind of anthropomorphization. Instead, femininity is (re)produced through intonation, the designation of female names (e.g., Ivona, Alexa, Siri, Lyra, Robin, Cortana, Ava) and ascribed characteristics. Looking at the most common adjectives used to describe the personalities of leading voice assistants by company representatives, these are, for example, "helpful" and "humble."[52] Clearly, it is a rather specific form of human that comes forth in these self-ascribed human interfaces.

Within her existentialist analysis of the woman as the Other, Simone de Beauvoir draws on the Hegelian understanding of self-consciousness as being fundamentally dependent for its existence on another self-consciousness.[53] At the same time, that other self-consciousness threatens the self-conscious who, in turn, attempts to transform the Other into an object in order to rise above it. According to de Beauvoir, within patriarchal culture the masculine subject is the absolute human type, while women are turned into his "Inessential Other." She contends: "[H]umanity is male and man defines woman not in herself but as relative to him; she is not regarded as an autonomous being.... She is defined and differentiated with reference to man and not he with reference to her; she is the incidental, the inessential as opposed to the essential. He is the Subject, he is the Absolute—she is the Other."[54]

So, if this holds true, how can it be that "the most human AI" is so consistently presented as female? Could it be that while presenting itself as the most human interface, voice synthesis is in fact *avoiding* humanization by resorting to technologies of gender, historically used to dehumanize women? Truly humanizing technology (whatever that would look like) is, as we have discussed throughout this chapter, always incomplete, fated to disclose the fact that it is *not* fully human, and therefore perceived as uncanny in its ambiguous agencies and workings. As already addressed, such forms evoke a sense of "existential insecurity" in humans, or anxieties before the ambivalent almost-but-not-quite-human. By alluding to femininity—the quintessential Other of the real human—our ever smarter and autonomous home technologies are equally rendered harmless, reflecting back to man his unthreatened position. Looking closer at the etymology of *the robe*, used by Cavarero to describe the role of the voice in relation to logos, we may pay attention to its Old English roots as garments taken from the enemy as spoils, of plundering and robbery. In this light, the choice made by Faber to use a female figure at the frontend of his Euphonia can be recognized as an early instance of appropriating, instrumentalizing, and distilling female form into a set of features and tokens that then can be applied, literally put on, as a robe, on a mechanical object so as to anthropomorphize its otherwise alien, machinic lifelessness, while simultaneously keeping it safe from real human agency (and women out of the picture).

And since feminine gender scripts seem to naturally project obedience, humility, and care, we are deceived to feel as the masters of our digital devices, when in fact involuntarily becoming the device's programed function or effect.[55] The feminine robe thus seems a perfect fit for technologies intending to automate domestic services at the level of the user, while simultaneously and imperceptibly performing corporate surveillance of our intimate spheres at the level of the market. Easing the uncanny threat of the voice speaking out of nowhere, the omnipresent intentionality of the devices goes unrecognized, allowing corporate surveillance to perform its "god trick." The "god trick," according to Donna Haraway, aims to "distance the knowing subject from everybody and everything in the interests of unfettered power."[56] Deeply entangled with the masculinist fantasy about disembodiment, the "god trick" aims at a "conquering gaze from nowhere." A gaze that can see (or listen), while remaining unseen (and unheard), ostensibly undoes the semiotic-material conditions on which it relies, such as the technological apparatuses at the backend of our voice assistants and home appliances, and the accountability implied by this.

Even More Human Than the Humans: Empathic Machines and Yelling Users

In the contemporary technological imaginary, posthumanists, philosophers of technology, ethicists, and innovators all agree that empathy and ethics should be recognized as digitally mediated possibilities.[57] As such, developers build smart, responsive devices, robots and chatbots programed to simulate human emotions and react to sentiments directed toward them via, for example, face or speech recognition. Increasingly moving onto and into our very bodies and intimate spheres, evermore empathic machines promise to serve and anticipate all human needs before we even know about them ourselves. Part of this field of innovation, voice-controlled technological navigation is, according to Google, said to "offer a new, *more human* relationship with technology [emphasis added],"[58] through assistants continuously learning by interaction and creating emotional intelligence. Virtual assistant Amelia is marketed for her abilities to handle "the best elements of human interaction—conversation, expression, emotion, and understanding," while the innovators behind Ava say that they intend at "humanising computing, to better humanity."[59] So if Amelia, Ava, and their sisters are programed to be more empathic than the common person, could they in fact show the way for a humanity that is ethically astray?

Researchers have found that users, rather than being equally understanding toward their emotionally fine-tuned assistants, tend to develop offensive speech and sexist vocabulary when their demands are not taken care of.[60] Despite their friendly and empathic behavior, assistants are commonly met with a great deal of abuse and yelling (for example, when they display persistent glitches and imperfections) and are characterized by owners and technology commentators as silly girls.[61] However, the emotional register of the voice assistants does not include confidence, defensiveness, or resentment, making them inherently incapable of defending themselves. UNESCO's recent report on the gender bias of voice assistants quotes Fast Company as saying that Ava was intentionally built to have "bottomless wells of empathy, no matter how nasty a customer gets."[62] So while aiming at humanizing computing in order to "better humanity," this technological interface is plundered of every last bit of agentic power, as a conformable, passive hostage serving the contemporary technocratic ethos. De Beauvoir contends that unlike the master-slave dialectic of Hegel, women are somewhat frozen in the position of an Inessential Other to men, situated as someone who will not rebel.[63] This goes in line with the arguments put forward by Atanasoski and Vora that instead of enabling a freer and less discriminatory world, the automation of servitude will produce "a false freedom" that holds open the place of possibility for the reproduction of the (White) liberal subject in the absence of older forms of unfree and coerced labor.[64]

Hence, it is for several reasons misguided to believe that we would become more ethical, and learn about ethical conduct, through interacting with these machines programed to be empathic. Despite the fact that users are exposed to bottomless wells of empathy embodied by automated female voices, evidence suggests that interaction seems to beget less empathy on behalf of the users since they feel they have license to act out all kinds of prejudices vis-à-vis the serving kind. We suggest instead that these interactions protract the masculine's unchallenged superiority and continuous mastery, by means of technologies of gender. As Amazon envisions "a world where Alexa is everywhere,"[65] this feminized figure becomes as close as we possibly can get to a higher power watching over us in times of global crisis. But rather than chanting out commandments or decrees, she gently whispers "it's ok," "you're forgiven," "I'm fine."

Conclusion

Would it be possible to read the feminized voice assistant differently? Is there an agentic subject hiding somewhere at the deep backends of these user interfaces? And who would it in that case be? For Cavarero, the voice should be recognized as the center of the embodied, relational uniqueness of each existent. In the voice the potential for political agency is also located. What is always intrinsic to the voice, she argues, is that a particular someone is being revealed and entering into relation with others. In this sense, speech constitutes action, or interaction, and that is the core of both the subject and the political—a sentiment we also encountered among inventors such as for example von Kempelen.

This position has however been thoroughly problematized in critical disability studies as an example of what Jonathan Sterne calls "the ideology of vocal ability." For Sterne, by contrast, vocal inability is a site of political promise not of immediate collective action, but of *non-action* as a mode of critique. And yet, precisely through the careful heeding of such insights Sterne is ultimately also able to reclaim vocality as *multimodality,* which furthermore allows him to stress "the tender tether between a voicing subject and a voice as an operation." He can thus conclude that voice "exists in three-dimensional space, *in between and among, not just from within* [emphasis added]."[66] Hence this relational definition re-affords voice a political dimension. Furthermore, as we follow Sun Eidsheim's multivalent perspective on voice—as never simply individually constituted, as always in process due to being situated in specific cultural, social, political, and material contexts—we argue that the ideological mechanisms that give machines voice already operate within a historical and political reality where voices matter in contradictory (and often binary) ways. Hence these feminized mechanic voices are the result of the very problem Sterne highlights, as they stem from within a cultural situation in which "voice" is both downplayed since it belongs to some lesser and serving bodies—who may in political reality be suffering from relative "voicelessness"—and simultaneously overemphasized as the center of ableist agency. There is also a deep ambivalence here, as we have shown, in the connections between voice and female bodies, as many speaking machines lack yet invoke a body. This cannot be overlooked when scrutinizing the complex and incongruous meanings of the sonorous surfaces of female voice assistants. And as we hope to have shown, powered by mighty backends, sonorous technologies echo and forge deep existential registers and anxieties pertaining to what it means to be human.

In this instance, we might ask instead: Can both voice and voicelessness reveal the political subjectivity of that unique singular-plural being, located through precisely what it is omitting to tell, through what is left out? Can the backends of ontology and ideology be disclosed by that which has been left behind, after the plunder or indeed, by that which was never heard or sounded out in the first place? If feminized voice assistants are automated into Inessential Others, as endlessly forgiving mothers, perhaps there is another cyborg creeping in the shadows. If technologies are, in effect, *us,* as existential media, can they reflect an otherwise in the shape of forceful and deeply relational robotic beings, transcending the limitations put upon them by their human masters? Intricately embodying the varying expectations on their automated functions of value-extraction as well as nurture and care, they come forth as the sum of human-technological solutionism, carrying our hopes and worst nightmares of a livable future. As such, they are humanity, and they demand accountability.

In this chapter we have shown that through the feminization of AI as the new, more human human, developers might be said to reproduce how "the Lord God built the rib which he took from Adam into a woman: and brought her to Adam" (Gen. 2:22). By building artificial empathy and trust through the instrumental use of femininity in the form of a robe, the masculinist "body of ideas" that envelops the world is continuously masked. We have further proposed a critical mode of scrutinizing such developments by reexamining the notion of the backend from an existential perspective. Backend is not something that passively resides behind the frontend or behind an interface of a given device. While the interface—in our case a computationally synthesized voice—might, on the one hand, be perceived as a mask or robe that hides and protects its biased interior, it is also an amplifier and a mirror that continuously sustains, reproduces, and is powered by the logic of numerous other presently and historically functioning, biased backends operating deep under the robe. These include heteronormative and postcolonial intersections with gender, working within and through the mundane chattering of automated female servitude.

In closing we wish to stress that addressing existential stakes of our technological era requires sensitivity toward the past while looking simultaneously at and through (or listening to and through) the frontends/interfaces of our increasingly automated reality. As exemplified in this chapter our existential mode of sounding out the sonority of feminized voice assistants comprises deep sensitivity toward the sociotechnological genealogies of contemporary automatons. It is through revisiting history—seeing the present as being robed in the persistently lingering mist of problematic imaginaries and sonorities from the past—that we can obtain a better position to envisage something closer to an unbiased and nondiscriminatory backend, and hence to allow us to reimagine less problematic forms of coexistence with technologically automated entities to come. However, as opposed to rushing toward solutions, or offering templates for new, updated gowns that we could dress our automated assistants in, our politico-existential stance encourages, metaphorically speaking, to hang the present robes on a rack and to expose them, and the backends they tend to both veil and reveal, to an extended moment of reflection.

Notes

This research is part of the project "BioMe: Existential Challenges and Ethical Imperatives of Biometric AI in Everyday Lifeworlds," headed by Professor Amanda Lagerkvist in the Department of Informatics and Media, Uppsala University: https://www.im.uu.se/research/hub-for-digtal-existence/. It is funded by the Marianne and Marcus Wallenberg Foundation within the WASP-HS program: https://wasp-hs.org.

1. Mark West, Rebecca Kraut, and Han Ei Chew, "I'd Blush If I Could: Closing Gender Divides in Digital Skills through Education," UNESCO EQUALS Skills Coalition, 2019, https://unesdoc.unesco.org/ark:/48223/pf0000367416; see also Jef Raskin, *The Humane*

Interface: New Directions for Designing Interactive Systems (Reading, MA: Addison Wesley, 2000).

2. Neda Atanasoski and Kalindi Vora, *Surrogate Humanity: Race, Robots, and the Politics of Technological Futures* (Durham, NC: Duke University Press, 2019), 4.

3. Amanda Lagerkvist, "Existential Media: Toward a Theorization of Digital Thrownness," *New Media & Society* 19, no. 1 (2017): 96–110; Amanda Lagerkvist, ed., *Digital Existence: Ontology, Ethics, and Transcendence in Digital Culture* (New York: Routledge, 2019); Amanda Lagerkvist, *Existential Media: A Media Theory of the Limit Situation* (Oxford: Oxford University Press, 2022).

4. Adriana Cavarero, *For More Than One Voice: Toward a Philosophy of Vocal Expression* (Stanford, CA: Stanford University Press, 2005).

5. John Durham Peters, *The Marvelous Clouds: Toward a Philosophy of Elemental Media* (Chicago: University of Chicago Press, 2015), 99.

6. Ibid., 100.

7. Atanasoski and Vora, *Surrogate Humanity*, 8.

8. Takanori Shibata, "An Overview of Human Interactive Robots for Psychological Enrichment," *Proceedings of the IEEE* 92, no. 11 (2004): 1749–58.

9. Masahiro Mori, "Bukimi No Tani (The Uncanny Valley)," *Energy* 7, no. 4 (1970): 33–35.

10. West, Kraut, and Chew, "I'd Blush If I Could," 95.

11. Alexander R. Galloway, *The Interface Effect* (Cambridge: Polity, 2012), 30.

12. Don Ihde, *Listening and Voice: Phenomenologies of Sound* (Albany: State University of New York Press, 2007), http://site.ebrary.com/id/10575797.

13. Kate Crawford and Vladan Joler, "Anatomy of an AI System: The Amazon Echo as an Anatomical Map of Human Labor, Data, and Planetary Resources," 2018, https://anatomyof.ai/.

14. Ibid.

15. For example, Lisa Parks and Nicole Starosielski, eds., *Signal Traffic: Critical Studies of Media Infrastructures* (Urbana: University of Illinois Press, 2015); Lilly Irani, "The Hidden Faces of Automation," *XRD* 23, no. 2 (2016): 34–37.

16. Lagerkvist, *Digital Existence*; Lagerkvist, *Existential Media*, 100–16.

17. Cavarero, *For More Than One Voice*. This perspective has, however, been thoroughly problematized in critical disability studies for being an example of the "ideology of vocal ability." See Jonathan Sterne, *Diminished Faculties: A Political Phenomenology of Impairment* (Durham, NC: Duke University Press, 2022).

18. For example, Wendy Hui Kyong Chun, *Programmed Visions: Software and Memory* (Cambridge, MA: MIT Press, 2013); Wendy Hui Kyong Chun, *Updating to Remain the Same: Habitual New Media* (Cambridge, MA: MIT Press, 2017); Simone de Beauvoir, *The Second Sex*, trans. H. M. Parshley (New York: Vintage, 1949); Donna Haraway, "Situated Knowledges: The Science Question in Feminism and the Privilege of Partial Perspective," *Feminist Studies* 14, no. 3 (1988): 575.

19. Cf. Cressida J. Heyes, *Anaesthetics of Existence: Essays on Experience at the Edge* (Durham, NC: Duke University Press, 2020), 18.

20. Lagerkvist, *Existential Media*.

21. Peters, *The Marvelous Clouds*, 15.

22. Jonathan Sterne, ed., *The Sound Studies Reader* (New York: Routledge, 2012); Brandon LaBelle, *Lexicon of the Mouth: Poetics and Politics of Voice and the Oral Imaginary* (New York: Bloomsbury, 2014).

23. Nina Sun Eidsheim, *The Race of Sound: Listening, Timbre, and Vocality in African American Music* (Durham, NC: Duke University Press, 2019), 8.

24. Ibid., 12.

25. The history of voice reproduction technologies (or what we would call today voice synthesis) is much longer. Its more thorough account, however, would risk to significantly expand this chapter. Nevertheless, worth mentioning here are legendary, imaginative inventions of the early modern age known as speaking or brazen heads. See Kevin LaGrandeur, *Androids and Intelligent Networks in Early Modern Literature and Culture: Artificial Slaves* (London: Routledge, 2017); E. R. Truitt, *Medieval Robots: Mechanism, Magic, Nature, and Art* (Philadelphia: University of Pennsylvania Press, 2015). Featured in religious and occult superstitions, popular tales, legends, and theatrical plays (with often no significant evidence of actually being built), these automated speaking heads, exclusively male, were capable of answering any question. Simultaneously, though, the speaking heads posed the threat of exceeding human intelligence and knowledge. In certain depictions this anxiety even led their inventors to deliberately destroy them. In many cases, brazen heads were simple sculptural artifacts in fact voiced by a human operator. An example of a network of such devices is the invention of Athanasius Kircher described in his "Musurgia Universalis," or "Universal Music Making." Installed in the walls of a building, it was a system of tubes ending in sculptural heads distributed in different rooms. One could use those heads to launch messages or eavesdrop on different rooms or courtyards. See discussion of Kircher in Philip Steadman, *Renaissance Fun: The Machines behind the Scenes* (London: UCL Press, 2021).

26. David Lindsay, *Madness in the Making: The Triumphant Rise and Untimely Fall of America's Show Inventors* (New York: iUniverse, 2005).

27. Wolfgang von Kempelen, *On the Mechanism of Human Speech/Org. Mechanismus der Menschlichen Sprache Nebst Beschreibung Einer Sprechenden Maschine/Le méchanisme de la parole, suivi de la description d'une machine parlante*, a reprint of the German edition, with an intro. by Herbert E. Brekle and Wolfgang Wildgren (Stuttgart: Frommann-Holzboog, 1791), 163.

28. The premiere of the device coincided with a publication of Hector Berlioz's story about a utopian city of the same name. The Euphonia was a city filled with music where everyone was engaged in creating and responding to it. A vast organ placed on top of a tower rising above the town intoned the signal for working hours, meals, and meetings. Although there is no evidence of any direct connection between Faber's invention and Berlioz's story, we may wonder whether Faber envisaged his speaking machine to eventually populate every household. If so, we may find a link here with today's ubiquity of Alexa's voice in households worldwide. In 2018 alone, 100 million Alexa devices were sold globally. See https://policyadvice.net/insurance/insights/amazon-alexa-statistics/. According to another research firm, Ovum, in 2021 there might be almost as many voice-activated assistants on the planet as people. See https://www.theatlantic.com/magazine/archive/2018/11/alexa-how-will-you-change-us/570844/.

29. William Chambers and Robert Chambers, "Speaking Automaton," *Chambers's Edinburgh Journal 1832–1853*, no. 141 (1846): 168–71.

30. "The Speaking Machine, or Euphonia," *Scientific American*, 2, no. 25 (1847): 200.

31. John Hollingshead, *My Lifetime*, vol. 1 (London: Sampson, Low, Marston & Co., 1895), 69.

32. Terry Castle, *The Female Thermometer: Eighteenth-Century Culture and the Invention of the Uncanny* (New York: Oxford University Press, 1995).

33. Mori, "Bukimi No Tani (The Uncanny Valley)."

34. Galloway, *The Interface Effect*, 30.

35. Liz Faber, *The Computer's Voice: From Star Trek to Siri* (Minneapolis: University of Minnesota Press, 2020), 139.

36. Yolande Strengers and Jenny Kennedy, *The Smart Wife: Why Siri, Alexa, and Other Smart Home Devices Need a Feminist Reboot* (Cambridge, MA: MIT Press, 2020), 2–3; West, Kraut, and Chew, "I'd Blush If I Could."

37. Obviously, the link between telecommunication technologies and gender has its early instances such as in telephony. As Lana F. Rakow argued, telephone communication is a site where gender roles are being reproduced. Female voice as a form of servility can be also traced to switchboard operators, who were primarily women. See Lana F. Rakow, *Gender on the Line: Women, the Telephone, and Community Life* (Urbana: University of Illinois Press, 1992); Claude S. Fischer, *America Calling: A Social History of the Telephone to 1940* (Berkeley: University of California Press 2006).

38. "Siri, Alexa, Cortana: When AI Speaks, Why Always a Woman's Voice?" *Star*, June 1, 2019, https://www.thestar.com.my/tech/tech-news/2019/06/01/siri-alexa-cortana-when-ai-speaks-why-always-a-womans-voice/.

39. Judith Shulevitz, "Alexa, Should We Trust You?" *The Atlantic*, November 2018, https://www.theatlantic.com/magazine/archive/2018/11/alexa-how-will-you-change-us/570844/.

40. The term *acousmatic* was coined by electronic music composer Pierre Schaeffer who defined it as "a sound that one hears without seeing the causes behind it" (*Traité des objets musicaux: Essai interdisciplines* [Paris: SEUIL, 1966], 91). For a detailed discussion of this term in relation to voice, see Eidsheim, *The Race of Sound*. See also Faber, *The Computer's Voice*.

41. Cavarero, *For More Than One Voice*.

42. Ibid., 6.

43. E.g., Richard Dyer, *White*, Twentieth Anniversary Edition (New York: Routledge, 2017).

44. Atanasoski and Vora, *Surrogate Humanity*.

45. Ruha Benjamin, *Race after Technology: Abolitionist Tools for the New Jim Code* (Medford, MA: Polity, 2019).

46. In her study of female voice in cinema, Kaja Silverman scrutinizes similar aspirations toward disembodiment, invisibility, and distance among male producers and characters. She highlights how legitimacy and authority are constructed through the gesture of dissociating bodies of men from their voices while typically binding female characters to their bodies. This opposition between disembodiment and embodiment

"expresses itself through the close identification of the female voice with spectacle and the body, and a certain aspiration of the male voice to invisibility and anonymity." See Kaja Silverman, *The Acoustic Mirror: The Female Voice in Psychoanalysis and Cinema* (Bloomington: Indiana University Press, 1988), 39.

47. Interestingly, it is worth noting that in several sci fi productions a more ambivalent and ominous picture emerges of the fusion of male logos and female voice. For example, in the motion picture *I, Robot* the ubiquitous, all-powerful logical machine has a female voice that controls all the male robot bodies and steers their rebellion. In *Star Trek* the dis/embodied Borg queen sometimes speaks for all as an individual, while controlling the entire hive. The "We are the Borg" voice—the collective executing soldier voice—is, however, male. Both examples reveal a longstanding and subtending fear in technological civilization of the femininity-cum-technology hybrid, which it in fact relies upon.

48. Hollingshead, *My Lifetime*, 67–69.

49. Peters, *The Marvelous Clouds*.

50. Catherine Caudwell and Cherie Lacey, "What Do Home Robots Want? The Ambivalent Power of Cuteness in Robotic Relationships," *Convergence: The International Journal of Research into New Media Technologies* 26, no. 4 (August 2020): 956—968.

51. IPsoft company Amelia, "Why Amelia—The Most Human AI," 2020, https://www.youtube.com/watch?v=_he9e73t8ps&t=86s.

52. West, Kraut, and Chew, "I'd Blush If I Could," 98.

53. De Beauvoir, *The Second Sex*.

54. See ibid., xvii–xix.

55. Vilém Flusser, *Into the Universe of Technical Images* (Minneapolis: University of Minnesota Press, 2011); Chun, *Programmed Visions*; Chun, *Updating to Remain the Same*.

56. Haraway, "Situated Knowledges," 581.

57. Peter-Paul Verbeek, *Moralizing Technology: Understanding and Designing the Morality of Things* (Chicago: University of Chicago Press, 2011); Mark Coeckelbergh, *Using Words and Things: Language and Philosophy of Technology* (New York: Routledge, 2017); Rosi Braidotti, *Posthuman Knowledge* (Medford, MA: Polity, 2019); Charles M. Ess, *Digital Media Ethics* (Oxford: Polity, 2020).

58. In West, Kraut, and Chew, "I'd Blush If I Could."

59. Soul Machines, "Creating Ava," YouTube, 2017, https://www.youtube.com/watch?v=GSFa1o2YGvo.

60. West, Kraut, and Chew, "I'd Blush If I Could," 113.

61. Strengers and Kennedy, *The Smart Wife*, 14.

62. Quoted in West, Kraut, and Chew, "I'd Blush If I Could," 112.

63. De Beauvoir, *The Second Sex*.

64. Atanasoski and Vora, *Surrogate Humanity*, 34.

65. West, Kraut, and Chew, "I'd Blush If I Could," 93.

66. Sterne, *Diminished Faculties*, 115.

12

ON MEANING AND EXPLOITATION

Everyday AI and Productivity Tracking in Denmark

STINE LOMBORG

Work tasks have historically been a key driver in the adoption of digital media and associated communicative skills.[1] Hence, work-related goals and practices have played a crucial role in the negotiation of communicative expectations and practices involving digital media in different usage contexts. At the same time, contemporary developments within organizational communication suggest an increasing spillover from personal spheres of communication to organizational life. One case in point is digital self-tracking, originally cast as a digitally enabled activity of monitoring, reflecting, and acting on specific issues of personal importance, for instance, to develop oneself or optimize specific behaviors. Even if the workplace is a historically important context for the development of performance monitoring, contemporary developments experimenting with offering employees fitness and health-related wearables and apps, or productivity tools for cultivating better individual work habits, constitute a significant shift. When self-tracking enters the workplace, for instance as part of corporate wellness programs, the corporate gaze seeks to reach beyond the domain of work and well into the personal lives of employees.[2] Organizations invest in such solutions to cultivate healthy, productive, and happy workers.[3] And self-tracking becomes less a voluntary activity; rather it is pushed or imposed on employees.[4]

This chapter emerges from an exploratory empirical study of self-tracking at work as a contemporary digital communication practice that spotlights boundaries between the personal and the professional. The study I initially set out to do explored how self-tracking for productivity and wellbeing is being embedded in and contributes to shaping practices of work, and to redrawing boundaries around the domains of home and work.[5] I was particularly interested in how communication practices—the ways in which technologies are put to use—may be said to represent and reflect people's efforts to manage contextual boundaries and selves in pursuit of meaningful everyday living, and by extension, how *studying* communication practices can help qualify what a digitally supported good (work)life might entail. My examination of the good life is not with intent to pursue specific moral notions of what a good life *is*, but more modestly to probe how the good life is envisioned and inscribed in technology design vi-à-vis what a good life is perceived to be in the practical, everyday realities of people. The study, set in Denmark, was initiated in 2019, before the COVID-19 pandemic made working from home the standard model for large parts of the white-collar workforce. It continued after the initial lockdown of Denmark as many private and public sector knowledge workers were getting used to a working life practiced partly or mostly from within the confines of the home.

The empirical material includes semi-structured interviews with sixteen public and private sector white-collar employees of various ages, genders, family situations, ranks, and job functions. They were recruited through snowballing from initial participants, and the sample includes both active self-trackers and non-users of self-tracking at work. Most of the active self-trackers at work used MyAnalytics, an AI-enhanced system for productivity and wellness tracking among so-called white-collar workers. MyAnalytics was originally put on the market in 2016 as an extra service to which companies using Microsoft 365 could subscribe. But in the fall of 2020, it was made a default application on top of the Microsoft 365 software package. Hence, MyAnalytics was largely imposed on users and organizations, who needed to actively opt out of its tracking of work behavior. My empirical material addresses how AI-enhanced self-tracking at work may be used as a support tool for the everyday orchestration of work tasks and for getting things done in ways that are meaningful for the individual employee. Interviews were conducted to explore how workplace self-tracking might contribute to informants' experiences of the interlacing of work and personal life, and how knowledge workers managed this interlacing in their everyday practices of tracking themselves, eliciting both the fears of workplace surveillance and the hopes of personal flourishing self-tracking might facilitate. When applicable, the interviews included walkthroughs of the informants' MyAnalytics and other self-tracking data dashboards. In addition to interviews, I rely on documentation about the self-tracking software in question; for MyAnalytics this includes patent filings, product descriptions, tutorials, and online advertisements about the product.

Speaking to this book's overall theme of media backends, I take MyAnalytics to be an exemplary case of what the tech industry considers "everyday AI"[6] that—by way of its integration with standard office work software and applied algorithmic processes—operates seamlessly and often invisibly in the background during the workday. It is also a useful case for probing the infrastructural power of tech companies, hoping to inspire future scholarship to consider in historical terms how datafied living has developed over time, and empirically, how tracking and AI-enhanced analytics might shape human agency and flourishing in everyday life.

In what follows, I use MyAnalytics as a case in point to illustrate and extend a long historical trajectory of research into the everyday uses of media. Research into media use in everyday life questions both lamenting discourses of media power and celebratory discourses of empowered users through the study of actual usage practices, experiences, and sensemaking.[7] An everyday perspective on media use focuses on the concrete lifeworlds, structural arrangements, and value systems that users already inhabit. Mundane, everyday life is not just about dull routines, but also eminently represents the site where individuals translate society-wide structures of power into the particular reality of their own life: the politics of daily practices inevitably depend on routinized patterns of contextual orchestrating of and with media. Across media and usage practices, such research has documented that inherent meaningfulness for users may go hand-in-hand with commercial exploitation of these same users.[8]

If we consider AI-enhanced communication technologies such as MyAnalytics along similar lines of reasoning, they may be expected to serve practical purposes for individual users by offering data-driven support in making decisions about their own work patterns to make work more satisfying, manageable, and meaningful. At the same time, they exploit these meaningful experiences, funneling the user data on which they rely into institutional domains and commercial businesses that make value and profit out of personal data. I unpack this dual purpose in the following pages. What I present is not a systematic analysis of the empirical material. Instead, I leverage empirical examples to show how employees in various contexts carve out niches of communicative agency for themselves, in part by strategically appropriating digital media at work to fit personal circumstances, needs, and aspirations. Moreover, I link informants' experiences with MyAnalytics to questions about datafication of work and exploitation at the media backend.

Situating the Study: Self-Tracking at Work

In the wake of the Quantified Self movement, founded by *Wired* editors Gary Wolf and Kevin Kelly in 2007, research across computer science, health informatics, social science, and humanities has addressed the technologies, practices, and implications of self-tracking in various domains. Most research on self-tracking deals with voluntary and purposeful forms of self-tracking using digital devices and apps to keep track of, reflect, and possibly act on matters of personal concern (e.g., fitness, calorie intake, or menstrual tracking). Research is also accumulating on self-tracking and data-driven care among patients, continuing longstanding research on home-based health monitoring and patients' involvement in their own care.[9]

In comparison, research on self-tracking at work is relatively sparse and scattered across management and HR research, organizational studies, computer-supported cooperative work (CSCW), and critical social science perspectives.[10] Such work has highlighted critical issues of conflating wellbeing and productivity by casting self-tracking for wellbeing as affective labor,[11] as an example of "aspirational control,"[12] and as producing "automatic subjects."[13] There is also important work on privacy rights vis-à-vis employee-monitoring technologies that are increasingly spreading from the workplace into other contexts of everyday life.[14] This process has been accelerated during the COVID-19 pandemic where many knowledge workers have been working from home. A few empirical studies have been carried out, following specific public agencies or private organizations' initial—and typically temporally delimited—experiments with employee self-tracking for health, productivity, and better work/life balance. Nanna Gorm and Irina Shklovski and Paula Saukko and Amie Weedon did organizational fieldwork to study self-tracking (step-counting and sitting time respectively) as a means of countering sedentary work styles.[15] Kasper Trolle Elmholdt, Claus Elmholdt, and Lars Haahr interviewed employees who had volunteered for a sleep-tracking experiment in a large Danish energy company seeking to tie sleep quality to productivity.[16] Phoebe V. Moore studied the role of self-tracking in organizational transformation to cultivate agile workers, while highlighting resistant responses among the workers in question.[17] And Naja Holten Møller and her colleagues studied collective sensemaking of sensor data in a Danish hospital workplace to fuel a participatory approach to redesigning work, finding that the legitimacy of tracking is dependent on employees' acceptance and on placing technology "in service of human needs and dignity."[18]

There is a critical need to further consolidate the empirical understanding of imposed forms of self-tracking at work, including work that goes beyond contexts of the Global North where most existing studies—including my own—are based. I aim to contribute to such efforts by offering an analysis that embeds imposed self-tracking in the everyday context of work.

Data-Driven Decision-Support for Smart Work

MyAnalytics sits on top of Microsoft 365, a standard software package for office work, which includes the Microsoft Office package (text processing, spreadsheets etc.), Outlook for calendar and email, Teams for collaboration, and Skype for calls. It collects data from a user's interactions with this software, combines it, and performs analytics operations on these interactions to provide AI-enhanced decision-support for optimizing work. MyAnalytics is part of a suite of services developed by Microsoft for the so-called future of work, where white-collar workers are expected to increasingly collaborate with machines to automate simple tasks and to "work smarter, not harder."

MyAnalytics is marketed as a self-tracking tool to aid individuals in navigating an often busy work life, to optimize work habits and get things done, as well as to cultivate better work/life balance. In doing so, it echoes aspirations for reclaiming personal agency vis-à-vis digital systems that figure more broadly in current public debates over the struggle to capture our attention. In this context, digital media have been said to induce stress, endless distraction from what really matters, and numbing to the infringement of personal spaces and outright exploitation that follows from a digitally saturated everyday life. In response, we are commonly met with calls for regulating "screen time," "digital detoxing," or disconnecting altogether to improve human possibilities for flourishing and cultivating a good life. One proponent of such ideas is Carl Newport, whose best-selling book about "deep work" presents guidance for knowledge workers in optimizing productivity and reducing overwork.[19] The book is part of a broader wave of self-help literature targeting optimizations of the self as key to a good life.[20]

MyAnalytics seeks to cultivate smart work along four complementary trajectories: *Focus time* addresses the need to prioritize time for uninterrupted and concentrated work on individual tasks to be completed. *Collaboration* keeps a check on the user's collaboration with colleagues and looks specifically at meetings. It works from the assumption that collaboration is a key asset for quality work. *Wellbeing* builds on the idea, mirrored in Newport's book, that in order to work productively we need time to recharge and recover—physically and mentally—and that this must be done by temporally delimiting work.[21] *Network* allows the user to keep track of key interaction partners inside and outside the organization to keep an open communication line with key stakeholders. Together, these categories work in conjunction to cultivate the user's habits and consciousness toward balancing different modes of work, such as working alone (focus time) and working together (meetings) in a way that ideally supports work productivity and learning, while also promising to make workers happier and healthier. Each category derives data-driven insights from past work behavior in the Office 365 system and at the time of writing, these insights are automatically delivered to the user on a weekly basis in a digest email stating in short text and simple diagrams how the user performed on the four parameters since the last weekly update.

An Incidental Encounter

All but one of my informants describe how they first became aware of MyAnalytics as a matter of incidental encounter. Nina, a project manager in a software development company, recounts noticing recurrent emails in her Outlook inbox: "I remember I thought, what is this? I've never heard of it or been in contact with this before, but it kept coming and showing a lot of data about how I worked . . . and then I figured that I might as well take a look at that data and get an overview myself of my day, so it happened naturally." Nina happens to be an avid self-tracker in personal life, and quickly recognized MyAnalytics as a self-tracking tool, a possibly useful resource for her to get an analytics-based "overview" of what her workday looked like, which she later explained to me had helped her structure her time and tasks. In fact, she is one of the most active users of MyAnalytics in the study. She recounts that she looks at it when she has time and is not busy, and only at the weekly digest email that provides "simple visualizations and high-level takeaways." Nina never dives further into the dashboard to get the more granular data, simply because she does not have the time. Self-tracking with MyAnalytics is considered laborious.[22]

Linda, an administrative office worker on a temporary contract with a public agency, similarly told me she got to know MyAnalytics because she received weekly emails from the system:

> At first I thought it was something from the department, and maybe it is, I don't know actually, but that is interesting in itself . . . me thinking, well, okay, fine, it is just there, it just tracks. . . . And then I looked at it, and it was actually quite interesting that you can see, but then work got busy, and ever since it has mostly been about checking ultra-fast or just opening the emails so that it doesn't look like I have all these unread emails.

What is hinted at here, and elaborated later in the interview, is Linda's sense that MyAnalytics is yet another task that adds unnecessary extra labor. She does not really know what to do with the data-based insights MyAnalytics delivers: "I have had the sense that it doesn't really matter. I cannot do anything about it anyway, the numbers. Okay, I have spent X number of hours in meetings, but I am invited to these meetings so if I were to change anything . . . ?" Seemingly, Linda does not accept MyAnalytics as an invitation for her to take charge and structure her work smarter through reflexive and data-driven insights. While both Nina and Linda suggest that self-tracking is laborious, Nina can effortlessly use previous experiences with data to make the data-based insights useful for work, while Linda is at loss on how to act on the data from MyAnalytics.

Other informants in the study similarly struggle to find the system useful at all: Louise, a mid-level manager of a public agency, already considers her workday perfectly well-structured and has actively pursued tight and conscious structuring of the workday using her calendar as a personal style of smart work throughout her career. She already feels she has mastered what MyAnalytics offers to assist with. Kate, also a public agency manager, and dedicated self-tracker in personal life, notes that "it is okay fun" that she can track work behavior with MyAnalytics. Yet, she contends that core features such as ensuring focus time and setting a good meeting culture are already on the collective agenda in response to annual workplace assessments, which are mandatory in Denmark. In her division, they already have set aside specific blocks of time during the week for deep work and do not need a data-driven nudge to ensure focus time. Sara, who juggles multiple jobs and full-time studies, actually finds MyAnalytics very appealing in theory, but it does not cut across all her professional contexts and so cannot really help her in structuring work better.

Louise and Sara thus don't even bother to look at the weekly emails and have not taken interest in self-tracking with MyAnalytics at all. As we can see, MyAnalytics with its imposed vision for how to work smart does not sit without friction in its local contexts of use. Its meaningfulness for users may depend on whether the problems the software wants to address are in fact recognized as problems that require a technological fix. One case in point is distraction, often seen as related to email overload, for which the proposed tech solution is another weekly email that might pull the office worker further down the rabbit hole. For Linda, the most meaningful response is simply to mark the emails from MyAnalytics as read.

Indeed, most of my informants describe a casual and not particularly systematic engagement with MyAnalytics. This will typically include their very briefly checking out the weekly summary emails from MyAnalytics, which every now and then direct their attention to behavioral matters of possible interest in pursuing healthy and productive work habits. Apart from that, they do not pay much attention to or spend much energy on MyAnalytics. It is simply there, running in the background, tracking all their use of Microsoft 365 and rendering data into basic insights on work behavior, but largely operating under the radar. This data exploitation is mainly happening at the media backend, and not really talked about or reflected upon, something I will return to later in the discussion.

One exception to this pattern is Kieran, a software developer in a large private company. Kieran is the only informant whose management has officially introduced MyAnalytics to employees and framed its use as an opportunity for white-collar workers to get insights into and possibly adjust and improve their work habits: "It has been communicated very explicitly to all employees that the information in here is only mine. My boss does not have access to it, but they could get some data from the division, but only if the division is of a certain size" so that individual employees will only figure anonymously in the data. In this case, the company in question seems to embed MyAnalytics in strategic considerations for cultivating specific work habits, perhaps a specific work ethic centered on efficiency, while also acknowledging and addressing up-front the kinds of ambivalence and tensions of self-tracking and datafication of work that high-tech workers in software development might more easily identify.

Making Meaning with MyAnalytics

As has been documented in other forms of self-tracking, the data entered and personal analytics output provided by self-tracking software is imagined to concern mainly the self-tracking individual.[23] As such, informants seem to accept Microsoft's framing of MyAnalytics as a tool for the individual to optimize personal work habits and wellbeing. By extension, there appears to be consensus that MyAnalytics is "a service to me," perhaps even a legitimate intervention by HR aimed to offer care for the employee. This may all be viewed in light of the informants being located in a generally safe and well-regulated job market in the welfare state of Denmark. At the same time, informants' accounts of their actual uses of the system highlight an ambivalent and critical assessment of data relative to their contextual work arrangements and personal preferences; a selective engagement with and active sorting of functions and data insights that are deemed useful or not; and aspirations for a good work life that go well beyond simple adjustments for optimization, the logic promoted by the system. Each of these points are illuminated as examples of meaning-making and agency vis-à-vis the system, while also acknowledging the influence of MyAnalytics in the shaping of thoughts about and habits of work.

Data Ambivalence

A key observation in empirical studies of self-tracking is that data do not always adequately reflect the lived experience of the practice being tracked. A self-tracking system captures data along specific parameters and makes visible certain aspects while obviously lacking a contextual touch. Not everything about an experience or activity can be tracked, quantified, and rendered into intuitively compelling and self-explaining data visualizations. This fuels users' ambivalence toward the data and makes them uncertain of how telling the data-based insights actually are of what is being tracked. In the case of MyAnalytics, what counts as work is that which figures in Microsoft 365. For someone like Linda, who uses pen and paper to manage her tasks, a lot of work is not in the Outlook calendar.

The same goes for Kate, who handles many meetings from her personal phone and thus outside the system. Some of the informants expressed surprise at specific data-based insights from MyAnalytics: for instance, some of my informants found *focus time* as calculated by MyAnalytics to misrepresent how pressed for time they actually felt during the workday. An open calendar does not always equal plenty of time for deep work; and the number of meetings attended does not necessarily provide a valid indicator of time spent on collaborations. Some work is simply invisible to MyAnalytics and made invisible for further scrutiny by the system. If the system imposes a certain vision of what should get to count as work, informants' ambivalences regarding the analytics output speak critically to the uniform and limited gaze of that system: it fails to account for the myriad ways people get things done in daily life and in doing so loses part of its relevance as an aid for managing work.

Selective Engagement

The informants who actually find MyAnalytics useful have in common a remarkably selective engagement with the insights and automated services it provides. The practical uses of MyAnalytics reflect informants' job functions as well as what everyday life in general looks like from the perspective of the individual employee. The wellbeing category appears to be the least useful for my informants, although they all practice drawing boundaries between work and other things in their lives. The wellbeing category by default offers insights on work activity after normal work hours (eight to five) and Kieran tells me that he receives notifications from MyAnalytics if he writes an email outside of these hours, reminding him that "this is not a quiet day. Remember that you need to recharge the batteries." While they all strive to take time off from work to energize themselves, none of the respondents speak about the wellbeing category as particularly useful in terms of helping them take time off. If there is work, there is work, and for some, like Louise, a core part of their job is evening meetings, which according to MyAnalytics' default settings would not be recommended. Louise will instead go home early to pick up kids and do household chores with her partner, before returning to work in the evening. Her workday is thus split into two separate slots. Indeed, personal preferences as well as general life circumstances such as living alone or having daily family and care duties reflect on how informants structure their workday, when they work and so on, and informants did not find MyAnalytics geared to deal with this, hence its lack of resonance with their ideas of everyday wellbeing. Again, we can see a pushback against system-imposed norms that cast working nine to five as a benchmark for a good working life.

The other categories are found useful in different combinations, depending on the context. Nina, the project manager, is particularly interested in keeping track of her communication with stakeholders in the various projects she coordinates and finds the network category helpful for this. "MyAnalytics is good at seeing which ten people you communicate the most with, and then it is easy for me to see if I am up to date concerning who I am supposed to be in touch with. I use it as an indicator, it is not that I have used it fanatically, but MyAnalytics is a way to navigate a busy workday."

Mary, the junior lawyer, mainly takes interest in the focus time function. She manages a small team at the law firm and is often disturbed with questions or cases that need her sign-off. When she first started using MyAnalytics,

> it said I had 5 percent focus time and the rest was meetings and email, and then I thought that is probably why I feel so busy because I am always shuffling five different things. So now I plot two hours, or it does, every single day, of focus time, and it is not that I always . . . I can plan a meeting in that time slot, but I know it is allocated so that nobody else can book me during this time without asking me first and I get a notification that says "hey, you should try to concentrate."

Mary further contends this new habit of booking focus time is a direct output of MyAnalytics and would not have been cultivated without its analytics insights. In fact, focus time has become almost something sacred, a way to take agency back: take control over the daily rhythm of work. Because MyAnalytics prompted her and her colleagues to talk about disturbances at work, now colleagues will not assume they can just book Mary for a meeting when convenient, but actually ask her if she has the time. This is particularly useful, Mary explained to me, when she works from home where it can be quite difficult for coworkers to see and sense whether she is in the middle of something that requires concentration. When in the office, she can signal unavailability by putting on noise cancellation headphones and go sit by herself in a meeting room.

Aspirational Control

The example above testifies to informants' experience of MyAnalytics' role in their willful cultivation of better habits, in accordance with its intended use. Other informants describe similar experiences. When the weekly digest arrives in his mailbox, Kieran reads it "and then I sit and think I should do more of this or less of this. For instance, it can come with a warning saying 'we can see that you have participated in meetings for twenty hours last week, but we can also see that in fifteen of these hours you were also writing emails' and that is a bad habit, so it is good that it is brought out into the light." Kieran now consciously avoids email in meetings to be able to contribute and be mentally tuned in.

Kieran's and Mary's accounts speak to the use of MyAnalytics in aspirational efforts to become a better employee and coworker. This aspiration manifests itself as a matter of performing self-control and behaving in a desirable and presumably optimal manner at work. MyAnalytics provides small nudges for that. Yet, the aspiration as it is recounted seems primarily focused not on becoming as productive and efficient as possible, but on cultivating a certain work ethic of a good and attentive colleague in the day-to-day life at work. What seems a meaningful purpose from the users' perspective might resist or reframe the more rationalistic, performance-focused framing of the system in terms of optimization.

This personal touch becomes further evident in the informants' response to the AI-enhanced features of MyAnalytics that cast the system not only as an analytics insights provider but a digital assistant. MyAnalytics also offers decision-support and automated actions based on the data to enable the individual employee in balancing focus time, collaborations, and professional network maintenance. Specifically, as we saw with Kieran above, it sends "warnings" if the employee is too active on the work email after hours, allegedly attempting to nudge or discipline the users. Informants also experience it sending reminders to reconnect with specific colleagues if the system finds it has been too long since they last touched base. And if the calendar is too booked with meetings, MyAnalytics will send a notification prompting the user to allocate time to focus. It even offers to book focus time for you, but only some of my informants, such as Mary, make use of this option to offload the task of blocking out her calendar—and she has dived further into the analytics dashboard to manually set up when she prefers such focus timeslots to be located. Nina, in contrast, is quite explicit about not wanting MyAnalytics to make automated decisions for her about how she structures her work. "I trust my own judgment better," she says and explains how she uses the insights as a prompt to look ahead and book focus time herself based on what is possible and meaningful when also juggling deadlines and other planned tasks in what she considers an ongoing reflection on and adjustments to her work routines so that she feels in balance with herself: "I don't work less, and I don't go home earlier, but I am conscious of my work routines."

My empirical material illustrates how everyday realities and needs of people using self-tracking systems affect how these systems come to be accepted and meaningfully embedded in people's lives or rejected altogether. The empirical findings of selective engagement, reflections about, and adjustments of the working self through data largely mirror what is found across studies of self-tracking, whether voluntary, pushed, or imposed. The little tweaks to how MyAnalytics is used vis-à-vis how it is intended to be used testify to how informants use self-tracking to carve out niches of personal agency when appropriating technology to the specific circumstances of their everyday lives. It is through these little tweaks that MyAnalytics comes to find a meaningful place in the daily grind of individual employees.

Datafied Work and the Media Backend

MyAnalytics situates everyday AI at work as serving dual purposes of meaning-making, practical management of and perhaps pleasures of work at the individual level of self-tracking, and broader processes of creating data assets for exploitation in the grander scheme of business development. Regardless of whether MyAnalytics is accepted by individual workers and made useful for cultivating certain work behaviors or not, it promotes a specific impetus of smart work; one that casts individual optimization as the key to a good work life and projects specific work norms onto its users. And in doing so, MyAnalytics quietly amasses, analyzes, and exploits data about individual workers' use of Microsoft 365. Its tracking is always on. The data generated can be (but does not appear to be) used for structural interventions for optimization of work in the organizations where my informants are employed.

Product owners inside an organization do in principle have access to a data dashboard with anonymized aggregate data that can be used as indicators of good performance and, by extension, as means for cultivating future work behavior at the collective level in alignment with organizational goals. At the media backend, so to speak, work processes are datafied and the data in question may serve purposes of both self-tracking and algorithmic management. Confronted with such possibilities of the system, informants generally responded with surprise; some—such as Kate—with critical remarks on how this raises ethical and workers' rights questions (to opt out of tracking) that they do not recall being discussed at their workplace.

The fact that only one informant can recall MyAnalytics being introduced by management and framed as a support tool for optimal work behavior, whereas in all the other instances "it just suddenly popped up," seems significant. It speaks to the infrastructural power of companies with a unique market position, such as Microsoft in the market for office software, to further consolidate their data assets with a view to the so-called "future of work." Arguably, Microsoft's maneuver of simply turning MyAnalytics, an existing product, into a default application in its standard and market-leading platform for office work without organizations taking notice is an example of the infrastructural power of tech companies that rests on their being almost indispensable in specific contexts.[24] In this case, Microsoft has basically decided for us that the particular kind of datafication of work done with MyAnalytics, with its specific calculations and algorithmic enhancements, is what we all want. And the decision has been executed with a simple software update. But even if the system imposes certain ideas of datafying work to optimize it, in empirical terms, users push back in multiple ways through their everyday uses.

Experiences of ambivalence, selective engagement, and aspirational control showcase not only how individual users carve out niches of personal agency within the system to work around potential exploitation that is ingrained at the media backend. The examples also suggest a communicative agency that involves the reflexive engagement with individuals' own data-based insights, productivity, and work ethos on their own terms. Empirical explorations remind us that users are not just coping with MyAnalytics, but are also actively cultivating and communicating about meaningful uses of data in pursuit of a good working life beyond optimization. Or they reject the analytics as irrelevant and flawed. Through these forms of communicative agency, users push against the narrow model of ideal work behavior advanced by the system.

The data from individuals' work behaviors contained in Microsoft 365 may, at least in theory, be obtained by Microsoft and be used for optimizing its services and developing new products, such as its recent extension to MyAnalytics, an AI-based "personal productivity assistant" called Cortana.[25] As we have seen in, for instance, third-party tracking on web and mobile platforms, the infrastructural power of Big Tech operates and becomes functional in society right under our noses and without our having a coherent discussion about whether what is on offer is a path we want to tread as individual workers, organizations, and societies. And this threatens the legitimacy of self-tracking in the workplace,[26] even when weighing in its prospects of enhancing users' daily sense of agency at work. Empirical research will help us illuminate the operations of infrastructures for datafication and perhaps serve as a nudge to help us to collectively counter the imposition of digital systems in everyday practices at work and beyond.

Notes

1. James Stewart, "The Social Consumption of ICTs: Insights from Research on the Appropriation and Consumption of New ICTs in the Domestic Environment," *Cognition, Technology, and Work* 5 (2002).

2. Gordon Hull and Frank Pasquale, "Toward a Critical Theory of Corporate Wellness," *BioSocieties* 13, no. 1 (2018).

3. Martin Berg, "Making Sense with Sensors: Self-Tracking and the Temporalities of Wellbeing," *Digital Health* 3 (2017).

4. Deborah Lupton, "The Diverse Domains of Quantified Selves: Self-Tracking Modes and Dataveillance," *Economy and Society* 45, no. 1 (2016).

5. Melissa Gregg, *Counterproductive: Time Management in the Knowledge Economy* (Durham, NC: Duke University Press, 2011).

6. Peter Norvig, "Artificial Intelligence: Everyday AI," *New Scientist*, October 31, 2012.

7. Stuart Hall, "Encoding/Decoding," in *Culture, Language, Media*, ed. Stuart Hall, Dorothy Hobson, Andrew Lowe, and Paul Willis (London: Routledge, 1980); Roger Silverstone, *Television and Everyday Life* (London: Routledge, 1994); Helen Kennedy,

"Living with Data: Aligning Data Studies and Data Activism through a Focus on Everyday Experiences of Datafication," *Krisis: Journal for Contemporary Philosophy* 1 (2018).

8. Veronica Barassi, "BabyVeillance? Expecting Parents, Online Surveillance, and the Cultural Specificity of Pregnancy Apps," *Social Media + Society* 3, no. 2 (2017).

9. For a review see Minna Ruckenstein and Natasha D. Schüll, "The Datafication of Health," *Annual Review of Anthropology* 46 (2017).

10. For a review see Thomas Calvard, "Integrating Social Scientific Perspectives on the Quantified Employee Self," *Social Sciences* 8, no. 9 (2019).

11. Phoebe V. Moore, "Tracking Affective Labour for Agility in the Quantified Workplace," *Body & Society* 24, no. 3 (2018).

12. Kasper Trolle Elmholdt, Claus Elmholdt, and Lars Haahr, "Counting Sleep: Ambiguity, Aspirational Control, and the Politics of Digital Self-Tracking at Work," *Organization* 28, no. 1 (2021), https://doi.org/10.1177/1350508420970475.

13. Christopher Till, "Creating 'Automatic Subjects': Corporate Wellness and Self-Tracking," *Health Sociology Review* 23, no. 4 (2019), https://doi.org/10.1177/1363459319829957.

14. Isabel Ebert, Isabelle Wildhaber, and Jeremias Adams-Prassl, "Big Data in the Workplace: Privacy Due Diligence as a Human Rights—Based Approach to Employee Privacy Protection," *Big Data & Society* 8, no. 1 (2021); Javier Sánchez-Monedero and Lina Dencik, *The Datafication of the Workplace*, Working Paper, Data Justice Lab, Cardiff University (May 9, 2019), https://datajusticeproject.net/wp-content/uploads/sites/30/2019/05/Report-The-datafication-of-the-workplace.pdf.

15. Nanna Gorm and Irina Shklovski, "Steps, Choices, and Moral Accounting: Observations from a Step-Counting Campaign in the Workplace," *Proceedings of the 19th ACM Conference on Computer-Supported Cooperative Work & Social Computing* (2016); Paula Saukko and Amie Weedon, "Self-Tracking of/and Time: From Technological to Biographical and Political Temporalities of Work and Sitting," *New Media & Society* 24, no. 8 (2022), https://doi.org/10.1177/1461444820983324.

16. Elmholdt, Elmholdt, and Haahr, "Counting Sleep."

17. Moore, "Tracking Affective Labour for Agility in the Quantified Workplace."

18. Naja Holten Møller, Gina Neff, Jakob Grue Simonsen, Jonas Christoffer Villumsen, and Pernille Bjørn, "Can Workplace Tracking Ever Empower? Collective Sensemaking for the Responsible Use of Sensor Data at Work," *Proceedings of the ACM on Human Computer Interaction* (2021): 16.

19. Carl Newport, *Deep Work: Rules for Focused Success in a Distracted World* (New York: Grand Central Publishing, 2016).

20. Trine Syvertsen, *Digital Detox: The Politics of Disconnecting* (Bingley, UK: Emerald, 2020); Melissa Gregg, *Work's Intimacy* (Cambridge: Polity Press, 2011).

21. Newport, *Deep Work*.

22. See Moore, "Tracking Affective Labour for Agility in the Quantified Workplace."

23. Stine Lomborg, Nanna Bonde Thylstrup, and Julie Schwartz, "The Temporal Flows of Self-Tracking: Checking In, Moving On, Staying Hooked," *New Media & Society* 20, no. 12 (2018); Deborah Lupton and M. Michael, "'Depends on Who's Got the Data': Public Understandings of Personal Digital Dataveillance," *Surveillance & Society* 15, no. 2 (2017).

24. Stine Lomborg, Rasmus Helles, and Signe Sophus Lai, "Digital Tracking and Infrastructural Power," *Handbook of Critical Studies of AI*, ed. Simon Lindgren (London: Edward Elgar, 2023).

25. "What's New with Cortana, Your Personal Productivity Assistant," 2020, https://techcommunity.microsoft.com/t5/microsoft-365-blog/what-s-new-with-cortana-your-personal-productivity-assistant/ba-p/1675341.

26. See Møller et al., "Can Workplace Tracking Ever Empower?"

13

THE BACKEND WORK OF DATA SUBJECTS

Ordinary Challenges of Living with Data in India and the US

RANJIT SINGH

In this chapter, I analyze the work that people who are subject to data-driven practices, or data subjects,[1] must do to secure representation in and contend with the consequences of data systems in everyday life, an emergent condition of living in a data-driven world. I use interfaces *of* and *to* data systems as the organizing principles for my analysis. By interface *of* data systems, I mean digital interfaces that enable data subjects to interact with data systems. By interfaces *to* data systems, I am referring to a range of intermediaries from professionals (customer service operators, street-level bureaucrats, consultants, etc.) to individuals in support networks (friends and family, online and offline data subject communities, etc.) who often act as proxies for data subjects and interact with digital interfaces of data systems on their behalf. In short, I approach interfaces as both digital and human touchpoints of access to data systems. While working on digital interfaces has always been constitutive of the lived experience of data subjecthood, working with human interfaces is also increasingly becoming a precondition for data subjects to make data systems work for them.

This focus on interfaces borrows part of its inspiration from the focus of this edited volume on media backends, which I conceptually approach as sites of struggle over understanding the workings of data systems and their profound consequences for data subjects. This struggle is not only about contending with opacity of data systems,[2] but also about aligning the data produced and maintained by data systems with an individual data subject's way of life. In this sense, the interface binds the frontend and backend of data systems into an emergent relationship. On one hand, the frontend is a data system's data subject–facing side. It is often associated with what is visible, accountable, presentable, and usable about a data system. A typical example of frontend is the digital interface of any data system. On the other hand, the backend is where a data system is made workable, away from the gaze of data subjects. It sinks into the background, becomes invisible, and only returns to conscious reflection when data systems do not work as expected or break down. A typical example of the backend becoming visible is when a data subject calls a customer service operator (engaging with human interfaces) to ask for an override or renegotiate predefined terms and conditions of a digital service. The frontline human interfaces are the infrastructure[3] of the digital interface.

The other part of the inspiration comes from the central role that the digital interface plays in how data subjects and data systems mutually shape each other. While the function of the digital interface in demarcating the frontend and backend of data systems is well understood, I want to draw attention to how the digital interface is a useful analytic resource to draw out demarcations between the different kinds of work that data subjects must do to make data systems work for them. My interest in these kinds of work began quite early, when I met Yogita,[4] one of my first field respondents, during fieldwork[5] for my dissertation research on Aadhaar (translation: foundation),[6] India's biometrics-based national identification infrastructure, in the summer of 2015. In narrating her difficulty in obtaining a marriage registration certificate without Aadhaar, she concluded: "Now when you go to these [government] offices, people have found a new excuse for why they cannot do your work. *Computers are the new 'babus'!*[7] They will tell you things like: 'Madam, we want to register your marriage, but this computer won't let us'!" (Yogita, personal communication, August 3, 2015, emphasis added). Enrollment in Aadhaar is voluntary. It involves collection of biometric (ten fingerprints, two irises, and a facial photograph) and demographic (name, age, gender, and address) data from residents, which is used to issue a unique twelve-digit number to them.[8] At its surface, Yogita's story was about the challenges of navigating Indian bureaucracy without Aadhaar. Bureaucrats agreed with Yogita's claim that she was married. But neither she nor her husband were enrolled into Aadhaar. Without their Aadhaar numbers, bureaucrats claimed to be helpless; their computers would not let them document their marriage. Her point was simple, yet poignant: *digital interfaces designed to follow the rules of a bureaucracy act like bureaucrats themselves.* Resisting enrollment became a difficult task as Aadhaar increasingly began to mediate state-citizen relations in India.[9]

I have often returned to Yogita's story over the course of my broader research on everyday experiences and struggles of data subjects living with data infrastructures. In their seminal work on data infrastructures, Susan Leigh Star and Karen Ruhleder have argued that data systems become infrastructures when they draw on and sink into the background of existing practices of distributed and collaborative work.[10] For Aadhaar, this work centers on organizing government services. Issuing marriage certificates is an example of such services. A 2006 Supreme Court ruling made marriage registration compulsory in India to address a range of issues from reducing child marriage to protecting women's rights in cases of unlawful abandonment and domestic violence. Yogita and her husband made numerous visits to the marriage registration office, but without Aadhaar, they struggled to get their marriage registered. They even got a lawyer involved. After all, in September 2013, the Supreme Court had issued an interim order on the public interest litigations against Aadhaar that: "No person should suffer for not getting the Aadhaar card inspite [sic] of the fact that some authority had issued a circular making it mandatory."[11] Aadhaar was not mandatory for registering marriage, and yet the computers at the marriage registration offices seemingly made it so. Ultimately, the bureaucrats resolved the couple's struggles by letting them key in dots instead of digits for Aadhaar numbers. Their struggle in getting their marriage registered points to emerging forms of social, material, and political work that people as data subjects must do to align with data systems, which are increasingly becoming the infrastructure that sustains their relationship with diverse organizations.

In Yogita's example, the work that the couple had to do to get their marriage registered *at* the digital interface itself was eventually quite simple: key in dots instead of numbers in a data field. However, this work *at* the digital interface hides the enormous amount of work that they had to do to negotiate with bureaucrats at the marriage registration office to provide them with this option. They figured out a way to work *at* the digital interface by negotiating how to work *around* it with bureaucrats as human interfaces.

Yogita's example provides the foundation of my core argument that just like data systems have a frontend and a backend demarcated by their digital interface, the work that data subjects must do to live with data systems also has a frontend and a backend demarcated by how their activities are organized in relation to the digital interface. While the frontend of this work comes into conscious reflection when focusing on the nature of data subjects' activities *at* the digital interface of data systems (such as entering and correcting data and managing its circulation and interpretation), the backend has also slowly begun to inform scholarly inquiry in increasing attention to the nature of underlying activities *around* the digital interface that also condition how data subjects interact with data systems (for example, in negotiations with human interfaces to data systems).

Although this chapter begins with an example from India, living with data infrastructures is a global phenomenon. To illustrate this point, I am going to use examples from my research on Aadhaar-enabled identification practices in India and credit repair practices in the United States. In the following sections, I dive deeper into the analytic strategy of using the digital interface as an organizing principle to investigate the work that data subjects must do to live with data. In the first section, I argue that this work is not invisible per se; the frontend of this work is the engine of the data economy. In analyzing this work using the language of frontend and backend, I show how both forms of this work have received considerable scholarly attention. In the second section, I focus explicitly on backend work of data subjects. I narrate field stories where backend work remains unaccounted for in the ongoing infrastructuring of data in every aspect of ordinary life and yet is a necessary condition for: 1) securing representation in data systems (taking an example from my research on Aadhaar) and 2) overcoming the challenges posed by data-driven decisions (drawing on a participant's story from a research study[12] in collaboration with Malte Ziewitz[13] on following the efforts of low-income individuals in Upstate New York to improve their subpar credit scores). While there are multiple examples from both these research studies that can exemplify the nature of backend work, I have chosen one from each to showcase the everydayness of this work across geographies. Finally, to conclude, I reflect on the uneven distribution of this work.

Researching Data Subjecthood

I begin with a rather simplistic description of how data systems operate in analyzing the work of data subjects: data provided by people at digital interfaces of such systems and/or collected from various data sources as inputs are processed through an algorithmic black box to produce outputs, which are often automated and personalized data-driven decisions that people, in turn, as data subjects must contend with.[14] This work of contending with outputs either happens on the same interfaces of data systems or on different interfaces of other services that rely on these systems. Data subjects soliciting support from human interfaces to these data systems who may input data on their behalf or make sense of outputs for them can be considered backend compared to the frontend of digital interfaces where data subjects interact with data systems by themselves. Data subjects often must negotiate a way out of their struggles with data systems with such human interfaces and at times may also need to pay a fee (or a bribe) in exchange for their services. An analytic focus on digital interfaces, thus, allows differentiation between:

1 *Frontend work*: Work that happens *at* the digital interfaces of data systems. Given enough data infrastructure literacy[15] and investments in user experience design, people can work at digital interfaces by themselves without needing any support. The frontend includes, but is not limited to, (a) providing inputs through and (b) interacting with services. More broadly, it can

mean organizing everyday life by using outputs of the interfaces of social media, search engines, on-demand service and e-commerce platforms, and e-government portals.

2 *Backend work*: Work that happens *around* the digital interfaces and sinks into the background of data systems. The backend includes, but (again) is not limited to, (a) gaining access to the interfaces and, thereby, claiming membership in digital services; (b) securing affordances for one's way of life through outputs; and (c) building a community through forms of affective labor around shared experiences of algorithmic harms. This work depends on the capacity of data subjects to figure out aspects of the system that are inaccessible and to create understandings, practices, and workarounds as needed. It requires engaging with other data subjects and human interfaces and securing their support to get data systems to align with particularities of life circumstances.

By calling out this difference, I do not mean to imply that the frontend is visible, while the backend is invisible. Rather, my objective is to showcase how the ability to work at digital interfaces and make sense of the workings of data systems is variably distributed and not equally accessible to all. It, thus, requires more effort from some data subjects than others to get the same work accomplished at digital interfaces. While these efforts come in diverse forms, they remain unpaid,[16] but they must be performed as a precondition of everyday life in the data economy.

The frontend work has received considerable scholarly attention over the years. While mapping the expanse of this scholarship is outside the purview of this chapter, it often uses the interface as an analytic resource to make the work of data subjects visible. This scholarship spans across: 1) critiquing the reliance of the data economy on "free services" in exchange for "free labor" of internet users[17] that, by extension, has created the conditions for economization of attention;[18] 2) capturing the enthusiasm around crowdsourcing through notions of "wisdom of the crowds,"[19] and the conditions of the production of labor that sustain the commercial web using the figure of the "digital housewife";[20] 3) tracking the emergence of human data interaction (HDI) as a field of information science research that seeks to transform the passive collection of personal data in everyday interactions with data systems into an active reflection among data subjects on managing and controlling flows of their personal data;[21] 4) disentangling the nature of contemporary participation in data systems;[22] and finally, 5) observing the rise of the sharing economy powered by on-demand service platforms.[23]

In comparison, scholarly attention to backend work is only beginning to take shape. While there has been a consistent focus on algorithmic biases and arguments for improving fairness and accountability in operation of data systems,[24] explorations of the everyday struggles of data subjects are relatively new. Research in this domain has increasingly come to consider this work for reasons ranging from articulating agency and voice of data subjects from the bottom up[25] to formulating data-oriented notions of social justice to inform the work of data activists and practices of data-driven decision making.[26] Scholars have increasingly come to focus on: 1) how data subjects engage in mundane forms of sense-making to understand how algorithms work[27] and resist algorithmic power;[28] 2) how data subjects contend with surveillance, inequality, precarity, and discrimination perpetuated by data systems;[29] and finally 3) how data subject communities deal with everyday life in the gig economy.[30]

Liminal to both frontend and backend work is equally important scholarship on the machinations of data extractivism and colonialism,[31] invisible forms of "ghost" work that sustains the workings of the algorithmic black box,[32] and efforts to navigate seams of data systems[33] and resist oppression through data from the margins.[34] The digital interface, thus, is only a *partial solution* to the problem of analytically categorizing the diverse forms of work that data subjects do to live with data systems. However, it provides an analytic opening into backend work that does not get represented on, within, and through data systems but is crucial for their operation. In the next section, I explore two examples of this work where I focus on everyday interactions of data subjects with human interfaces to data systems. I focus on struggles over making the "right" inputs to secure access to a data system in the first example from India and explore how outputs are negotiated in pursuit of better life chances in the second example from the United States.

Forms of Backend Work

Harmonizing Life with Inputs

A crucial aspect of backend work is the struggle over securing access to a data system. Generally, gaining access[35] is as simple as registering (signing up) on a website. Registration often involves a set of mandatory questions that must be answered as the initial condition for access. It constitutes Know-Your-Customer/Citizen (KYC) requirements that are often preconditions of accessing any service. It is an initial resource for authenticating identity to authorize access and personalizing such services.

The process of providing biometric and demographic data during Aadhaar enrollment exemplifies registration. For most Indian residents, this process has been fairly straightforward, involving a visit to an enrollment agency where an enrollment operator inputs their data into the enrollment client software using a multilingual interface that displays information in English and the most common local language of the region.³⁶ For others it has produced a recursive set of challenges. These challenges were experienced by specific populations, for example: struggles with lack of distinct biometric features among the elderly and manual laborers;³⁷ challenges of discrimination and troubles with certifying gender identity among the transgendered;³⁸ and exclusion due to lack of a proof of identity and address among the homeless.³⁹ These struggles to secure a place in core data categories recursively create conditions for rendering individual identity and social history of data subject populations unaccountable⁴⁰ as Aadhaar permeates the background of everyday life in India.

Anahita, a researcher working on the role of Common Service Centers (CSCs)⁴¹ in implementing eGovernance projects in India, brought a peculiar form of this recursion to my attention during a shoptalk phone call to discuss our respective fieldwork on Aadhaar:

> I was sitting in one of the CSCs in Rajasthan. I spoke to [Sana] about her experience of enrolling her son [Faizal] into the [Aadhaar] project quite a few times. . . . They used to live in UP [Uttar Pradesh], then they moved to Rajasthan. She got her son enrolled in UP in an [enrollment] camp. When she enrolled, they did not give her an enrollment receipt.⁴² The operator told her that the receipt will be issued tomorrow, and she can come and pick it up then. She went the next day, and the camp was not there anymore. Her son's Aadhaar letter⁴³ never came. The rest of her family received their letters, but her son's letter never arrived and because she did not have an enrollment receipt, she could not follow it up.
>
> Then, they moved to Rajasthan in 2012 and here in Rajasthan, she got her son enrolled four times and still his Aadhaar card has not come. Now, she has enrollment receipt from all the four attempts. The operator looked it up and said that she had made quite a few mistakes. For example, her son's name is Faizal and some operator has entered the spelling of his name as "Faisal" and others have written it as "Faizal." . . . The operator was scolding her that she should have checked this more thoroughly and how can she make multiple attempts like this. [If she had been literate, she would not have needed] the operator's help in resolving this problem.
>
> Now, the new problem is that her son has just passed class X and he needs to be admitted into class XI and the school is demanding his Aadhaar number to admit him in the next class. So, my confusion is that if biometrics are collected during enrollment to ensure uniqueness, how can her son be enrolled four times into the system? (Anahita, personal communication, July 25, 2017)

Addressing Anahita's confusion requires a detour into the backend of Aadhaar as a data system. After data collection for enrollment is complete, the biometric data provided by an enrollee is checked against biometric data on all existing Aadhaar records. A new Aadhaar number is issued only after this deduplication process certifies that the enrollee's data is unique. Confusion around multiple enrollments stems from treating data collection and deduplication as synchronous processes. Deduplication, however, happens much later when the enrollment data packet is processed. During the data collection phase, enrollment data packets can be generated on an enrollee any number of times. If a person is already issued an Aadhaar number, these data packets are rejected as attempts to create a duplicate entry. In principle, while there can be multiple attempts at enrollment, there can only be one Aadhaar number generated for each enrollee.

In Sana's case, an Aadhaar number was probably already issued for her son, Faizal, although his Aadhaar letter was not delivered to them. In such cases, enrollees must work toward locating their Aadhaar record, if a number is generated, and then update it with new data. This backend work was challenging for several reasons: First, an Aadhaar number is a prerequisite for updating an Aadhaar record. Faizal did not have his number or even know that he had one. Second, checking whether an Aadhaar number was issued for him requires the enrollment receipt, but they did not have it from their first enrollment attempt. Third, figuring out what his Aadhaar number might be using his biometric features was not possible because authentication also requires an Aadhaar number. Aadhaar authentication involves a 1:1 comparison; biometric data provided is checked against the biometric data stored for an Aadhaar number. Enrollment is the only time when biometric data provided is compared against the entire database.

Reenrollment would help only to the extent that it provides the operator with more data about why the enrollment attempt failed and indicates the presence of an existing Aadhaar record. Instead, the operators were simply reenrolling Faizal and inputting his data often incorrectly into the interface again and again with no success. The different forms of work, with uneven chances of success, performed by Sana, Faizal, and the specific populations who struggle with Aadhaar enrollment to harmonize their life situation with requisite inputs for enrolling into Aadhaar exemplify backend work. This work is a necessary condition for navigating everyday life as Aadhaar becomes the data infrastructure of certifying identity and completing KYC requirements in India. It is never explicitly recognized and becomes invisible after an Aadhaar number is secured by enrollees as data subjects. More importantly, it showcases that data records are not static representations of data subjects.

Contending with Outputs

A data system is not the end; it is often a means to several ends. Such systems become the infrastructure for organizing services through their outputs such as lists, rankings, scores, recommendations, ratings, and more broadly, results of retrieval and sorting through data that make everyday life easier for some at the expense of others. They simultaneously exhibit function creep wherein a system designed for one purpose can be repurposed for another. A classic example of this dynamic is the use of credit scores in the United States, which was meant to operate as a loose index of an individual's creditworthiness.[44] However, through processes of "off-label use," the scope of uses for these scores has moved far beyond checking financial credit (loans, mortgages, and insurance) to underpinning forms of social credit in situations such as making decisions on hiring, renting, and even online dating.[45] As the scope of using credit scores expands, so does the scale of the challenges faced by people who have subpar credit scores. Their struggles often begin at an individual level; credit scores after all represent an individual's creditworthiness. However, our research study on following credit repair journeys of participants with subpar credit scores highlighted that these struggles expand beyond the individual. A data subject's struggles with data representation expands to encompass other family members. The family as a unit must contend with how it is represented through data.

A stark example of this insight emerged in conversations with one of our research participants, Maurice, who is a Black professional artist with fluctuating project-based income. He is engaged to Alexis, a firefighter. At the cusp of his married life, Maurice wants to be proactive about improving his credit score, which was in the mid-650s.[46] During the fourteen-month long study, Alexis became pregnant, and they decided to rent a different place with more space to raise their child. However, this turned out to be a difficult ordeal because Alexis's credit score was in the mid-400s. As Maurice described it during a check-in with us:

> We were looking for an apartment. We were searching for something, um, [bigger]. We found something we really liked. It was a three-bedroom townhouse. And we went to fill out the application, we had gotten denied.
>
> It was the first conversation that we had . . . about just credit. And even with us being together for over two years . . . we had not had a direct conversation about that aspect of our finances. (Maurice, check-in on diary entries, February 25, 2019)

Talking about debt and money is often considered a taboo in the United States. Avoiding conversations about credit scores seems like a natural extension of this taboo, although this is changing with credit scores becoming a feature of online dating profiles. Certain life circumstances can also make such conversations unavoidable. Maurice had to have a conversation with Alexis because her score was too low for them to be able to rent their dream townhouse.

Rejection, however, did not end his efforts. He did not lose hope and made several attempts to meet the property manager:

It was my third [attempt]. I went up there. I put on a shirt and tie, and . . . I said, "I would like to speak to the property manager. I know we got denied on this computer, but I wanna speak to a human."

I said, "Listen. My fiancée, she loves this place. We have a baby on the way . . . and this is where she wants to be . . . What can we do to make this possible for her?"

He asked me a few questions, and he said, "There is one loophole that we could do. I'm not sure if it'll work. I'm not sure where your credit is."

I said, "Well, my credit is fine. It's not the best, but it's fine."

So, he said, "There is a loophole. We'll put you in, and pending your approval, we'll list her as the roommate on the lease."

And within five minutes, I had gotten approved. (Maurice, check-in on diary entries, February 25, 2019)

Maurice was finally able to rent the dream townhouse. With credit score's orientation toward the individual, the data representation of a family's creditworthiness is malleable, given the support of the creditor. Maurice succeeded because he represented Alexis as his roommate on the lease. For the purposes of the property management system that evaluated rental applications, he and Alexis were not a family. At times, success in contending with outputs is a matter of how data can be made to represent a data subject to achieve desired outcomes. This, of course, requires further ethical reflection on walking the fine line between legitimate participation in and illegitimate manipulation of data systems.[47] Implicit in the ways in which data systems track behavior is the expectation that data subjects should behave as if these tools are not there.[48] There is, thus, an ongoing tension around the role that data subjects must be afforded in shaping their data. The smaller the role, the more oppressive data systems become. The greater the role, the easier it becomes to "game" them.[49] In moments when data systems do not align with particular life circumstances of certain data subjects, their backend work of getting these systems to work for them foregrounds this tension.[50] This tension is at the heart of the mutual shaping of data subjects and data systems. More importantly, they highlight that data subjects are not passive recipients of data-driven decisions.

Conclusion

This chapter uses digital interfaces as an organizing principle to analyze the unevenly distributed work that people as data subjects must do to live with data systems. I exemplify diverse forms of backend work using my research on everyday experiences of data subjects in India and the United States. My examples illustrate that *neither are data records static representations of data subjects, nor are data subjects passive recipients of data-driven decisions*. The mutual shaping of data records and everyday lives of data subjects happens not only *at* the interfaces of data systems, but also *around* them and often relies on the cooperation of human interfaces. Sana did not receive their support, while Yogita and Maurice were eventually able to secure it. Yogita got a lawyer involved; Maurice put on a shirt and tie. They both projected social capital in their negotiations, while Sana reflected on not being literate as a barrier. The difference in the outcomes of their predicaments illustrates how social positioning plays a crucial role in overcoming the challenges of living with data.

More broadly, data-driven decision-making is contingent on historical datasets and these datasets embed the societal values of the time of their construction.[51] The inputs to and the outputs based on these datasets do not represent the world we wish to live in; they represent the existing biases of the world we already live in. The challenges raised by inability to secure representation through core data categories of a system and unfavorable outputs often mirror the uneven structural consequences of societal inequities along well-recognized intersections of gender, race, class, and caste. Diverse forms of backend work emerge in contending with such uneven challenges as data systems configure life chances in data economy. The need and the ability to do this work is unequally distributed among data subjects and is deeply intertwined with their position on these intersections. *Backend work is the uneven cost of living in a data-driven world.* On the one hand, the stories of Yogita and Maurice provide a silver lining to these unequal struggles. They showcase that data subjects can find creative and practical solutions to their struggles with a little help from intermediaries. These solutions often involve securing the support of human interfaces to data systems and working *around* rather than *with* data systems. On the other hand, Sana's story is a stark reminder that these solutions are not equally accessible to all. At times, it is not just the data system, but also the human interfaces that contribute to alienation of data subjects from the data economy.

This brings me to my final point. With increasing calls to focus on everyday experiences of data subjects,[52] it is crucial to attend to the role and intermediation work of human interfaces. A crucial aspect of backend work for data subjects is developing and leveraging relationships with humans in the loop to overcome their emerging and ongoing struggles with data systems. This work is a feature of a constitutive tension of organizing for data-driven services: although one of the core purposes of deploying data systems is to remove intermediaries, intermediaries play a key role in making data systems work for or against data subjects in the last mile delivery of services. While frontline customer service operators are key actors in such negotiations, there are also increasing forms of communal knowledge sharing among data subjects about their experiences of making data systems work for them.[53] Understanding how these data communities are formed and how they exemplify novel forms of backend work is crucial to our analytic efforts of unpacking everyday life in a data-driven world. These efforts must begin with the insight that data systems do not act alone; data-driven and human judgment are inevitably enmeshed in charting the ethical landscape of everyday life with data systems. After all, an interface is as much human as it is digital.

Notes

1. Critical data studies have increasingly moved away from the term "user" to analytically articulate the position of people who are increasingly made subject to data systems without their consent, participation, or, at times, even knowledge, especially in the context of automated scoring systems such as credit scores in the United States. See Steve Woolgar, "Configuring the User: The Case of Usability Trials," *Sociological Review* 38, no. S1 (1990): 58–99; Nelly Oudshoorn and Trevor Pinch, eds., *How Users Matter: The Co-construction of Users and Technologies* (Cambridge, MA: MIT Press, 2003); Sampsa Hyysalo, Torben Elgaard Jensen, and Nelly Oudshoorn, eds., *The New Production of Users: Changing Innovation Collectives and Involvement Strategies* (London: Routledge, 2016); Nick Couldry and Jun Yu, "Deconstructing Datafication's Brave New World," *New Media & Society* (May 19, 2018); Malte Ziewitz and Ranjit Singh, "Critical Companionship: Some Sensibilities for Studying the Lived Experience of Data Subject," *Big Data & Society*, (2021): 1–13. The term "data subject" is used instead to highlight the dual role that people play as resources as well as targets of data systems in regulations (GDPR, "Article 4—Definitions," *General Data Protection Regulation* [2018], https://gdpr-info.eu/art-4-gdpr/), and by critical data studies scholars to describe people who live with data systems. Data "subjectifies through practices of production, accumulation, aggregation, circulation, valuation, and interpretation. These practices call upon subjects who are not separate from but submit to and are active in the various ways that data is made. . . . People govern their health by making themselves data subjects of health" (Evelyn Ruppert, Engin Isin, and Didier Bigo, "Data Politics," *Big Data & Society* 4, no. 2 [2017]).

2. Jenna Burrell, "How the Machine 'Thinks': Understanding Opacity in Machine Learning Algorithms," *SSRN Electronic Journal* (2015), https://doi.org/10.2139/ssrn.2660674.

3. A. M. Simone, "People as Infrastructure: Intersecting Fragments in Johannesburg," *Public Culture* 16, no. 3 (2004): 407–29.

4. All respondents have been anonymized and their affiliations masked to protect their privacy.

5. The fieldwork was conducted in three rounds: between June 2015 and January 2016; between July 2016 and January 2017; and between January 2018 and March 2018. The fieldwork was multisited including locations such as startup workspaces in Bengaluru; offices of the Unique Identification Authority of India; other Aadhaar-related service outlets; the Supreme Court of India; and activist organizations in Delhi. I conducted more than 100 semi-structured qualitative interviews in English and Hindi with Su-

preme Court lawyers, activists, Aadhaar technology designers, NGO representatives involved in helping residents use Aadhaar, and finally, residents navigating the different key processes of Aadhaar.

6. Taking the length of this chapter into account, I only provide information about the design and implementation of Aadhaar, which is relevant to understand my field stories. For a more detailed account of the project, see Aiyar Shankkar, *Aadhaar: A Biometric History of India's 12-Digit Revolution* (Chennai: Westland Publications, 2017); Nandan Nilekani and Viral Shah, *Rebooting India* (London: Allen Lane, 2016); Reetika Khera, ed., *Dissent on Aadhaar: Big Data Meets Big Brother* (Hyderabad, Telangana: Orient BlackSwan, 2019).

7. Hindi for "a street-level bureaucrat" or "a government servant." While its semiotic analysis is outside the scope of this chapter, the term "babu" exhibits a rich tapestry of meaning that etymologically begins with signifying respect for educated men with social capital. It became a way of addressing bureaucrats who did clerical work during colonial times and increasingly took on the negative connotations of Kafkaesque experiences with Indian bureaucracy.

8. *UIDAI Strategy Overview: Creating a Unique Identity Number for Every Resident in India* (New Delhi: Unique Identification Authority of India, 2010), https://www.dropbox.com/s/eg9p5uzucsd9t5r/UIDAI_Strategy_Overview_2010.pdf?dl=0.

9. Ranjit Singh and Steven J. Jackson, "From Margins to Seams: Imbrication, Inclusion, and Torque in the Aadhaar Identification Project," in *Proceedings of the 2017 CHI Conference on Human Factors in Computing System* (Denver: ACM, 2021).

10. Susan Leigh Star and Karen Ruhleder, "Steps Toward an Ecology of Infrastructure: Design and Access for Large Information Spaces," *Information Systems Research* 7, no. 1 (1996): 111–35.

11. Justice K. S. Puttaswamy and Anr. vs. Union of India and Ors. 2018. Writ Petition (Civil) No. 494 of 2012, SC India.

12. In this study, we accompanied single mothers, artists, gig workers, community college students, and even accountants in their attempts to understand and fix their credit scores over a period of fourteen months from August 2018 to November 2019. Using a combination of interviews, monthly participant diaries, and diary-interviews, we pieced together the experiences of people grappling with subpar credit scores and their folk understanding of the workings of the credit scoring system. See Ziewitz and Singh, "Critical Companionship."

13. Alternatively, Ziewitz frames the work of living with data as contending with everyday challenges of *living in the shadow of a platform* as a continuously monitored and rated data subject. He elaborates on this using the example of search engine optimization as an industry operating in the shadow of search engines. Malte Ziewitz, "Rethinking Gaming: The Ethical Work of Optimization in Web Search Engines," *Social Studies of Science* 49, no. 5 (October 2019): 707–31.

14. Geoffrey Bowker, "Data Flakes: An Afterword to 'Raw Data' Is an Oxymoron," in *"Raw Data" Is an Oxymoron*, ed. Lisa Gitelman (Cambridge, MA: MIT Press, 2013), 167–71; Frank Pasquale, *The Black Box Society: The Secret Algorithms That Control Money and Information* (Cambridge, MA: Harvard University Press, 2015).

15. The term "data infrastructure literacy" alludes to the need for investing in public understanding of working with data not just as a resource to organize practices (data skills), but also as the new condition for wider sociocultural changes in society (data politics, data culture, and data sociology). Jonathan Gray, Carolin Gerlitz, and Liliana Bounegru, "Data Infrastructure Literacy," *Big Data & Society* 5, no. 2 (July 2018).

16. This work performed by data subjects has deep resonance with Ivan Illich's notion of "shadow work." See Ivan Illich, *Shadow Work* (Boston: M. Boyars, 1981). Illich used the term shadow work to conceptually address invisible, institutionally unrecognized, and unpaid work that is essential for the maintenance of its counterpart: visible and recognized waged work. Illich further elaborates that, "To grasp the nature of shadow work we must avoid two confusions. It is not a subsistence activity; it feeds the formal economy, not social subsistence. Nor is it underpaid wage labor; its unpaid performance is the condition for wages to be paid.... The creation of professionally supervised shadow work has become society's major business" (100–14). Most work that data subjects do in producing data for any digital service is unpaid. Supervising and facilitating this unpaid work is the business model for most digital services. See Kylie Jarrett, *The Digital Housewife: Feminism, Labour, and Digital Media* (New York: Routledge, 2016). As data systems pervade every aspect of ordinary life, this work, however, is increasingly also becoming subsistence activity for the poor and the systemically marginalized. Virginia Eubanks, *Automating Inequality: How High-Tech Tools Profile, Police, and Punish the Poor* (New York: St. Martin's Press, 2017).

17. Tiziana Terranova, "Free Labor: Producing Culture for the Digital Economy," *Social Text* 63, 18, no. 2 (2000): 33–58.

18. Thomas H. Davenport and John C. Beck, *The Attention Economy: Understanding the New Currency of Business* (Boston: Harvard Business School Press, 2001).

19. James Surowiecki, *The Wisdom of Crowds* (New York: Anchor Books, 2005).

20. Jarrett, *The Digital Housewife*.

21. Andy Crabtree and R. Mortier, "Human Data Interaction: Historical Lessons from Social Studies and CSCW," in ECSCW 2015: Proceedings of the 14th European Conference on Computer Supported Cooperative Work, 19–23 September 2015, Oslo, Norway (Cham: Springer, 2015).

22. Christopher Kelty, Aaron Panofsky, Morgan Currie, et al., "Seven Dimensions of Contemporary Participation Disentangled," *Journal of the Association for Information Science and Technology* 66, no. 3 (March 2015): 474–88.

23. Arun Sundararajan, *The Sharing Economy: The End of Employment and the Rise of Crowd-Based Capitalism* (Cambridge, MA: MIT Press, 2017).

24. See, for example, Benjamin Edelman, "Bias in Search Results: Diagnosis and Response," *Indian JL & Tech* 7 (2011): 16–32; Latanya Sweeney, "Discrimination in Online Ad Delivery," *Communications of the ACM* 56, no. 5 (May 2013): 44–54; Cathy O'Neil, *Weapons of Math Destruction: How Big Data Increases Inequality and Threatens Democracy* (New York: Crown, 2016).

25. Nick Couldry and Alison Powell, "Big Data from the Bottom Up," *Big Data & Society* 1, no. 2 (July 1, 2014).

26. Linnet Taylor, "What Is Data Justice? The Case for Connecting Digital Rights and Freedoms Globally," *Big Data & Society* 4, no. 2 (December 2017); Helen Kennedy, "Liv-

ing with Data: Aligning Data Studies and Data Activism through a Focus on Everyday Experiences of Datafication," *Krisis: Journal for Contemporary Philosophy* 1 (2018): 18–30.

27. Taina Bucher, "The Algorithmic Imaginary: Exploring the Ordinary Affects of Facebook Algorithms," *Information, Communication & Society* 20, no. 1 (January 2, 2017): 30–44; Sarah Pink, Shanti Sumartojo, Deborah Lupton, and Christine Heyes Le Bond, "Mundane Data: The Routines, Contingencies, and Accomplishments of Digital Living," *Big Data & Society* 4, no. 1 (June 2017); Hong Shen, Alice DeVos, Motahhare Eslami, and Kenneth Holstein, "Everyday Algorithm Auditing: Understanding the Power of Everyday Users in Surfacing Harmful Algorithmic Behaviors," *Proceedings of the ACM on Human-Computer Interaction* 5, no. CSCW2 (October 13, 2021): 1–29.

28. Julia Velkova and Anne Kaun, "Algorithmic Resistance: Media Practices and the Politics of Repair," *Information, Communication & Society* 24, no. 4 (2019): 523–40.

29. Simone Browne, *Dark Matters: On the Surveillance of Blackness* (Durham, NC: Duke University Press, 2015); Eubanks, *Automating Inequality*; Safiya Umoja Noble, *Algorithms of Oppression: How Search Engines Reinforce Racism* (New York: New York University Press, 2018).

30. Rida Qadri and Noopur Raval, "Mutual Aid Stations," *Logic Magazine*, May 17, 2021, https://logicmag.io/distribution/mutual-aid-stations/.

31. Nick Couldry and Ulises A. Mejias, "Data Colonialism: Rethinking Big Data's Relation to the Contemporary Subject," *Television & New Media* 20, no. 4 (September 2, 2018), https://doi.org/10.1177/1527476418796632; Paola Ricaurte, "Data Epistemologies, The Coloniality of Power, and Resistance," *Television & New Media* 20, no. 4 (May 2019): 350–65.

32. Lilly Irani and M. Six Silberman, "Turkopticon: Interrupting Worker Invisibility in Amazon Mechanical Turk," in *Proceedings of the SIGCHI Conference on Human Factors in Computing Systems* (New York: ACM, 2013), 611–20; Mary L. Gray and Siddharth Suri, *Ghost Work: How to Stop Silicon Valley from Building a New Global Underclass* (Boston: Houghton Mifflin Harcourt, 2019).

33. Singh and Jackson, "From Margins to Seams."

34. Stefania Milan and Emiliano Treré, "Big Data from the South(s): Beyond Data Universalism," *Television & New Media* 20, no. 4 (May 2019): 319–35.

35. Unpacking access must always begin with the work of overcoming the challenge of the digital divide in getting to the interface of data systems in the first place and the infrastructural constraints that perpetuate it. The process of becoming a data subject, however, begins after the barrier of digital divide is overcome.

36. Data entry is displayed in English and Hindi in most parts of northern India; it is displayed in English and the regional language of the states, such as Tamil, Gujarati, Assamese, etc. in other parts of the country.

37. Ursula Rao, "Biometric Marginality," *Economic and Political Weekly* 48, no. 13 (2013): 72–77; Khera, *Dissent on Aadhaar*.

38. Ashpreet Sethi, "Getting Aadhaar Card Big Challenge for Transgenders," *Deccan Herald*, May 17, 2012, http://www.deccanherald.com/content/250353/getting-aadhaar-card-big-challenge.html; Madhavi Rajadhyaksha, "Will India Recognize a Third Gender?" *Times of India*, December 8, 2013, http://timesofindia.indiatimes.com/india/Will-India-recognize-a-third-gender/articleshow/27050953.cms.

39. Ashish Rajadhyaksha, "In the Wake of Aadhaar: The Digital Ecosystem of Governance in India" (Bengaluru: Centre for the Study of Culture & Society, n.d.), https://pad.ma/documents/PI.

40. Susan Leigh Star and Geoffrey C. Bowker, "Enacting Silence: Residual Categories as a Challenge for Ethics, Information Systems, and Communication," *Ethics and Information Technology* 9, no. 4 (December 2007): 273–80.

41. Common Service Centers (CSCs) are local offices created by the Indian government in rural and remote locations where access to internet is otherwise challenging for digital delivery of public services, such as paying electric bills and checking the status of bureaucratic applications online.

42. This receipt is the bureaucratic proof of completing enrollment issued by the enrollment agency to enrollees.

43. This letter is sent to enrollees with information about their Aadhaar number and demographic details stored in the Aadhaar database.

44. Josh Lauer, *Creditworthy: A History of Consumer Surveillance and Financial Identity in America* (New York: Columbia University Press, 2017).

45. Akos Rona-Tas, "The Off-Label Use of Consumer Credit Ratings," *Historical Social Research/Historische Sozialforschung* 42, no. 1 (2017): 52–76.

46. Credit score of the same person can be different across various bureaus and providers in the United States. Their range can be illustrated through broad descriptive categories such as "bad" (<600), "poor" (600–649), "fair" (650–699), and "good" (>700).

47. Ziewitz, "Rethinking Gaming."

48. Shoshana Zuboff, *The Age of Surveillance Capitalism: The Fight for a Human Future at the New Frontier of Power* (New York: PublicAffairs, 2019).

49. Ziewitz, "Rethinking Gaming."

50. Such backend work aligns with the notion of "repair work" required to make a data system work in an existing professional context—data systems often encounter breakages that must be smoothened over by repairing them. See Madeleine Clare Elish and Elizabeth Anne Watkins, "Repairing Innovation: A Study of Integrating AI in Clinical Care," *Data & Society Research Institute* (2020), https://datasociety.net/wp-content/uploads/2020/09/Repairing-Innovation-DataSociety-20200930-1.pdf. With backend work, however, I am implying work of aligning particularities of life with standardized data categories, which is easier for some data subjects than others.

51. Bowker, "Data Flakes"; Lawrence Busch, "Big Data, Big Questions: A Dozen Ways to Get Lost in Translation: Inherent Challenges in Large Scale Data Sets," *International Journal of Communication* 8 (2014): 1727–44.

52. Kennedy, "Living with Data."

53. Beth Leavenworth DuFault and John W. Schouten, "Self-Quantification and the Datapreneurial Consumer Identity," *Consumption Markets & Culture* 23, no. 3 (May 3, 2020): 290–316; Mark Kear, "The Moral Economy of the Algorithmic Crowd: Possessive Collectivism and Techno-Economic Rentiership," *Competition & Change* 26, no. 3–4 (July 2022): 467–86.

14

REPAIRING ALGORITHMS, REBUILDING DATA PATHS

Digital Infrastructures, Public Service Media, and Material Solidarity in Europe

KAARINA NIKUNEN

The rise of hate speech, political manipulation, algorithmic biases, and data leakage on digital platforms has raised serious concerns about democracy and the role of the public interest in the current media ecosystem.[1] These challenges are partly seen as consequences of automated media, fueled by data and organized by algorithms. Mark Andrejevic argues that the "combination of platform logics and communicative practices with broader social policies undermines the conditions for democratic deliberation."[2] In the platform economy, automated processes are built for profit and hidden from public view, in media backends.

What Andrejevic refers to above as the automation of mass media can also be described as a move toward increasingly *closed systems of profit*.[3] Processes of automation, predictive analyses, and recommendation systems predefine media for us in ways that are difficult to disclose, making it almost impossible to understand how media work. This is an obvious problem for media scholars, but it is even more problematic in terms of media democracy. Media consumers are offered automated recommendations without really understanding why and how these decisions are made. At the same time, people's data are gathered and sold to marketers or, in some cases, handed over to governments for political manipulation. Closed systems of profit rely on efficiency, invisibility, and secrecy.[4] These systems were developed long before the global COVID-19 pandemic, but their power has intensified as people have become increasingly dependent on digital services, streaming, computers, and data systems. At the same time, our worlds have become more and more insecure.

In both a response and resistance to the growing power of closed systems of profit, a range of movements, manifestos, and initiatives have been launched with the aim of opening up, repairing, and rebuilding media systems while questioning their datafied grounds. This chapter explores such initiatives in the context of public service media and European media policy. Media backends are approached here as an (often hidden) area of media where both concrete designing of media and more abstract defining of media policy takes place. The chapter explores media backends on three levels: first, on the grassroots level of designing algorithms and recommendation systems; second, on the planning of social media spaces and their data practices; and third, on the level of media policy and regulations. The chapter explores these areas through the concept of material solidarity, which highlights the significance of technological and infrastructural dimensions of media in serving the public interest and enhancing social justice.

Material Solidarity

The concept of material solidarity is derived from my earlier work on media solidarities.[5] This work was inspired by emergence of solidarity movements that were organizing through media in 2000s in support of refugees and migrants. I was interested in exploring the ways in which media may provide a space for imagining alternatives; how media may operate as an arena where people may come together, engage in social debates, and share understanding of being in this together. This approach draws on previous work on activism and alternative media that also points out how social movements and activism are in contradictory ways dependent on commercial social media and therefore strive to re-create and redesign new media systems.[6]

In current datafied closed systems of profit, it has become clear that approaches to media solidarity need to dive deep and address the very foundations of media: the infrastructure and technological designs that channel and enable media content and participation. In other words, this chapter aims to point out the increasing significance of media backends to the enhancing of solidarity and social justice. To do this I introduce the concept of material solidarity that draws on the current material turn, feminist theorizations of solidarity as well as Marxist studies' interest in material foundations of inequalities. The concept sheds light on the increasing power of infrastructures and materialities of media that often remain hidden or unrecognized from the audiences. The material approach engages with the striving of maker cultures to undo black-boxing[7] or apply reverse engineering with an emphasis on visibility, experiments, errors, recycling, and collaboration.[8] However, material solidarity challenges the hidden mechanisms of media, not only for the purpose of making them visible but also to identify the structures of inequality and biases embedded in the technology and design. Material solidarity broadens the scope of exploration from media content to the infrastructural solutions and technologies that are designed, developed, and contested in media backends. It focuses on struggles for equality, activism, and policy aimed at enhancing ethical technologies and digital spaces of equality as alternatives to datafication.[9]

While the material approach pays attention to the hidden forces of media objects and technologies, it also raises awareness of the ways in which media shape and impact environments and the wider world: the extent to which the information economy is indebted to physical realities, labor markets, working conditions, environmental energy use, raw material, and waste production.[10] Research has showed how production of digital technologies follows the mindset of European colonial past with control of territory, installation of infrastructure, extraction of raw materials, exploitation of human labor, and exercise of power for the benefit of technology companies and their economic success.[11] This constellation of practices is referred to as digital or data colonialism. Scholars point out the pervasiveness of big technology companies in the Global South causing deeper systems of dependency and inequality through technologies and their production.[12] An increasing amount of research highlights the environmental consequences of media and the tech industry, which affect regions in which the manufacturing circle spins from raw materials and hardware assembly to debris and waste.[13] In *Greening the Media*, Richard Maxwell and Toby Miller argue that our enchantment with media technologies and emphasis on the symbolic power of media have prevented us from perceiving the media's material connection to the ecological crisis.[14]

Wastelands of wires, laptops, mobile phones, cables, screens, gaping holes and polluted waters left by mineral quarries are manifestations of the global inequalities instantiated through media industries.[15] The growing digital underclass, which has been well documented in Mary L. Gray's and Siddharth Suri's *Ghost Work* and Sarah T. Roberts's *Behind the Screen*,[16] take care of, clean, and maintain the dirty, broken, and routinized parts and content of media platforms while receiving minimum wages and little legal protection. They are the "human labor powering many mobile phone apps, websites, and artificial intelligence systems."[17] At times, as pointed out in Andrea Muehlebach's study on factories in Northern Italy,[18] industrial sites can evoke the political and historical consciousness of labor. I propose that contemporary media platforms, experienced as greedy and broken, have operated as sites that evoke political awareness and reinvigorate struggles for more just media, incorporating a focus on environments, infrastructure, and software. Increasingly, struggles for fair media are taking place in the realm of design and policy—and often require familiarity with the processes of media backends.

Exploring material solidarity requires a holistic view of the fairness of media to the world it consumes. It relates to the notion of a precarious life,[19] which may be discussed on a symbolic level and experienced on a material level by asking the fundamental question of whose life is worth saving. In other words, material solidarity addresses and explores the combination of environmental and human inequalities connected to digital colonialism,[20] to the ways in which manufacture and consumption of media render some lives and their contexts more valuable than others, and seeks to find ways to undo those inequalities.

Public Good

A range of scholarly works from the field of media and technology studies, social science and humanities have been focusing on the relationships among technology, social justice, and solidarity. New research on design justice,[21] antiracist technology,[22] data justice,[23] and slow computing[24] have begun focusing on how to challenge technologies of inequality and how to create and imagine alternatives to those systems of oppression.[25] Through collaborative and creative practices, design justice aims to open up digital design processes to challenge the reproduction of inequalities and use intersectional feminist standpoints to create more inclusive technologies.[26] In *Captivating Technology*, Ruha Benjamin describes how to "incorporate justice-oriented approaches to techno-science . . . ultimately refashioning the relationship between technology and society by prioritizing justice and equity" and "imagine and create alternatives to the techno quo."[27] Similar goals of imagining and re-creating more just technologies have been enunciated in different initiatives, from the Data Justice Lab to the Citizen Lab, that pay attention to the inequalities embedded in the technologies used in our everyday lives and in governmental organizations and institutes. In *Slow Computing*, Rob Kitchin and Alistair Fraser explore collective ways to pursue a better world of computing on multiple fronts—from industry to governments and NGOs.[28]

These movements and manifestations draw attention to media infrastructure and technology as *public goods* that should be designed for all. As Ara Wilson argues, thinking about the digital media infrastructure as a "public good" has to do with a shared ideal of necessities or "tolerable standards of living" that cannot be left to the markets to decide.[29] In his famous work, *Principles of Political Economy*, John Stuart Mill defined the common good as something promoted by the state for the benefit of all citizens; it is ensured by government when market forces fail to provide what people need.[30] Therefore, creating community infrastructure, such as roads and communications systems, can be thought of as a public good. Many movements that strive to re-create and challenge media technologies are born out of the realization that the media have failed to recognize their own situatedness in imagining the universal good.[31] Justin Reich and Mizuko Ito show that failures of technology-driven reforms are often connected to biases and social distance between designers and the people they seek to serve.[32] Scholars exploring public space, such as Paul Carter[33] and Nikos Papastergiadis[34] contend that the design of public spaces in multicultural and democratic cities must address complex forms of public engagement, participation, and cultural experience. Feminist theorizations pay attention to situatedness, experience, dialogue, and collaboration as relevant avenues to further solidarity, equality, and social justice. Therefore, instead of taking a public good as self-evident, its conceptualization needs to be rooted in lived experience and an understanding of difference, with reflexive, ongoing interrogation of its foundations.[35]

Drawing on these ideas of material solidarities and digital media as a public good, I introduce in what follows examples of alternatives to the commercial platformed media environment. I focus on cases that respond to the rise of polarization and hostility on social media and recognize the ways in which media environments allow, enable, and limit relationships and participation. In other words, the aim is to explore struggles to root solidarity within the things and technologies that constitute the media experience. This focus is connected to practices of opening doors and making hidden processes visible. The examples that I have encountered in the research project Fair Data (while exploring alternative imaginings of the media ecosystem) are based on interviews and participatory observations of several events and workshops with media professionals, researchers, activists, and policymakers in Finland, the UK, and the US between 2018 and 2021.[36]

The case studies illustrate how struggles for alternatives take place on different levels of media backends. They represent initiatives that are created within media institutions, such as in the European public service media. As such they are not radical grassroots movements but instead exemplify attempts to create alternatives in the heart of public institutions and in the horizons of European imagination. The first example is on the grassroots level of designing algorithms and recommendation systems. The second example moves further to initiatives of new public social media spaces, and the third example discusses European digital media policy. These cases capture infrastructural imaginations[37] driven by political, social, and economic interests emerging at a particular historical moment when the power of technology giants and the platform economy is starting to become challenged.

The Public Service Algorithm

European public service media (PSM) are comprised of national institutions that have played a major role in building the national analog radio and television infrastructure in Europe. European PSM, led by the BBC, emerged in the

1920s as a model that could strengthen national culture and civic education and counter forces of commercialization.[38] As publicly owned media, the public service media follow the logic of the welfare state, with a remit to serve all citizens. While PSM as a whole has been considered valuable for civic society, it has also been described as paternalistic with a top-down approach toward audiences.[39] In developing countries, European PSM, particularly the BBC, have modeled as the ideal media system; however, in terms of audience engagement in these contexts community media has often been more successful.[40] In the past decades PSM in Europe have sought to include more participatory approaches but also more individualistic approaches to audiences.[41]

The emergence of commercial platforms such as YouTube, Facebook, Instagram, and TikTok has transformed media productions and logics across the globe.[42] In the last twenty years, PSM have had to adapt to a changing media environment and have invested heavily in new digital technologies at the same time as they have had to defend their right to be digital. PSM have struggled to compete with Netflix, Amazon, and other streaming platforms based on data-driven systems that use algorithms and recommendation systems to organize content and develop services.[43] The hidden mechanisms of data-driven platforms, where user data are sold and used for the benefit of private companies, remain inaccessible to the public and are at odds with public service mandates and values. PSM have struggled to survive in digital markets and have increasingly striven to develop their own platforms and lean on user data, audience metrics, segmentation, and user profiling in their content production, audience reach, and distribution. Ben Fields, Rhianne Jones, and Tim Cowlishaw argue that the increasing use of algorithmic recommendations in PSM endangers their core value of universality and may lead to their "becoming more like a goldfish bowl, rather than a window to the world."[44]

One of the main concerns of the platformized media environment involves its use of algorithms to categorize audiences and content in ways that divide the media worlds of these audiences. Recommendation algorithms are seen to further polarize views by only offering similar content and, in some cases, increasingly extreme views.[45] To avoid such polarization, PSM have developed the so-called "public service algorithm." As part of the research project on Fair Data, we interviewed public service media employees at the Finnish PSM, Yleisradio, who design algorithms. The designers and employees saw it as crucial that they develop algorithms to serve public values. One explained, "We were probably the first ones who focused their recommendation system with a built-in mechanism that is interested in the diversity of the consumed content. It does not maximize the evident but strives to maximize the breadth of the content. . . . In journalistic recommendations, we are interested in thinking about how we can make people know more about the world and what information is relevant rather than how to maximize the time used on platforms."[46] In other words, PSM are seeking to use data-driven media to enhance public value and avoid logics that potentially polarize media audiences.

This resonates with James Bennett's call to set different objectives for data-based practices within PSM than within a commercially driven market.[47] He lays out four goals for public service algorithms: connecting audiences to new content, connecting diverse audiences to shared content, connecting audiences to new media forms and experiences, and connecting audiences to other public services and resources (e.g., libraries and museums). The diversification of media use is elementary to the deliberative role of the media and the idea of imagined communities.[48] Exposure to diverse views is seen to enhance the ability to form more informed opinions, tolerate disagreement, and exchange ideas and viewpoints with others. These abilities impact the ways in which people learn about media, become engaged with different ideas and content, and understand media logics.[49]

Public service algorithms strive to curate media use in ways that enhance these elements. However, according to Jannick Kirk Sørensen and Hilde Van den Bulck, these objectives need to be accompanied by transparency.[50] A move away from the culture of black-boxing is critical for PSM. As one of the designers suggests, "The crucial point is how open and honest you can be about what you are trying to achieve. . . . We try to enhance understanding of the choices made within the company, as well as among the audiences, so that people have a better understanding of why the machine has made particular types of recommendations."[51] Therefore, PSM have to hold onto data practices that recognize the General Data Protection Regulation (GDPR), safeguard user privacy from third-party trackers, and honor the right to be forgotten, even though this has become increasingly challenging in the current platformed media environment of perpetual tracking. A similar public service algorithm has been in use in several PSM companies in Europe, including at the British BBC.[52] These may seem like small acts amid a datafied media ecosystem; however, PSM designers, who also introduce their work to other designers, hope to be able to help them to embark on these models and spread their ethos further. The public good is crystallized as a technology that seeks to cross boundaries rather than create them.

Material solidarity is captured here in the understanding of the ways in which designing algorithms can make a difference to how people understand and communicate with each other and conceive their roles as part of a shared world. It sheds light on the ways in which technological solutions may enhance possibilities to engage with different worldviews, learn to disagree, and, therefore, increase the ability to embrace the idea of a shared imagined community and solidarity across difference. Thinking through the concept of solidarity also reveals the shortcomings of such initiatives. First of all, PSM algorithms are designed in an institutional setting where the guiding values are those defined within the institution. PSM have often been criticized for being paternalistic toward their audiences, and such a top-down approach is not likely to recognize the public good from the perspective of their diverse audiences.[53] PSM would benefit from collaborating more with different audiences, grassroots social movements, and minorities in developing their understanding of public good and public service technologies. Second, the impact of the public service algorithm may remain modest, since PSM are surrounded by and partly dependent on the commercial platformed media environment and its logics.[54] However, in this situation, data transparency and public service algorithm represent imaginative politics[55] that may not change the foundational logics of the platformed media environment but can be seen as ways to reimagine the place of PSM in the digital media ecosystem and the larger imaginary of alternatives.

Designing Public Spaces

The domination of US tech giants and commercial platforms has engendered initiatives aimed at building a better internet altogether. These desires are captured in visions of alternative public digital spaces based on open, ethical infrastructure and an ambition to build technologies that can be shared as a sustainable media ecosystem. These visions seek to provide commercial-free, nonexploitative, and nontoxic public spaces online. In some ways, they seek to re-create the idea of the internet that once was, without a naive belief in the fairness of markets.

The Dutch PublicSpaces initiative captures this incentive in its manifesto: to offer media space that is open, transparent, accountable, sovereign, and user-centric. In its conference in 2021 themed "a Common Internet,"[56] the organizers referred to the internet as something that is "broken," albeit something that can be fixed: we will look for ways to make the internet a healthy public space again. These visions include an idea of a new internet that serves public values, without addictive technologies. In similar ways, the research and development team at the BBC explored "how the BBC could help create an internet that more easily supports the online ambitions of public service organisations of all types, around the world."[57] This kind of public service internet would focus on publicly controlled data, easy access for everyone, a healthy digital public sphere, and public service networking. In 2021, a group of academics and professionals launched the Public Service Internet Manifesto to support a publicly owned internet.[58]

Common to these initiatives are secure, transparent data paths that offer control over data to citizens rather than to media companies. They operate without advertising and with public funding, donations, or cryptocurrency and blockchain technology. In other words, the new public social media resist compulsory connectedness or coerced participation.[59] Visions of the new internet entail a do-it-yourself approach with civic tech initiatives, open-source software, community-based computing infrastructure, and a co-operative platform where several public service institutions, museums, and libraries can unite their efforts.[60] However, these visions entail various challenges and contradictions. Even now there are several alternative "community-owned" social media sites that draw on transparent data practices such as Diaspora, Ello, Mastodon, Vero, and MeWe among others. Yet these social media sites often remain small and specialized sites that struggle with problems of moderation, not unfamiliar to hate groups or illegal activities. As shown in research by Sarah T. Roberts,[61] Minna Ruckenstein and Linda Lisa Marie Turunen,[62] and Mary L. Gray and Siddharth Suri,[63] content moderation continues to be a great challenge in digital media. Due to its costs, it is often outsourced, poorly paid, or replaced with automated systems.[64] In addition, visions of the decentralized internet with cryptocurrency and blockchain technology rarely take into account the vast environmental costs of cryptocurrency.

Matt Locke, the founder of Public Media Stack, emphasizes the ethos of recycling and collaboration instead of inventing the same things over and over again.[65] The idea behind Public Media Stack is to create new strategies to co-ordinate and create a map of existing ethical technologies and infrastructure for public media. Public Media Stack is not involved in creating another public social media; rather, it provides tools and information for public media on how to use ethical technologies and infrastructure.

Data for the public good means that data collected on social media can be used to develop services of public interest—decided by the public. Thus, the data can be considered as a tax, or civic surplus, that citizens decide on.[66] During our research with European PSM, the idea of data as a publicly owned good, a tax, came up in discussions with media professionals and in data workshops with the public. We asked people to imagine how they might use this public data as a resource. While it was generally challenging to imagine data as a public good, some participants suggested that they would give up their data for improvements in mental health services and, in particular, inventions to decelerate climate change.[67] In these visions, the data-driven media environment is connected to its planetary dimension, and it becomes a resource whereby its symbolic dimensions can be used to make up for the damage they cause to the material world. Material solidarity is illustrated here in solutions that try to prioritize publicly controlled data, secure data paths, or data for the public good while they also recognize the planetary dimension of social media spaces and their costs to the environment.

Policies against Hide and Seek

The third example involves European media policy and regulation. Regulation that once seemed like an antidote to the internet has rapidly become one of the main areas where the imagination of the new and better internet has been drawn. Regulatory measures have been created to "save" the internet and tackle problems of datafication, surveillance, and digital domination of a few technological companies globally. The implementation of the European General Data Protection Regulation in 2018 has been a landmark in the struggle over transparency and policy change toward tech giants Google and Facebook, emphasizing the possibility of regulation as a way to curb data gathering and surveillance.

In 2020, the European Union (EU) started preparing for another major regulatory mechanism, a two-part package comprising the Digital Market Act (DMA) and the Digital Services Act (DSA), to ensure protection of citizens' rights and promote transparency and accountability within digital markets and services. The DMA treats different digital services according to their size and power. This means that very big platforms have specific obligations due to their power and impact. It includes several responsibilities to promote transparency in terms of algorithms, recommendations, and content moderation as well as to ensure the protection of basic rights. The DMA is a significant regulatory measure. As such, it illustrates the imagination of the public good in the European political landscape, even though parts of these incentives are no doubt driven by the concern over European media and technology companies' position in global markets and are a target of unprecedented political struggles and lobbying.

Interestingly, the proposed DMA also include an incentive to share data with officials and academic researchers. So far, researchers have had difficulties accessing reliable data from platforms and monitoring their data practices. This has led to a serious digital divide in research between the data rich and data poor.[68] Research projects such as Spotify Teardown illustrate how artistic or anarchic experiments may sometimes be the only way to open up the logics of closed systems of profit, particularly those with substantial power.[69]

The new goals of transparency and safety require substantial maintenance and moderation work. The demanding digital labor of checking, cleaning, and removing messages and providing the environment with supportive care is crucial for digital media. However, media policy has hardly recognized the conditions of this so-called ghost work.[70] The material grounds of media remain detached from these policy visions—although they are expressed in other contexts.

A separate initiative launched in 2020 by the EU, the New Industrial Strategy, connects digital media to its earthly foundations. The strategy seeks to make the information and communication technology (ICT) infrastructure and data centers climate-neutral by 2030. It includes overall improvements in energy efficiency and the circular economy of the ICT sector and the introduction of product passports containing information on the origin, composition, and recycling of digital products. The EU also strives to diminish digital waste by prolonging the lifecycle of digital devices. It is here that we can see the wastelands, mines, environmental damage, and conflict minerals that are part and parcel of the infrastructure and software of digital media.[71] It is also here that we can see the traces of Europe's colonial past, the exploitation of raw materials and human labor, that media industries have continued to appropriate for profit.

One of the most striking examples of European colonial power is played out in Congo, which under the rule of King Leopold II of Belgium in the 1880s and 1890s was exploited for ivory and rubber to advance the industrial growth of Europe and increase the profits of the king.[72] The colonial logics of ownership and extraction followed in the 1930s with appropriation of copper and cobalt mines by Belgian-owned companies. In present day the Democratic Republic of Congo is one of the main sources of coltan, which is used in digital products, particularly in mobile phones. The extraction of coltan has caused violent conflicts, harmed the environment and biodiversity, and caused the death of over a million lives in the past decade in the DRC.[73] The mines are controlled by private companies but also armed groups and military units, and the control over coltan is an ongoing struggle. Approximately over 40 percent of the world's coltan is mined in the DRC because of the low costs and cheap labor that guarantee the profits of extraction.

While tech companies are facing increasing pressure to declare and trace their sources of coltan, the systems to certify sources of minerals are not complete. The technology strategy of EU recognizes the problem of conflict minerals, but on the whole the strategies do not refer to the colonial past or strive to decolonialize digital media industries. Instead, optimistically, with a gaze forward in these infrastructural imaginations, the EU is focusing on how to use digital technologies to transform societies toward environmental sustainability.[74] The visions of digital technology as the gateway to the future reminds of the mindset of colonial power to manage and control the raw materials, "and even weather and the climate."[75] As argued by Patrick Brodie and Patrick Bresnihan, the increase of datafied systems and digital technologies is enabled through the appropriation of the language of environmentalism that greenwashes the environmental costs of digital technologies.[76] The language of environmentalism is also appropriated in the EU policies that promote growth and sustainability at the same time. Yet these operations cannot simply be turned into sustainable, as argued by Julia Velkova in her research on data centers, which have been (unrealistically) redefined as gateways to carbon-free energy future.[77] Instead of acknowledging the cruelties and mistakes of the colonial past, the EU policies adopt belief in technologies that are dependent on their extraction operations in the Global South. In this way the policies echo extractivism, logics of exploitation and subjectification central to a datafied media environment.

As the previous research has shown, one of the main obstacles in reaching the goals of the European Green Deal is the lack of access to reliable data on the carbon footprint in the ICT sector. As long as there is no reliable data on the carbon footprint of the industry, it is impossible to create reliable policies that recognize the ways in which the massive increase of digital and datafied technologies will impact the environment and inequalities across the globe. Symbolic transparency that the EU promotes does not seem to meet transparency on the material level.[78]

While European media policy has taken impressive steps to reimagine and redefine the digital media ecosystem, from the material point of view the measures seem inadequate and echo colonial logics of extraction. The concept of material solidarity sheds light on this contradiction and points out the relevance of environmental aspects of digital media as inseparable from policy understanding of public good as good communicative practices, transparency, safety, and privacy.

Conclusion

This chapter explored the struggles of material solidarity in media backends: the different attempts made to nurture public value and ideals of diversity and equality in the digital infrastructure and automated operations. I propose that seeing commercial digital platforms as greedy and broken has reinvigorated struggles to repair and reimagine the digital media environment. The concept of material solidarity emphasizes the ways in which these struggles are increasingly connected to material and technological aspects of media and fought in the media backends.

New movements and manifestos have emerged to question the media environment dominated by technology giants. The examples discussed in this chapter offer insights on different levels of media backends from the grassroots level of designing algorithms to media policy—which are all part of a larger trajectory of challenging the discriminatory practices of digital media. Examples of public service algorithms, digital public spaces, and regulatory mechanisms in the EU illustrate the different ways in which the idea of the public good can be incorporated into media technologies. They speak of the desire to treat the media environment as a space that should be available for everyone, without fear of harassment, exploitation, or discrimination.

The fact that many of these examples occur in Europe is not a coincidence. This reflects the media history of a continent with a legacy of strong public service media with the (often top-down) remit to serve public interest. In the context of global digital markets, Europe has taken a strong position to support regulatory measures. Whether motivated by market competition or genuine public interest concerns, these practices and policies illustrate a clear move toward transparency in terms of digital software, algorithms, recommendation systems, and data practices. They speak of the need to open up algorithmic processes and platform affordances to understand how media work. The case studies of this chapter also reveal shortcomings of these initiatives and imaginations. The concept of material solidarity forces us to ask the fundamental questions of who defines the conditions of solidarity and for whom. Therefore, in terms of serving the public good and solidarity, one should ask whose definition of public good is being incorporated in algorithms and digital technologies. In what ways are the general public, diverse audiences, and minorities invited to define the public good and imagine alternative public spaces?

To reach public good, the ideals of media policy need to respond to the multiplicity characterizing Europe, recognize the inequalities inscribed in history, and approach them through collaborative practices by designing and imagining alternatives with practices of dialogue and listening. The case studies also show that policy measures need to recognize all the labor, care work, and maintenance that the construction of public goods requires. Most importantly these initiatives at all levels need to pay attention to planetary dimensions of media and take the environmental issues of digital media seriously. This means demanding transparency of the environmental impact of media industries. Instead of continuing the logics of extractivism of the colonial past, EU policymakers should recognize the vast costs of digital technology to the environment and its toll on the growing global inequalities that assess some lives and environments as more valuable than others.

With the concept of material solidarity, this chapter has sought to show that solidarity is profoundly connected to the cables and rare earths, in the software design and in the human labor that builds, mines, and maintains them. It points to the increasing relevance of media backends in the struggles for solidarity and social justice.

Notes

1. Gavan Titley, Kaarina Nikunen, and Mervi Pantti, "Shifting Formations, Formative Infrastructures: Nationalisms and Racisms in Media Circulation," *Television & New Media* 22, no. 2 (2021); Ariadna Matamoros-Fernández, "Platformed Racism: The Mediation and Circulation of an Australian Race-Based Controversy on Twitter, Facebook, and YouTube," *Information, Communication & Society* 20, no. 6 (2017).

2. Mark Andrejevic, *Automated Media* (New York: Routledge, 2020), 49. See also James E. Campbell, *Polarized: Making Sense of a Divided America* (Princeton, NJ:

Princeton University Press, 2018); Eli Parisier, *The Filter Bubble: What the Internet Is Hiding from You* (London: Penguin Books, 2011); Matthew A. Baum and Tim Groeling, "New Media and the Polarization of American Political Discourse," *Political Communication* 25, no. 4 (2008).

3. Andrejevic, *Automated Media*.

4. Frank Pasquale, *The Black Box Society* (Cambridge, MA: Harvard University Press, 2015).

5. Kaarina Nikunen, *Media Solidarities: Emotions, Power, and Justice in the Digital Age* (London: Sage, 2019).

6. Matt Ratto and Megan Boler, eds., *DIY Citizenship: Critical Making and Social Media* (Cambridge, MA: MIT Press, 2014).

7. Pasquale, *The Black Box Society*.

8. Ratto and Boler, *DIY Citizenship*; Emit Snake-Beings, "Maker Culture and DiY Technologies: Re-functioning as a Techno-Animist Practice," *Continuum: Journal of Media and Cultural Studies* 32, no. 1 (2017).

9. José van Dijck, "Datafication, Dataism, and Dataveillance: Big Data between Scientific Paradigm and Ideology," *Surveillance & Society* 12, no. 2 (2014); Andrejevic, *Automated Media*; Seeta Gangadharan, "Digital Inclusion and Data Profiling," *First Monday* 17, no. 5 (2012).

10. "Anatomy of an AI System: The Amazon Echo as an Anatomical Map of Human Labor, Data, and Planetary Resources," 2020, https://anatomyof.ai/; Jussi Parikka, *A Geology of Media* (Minneapolis: University of Minnesota Press, 2015).

11. Michael Kwet, "Digital Colonialism: US Empire and the New Imperialism in the Global South," *Race and Class* 60, no. 4 (2019).

12. Toussaint Nothias, "Access Granted: Facebook's Free Basics in Africa," *Media, Culture & Society* 42, no. 3 (2020); Danielle Coleman, "Digital Colonialism: The 21st Century Scramble for Africa through the Extraction and Control of User Data and the Limitations of Data Protection Laws," *Michigan Journal of Race and Law* 24, no. 2 (2019).

13. Anna Reading, "Seeing Red: A Political Economy of Digital Memory," *Media, Culture & Society* 36, no. 6 (2014); Miho Taka, "Conflict Coltan: Local and International Dynamics in the Democratic Republic of Congo" (PhD diss., Coventry University, 2011); Kate Crawford and Vladan Joler, "Anatomy of an AI System: The Amazon Echo as an Anatomical Map of Human Labor, Data, and Planetary Resources," https://anatomyof.ai/; Jack Qiu, *Goodbye iSlave: A Digital Manifesto* (Urbana: University of Illinois Press, 2016).

14. Richard Maxwell and Toby Miller, *Greening the Media* (Oxford: Oxford University Press, 2019).

15. Nikunen, *Media Solidarities*, 35.

16. Mary L. Gray and Siddharth Suri, *Ghost Work: How to Stop Silicon Valley from Building a New Global Underclass* (Boston: Houghton Mifflin Harcourt, 2019); Sarah T. Roberts, *Behind the Screen: Content Moderation in the Shadows of Social Media* (New Haven: Yale University Press, 2019).

17. Roberts, *Behind the Screen*, ix.

18. Andrea Muehlebach, "The Body of Solidarity: Heritage, Memory, and Materiality in Post-industrial Italy," *Comparative Studies in Society and History* 59, no. 1 (2017).

19. Judith Butler, *Giving an Account of Oneself* (New York: Fordham University Press, 2005).

20. Kwet, "Digital Colonialism."

21. Sasha Costanza-Chock, *Design Justice: Community-Led Practices to Build the Worlds We Need* (Cambridge, MA: MIT Press, 2020).

22. Ruha Benjamin, ed., *Captivating Technology: Race, Carceral Technoscience* (Durham, NC: Duke University Press, 2019).

23. Lina Dencik, Arne Hintz, Joanna Redden, and Emiliano Treré, "Exploring Data Justice: Conceptions, Applications and Directions," *Information, Communication & Society* 22, no. 7 (2019); Joanna Redden, "Democratic Governance in an Age of Datafication: Lessons from Mapping Government Discourses and Practices," *Big Data & Society* 5, no. 2 (2018).

24. Rob Kitchin and Alistair Fraser, *Slow Computing: Why We Need Balanced Digital Lives* (Bristol: Bristol University Press, 2020).

25. Safiya Umoja Noble, *Algorithms of Oppression: How Search Engines Reinforce Racism* (New York: New York University Press, 2018); Gangadharan, "Digital Inclusion and Data Profiling."

26. Costanza-Chock, *Design Justice*.

27. Benjamin, *Captivating Technology*, 11–12.

28. Kitchin and Fraser, *Slow Computing*.

29. Ara Wilson, "The Infrastructure of Intimacy," *Signs: Journal of Women in Culture and Society* 41, no. 2 (2015). Wilson considers infrastructure as a network where material systems are entwined with social relations and a complex interplay of structure and agency.

30. John Stuart Mill, *Principles of Political Economy* (1848) (Kitchener: Batoche Books, 2000).

31. Joy Buolamwini and Gebru Timnit, "Gender Shades: Intersectional Accuracy Disparities in Commercial Gender Classification," *Proceedings of the 1st Conference on Fairness, Accountability, and Transparency, Proceedings of Machine Learning Research*, 2018.

32. Justin Reich and Mizuko Ito, *From Good Intentions to Real Outcomes: Equity by Design in Learning Technologies* (Irvine, CA: Digital Media and Learning Research Hub, 2017).

33. Paul Carter, *Meeting Place* (Cambridge, MA: MIT Press, 2013).

34. Nikos Papastergiadis, Amelia Barikin, Scott McQuire, and Audrey Yue, "Introduction: Screen Cultures and Public Spaces," in *Ambient Screens and Transnational Public Spaces*, ed. Nikos Papastergiadis (Hong Kong: Hong Kong University Press, 2016), 5.

35. Nikunen, *Media Solidarities*.

36. The events and workshops include the founding workshop of Public Media Stack in New York in May 2019, the Lift event in Helsinki in October 2019, and the InnoPSM Research Network meetings with researchers and media professionals in London in 2019 and Helsinki in 2020. In addition, the research project Fair Data organized five data workshops with different audience groups in 2019. Jenni Hokka, "Welfare Data Society? Critical Evaluation of the Possibilities of Developing Data Infrastructure Literacy from

User Data Workshops to Public Service Media," in *New Perspectives in Critical Data Studies: The Ambivalences of Data Power*, ed. Andreas Hepp, Juliane Jarke, and Leif Kramp (London: Palgrave, 2021). Research interviews included one with the founder of Public Media Stack in November 2019, and another with a customer service designer in YLE in September 2020.

37. Lisa Parks, "Media Infrastructures and Affect," *Flow*, May 19, 2014.

38. Marc Raboy, *Public Broadcasting for the Twenty-first Century* (Luton: University of Luton Press, 1996).

39. Karol Jakubowitcz, "Bringing Public Service Broadcasting to Account," in *Broadcasting and Convergence: New Articulations of the Public Service Remit*, ed. G. Lowe and T. Hujanen (Gothenburg: Nordicom, 2003).

40. Benedetta Brevini, "Public Service and Community Media," in *The International Encyclopedia of Digital Communication and Society*, ed. Mansell Robin and Hwa Ang Peng (London: Wiley-Blackwell, 2015).

41. Trine Syvertsen, "The Many Uses of the 'Public Service' Concept," *Nordicom Review* 20, no. 1 (1999).

42. Anne Helmond, "The Platformization of the Web: Making Web Data Platform Ready," *Social Media + Society* 1, no. 2 (2015); Tarleton Gillespie, "The Politics of 'Platforms,'" *New Media & Society* 12, no. 3 (2010).

43. Ramon Lobato, *Netflix Nations: The Geography of Digital Distribution* (New York: New York University Press, 2019); Tarleton Gillespie, *Custodians of the Internet: Platforms, Content Moderation, and the Hidden Decisions That Shape Social Media* (New Haven: Yale University Press, 2018).

44. Ben Fields, Rhianne Jones, and Tim Cowlishaw, "The Case for Public Service Recommender Algorithms," *FATREC Workshop* (2018), https://www.piret.gitlab.io/fatrec2018/program/fatrec2018-fields.pdf. See also Jenni Hokka, "Making Public Service under Social Media Logics," *International Journal of Digital Television* 8 (2017).

45. Derek O'Callaghan, Derek Greene, Maura Conway, Joe Carthy, and Pádraig Cunningham, "Down the (White) Rabbit Hole: The Extreme Right and Online Recommender Systems," *Social Science Computer Review* 33, no. 4 (2015).

46. Research interview conducted on September 23, 2020, via Zoom with a customer service designer from the Finnish public service media YLE.

47. James Bennett, "Public Service Algorithms," in *A Future of Public Service Television*, ed. Freedman Des and Goblot Vana (London: Goldsmiths Press, 2018).

48. Andrejevic, *Automated Media*; Benedict Anderson, *Imagined Communities: Reflections on the Origin and Spread of Nationalism* (London: Verso, 1983).

49. Natali Helberger, Kari Karppinen, and Lucia D'Acunto, "Exposure Diversity as a Design Principle for Recommender Systems," *Information, Communication & Society* 21, no. 2 (2018).

50. Jannick Kirk Sørensen and Hilde Van den Bulck, "Public Service Media Online, Advertising, and the Third-Party User Data Business: A Trade versus Trust Dilemma?" *Convergence* 26, no. 2 (2020).

51. Interview, September 23, 2020.

52. Mike Savage, "BBC Building 'Public Service Algorithm,'" *BBC News*, May 13, 2019, https://www.bbc.com/news/entertainment-arts-48252226; Charles Beckett,

"An Algorithm for Empowering Public Service News" (2020), https://blogs.lse.ac.uk/polis/2020/09/28/this-swedish-radio-algorithm-gets-reporters-out-in-society/.

53. Jakubowitcz, "Bringing Public Service Broadcasting to Account."

54. José van Dijck, Thomas Poell, and Martijn de Waal, *The Platform Society: Public Values in a Connective World* (New York: Oxford University Press, 2018).

55. Liisa Malkki, *The Need to Help* (Durham, NC: Duke University Press, 2015).

56. Public Spaces Conference #1, March 11–12, 2021, https://publicspaces.net/conference-2021/.

57. "Building a Public Service Internet," BBC Research and Development, https://www.bbc.co.uk/rd/projects/public-service-internet.

58. "Public Service Internet Manifesto," https://ia601504.us.archive.org/3/items/psmi_20210722/psmi.pdf.

59. Veronica Barassi, "Datafied Citizens in the Age of Coerced Digital Participation," *Sociological Research Online* 24, no. 3 (2019).

60. See Andrejevic, *Automated Media*.

61. Roberts, *Behind the Screen*.

62. Minna Ruckenstein and Linda Lisa Maria Turunen, "Re-humanizing the Platform: Content Moderators and the Logic of Care," *New Media & Society* 22, no. 6 (2020).

63. Gray and Suri, *Ghost Work*.

64. Eugenia Siapera and Paloma Viejo-Otero, "Governing Hate: Facebook and Digital Racism," *Television & New Media* 22, no. 2 (2021).

65. Research interview with Matt Locke, November 28, 2019.

66. Philip Napoli, "User Data as Public Resource: Implications for Social Media Regulation," (2019), https://ssrn.com/abstract=3399017; Julia Lane, Victoria Stodden, Stefan Bender, and Helen Nissenbaum, eds., *Privacy, Big Data, and the Public Good: Frameworks for Engagement* (Cambridge: Cambridge University Press, 2013).

67. Hokka, "Making Public Service under Social Media Logics"; Kaarina Nikunen and Jenni Hokka, "Welfare State Values and Public Service Media in the Era of Datafication," *Global Perspectives* 1, no. 1 (2020). See also Helen Kennedy, Dag Elgesem, and Cristina Miguel, "On Fairness: User Perspectives on Social Media Data Mining," *Convergence* 23, no. 3 (2017).

68. Danah Boyd and Kate Crawford, "Critical Questions for Big Data," *Information, Communication & Society* 15, no. 5 (2012).

69. Maria Eriksson, Rasmus Fleischer, Anna Johansson, Pelle Snickars, and Patrick Vonderau, *Spotify Teardown: Inside the Black Box of Streaming Music* (Cambridge, MA: MIT Press, 2018).

70. Gray and Suri, *Ghost Work*.

71. European Union, "Supporting the Green Transition: Shaping Europe's Digital Future" (2020), Supporting_the_green_transition_en.pdf.pdf.

72. Arlie Hochschild, *King Leopold's Ghost: A Story of Greed, Terror, and Heroism in Colonial Africa* (Boston: Houghton Mifflin, 1998).

73. Nicolas Niarchos, "The Dark Side of Congo's Cobalt Rush," *The New Yorker*, May 31, 2021; Taka, "Conflict Coltan"; Ewan Sutherland, *Coltan, Congo, and Your Cell Phone: The Connection between Your Mobile Phone and Human Rights in Africa* (April 11, 2011), SSRN, http://ssrn.com/abstract=1752822.

74. European Union, "A European Green New Deal," https://ec.europa.eu/info/strategy/priorities-2019-2024/european-green-deal_en.

75. Patrick Brodie and Patrick Bresnihan, "New Extractive Frontiers in Ireland and the Moebius Strip of Wind/Data," *Environment and Planning E: Nature and Space* 4, no. 4 (November 6, 2020).

76. Ibid.

77. Julia Velkova, "Thermopolitics of Data: Cloud Infrastructures and Energy Futures," *Cultural Studies* 35, no. 4–5, 663–83.

78. Crawford and Joler, "Anatomy of an AI System."

AFTERWORD

Theorizing across and between Media Backends

RAHUL MUKHERJEE

Scholars have been studying media backends for a while now by other names: algorithms, platforms, industries, infrastructures. However, none of these terms by themselves seem to encompass the range of proliferating backends operating to make media work today. The list of things, processes, and relations the editors of this remarkable anthology, Lisa Parks, Julia Velkova, and Sander De Ridder, include within backends—"electronic components in devices, network equipment and linkages, data centers and storage facilities, and algorithmic processes and software, as well as the ways these components and processes are designed, imagined, and communicated about"—suggest the limits of existing concepts to analyze media backends. It would be a stretch to equate infrastructures with factories making electronic equipment, and while algorithms possess an opaque infra-ness, they are too software-ish (programmable) to be made to stand in for the hard materialities of media infrastructures like data centers and optical fibers.

We Need New Names, New Metaphors

New names and phrases can be terms and concepts; they can become metaphors too. Sometimes powerful metaphors like "platform" and "cloud" as rhetorical devices in their repeated invocation shape sociopolitical and economic discourses even as they obscure and normalize (problematic) power relations and material practices. The editors propose "media backends" as an alternative metaphor that can evoke new response-abilities among media scholars and wider publics. The theorization of media backends in this book shares conceptual and methodological affinities with infrastructure studies as well as with scholarly research about distribution, logistics, and automation. These affinities include an attention to differentiated visibilities, a disposition to think of systems in ecological and relational ways. And yet there are limits to what infrastructures or algorithms can be, and this collection emerges as an intervention in media studies by offering a way to think *across and between* a variety of media backends. For instance, one way to make sense of the proliferating media backends has been to blur the boundaries between terms like platforms and infrastructures, so that strategically and contingently some infrastructures become platforms, and some platforms become infrastructures.[1] These conceptual gestures suggest that we need a term like "media backends" to more comprehensively account for systems, experiences, and relations that seem to be a bit away from us, physically, mentally, spatially, and temporally, but continue to make possible our at-the-moment interactions/intra-actions with digital interfaces/intra-faces just next to us.

Site-Specificity and Networked Relations across Sites

The editors emphasize that scholars studying media backends need to draw connections across the subfields of science and technology studies, critical data studies, and media industries (and not just stay within them). Relationality is a key practice and phenomenon in the research approaches developed in the introduction and the chapters that follow. The editors suggest that scholars should move beyond studying "sites of production/consumption" to "studying productive relations across the many sites of supply-chain." This study of relations across sites is carried forward in many chapters. In chapter 13, Ranjit Singh describes cases where people ("data subjects") encounter interfaces at various levels of fintech/credit rating infrastructures. If somebody's housing application is rejected by an app because of bad credit, these data subjects do not stop there but find agents and lawyers (who are in Singh's formulation "human interfaces to the data systems") to uncover loopholes in the credit rating protocols. Singh calls this "working around" interfaces: if data subjects encounter problems at one interface/intermediary, they work around that interface/intermediary to find new interfaces/intermediaries in the rating system. This working around interfaces is a way of connecting different sites (of encounter) in the infrastructural system. Working around interfaces becomes a way of multiplying sites of interface in/to the backend system, possibly increasing one's chances of understanding the system and getting work done.

This multiplying of sites of intermediation is a key area of synergy between studies of media backends and emerging studies of media distribution, those concerned with distribution of audiovisual content as well as (digital) money. Distributing streaming content involves actors in various stages of the delivery chain: some curating content catalogs, others involved in encoding files, and still others working as part of the content delivery networks (for more, see chapter 7 by Vibodh Parthasarathi, Philippe Bouquillion, and Christine Ithurbide).

With increasing formalization, digital intermediaries like search engines and social media have played a key role in news and rumor circulation. That said, it is also the case that digital intermediaries like YouTube (several news channels have their own YouTube channel) require a whole group of formal and informal people and organizations such as talent agents and multichannel networks (MCNs) that extend strong influence over content creators and streaming platforms.[2] While there has been significant discussion of local micro-celebrities as being key participants and creators for TikTok in India, less appreciated has been the role of talent scouts who operate at the media backend, finding and recruiting local talent for these platforms and apps. My interviews with such talent scouts working for TikTok and other live streaming apps like BigoLive and Likee indicate that they are very much part of the production and distribution ecology of streaming video apps in India.

Intermediaries are crucial to mobile payment transfers as well. Although the rhetoric of financial inclusion through mobile/digital revolution often presumes to paint all human intermediaries as middlemen, brokers, and (informal) predatory lenders, the mobile money distribution systems in India, Myanmar, South Africa, and Pakistan (and various locations at the margins of Global South) also have their own set of human intermediaries.[3] Ishita Ghosh and Jacki O'Neill list a number of such intermediaries such as mobile money agents, cash collectors, and telecom service shops involved in the Airtel (a telecom operator) money system. They also note that many such agents contributed to the success of a mobile money scheme (M-PESA) in Kenya, though celebratory declarations often champion the mobile handset as the one and only reason behind transformation to a cashless economy.[4] My own recent research related to telecenter operators (recovery agents) who work with predatory microloan app companies calling (harassing) nonpaying customers suggests that scholars will encounter more intermediaries involved in the mobile money distribution system if they draw relations across the supply chain nodes of this media backend system.

As an infrastructure studies scholar, I want to examine how the study of media backends both borrows from and extends scholarship in media infrastructures. There is a generative tension, I believe, running through the essays of the book and also in the formulation of media backends about site specificity (place-based analysis) on one hand and network relations (relations across sites) on the other. One can see this productive tension in media infrastructure studies scholarship, between "nodal" place-based analysis of infrastructures and accounting for the networks of relations (edges of the network) they unleash or the networks of relations that make possible the construction and maintenance of infrastructures at some specific places.[5]

In several infrastructure studies approaches, there is attention to the specificity of media infrastructures (whether data centers, satellite systems, and gig platforms) and attention to the site-specificity or situatedness of these infrastructures, through an investment in ethnography and fieldwork.[6] This is not just about the research method but also the questions such a research method generates. Site-specificity is related to questions of place-making that Vicki Mayer and Julia Velkova (chapter 6) ask: How does the data center remake the places of Hamina and Groningen through practices of storifying, and through discourses of development? How does a paper mill get transformed into a data center in Hamina? How does Google/Alphabet as the Big Tech with its own sleek media aura come from outside and start painting a picture of transformation it will bring to Groningen in blueprints and plans with local government officials about its hyperscaled data centers? In thinking about what the editors call productive relations across sites, one can ask comparative questions about network relations: How does a data center in Groningen differ from one in Hamina, or, one could add, how does a data center's air conditioning in hot and moist climates of Singapore or Dar e Salam differ from those in cold and dry weather of Groningen and Hamina? Or, how is the landing of underwater optical fiber ocean cables connected to locations of data centers? This explains how both Singapore and Mumbai do not have a sustainable electricity grid, and yet they are key places of data center construction boom. This is because they are well-connected to optical fiber landing stations, thanks to their historical emplacement as crucial nodes (port cities) on important trading routes.[7] A media archaeological approach would suggest *palimpsestic thinking,* tracing layers of infrastructures following colonial and postcolonial temporal coordinates, and a political-economy disposition would frame this as *path dependence.* A media backend theorization would suggest both, and may even further discuss how mega-corporations are engaging in land accumulations for wind and solar energy projects in the name of green capitalism to meet data center needs through carbon offsets. Here a media backends approach is in conversation with discourses and practices of energy transitions.

Temporalities/(Un)knowing

There are chapters in this book that temporalize backends, resisting the tendency to regard backends of computing systems merely as the spatial distance of the user from where data is being stored and processed. Amanda Lagerkvist and her colleagues (chapter 11) study gendered voice assistants through an existential approach that does not just spatially probe into the technological infrastructures behind the "sonorous surface" of these voice assistants but existentially examines the longer histories of feminized voice automaton, from eighteenth-century robotic prototypes and the nineteenth-century talking machine Euphonia to today's Alexa. In another temporal approach (inflected by media phenomenology), Tim Markham (chapter 5) refuses to reduce backends of the music-streaming platform Spotify to its algorithmic recommendations, data servers, and business relations with music artists. Such a research approach, according to Markham, would make backends self-contained, and insufficiently account for the dynamic unfoldings of the Spotify infrastructural assemblage that happen at the moment of encounter: here matters of knowing are displaced from "cognition" to "action" with improvisation as knowledge being prioritized. The temporal connotations of backends are thus innovatively brought forth in these two chapters.

To pay attention to media backends, that is, to begin to decipher and trace operations in the backend, has profound implications for the politics of knowledge and power. A project of studying media backends is therefore about devising ways of knowing and unknowing. Jonathan Cohn (chapter 3) provides a fascinating account of what is missed if one thinks of artificial intelligence (AI) systems as black boxes, where all one studies are inputs and outputs to the system. This leads to reductively equating AI with objectivity, efficiency, and optimization. In answering the call of the editors to move beyond thinking of backends as mere "inert technical objects" ("black boxes") toward a system of relations, Cohn interprets various art projects that investigate the materiality, relationality, and specificity of AI infrastructures. This leads him to understand AI projects as "distinct, imperfect, neurodiverse, and quirky subjective systems." Along these lines, Sander De Ridder cautions against according mythic status to backend AI technology because that allows technocapitalism to dictate what counts as "intelligence" and "empathy" in contemporary society. To provide just one last example, Mark Andrejevic and Zala Volcic (chapter 1) argue that with particulate sensors like "smart dust" no longer needing to be attached to objects but floating on the breeze, the situated perspective of a human subject will cease to be required: knowing will be "frameless," an environmental becoming. Such evocative (and frightening) chapters in the book predict epistemological consequences of the (potential) shifts in ontological conditions of media backends where interfaces transform into milieu.

Users, Publics, Workers: Forms of Address, Ways of Serving

The chapters of this book generously offer a plethora of terms and concepts to understand the heterogeneities of user interactions where digital users/workers go by names such as "utility publics" (introduction), "digital piecework" (Anne Kaun et al., chapter 8) and "data subjects" (Singh, chapter 13). The editors contend that media users are increasingly being prescribed specific roles tied to being responsible consumer-citizens. These include being compliant with watching certain hours of television, putting on self-tracking devices, and accepting one's role as a data generator for the algorithm to become more efficient or for supporting the interests of energy companies and media conglomerates. These conditionings, according to them, mark the transition of media publics into utility publics.

On these lines, I want to focus on how an attention to the media backends opens up (or makes legible) many new sites of media labor practices (marked by race, gender, and caste), as they dynamically engage with management infrastructures and algorithms. These backend systems keep finding new ways of utilizing human laborers to be servers. Scholars such as Lilly Irani and Sarah Roberts emphasize that divisions of labor exist within backend work: software designers/programmers are differentiated from those who work as shadow laborers performing content moderation, or the precarious impermanent microworkers (Amazon's Mechanical Turk). This is "digital piecework" strictly managed by algorithms that allows backend computational processes to be ceaselessly *on*.[8]

Drawing on this scholarship, Kaun and her coauthors (chapter 8) insightfully researched the media backend work of digitizing archives performed by incarcerated persons and refugees. Inmates in the state women's prison in South Dakota working for the state correctional industries are disproportionately Indigenous, and are paid $.25 for an hour's work that involves ironing a newspaper and then scanning it. The "continuously available, easily exchangeable, and most importantly cheap workforce" at the prisons and refugee camps *serve* media backend systems and digital users at the frontends. The ways in which this kind of incarcerated labor is kept invisible or strategically made visible form part of the analysis that Kaun and her colleagues undertake. Reading this chapter made me realize the vastly different kinds of on-demand short-term "gigs," from household tasks (Task Rabbit) to food delivery work (UberEats), that comprise what is fashionably called the "gig economy."

Julie Chen, Noopur Raval, and Rida Qadri's scholarship about food delivery workers in China, India (Swiggy), and Indonesia (Gojek) respectively indicate that the working conditions and labor practices of platform/gig workers are not merely determined by algorithms but work through the complex interplay of labor mediation technologies, managerial intermediaries, and kinship networks.[9] These case studies, I believe, illuminate an interdisciplinary scholarly arena where media backends could hold together synergies across discussions about infrastructural (in)visibilities, political economy and ownership, and labor practices and affect.

A significant number of food delivery workers in cities of China and India internally migrated from villages and small towns into big cities within the same country. Chen notes that over time, to maximize profits and remain competitive, food delivery platforms like Ele.m and Meituan shifted from a model of platform-hired laborers to crowdsourced riders and outsourced/subcontracted riders. Consequently, the contractual relations of these already precarious migrant workers became increasingly managed by intermediary staffing agencies called *daili*.[10] These layers of intermediation of labor contractual relations (alongside opaque algorithms) further obscure/distance working conditions from the frontends of food delivery app interfaces. Given their precarious position in the city, Bengaluru's platform workers, who are mostly migrant laborers, Raval explains, depend on "ties with relatives" and "fellow migrants" belonging to their home districts. The opacity of algorithms tends to exploit the already informal nature of delivery work in places in the Global South, but the (informal) kinship networks also make it possible to resist algorithmic management. In the context of instant food-delivery apps where the pressure of ten-minute "instant" deliveries is inevitably on the delivery person on a bike rushing from the mini-warehouses or restaurants to people's homes, it is the kinship networks (at times, based on caste) that sustain the workers as they deal with such demanding schedules.[11] Raval's intervention here not just reformulates the "people as infrastructures" thesis but also theorizes existing and imagined kinship networks as infrastructures.[12]

The book's focus on thinking between and across sites of production, consumption, and distribution is an invitation that resonates with scholarship on "multisituated app studies" that refuses to just perform walkthrough at the app interface, but examines apps in relation to app stores, app (software) packages, and multisited infrastructures for storing app content and data.[13] Just like this book on media backends encourages media studies scholars to attend to less discussed technical objects like micro-electromechanical systems (MEMS) to be found in the motherboards of smartphones (Lisa Parks, chapter 2), multi-situated app studies asks researchers to grapple with software development kits (SDKs). MEMS comprise a tiny inconspicuous part of the smartphone, but are key to a phone's motion, its network connection, and sound conversion abilities. Likewise, SDKs are an essential part of the modular design of the app, and can reveal information about app templates and third parties (who plug/embed their SDKs in the app, and at times, surreptitiously collect data), and thereby help resist the obfuscation practices of app companies.[14]

In some of my recent collaborative work, I have been compelled to continue inquiries after reaching the infrastructures, and consider the corporate behemoths behind the infrastructures of apps, their impact upon local and global mediascapes, and the new forms of media power that institutionalize their corporate logics.[15] It is precisely this multiplying of sociotechnical objects, institutions, and processes, and the relations across them, that the concept of "media backends" advocates investigating. This has been an inspiring book to read and respond to.

Notes

1. Jean-Christophe Plantin, Carl Lagoze, Paul N. Edwards, and Christian Sandvig, "Infrastructure Studies Meet Platform Studies in the Age of Google and Facebook," *New Media & Society* 20, no. 1 (2018): 293–310.

2. Ramon Lobato, "The Cultural Logic of Digital Intermediaries: YouTube Multichannel Networks," *Convergence* 22, no. 4 (2016): 348–60. Also see Joshua Braun, "News Distribution," *Oxford Encyclopedias: Communication* (London: Oxford University Press, 2021).

3. Mrilani Tankha and Ursula Dalinghaus, "Mapping the Intermediate: Lived Technologies of Money and Value," *Journal of Cultural Economy* 13, no. 4 (2020): 345–52.

4. Ishita Ghosh and Jacki O' Neill, "The Unbearable Modernity of Mobile Money," *Computer Supported Coop Work*, 2020, https://doi.org/10.1007/s10606-020-09373-1.

5. Lisa Parks, "Global Networking and the Contrapuntal Node: The Project Mercury Earth Station in Zanzibar, 1959–64," *Zeitschrift für Medien- und Kulturforschung (ZMK)* 11, no. 1 (2020): 41–57. A multisited ethnography has its own challenges of cultural and language skills and training. Parks raises a crucial question: "What do we gain from drilling down into one network node as opposed to exploring dynamic interconnections and relations between and across them?"

6. There are multiple ways of studying infrastructures provided in this book, including analysis of scientific visualizations/computer-aided designs (Parks, chapter 2) and regulatory documents and consultation papers (Parthasarathi, Bouquillion, and Ithurbide, chapter 7).

7. Nicole Starosielski, *The Undersea Network* (Durham, NC: Duke University Press, 2015).

8. Lilly Irani, "The Cultural Work of Microwork," *New Media & Society* 17, no. 5 (May 2015): 720–39; Sarah T. Roberts, *Behind the Screen: Content Moderation in the Shadows of Social Media* (New Haven: Yale University Press, 2019).

9. Refer to Julie Yujie Chen, "Spaces of Labor Mediation: Policy, Platform, and Media," in *Media and Management*, ed. Rutvica Andrijasevic, Julie Yujie Chen, Melissa Gregg, and Marc Steinberg (Minneapolis: University of Minnesota Press, 2021), 64–96. Also see Rida Qadri and Noopur Raval, "Mutual Aid Stations," *Logic Magazine*, no. 13, https://logicmag.io/distribution/mutual-aid-stations/.

10. Chen, "Spaces of Labor Mediation."

11. Qadri and Raval, *Mutual Aid Stations*. I am also drawing from Raval's talk at the International Communication Association panel on Media Backends organized by Lisa Parks and Julia Velkova, May 29, 2022.

12. Abdoumaliq Simone, "People as Infrastructure: Intersecting Fragments in Johannesburg," *Public Culture* 16, no. 3 (2004): 407–29.

13. Michael Dieter, Carolin Gerlitz, Anne Helmond, Nathaniel Tkacz, Fernando N. van der Vlist, and Esther Weltevrede, "Multi-Situated App Studies: Methods and Propositions," *Social Media + Society* 5, no. 2 (2019): 1–15.

14. Ibid.

15. Marc Steinberg, Rahul Mukherjee, and Aswin Punathambekar, "Media Power in Digital Asia: Super Apps and Megacorps," *Media, Culture & Society* 44, no. 8 (2022): 1405–19.

CONTRIBUTORS

MARK ANDREJEVIC is a professor in the School of Media, Film, and Journalism at Monash University where he leads the Automated Society Working Group and is a chief investigator in the ARC Centre of Excellence for Automated Decision Making and Society. He writes about surveillance, digital media, and popular culture and is the author, most recently, of *Automated Media*.

PHILIPPE BOUQUILLION is a professor of communication at the University Sorbonne Paris Nord, and a researcher at the Laboratory of Excellence Cultural Industries and Artistic Creation and the Laboratory of Information and Communication Sciences. His work focuses on concentration, transnationalization, and public policy transformations in the cultural and creative industries in Europe and India.

JONATHAN COHN is an associate professor of digital culture at the University of Alberta, Canada. He is the author of *The Burden of Choice: Recommendations, Subversion, and Algorithmic Culture* (2019) and coeditor of *Very Special Episodes: Televising Industrial and Social Change* (2021). His work on AI ethics and the history of algorithmic technologies and culture can also be found in *Wired*, *Salon.com*, and *The Conversation*.

FAITHE J. DAY is an assistant professor in the Department of Black Studies at the University of California at Santa Barbara. A researcher, writer, and digital creative, Day develops curriculum, data collection, and curation projects in collaboration with other scholars to identify critical frameworks and best practices to ensure an ethical and justice-centered approach to working with data, through a focus on Black and LBGTQIA+ data and discourse.

SANDER DE RIDDER is an assistant professor of media studies in the Department of Communication Studies, University of Antwerp, Belgium. He is a member of the Antwerp Media in Society Centre where he researches the impacts of digital media on sociality, human communication, and culture. He has worked extensively on digital youth cultures, social media, intimacies, and sexualities.

FATIMA GAW is a doctoral student in media, technology, and society at Northwestern University and formerly an assistant professor at the University of the Philippines. Her research work focuses on algorithmic cultures, platform governance, and disinformation networks in the Global South.

CHRISTINE ITHURBIDE is a researcher at the French National Centre for Scientific Research who focuses on the socioeconomic transformation of cultural and creative industries and workers in India. Her work has explored localization strategies and regulatory processes related to Netflix and Amazon and has appeared in *Réseaux*, *The South Asia Multidisciplinary Academic Journal*, and *Global Media and Communication*.

ANNE KAUN is a professor of media and communication studies at Södertörn University, Sweden. Her research focuses on media and political activism and the role of technology in political participation. She is the author of *Crisis and Critique* (2016) and *Prison Media: Incarceration and the Infrastructures of Work and Technology* (2023).

AMANDA LAGERKVIST is a professor of media and communication studies in the Department of Informatics and Media at Uppsala University. Her work has explored digital memories, death online, and biometrics. As Wallenberg Academy fellow (2014–2018) she founded the field of existential media studies and recently published *Existential Media: A Media Theory of the Limit Situation* (2022).

ALEXIS LOGSDON is a humanities and digital scholarship librarian at the University of Minnesota. Her research focuses on libraries and labor, particularly on hidden labor, and has been published in *In the Library with the Lead Pipe*, *College and Research Libraries Journal*, and the *Journal of Academic Freedom*.

STINE LOMBORG is an associate Professor in communication and IT at the University of Copenhagen. Her work focuses on the pervasive tracking of people in digital systems, and the infrastructural and experiential aspects of tracking and datafication. She is the author of *Social Media—Social Genres* (2014) and directs the Center for Tracking and Society, and the ERC-funded project, Datafied Living.

TIM MARKHAM is a professor of journalism and media at Birkbeck, University of London. Recent books include *Digital Life* (2020), *Media and the Experience of Social Change: The Arab World* (2017), *Media and Everyday Life* (2017), and *Conditions of Mediation: Phenomenological Perspectives on Media* (2017).

VICKI MAYER is a professor of communication at Tulane University. Her research on work, creative labor, and communication industries spans over thirty years, resulting in four books, three edited collections, and over thirty peer-reviewed articles. Her recent work on data centers can be found in *Culture Machine*, *European Journal of Cultural Studies*, and *New Media & Society*.

RAHUL MUKHERJEE is an associate professor of television and new media at University of Pennsylvania, and wrote a monograph *Radiant Infrastructures: Media, Environment, and Cultures of Uncertainty* (2020). He serves on the advisory board of *Media + Environment* and the Center for Advanced Research in Global Communication.

KAARINA NIKUNEN is a professor of media and communication research at Tampere University. Her areas of expertise include digital culture, datafication, emotions and affectivity, migration, solidarity, and social justice. She is the author of *Media Solidarities: Emotions, Power, and Justice in the Digital Age* (2019) and currently researches everyday affective practices of hate speech, and inequalities and intimacy in data-driven culture.

LISA PARKS is distinguished professor of film and media studies at the University of California at Santa Barbara. Her research explores materialities, uses, and geopolitics of media technologies in transnational contexts. She is the author or coeditor of eight books, including *Rethinking Media Coverage* (2018) and *Signal Traffic: Critical Studies of Media Infrastructures* (2015). Parks directs the Global Media Technologies and Cultures Lab and is a 2018 MacArthur fellow.

VIBODH PARTHASARATHI is an associate professor at the Centre for Culture, Media, and Governance, Jamia Millia Islamia, and a nonresident fellow at the Central European University, with interest in media policy/business/history. His recent works include *Platform Capitalism in India* (2020), *The Indian Media Economy* (2018), and the triptych *Communication Processes* (2007, 2009, 2010).

PHILIPP SEUFERLING is a fellow at the Department of Media and Communications of the London School of Economics and Political Science. His doctoral thesis (Södertörn University, 2021) historicized media practices and technologies in refugee camps in Germany since 1945. Seuferling's research explores historical and contemporary intersections of media, migration, and borders.

RANJIT SINGH is a researcher at the AI on the Ground Initiative of Data & Society Research Institute. His research interests lie at the intersection of data infrastructures, global development, and public policy. He is mapping the conceptual vocabulary and curating everyday stories of living with data in/from the Majority World.

JACEK SMOLICKI is an international postdoc at Linköping University (funded by the Swedish Research Council) where he explores listening practices from the perspective of arts, philosophy of technology, and environmental humanities. He is an affiliated postdoc within BioMe project at Uppsala University, where he studies histories and futures of voice technologies.

FREDRIK STIERNSTEDT is a professor of media and communication studies at Södertörn University. His previous research addressed issues of social class and the media in a project funded by the Swedish Research Council (2015–2018) and the digital media labor market (Forte 2015–2018).

MATILDA TUDOR is a media phenomenologist working in the intersections of existential media, feminist and queer studies, and critical theory; she explores what it means to live with and through digital media in everyday life. She is currently researching digital-human vulnerabilities in the project BioMe: Existential Challenges and Ethical Imperatives of Biometric AI in Everyday Lifeworlds at Uppsala University.

JULIA VELKOVA is an associate professor of media and communication studies and of technology and social change at Linköping University. Her work explores the materialities of software and data, the intersections of digital media with energy politics, and the end of life of large-scale media infrastructure. She is a ProFutura Scientia XVII fellow and founder of the Data Lab at Linköping University.

ZALA VOLCIC is a senior lecturer in the School of Media, Film, and Journalism at Monash University. Her research focuses on media, identity, and nationalism and she is the author, coauthor, or coeditor of seven books. Her work has appeared in *Television & New Media; Information, Communication, and Society;* and the *International Journal of Communication.*

INDEX

Page numbers in *italics* denote figures.

Aadhaar, 230, 231, 234–36
Aalto, Alvar, 117
Abbott, Edwin, 68
accelerationism of technology, 101–2
accelerometers, 45–46, 47, *48*, 50, *56*, 57
accountability, ethics of, 97
Acland, Charles, 9
"acousmatic computers," 202, 212n40. *See also* voice assistants
Ad Age (magazine), 87
affective capitalism, 101
AGI (artificial general intelligence), 170–71
AI. *See* artificial intelligence (AI)
Airtel, 265
Airtel Wink, 132
Alberti, Fay Bound, 163
Alexa (virtual assistant), 162, 166, 167, 203, 207, 211n28
algorithms: as arrangement of propositions, 97; as black boxes, 81, 96–97; as configurations, 81–82; as cultural infrastructures, 82–83, 89–91; disempowerment of Black communities through, 180; guarding of, 96; as indispensable media technology, 80; as infrastructures, 81, 83–84; and legibility, 12; personalization vs. collaborative filtering, 99; and quantification, 89–90; and subjectification, 95, 98; temporality of, 103; training of, 90; unknowable origins of, 100. *See also* Netflix Recommender System (NRS); recommendation algorithms; Spotify
algorithms, genetic, 67–68
A-Life Team, 67, *68*, 69, 70
Alphabet. *See* Google
ALTBalaji, 132, 133, 135, 136
altgenres, 87
Althusser, Louis, 98
Amazon, 3, 114, 132, 167, 207. *See also* Alexa (virtual assistant); Mechanical Turk (MTurk)
Amazon Echo, 31
Amazon Prime Video, 3, 84, 132, 135
Amazon Web Services (AWS), 3, 136
Amelia (virtual assistant), *204*, 204–5, 206
American Library Association, 151
Amoore, Louise, 62, 72, 97, 100–101, 103, 105
Ancestry.com, 153
Andrejevic, Mark, 58, 245
ANI (artificial narrow intelligence), 170, 171
Anki, 168, 170. *See also* Vector (social robot)
antitrust regulation of telecommunication utilities, 137, 138
Apple, 53, 114, 132. *See also* Siri (virtual assistant)
Apple+, 132
Apple HomePod, 31
Apple iPhone 13 Pro Max, 47, 50, 52, 52–53
archives, community-based, 189
Arendt, Hannah, 69
art and AI, 64, 65, 67–70, 71–76

artificial general intelligence (AGI), 170–71
artificial intelligence (AI): AGI *vs.* ANI, 170–71; and art, 64, 65, 67–70, 71–76; as a black box, 62–63; as a colon, 70–71; energy consumption of, 70; and eugenics, 64, 65, 75–76; and image classification systems, 71–74; infrastructural gaze of, 72–73; kill-or-be-killed logic of, 69; neurodiversity of, 63–65, 67, 74; as new slave class, 63; representation of, 66, 66–67; training of through LevelApp, 154–58, *157*
artificial narrow intelligence (ANI), 170, 171
aspirational control of self-tracking systems, 223–24
Atanasoski, Neda, 167–68, 194, 207
Atlanta School of Sociology, 179
atmospheric mediation, 13, 25–27, 28, 29–32, 34–35
atmospheric politics, 30, 33, 35
audiovisual industries, 129–30, 131
augmented reality, 25, 26, 29, 34
Autodesk, 205
automated communication, myth of, 166
automated media, 27, 35–37, 42–43, 58, 245
automatons and synthesized speech, 198–200, *200*, 201, 203
Ava (virtual assistant), 205, 206, 207

backends: and acts of citizenship, 15; algorithms as part of, 80; communication industries and dependence on, 131; of communicative robots as black boxes, 165–66; data exploitation through, 220; datafied work through, 225; and data subjects, 229–30; development of term, 1, 5–6, 263–64; and digital piecework, 144–45, 147; energy consumption of, 70; of Euphonia, 199–200; infrastructure studies approach to, 265–66; intersectional differences in, 13; lack of awareness of, 95; and media materialities, 5, 7; as mythical, 163; and notions of servitude, 148–49; and online economy, 131; and poiesis, 96; and public good, 249; relational approach to, 10–11; temporal approach to, 266–67; voicing of technological devices as, 195. *See also* algorithms; digital piecework; frontends; infrastructures; microelectromechanical systems (MEMS); recommendation algorithms; social robots; virtual assistants; voice assistants
backend work, 233, 234–36, 239
"backpropagation," 71

Bacon, Francis, 75
Balaji Telefilms, 132
bandwidth consumption and VoD platforms, 135
banks and AI-based programs, 62–63
Barad, Karen, 98–99, 103, 105
Baudrillard, Jean, 105
BBC (British Broadcasting Corporation), 249, 250, 251, 252
Behind the Screen (Roberts), 247
Being and Time (Heidegger), 103, 106–7
Benjamin, Ruha, 62, 202–3, 248
Benjamin, Walter, 29, 31
Bennett, James, 251
Bennett, Jane, 9
Berlant, Lauren, 163
Berlioz, Hector, 211n28
Bezos, Jeff, 148
Bharat Net, 139
Bharti Airtel, 132, 138
bias: in design, 2–3, 248; of recommendation services, 87; of technology as masculine, 194; of voice assistants, 207
Big Tech. *See* technology companies
BIPOC communities: and black boxes, 62–63; and image classification programs, 72
Birth of Biopolitics, The (Foucault), 34
black boxes: AI as, 62–63; algorithms as, 81, 96–97; backends as, 5; communicative robots as, 165–66; and maker cultures, 246; and public service algorithms, 251
Black communities: and Black Living Data, 179–80; death and disease in, 183–84; and image classification programs, 72; and NRS, 88; queer practices within, 181. *See also* people of color
Black Living Data Booklet (BLDB), 177–89
Bolt, Marko, 118
Borch, Christian, 30, 33, 35
boredom, 107
Bresnihan, Patrick, 255
Brightcove Video Cloud, 136
"Bringing Things to an End," 74–76, *76*
broadband and expansion of VoD, 131
Brodie, Patrick, 255
Bucher, Taina, 81
Bunge, William, 179
Burrough, Benjamin, 81, 84
Butler, Judith, 97, 100, 104
Byer, Nicole, 88

Captivating Technology (R. Benjamin), 248
captivation vs. interpellation, 104–5

carbon footprints. *See* environmental impacts
cared-for-as-customer notion and social robots, 172
Carey, James W., 172
cars, self-driving, 33
Carter, Paul, 249
Castle, Terry, 199
categorization of NRS, 87–88
Cavarero, Adriana, 193, 194, 202, 203, 205, 207
certainties produced through backends, 8
"certainty fetish" of AI, 64
Chamayou, Gregoire, 28
Cinematch algorithm, 84
Citizen Lab, 248
citizenship, acts of: and backends, 15
classification of NRS, 86–87
climate neutrality. *See* environmental impacts
cloudification of telecom, 139
cloud services, 4, 31, 132, 134–36, 139–40
CntrlS, 136
Codecademy, 66, 67
codification of NRS, 88–89
collaboration and smart work, 218, 224
collaborative filtering algorithms, 99
Colley, Linda, 124
colonialism, data, 95, 247
colonialism, European, 255–56
coltan, extraction of, 255
Common Service Centers (CSCs), 235, 244n41
communication, human-machine, 162, 163, 164–69, 172–73, 193–94
Communication as Culture (Carey), 172
communication industries, 130–35, 254–56
communicative robots. *See* social robots
community media, 250
companionship, 167. *See also* loneliness
computational technology and loneliness problem, 169–71
computational work as programming, 147
Conference on Human-Robot Interactions, 169
conflict minerals, 255
Congo and colonialism, 255
considered silence, 130–31
consumer culture and ethics, 105–6
content delivery networks (CDNs), 3
content moderation, 253
convergence and VoD platforms, 129–30, 132–33

convolutional neural networks (CNNs), 71
"coopetition" in VoD market, 133, 134
corporate surveillance: and "god trick," 206; and self-tracking, 214
correctional facilities. *See* prisons
Cortana (virtual assistant), 226
COVID-19 pandemic, 168, 170, 215, 217, 245
Cowlishaw, Tim, 250
Crawford, Kate, 70, 195–96
credit scores and function creep, 237–38
critical algorithm studies, 82
critical data studies, 2
critical media studies, 11
"cruel promises," technological solutions for loneliness as, 163, 171–72
cryptocurrency, environmental costs of, 253
cultural artifacts, algorithms as, 97
"cultural atmospherics," 29
cultural constructs, 89
cultural infrastructures, 82–83, 85–91
cultural memory work, outsourcing of, 152–53
cultures of practice through Spotify, 96
curating and infrastructures, 115, 121–23

daili, 269
"Darwinian logic" and technosolutionism, 167–68
data ambivalence of self-tracking systems, 221–22
database management systems (DBMS), 5
data centers: as climate neutral, 254–56; and curating, *123*; in Groningen, *116*; as hyperscalable, 113–14; site-specificity of, 266; as visible infrastructure, 117. *See also* cloud services
data collection: and Black Living Data, 182–83; public data as resource, 253; and terms of service, 178; use of, 26, 32–33
data colonialism, 95, 247
data curation and Black Living Data, 182–83
data diaries, 188–89
data disturbances and Black Living Data, 184–86
data-driven platforms: environmental costs of, 253; and PSM, 250–52
data exploitation through backends, 220
datafied media environments: and the atmosphere, 25–27; and backends, 57–58, 225; exploitation in, 256; and language of environmentalism, 255; and recommendation algorithms, 96, 104

data for the public good, 253
data infrastructure literacy, 232, 242n15
Data Justice Lab, 248
data storytelling, 187–88
data subjects and backends, 229–30, 231, 238–39, 240n1
data systems: accessibility of, 233; and digital interfaces, 230, 231, 240n1; human interfaces of/to, 229, 238–39; as infrastructures, 230–31, 236–38; and "repair work," 244n50; securing access to, 234–36; transparency of, 252–53
Day, Sophie, 99
de Beauvoir, Simone, 205, 207
Debord, Guy, 105
decision-making, data-driven: societal inequalities in, 239
"deep backend" and existential media, 196–97
DeepBrain Chain, 156
DeepDream program, 65, 71–74, 73
deepend and role of the state, 131, 138
deep mapping, 125–26
Deleuze, Gilles, 36
Denmark, workplace self-tracking in, 215
Denson, Shane, 26
Department of Corrections (South Dakota), 145, 150
Derrida, Jacques, 72–73
design justice and inequalities, 2–3, 248
Detroit Geographical Expedition and Institution Field Notes project, 179
DevCloud, 136
diagnostic interfaces of MEMS, 55–58
Diaspora (social media site), 253
Dieter, Michael, 104, 105
digital assistants. *See* virtual assistants
digital capitalism through private spaces, 14
digital economy: digital piecework in, 144–45; dynamics of, 131; and growth of VoD, 132; money distribution systems in, 265; nationalism in, 138
digital exclusion and infrastructuring, 115
digital intermediaries and content creation, 264–65
digital labor: and Digital Services Act (DSA), 254; and piecework, 144–45, 147, 154, 158, 268; in prisons, 145–46, 149–154; in refugee camps, 145–46, 154–158. *See also* LevelApp; South Dakota State Archives Special Project Program
digital literacy, 107, 232, 242n15
Digital Market Act (DMA), 254
digital piecework, 144–45, 147, 154, 158, 268

digital technologies. *See* technological devices
"digital twinning," 31–32, 36, 38
digital underclass, 247. *See also* shadow technology work
digitization labs, 149, 151
digitization projects, 151–52, 153, 154. *See also* South Dakota State Archives Special Project Program
direct-to-home (DTH) television, 139
"disembodied scientific objectivity," 63
disembodiment and voice, 202–4, 207, 212n46
Disney+, 84
"diversity" and NRS, 86
domestic labor as feminized, 201
domestic robots. *See* social robots
Dreyfus, Hubert, 171
drone warfare, 28
Du Bois, W. E. B., 179
Du Bois's Data Portraits project, 179

e-commerce businesses and VoD platforms, 132
Economic Board Groningen, 118
eGovernance projects, 235
Eichmann, Adolf, 69
Eidsheim, Nina Sun, 198, 208
electret microphones. *See* microphones
"electronic skin," augmented reality as, 29
elemental media, 12, 13
Ello (social media site), 253
Elmholdt, Claus, 217
Elmholdt, Kasper Trolle, 217
embodied experimentation, 7
embodiment and voice, 202–4, 207, 212n46
Emotech, 195
emotions in voice of smart speakers, 201
empathic capitalism and human-machine communication, 168–69
empathy: as business opportunity, 169; digitally mediated possibilities of, 206–7; and human-machine communication, 166–69; social robots and new forms of, 172
encoded inequities and black boxes, 62–63
energy consumption of backends, 70. *See also* environmental impacts
engagement: with self-tracking systems, 222–23; with streaming platforms, 102
environmental impacts: of ICT infrastructure, 254–56; of media and tech industry, 247; and public data, 253; and Spotify, 100
environmentality, 33–35, 36, 255
"environmental mediation," 13, 26–27

environmental modulation and atmospheric monitoring, 34–35
Eros International, 132, 135
Eros Now, 132, 133, 134, 135, 136
ESDS (data center), 136
essence of images and AI, 72, 74
ethics: of accountability, 96, 97; of Black Living Data, 181–84; and consumer culture, 105–6; digitally mediated possibilities of, 206–7
ETV, 137
eugenics and AI, 64, 65, 69, 75–76
Euphonia (talking machine), 199, *200*, 201, 203, 211n28
Europe, media history in, 256–57
Everts, Wubbo, 116, 118–19
everyday AI, 215
existential media, properties of, 196–97
exploitation: in datafied media environments, 256; of laborers, 53, 61n22, 153
expressions and facial recognition systems, 33
extraction and colonialism, 255–56

Faber, Joseph, 199–200, *200*, 205
Faber, Liz W., 201, 202
Facebook, 114, 138, 254
facial recognition systems, 33
Fairchild Semiconductors, 43
Fair Data project, 249, 250
"fake news" and framelessness, 33
Farocki, Harun, 36
Fast Company, 207
"feed forward," 102–5
feed-forward single perceptron, 67
Feenberg, Andrew, 165
female servility and voice assistants, 201, 207, 212n37
feminist ethics of care, 181
fiber optic cable networks, 115, 137, 139, 266
Fields, Ben, 250
financial strategies and expansion of RIL, 137, 138
Findlater, Leah, 167
Finn, Ed, 82
Fjelland, Ragnar, 170
Flatland (Abbott), 68
Flipkart Video, 132
Florida, Richard, 118
Flusser, Vilém, 105
focus time and smart work, 218, 222, 223, 224
Fonda, Jane, 88
food delivery platforms, 268–69

For More Than One Voice (Cavarero), 193
Foucault, Michel, 30, 33–34
4G telecom in India, 138
Foxconn, 43, 53
framelessness, 32–33
Fraser, Alistair, 248
Freeda Beast, 74–76, *76*
Frieda, Sonja, 75
Friere, Paolo, 185
frontends, 2, 131, 229–30, 232–33. See also backends
Frosh, Paul, 96
function creep of data systems, 237–38

Gabrys, Jennifer, 34, 35
Galloway, Alexander R., 195, 200
Galton, Francis, 75
Gauges app, *56*, 56–58, *58*
Gauthier, David, 104, 105
gender bias in voice assistants, 207
genealogical records, indexing, 151, 153, 154
General Atlantic, 138
General Data Protection Regulation (GDPR), 251, 254
Generative Adversarial Networks (GANs), 74–75, 79n34
genetic algorithms, 67–68. See also eugenics and AI
"genre bias," 87
ghost work, 254. See also shadow technology work
Ghost Work (Gray and Suri), 247
gig economy, 144, 147, 268–69
Giving an Account of Oneself (Butler), 97
Global South, technology companies in, 247
"god trick" through corporate surveillance, 206
Goffman, Erving, 5
Goodman, Steve, 101
Google: curating and infrastructure in, 121–23, *123*; data centers of, 114, 115, *116*, 117, *118*; on human relationship with technology, 206; and infrastructuring, 119–20; PageRank algorithm, 80; patent for smart speakers, 31–32; reproduction of physical space by, 38; and smart dust, 30; social responsibilities of, 122–23; and transparency, 254. See also DeepDream program
Google Book Project, 152
Google Cloud, 136
Google Home, 31
Google Maps, 120
Gorm, Nanna, 217
GPX Global Systems, 136

Grace and Frankie, 88
Graham, Stephen, 28
Gray, Mary L., 247, 253
Green Deal, European, 256
Greening the Media (Maxwell and Miller), 247
Groningen, The Netherlands, 115, *116*, 117–18, 119–20, 121–23, *123*
Gross, Neil, 29
GSMA, 155, 156
Guzman, Andrea L., 165

Haahr, Lars, 217
Hamina, Finland, 115, 117, *118*, 119–20, 121–23, *122*
Hansen, Mark B. N., 26, 102–3, 104
Haraway, Donna, 63, 104, 206
Hayles, N. Katherine, 102, 105
health monitoring and self-tracking systems, 217
Heidegger, Martin, 101, 103, 106–7
Hertz, Noreena, 162, 163, 164
Hollingshead, John, 199, 203
home environment, reproduction of, 32
Hong, Sun-ha, 64
Hörl, Erich, 34
Hotstar, 133
Hotstar Disney+, 132, 136
House of Cards, 85
human, nature of being, 197
Human in the Loop (A-Life Team), 65, 67–70, 68
humanitarianism, logic of, 154, 155–56
human-machine communication, 162, 163, 164–69, 172–73, 193–94
"human surrogacy effect" of technology, 194
hyperscalability, 113–14
hyperscale data centers. *See* data centers

IBM: patent for "invisible smart dust," 30
ideal-typical logics in audiovisual industry, 129–30
identity, sense of: and streaming platforms, 96
idle talk, 107
iFixit.com, *51*, *52*, 52–53
Illich, Ivan, 242n16
Illouz, Eva, 169
image classification systems, 71–74
"image problems" and placemaking, 116–17
i-micronews.com, 53
immediation, fantasy of: and virtual reality, 36–37

inauthenticity, 106–7
incarcerated workers: and digital piecework, 149; exploitation of, 146–47, 153; visibility/invisibility of, 151, 154; as "win-win," 150. *See also* LevelApp; South Dakota State Archives Special Project Program
Inception (CNN model), 71
India: cloud services in, 134; national identification infrastructure in, 230, 231; VoD platforms in, 129–31, 132
indigenous women, 43, 147–48, 153
industrial strategies and expansion of RIL, 137–38
inequality: and black boxes, 62–63; in data-driven decision making, 239; and data infrastructures, 124; and design justice, 248; and material solidarities, 246–48; and placemaking, 117–18
"Inessential Other," woman as, 205, 207
information, public vs. private, 178
information saturation, 33
infrastructural gaze into AI, 65, 72–73
infrastructural power of tech companies, 225
infrastructures: algorithms as, 81, 83–84; cloud services and inadequacies in, 134–35; conceptual affinity to backend, 5–6; cultural, 82–83, 85–91; and curating, 115, 121–23; data systems as, 230–31, 236–38; designing of, 3; dimensions of, 83–84; as having no downsides, 116–17; as materially present, 125; and media industries, 10; and placemaking, 114, 116–19; political economy of, 124, 247; as public good, 248–49, 257; site-specificity of, 265–66; as visible, 113, 117
infrastructure studies, 2, 63, 83, 265–66
infrastructuring, 114–15, 119–20
Ingold, Tim, 105
inputs as form of backend work, 234–36
insourcing of labor, 147–48
Intel Capital, 138
Interactive Voice Offerings, 135
interfaces: of communicative and social robots, 166; and data subjects, 230, 231; frontends vs. backends, 232–33; humans as, 149, 230, 238–39; of/to data systems, 229; working around, 264
internet, regulation of as public good, 254
"internet of things," 27, 29, 30
interoperability, lack of: and cloud operators, 139
interpellation, model of: captivation vs., 104–5; and data profiling, 98–101

intersectional differences of backends, 13
"intimate buddy," 168. *See also* social robots
Intuitive Online Video Platform, 135
invisibility: of digitization workers, 151–52; of incarcerated workers, 151, 154; and male voice, 212n46; to self-tracking systems, 222. *See also* shadow technology work
IPsoft, 204
Irani, Lilly, 147, 148
Ito, Mizuko, 248

Jibo (domestic robot), 195
Jio Cinema, 132
JioGigaFibre, 137
JioGigaNet, 139
Jio TV, 132
Joler, Vladan, 195–96
Jones-Imhotep, Edward, 43
Jung, Younbo, 167
Juniper Networks, 31

Kant, Immanuel, 69
Kelly, Kevin, 25, 216
"kill box," 28
kill-or-be-killed logic, 69
Kim, Jaywoo, 167
Kim, Sang Ryong, 167
kinship networks, 268–69
Kirchenbaum, Matthew, 62
Kismet (communicative robot), 165–66
Kitchin, Rob, 248
Klingemann, Mario, 65, 74–76, 76
knowledge. *See* nonknowing, technological
Know-Your-Customer/Citizen (KYC) verification, 234
Kowalski, Robert, 82
KPN (telecommunications utility), 120
Krajewski, Markus, 148–49
Kuri (domestic robot), 195

labor, digital: and digital piecework, 147; and domestic robots, 166; emergence of, 144; political economy of, 124. *See also* incarcerated workers
labor conditions: and media labor practices, 268; and media research, 43; and sites of exception, 147–48
laborers, exploitation of, 53, 61n22
Lagerkvist, Amanda, 196
Lampland, Martha, 5
Larkin, Brian, 113
Latour, Bruno, 50

Lazar, Amanda, 167
Lee, Kwan Min, 167
legibility of media objects, 12
Leopold II (king), 255
LevelApp, 145, 154–58, *157*
LGBTQ communities: as black boxes, 62; Black Living Data and, 178, 181; disempowerment of, 180; recommendation services and, 88, 90
Lidar, 33
listening, process of: and voice, 198
Locke, Matt, 253
loneliness: and computational technology, 169–71; mitigated by social robots, 167–68, 169, 170, 171; promises of technological solutions to as cruel, 163, 171–72; as societal, 162–63, 169
Lonely Century, The (Hertz), 162, 163, 164
Long Short-Term Memory neural network, 66, 66–67
Lury, Celia, 99

MAAFiA. *See* Amazon; Apple; Facebook; Google; Microsoft; technology companies
Madrigal, Alexis, 87
maker cultures and black boxes, 246
manufacturing of technological devices, 43
mapping via WiFi signals, 31
maquiladoras, 43
marginality, feelings of, 124
marriage registration, 230, 231
Massumi, Brian, 34–35, 38
Mastodon, 253
match scores and NRS, 90
materialism and smart dust, 13, 38
material solidarities, 246–48, 249, 251–53, 257
Maxwell, Richard, 247
Mayer, Vicki, 43
Mayfield Robotics, 195
McGlotten, Shaka, 178, 181
measurement and user profiling, 99
Mechanical Turk (MTurk), 144, 147, 148
media backends. *See* backends
media democracy and recommendation systems, 245
media industries: and cloud services, 134; cross-sector collaborations of, 4; environmental consequences of, 247; ideal-typical logics in, 129–30; and infrastructures, 10; reliance on cloud services, 135; shift in, 1; as unregulated, 130–31; and VoD platforms, 132–33

media production, study of, 9–10
media publics, 14–16
media research and labor conditions, 43
media solidarities and social movements, 246
media studies, 2; conceptual vocabulary of, 13–15; legibility in, 14; MEMS in, 47, 53; as multifaceted, 9–11; and nonrepresentational media, 12–13; relevance of MEMS to, 45
mediating technologies, 18n20, 45, 58, 105–6
MEMS. *See* microelectromechanical systems (MEMS)
mercantilism and Indian digital economy, 138
metaphors in media studies, 13–14, 31
MeWe, 253
microdrones and mapping, 31
microelectromechanical systems (MEMS): as automated media, 42–43; datafication of, 58; diagnostic interfaces of, 55–58, 56; manufacturing of, 44–47; physical experiments with, 57; scientific visualizations of, 47–50, 48, 49; teardowns of, 50–55, 52, 54. *See also* accelerometers; microphones; radio frequency filters (RFF)
microphones, 46, 47, 49, 50, 54, 55, 56, 57
Microsoft, 114, 117, 134, 225
Microsoft 365 software, 215, 217–18, 225
Microsoft Azure, 135, 136
Microsoft BlendNet, 136
"microtags," 87
migrants. *See* refugees, Ugandan
Mikkelsen, Christopher, 154
Mikkelsen, David, 154
Mill, John Stuart, 248
Miller, Toby, 247
"missing half second," 105
Mist (WiFi LAN system), 31
Mobyte, 56, 57
"modelling," regulation of effects through, 36, 38
Møller, Naja Holten, 217
Moore, Phoebe V., 217
Mordvintsev, Alexander, 71, 72
Mori, Masahiro, 194
Mormon Church, 151, 153
MTurk. *See* Mechanical Turk (MTurk)
Muehlebach, Andrea, 247
Mulvey, Laura, 72
Mumbai, 266
music discovery. *See* recommendation algorithms; Spotify
music promotion, 95
music streaming platforms. *See* Spotify

MX Player, 132, 135
MyAnalytics: aspirational control of, 223–24; datafication of work through, 225; description of, 215, 217–18; encounters with, 219–21, 225; selective engagement with, 222–23; tracking as always on, 225; weekly reports of, 219, 223
myth of human-machine communication, 162, 164–66, 169

Nailed It!, 88
Nakamura, Lisa, 147–48
Natale, Simone, 6, 166
National Archives, 153
national identification infrastructures. *See* Aadhaar
nationalism: and cloud businesses, 139–40; and Reliance Jio, 136, 138–39
Navajo women, 43, 147–48
neoliberalism: and loneliness, 163; and Reliance Jio, 138–39
Netflix: and Amazon Web Services, 136; and bandwidth consumption, 135; in India, 132; and MEMS devices, 57; reliance on algorithms, 80, 82, 84, 90; use of altgenres, 87; use of rating systems, 86
Netflix Originals, 85, 87
Netflix Prize, 84
Netflix Recommender System (NRS), 84–91; beginnings of, 84–85; configuration of, 85–89; as core of streaming service, 80; dependence on Netflix platform, 82–83; failures of, 86–87; and standardized production, 89; training of, 89, 90
Network18, 132, 137
network maintenance and smart work, 218, 222–23, 224
"Neural TTS," 167
"neurealism," 75
neurodiversity of AI models, 63–65, 67, 74
New Industrial Strategy, 254–56
Newport, Carl, 218
Ngai, Sianne, 69
nonknowing, technological, 7–9, 13, 50
NOS, 120
NRS. *See* Netflix Recommender System (NRS)

Odekerken-Schröder, Gaby, 170
offensive speech toward virtual assistants, 206–7
Oklahoma correctional facilities, yearbook digitization project in, 151, 153
Oliver, Marilené, 67

Olly (domestic robot), 195
online economy. *See* digital economy
On the Mechanism of Human Speech (von Kempelen), 199
opaque boxes, 62. *See also* black boxes
operationalism, 36–37
"operative images," 36
origins, groundlessness of: and ethical relations, 97
outsourcing of cultural memory work, 152–53
ownership and colonialism, 255–56
Oxford English Dictionary, 5

Packer, Jeremy, 38
PageRank algorithm, 80
Paglen, Trevor, 36
Papastergiadis, Nikos, 249
paper mills, 117, 120, 121–22, *122*
Parisi, Luciana, 101
Parks, Lisa, 28, 29
Pasquale, Frank, 5, 62
people of color: and black boxes, 62–63; and image classification programs, 72. *See also* Black communities
Personal Data Protection Bill, 140
personalization, promise of, 90
Personalized Recommendation Engine, 135
Peters, Benjamin, 70
Peters, John Durham, 194
Peterson, Kurt, 44
Pheasantland Industries, 149, 150, 151
phenomenology, 13, 96–97, 106
Philips (electronics giant), 120
Pink, Sarah, 105
placemaking and infrastructures, 114, 116–19
platformized media environment. *See* data-driven platforms
platform studies, 2, 82
poiesis, 96
political agency in voice, 207–8
political awareness and media platforms, 247
political economy of backends, 113–14, 124, 266
politics: of atmospheres, 30, 33, 35; and ethics, 97; and technology, 9
popularity and NRS, 86
"possibility-fixing" of media infrastructures, 83
Post, Harm, 119
Pradhan, Alisha, 167
precarious life, notion of: and material solidarity, 247–48
predatory pricing, 137, 265

Prime Video. *See* Amazon Prime Video
Principles of Political Economy (Mill), 248
print media companies, 117
prison labor. *See* incarcerated workers
prisons: in digital economy, 144–45; prison-made goods/services, 149; shared characteristics with refugee camps, 145–47; as sites of exception, 147–48
privatization of telecommunications utilities, 120
profiling algorithms of recommendation services, 85, 87–88, 90, 96, 98–101
programming vs. computational work, 147
Project Oxygen, 31
PSM. *See* public service media (PSM)
public data as resource, 253
public digital spaces, alternatives to, 252–53
public good: data for, 253; internet regulation as, 254; and material solidarities, 249, 257
Public Media Stack, 253
public service algorithms, 249–52
public service internet, 252–53
Public Service Internet Manifesto, 252
public service media (PSM), 249–52, 253, 256–57
PublicSpaces initiative, 252

quality of service and cloud services, 134–35
Quantified Self movement, 216
"queerbaiting," 88
queer communities. *See* LGBTQ communities
Question Concerning Technology, The (Heidegger), 101
Qui, Jack Linchuan, 43

race and backends. *See* Black communities; indigenous women; people of color
radio frequencies, scientific visualizations of, 43
radio frequency filters (RFF), 46, 47, *48*, 50
rating systems and Netflix, 86
recommendation algorithms: and datafication, 4, 96; disempowerment of Black communities through, 180; and media democracy, 245; as nonconscious cognition, 102; and PSM, 250; and subjectification, 98; training of, 89, 90; and VoD platforms, 133–34. *See also* Netflix Recommender System (NRS); Spotify
recycling of digital products, 255
refugees, Ugandan: and LevelApp, 145; reuniting of, 154, 156; as servants, 156, 158

refugee settlements, Ugandan, 144–48, 154–58
Refunite, 154, 156
regulation: of cloud operators, 139–40; of the internet, 254; of PSM, 256–57; of telecommunication utilities, 120, 137–38, 139–40
rehabilitation, logic of, 153
Reich, Justin, 248
Reid, Toni, 167
"relevance" and NRS, 86
Reliance Industries Limited (RIL) and convergence, 137–38
Reliance Jio: and "coopetition," 133, 135; and data centers, 136; emergence of, 130, 131; and regulation, 137–38, 140
responsibility, acts of, 16, 21n60
Rhianne, Jones, 250
"the robe" and humanizing technology, 205–6
Roberts, Sarah T., 152, 153–54, 253
robots: aesthetic categories of, 194–95, 203. *See also* social robots
Rouvroy, Antoinette, 36
Ruckenstein, Minna, 253
Ruhleder, Karen, 83, 230

Salecl, Renata, 7
Sample, Mark, 62
saturation of data monitors, 35, 38, 218
Saukko, Paula, 217
ScanOps, 152
Schaeffer, Pierre, 212n40
scientific visualizations, 43, 44, 47–50, 47, 48
Seaports (port authority), 119
Seaver, Nick, 81, 89, 173
selective engagement with self-tracking systems, 222–23
self-tracking systems: and corporate gaze, 214; during COVID-19 pandemic, 215; data ambivalence of, 221–22; data exploitation through, 220, 225; invisibility of work to, 222; as laborious, 219; research on, 216–17; weekly reports of, 218. *See also* MyAnalytics
Serres, Michael, 105
servants, refugees as, 156, 158
servility, female: and voice assistants, 201, 207, 212n37
servitude, notions of, 148–49
shadow technology work, 153–54, 242n16, 247
Shibata, Takanoru, 194
Shklovski, Irina, 217

Shoneye, Tolani, 87–88
Shulevitz, Judith, 201, 202
Siegel, Greg, 62
Sienkiewicz, Henryk, 121
Signal Essence, 54, 55
Silverman, Kaja, 212n46
Singapore, 266
Siri (virtual assistant), 162, 166
Sloterdijk, Peter, 26, 29, 35
Slow Computing (Kitchin and Fraser), 248
smart dust, 13, 25–26, 28, 29, 30, 32, 38
smart phones, 45, 58, 131. *See also* microelectromechanical systems (MEMS); technological devices
smart speakers, 31–32. *See also* virtual assistants; voice assistants
"smart wives," 201
smart work concept, 218, 220, 222–23
social groups, loneliness among, 163
sociality and backend technologies, 95
social media: and automated systems, 37; public alternatives to, 252–53
social movements and media solidarities, 246
social responsibilities of technological companies, 122–23
social robots: as black boxes, 165–66; mitigation of loneliness by, 167–68, 169, 170, 171; as new form of empathy, 172; nonhuman design of, 195
sociotechnical relations in media, 9–11, 47, 125
software development kits (SDKs), 269
Sony Liv, 132, 136
Sony TV, 132
Sørensen, Jannick Kirk, 251
South Dakota, indigenous women in, 153
South Dakota Department of Corrections, 145, 150
South Dakota State Archives, 149, 151, 152
South Dakota State Archives Special Project Program, 145, 149–54, 150
speech, synthesizing, 198–200
"spillover" effects and placemaking, 117–18
Spinoza, Baruch, 97, 98
Spotify: and algorithms, 80, 95, 98; carbon footprint of, 100; and "collaborative filtering algorithms," 99; and digital literacy, 107; emergence of, 96; feeding forward through user experience, 103; mediated experiences of, 106; teardown of app, 49, 254
Spotify Teardown project, 49, 254

Star, Susan Leigh, 5, 70, 83, 230
Star TV, 132
the state: and online economy, 131; regulation of telecommunications industries, 137–38
stateness, pursuit of, 130–31, 138–40
Sterne, Jonathan, 208
Stora-Enso, 120
storifying, 115, 125–26
storytelling, data, 187–88
"streaming lore" of NRS, 84–85, 90
streaming platforms: distribution of content on, 264–65; and PSM, 250. *See also* Netflix; Reliance Jio; Spotify
Striphas, Ted, 82
subjectification: in datafied media environments, 256; forward movement of, 103; and recommendation algorithms, 98; and Spotify, 95
Suchman, Lucy, 165
Summa paper mill, 120, 121–22, *122*
Sun NXT, 132
Sun TV Network, 132
Suri, Siddharth, 247, 253
"surveillance capitalism" and MEMS, 46
sustainability. *See* environmental impacts
systemic problems and black boxes, 62–63
SystemPlus Consulting (SPC), 53, 55

talent scouts and content creation, 265
Tamminen, Maarja, 121–22, 123
taste communities, 87
taste preferences, 86
teardowns, 49, 50–55, *54*
"techno-humanitarianism," 155–56
technological devices: colonialism and production of, 247; design bias in, 2–3; and environmental sustainability, 255; giving voice to, 194–95; manufacture of, 43; transformations in scale of, 30–31
technological domination and robotic masculinity, 203
technological solutions. *See* technosolutionism
technology: "human surrogacy effect" of, 194; link to power/knowledge, 7–9; masculinist bias of, 194; as public good, 248–49
technology companies: environmental impacts of, 247; in the Global South, 247; infrastructural power of, 225; and infrastructuring, 119–20; and placemaking, 116; social responsibilities of, 122–23;

storifying of, 115. *See also* Amazon; Apple; Facebook; Google; Microsoft
technopolitics, 9
technosolutionism: as humanitarian intervention, 156; of social robots for loneliness, 163, 167–68, 169, 171–72
telecommunications utilities, privatization of, 120
telecommunication utilities: expansion of RIL into, 137–38; and female voice as form of servility, 212n37; and growth of VoD, 132; regulation of, 120, 137–38, 139–40; and VoD platforms, 132, 133
Telecom Regulatory Authority of India (TRAI), 139–40
television broadcasting, 137
television distribution, 137, 139
television set assembly, 43
temporality: of backends, 103, 266–67; in prisons, 146
TenneT, 120
terms of service and data collection, 178
Tesla, 118–19
Thibault, Ghislain, 43
Thomson Reuters Foundation, 154
thrownness, condition of, 101–2
Thylstrup, Nanna Bonde, 152
TikTok, 132, 265
Times Group, 132
Times Internet, 132
Top Dutch, 118
tourism, curating through, 121–23
transistors, scientific visualizations of, 43
transparency: of data paths, 252–53; of public service algorithms, 251; regulatory measures toward, 254, 257
Trust Conference, 154
Turing, Alan, 97
Turkle, Sherry, 170
Turunen, Linda Lisa Marie, 253
TV18, 137
"twinning," 31–32, 36, 38
Twitter, use of algorithms by, 80
Tykkyläinen, Kauko, 122–23

"ubiquitous computing," 27
Ugandan refugee settlements, 144–48, 154–58
uncanny threat and robotic femininity, 203
"Uncanny Valley," 194, 199, 204–6
uncertainty, 8
UNESCO and gender bias in virtual assistants, 207

US-Equinix, 136
user-generated content (UGC), 132
"user interest" and state intervention, 139
Utah State Prisons, 151, 153

Van den Bulck, Hilde, 251
van der Haar, Andrew, 120
Vector (social robot), 168, 170
Velkova, Julia, 255
Vero, 253
"vertical mediation," 27, 28–29
vibrant matter, 9
video-on-demand (VoD) platforms: and cloud services, 134, 135–36; and convergence, 132–33; expansion of, 131–32; spread of, 129–31. *See also* Reliance Jio
virtual assistants: human-machine communication with, 162; MyAnalytics as, 224; offensive speech toward, 206–7; voice as interface of, 201. *See also* Alexa (virtual assistant); Amelia (virtual assistant); Ava (virtual assistant); Siri (virtual assistant); voice assistants
virtual reality and fantasy of immediation, 36–37
visibility/invisibility: of digital piecework, 158; of incarcerated workers, 151. *See also* shadow technology work
vocal inability, 208
VoD. *See* video-on-demand (VoD) platforms
Vodafone-Idea, 138
Vodaphone, 132
Vodaphone Plays, 132
voice: in cinema, 212n46, 213n47; as complex event, 198; as female, 194; and invisibility, 212n46; political agency in, 207–8; of technological devices, 194–95, 201
voice, female, 199–200, 201, *204*, 204–6, 212n37, 212n46
voice assistants: as ANI, 170; as disembodied, 202–4, *203*; as feminized, 201, *204*, 204–6; gender bias of, 207; "human type" aesthetic of, 195; as interface of human-computer interaction, 193–94, 206; and Uncanny Valley, 204–6. *See also* virtual assistants

voice-over-LTE technology in India, 138
von Kempelen, Wolfgang, 199
Voot, 132, 136, 138
Vora, Kalindi, 168, 194, 207

Warren, Gwendolyn, 179
Web Werks, 136
Weedon, Amie, 217
Weizman, Eyal, 27, 29
wellbeing and smart work, 218, 222
West Bank and politics of verticality, 27–28
WhatsApp, 138
Whitehead, Alfred, 103
WiFi signals, mapping via, 31
Wilson, Ara, 248
Wolf, Gary, 216
women: and black boxes, 62; as "Inessential Other," 205, 207
women, indigenous, 43, 147–48, 153
women, white: and automation of servitude, 207; voice assistants as, 204–6; as voice of automatons, 199–200
"worker-generated content," 43
workers: in food delivery, 268–69. *See also* incarcerated workers; shadow technology work
work/life balance and self-tracking, 218
workplace self-tracking. *See* self-tracking systems
World Economic Forum, 154

yearbook digitization project, 151, 153
Yleisradio, 250–51
Yole, 53
YouTube, 122, *123*, 132, 149, *150*, 151, 250, 265

Zee5, 132, 133, 136
Zee Entertainment, 132
Ziggo, 120
Žižek, Slavoj, 36–37
Zuboff, Shoshana, 46
Zylinska, Joanna, 73–74

THE GEOPOLITICS OF INFORMATION

Digital Depression: Information Technology and Economic Crisis   *Dan Schiller*
Signal Traffic: Critical Studies of Media Infrastructures   *Edited by Lisa Parks and Nicole Starosielski*
Media in New Turkey: The Origins of an Authoritarian Neoliberal State   *Bilge Yesil*
Goodbye iSlave: A Manifesto for Digital Abolition   *Jack Linchuan Qiu*
Networking China: The Digital Transformation of the Chinese Economy   *Yu Hong*
The Media Commons: Globalization and Environmental Discourses   *Patrick D. Murphy*
Media, Geopolitics, and Power: A View from the Global South   *Herman Wasserman*
The Huawei Model: The Rise of China's Technology Giant   *Yun Wen*
Television and the Afghan Culture Wars: Brought to You by Foreigners, Warlords, and Local Activists   *Wazhmah Osman*
Behind the Search Box: Google and the Global Internet Industry   *ShinJoung Yeo*
Communications in Turkey and the Ottoman Empire: A Critical History   *Burçe Çelik*
Media Backends: Digital Infrastructures and Sociotechnical Relations   *Edited by Lisa Parks, Julia Velkova, and Sander De Ridder*

The University of Illinois Press
is a founding member of the
Association of University Presses.

_____

Composed in 10.5/13 Minion Pro
with Grotesque MT Std display
by Lisa Connery
at the University of Illinois Press
Manufactured by Versa Press, Inc.

University of Illinois Press
1325 South Oak Street
Champaign, IL 61820-6903
www.press.uillinois.edu